ADDING IN
TO INJU

ADDING INSULT TO INJURY

Nancy Fraser Debates
Her Critics

◆

NANCY FRASER

EDITED BY KEVIN OLSON

VERSO
London • New York

First published by Verso 2008
© the collection Verso 2008
© individual contributions the contributors
All rights reserved

1 3 5 7 9 10 8 6 4 2

Verso
UK: 6 Meard Street, London W1F 0EG
USA: 20 Jay Street, Suite 1010, Brooklyn, NY 11201
www.versobooks.com

Verso is the imprint of New Left Books

ISBN-13: 978-1-85984-223-2 (pbk)
ISBN-13: 978-1-85984-728-2 (hbk)

British Library Cataloguing in Publication Data
A catalogue record for this book is available from the British Library

Library of Congress Cataloging-in-Publication Data
A catalog record for this book is available from the Library of Congress

Typeset by Hewer Text UK Ltd, Edinburgh
Printed in the USA by Maple Vail

In memory of Richard Rorty and Iris Marion Young,
their voices live on in our conversation

CONTENTS

ADDING INSULT TO INJURY:

An Introduction

Kevin Olson

The political storms of the last several decades have subjected received understandings of social justice to repeated poundings. In the 1960s and 1970s, New Leftists exploded the confines of social-democratic conceptions that had prioritized distributive injustices and class inequality. Rejecting economism, they problematized such mainstays of capitalist culture as consumerism and sexual repression, "the achievement ethic" and "social control," while the "new social movements" that followed them expanded the purview of justice to encompass relations of gender, sexuality, and ethnicity. Later, in the 1980s, social-democratic views of distributive justice faced a different sort of challenge from the Right. Seeking to roll back hard-won social-welfare entitlements, neoliberals combined elements of an older vision of society, premised on personal responsibility, with a new ideology of flexibility aimed at liberating market forces from public control. From the Left, meanwhile, multiculturalists mounted a critique of "difference-blind liberalism." Treating liberal constructions of public space as discriminatory, they joined "difference feminists" and indigenous movements in promulgating a new understanding of justice, centered on the recognition of group specificity. Soon, however, with the fall of Communism seeming to delegitimate the whole problematic of social equality, ethnonationalists and religious communitarians adapted the recognition model to other, less difference-friendly, ends. Still later, the new millennium spawned myriad challenges to the standard Westphalian framing of questions of justice, which cast them as matters internal to territorial states. Caught between genocide and militarized humanitarianism, purdah and the "war on terror," human-rights activists and international feminists foregrounded transborder injustices, as did critics of structural adjustment and the WTO. Before long, however, the insistence on transnational injustice provoked a backlash. Struggling with insecurities unleashed by

corporate-led economic globalization, the wealthy polities of the North
Atlantic became hotbeds of anti-immigrant nativism. Embracing nation-
alisms of country and continent, of ethnos and demos, many in the
former heartlands of social democracy now seek to put the genie of
post-Westphalian justice back into the bottle.

What remains, in the wake of these political upheavals, of once
well-defined understandings of social justice? If the pattern of
contestation suggests the continuing relevance of the left/right division,
it also reflects the absence of any shared vision of justice on the Left.
Today, in fact, we find little agreement among progressives as to what
counts as a genuine injustice, let alone as to how to overcome it. While
some emphasize new permutations of sexism and homophobia, others
are more concerned with ongoing legacies of colonialism and
imperialism. Then, too, while some left-wing currents stress burgeoning
industrial exploitation in the global South, others highlight the rise
there of mega-slums utterly cut off from formal work, and still others
underscore the differential effects in the North of a post-industrial,
post-egalitarian, post-welfare economy.

Certainly an adequate approach must capture all such core, defining
inequities of the present era. But which understanding of justice can
encompass them all? Which conception can best advance the central
task of critical theorizing: the self-clarification of the struggles and
wishes of the age?

If the answer remains obscure, two camps persist in appealing to
familiar styles of thinking. One camp, focused on combating economic
inequality, remains attached to the social-democratic paradigm of
redistribution. The other, more concerned to battle the stigmatization
of depreciated cultures, espouses the difference-sensitive paradigm of
recognition. Each has its insights and blind spots.

The redistribution conception has venerable forebears: utilitarians and
Fabians, progressives and populists, utopians and Marxists, socialists and
social-democrats, anti-imperialists and developmentalists, labor
movements of every stripe. Shaped by the industrial-revolution-era
conjunction of factory production, unregulated markets, and
concentrated wealth, this paradigm foregrounded *injuries* inflicted by
the capitalist system. Associated primarily with the politics of class, it
understood justice as concerned centrally with assuring the fair allocation
of resources, opportunities, and goods.

This approach still retains considerable traction. Despite major
shifts in the mode of capital accumulation, issues of workers' rights,
workplace safety, job security, and the just distribution of goods and
bads are still very much with us. Wealth is still lopsidedly distributed

and severe poverty still runs rampant, while the power of labor unions has declined and reforms won in previous eras have been eroded. Meanwhile, the conjoint globalization of capitalist economy and communications media is lending new salience to stark patterns of world inequality. Small wonder, then, that many social-justice movements continue to couch their claims in the idiom of redistribution.

Nevertheless, some progressive social movements have found the redistribution paradigm wanting. More concerned with *insults* than injuries, cultural feminists, multiculturalists, and "queers" aim to combat the depreciation of their identities, ways of life, and social contributions. Forms of institutionalized disrespect not reducible to maldistribution, these harms were largely overlooked by social democracy. Determined to attack them frontally, claimants have elaborated another paradigm of social justice centered on recognition. Focused on the discursive construction of hierarchy, the recognition paradigm replaces the older economistic social imaginary with a culturalist view of society as a symbolic ordered matrix of unequally valued identities. By this shift, it makes visible, and opens to criticism, status hierarchies that were occluded by the earlier paradigm.

This approach, too, has its insights and blind spots. On one hand, the recognition paradigm has proven capable of unmasking false universalisms that entrench hegemonic values and privilege dominant cultures. On the other hand, it has tended to reify identities and to displace struggles against maldistribution, which its proponents sometimes view as a mere secondary effect of misrecognition. Understandably, therefore, many proponents of redistribution remain skeptical of the newer paradigm.

Here, then, are two familiar conceptions of social justice, mirror images of each other. On one side stands an egalitarian conception rooted in a century-and-a-half-old critique of the capitalist economy, which holds that maldistribution underlies misrecognition. On the other side stands a newer tradition of difference-sensitive criticism, centered on the symbolic construction of hierarchy, which holds that misrecognition drives maldistribution. Viewed this way, each as impugning the other, the two paradigms of justice have often been counterposed as antithetical and incompatible.

That, at least, was the widely felt sense in 1995, when Nancy Fraser published the essay that opens this volume, "From Redistribution to Recognition?" Hailed as a major intervention even by those who disagreed with its core propositions, this essay aimed to lay bare the deep conceptual underpinnings of the antagonism between multiculturalists and social democrats. Seeking to clarify what was at stake, Fraser located the roots of this rift in an epochal alteration in the grammar of political claimsmaking. Naming this the "shift from redistribution to recognition," she proceeded to diagnose the uncoupling in the post-1968 era of those two conceptions of justice. But her aim was not merely diagnostic. In her attempt to chart a path beyond sectarian rivalries, she also proposed to reconstruct our understanding of justice so as to incorporate the insights of both camps. Claiming that major axes of injustice were two-dimensional, rooted simultaneously in the political economy and the status order, she insisted that struggles for justice could not succeed unless they combined a politics of redistribution with a politics of recognition. Devising such a politics requires some subtlety, however, as Fraser discerned real tensions between those two orientations. Seeking to overcome what she called "the redistribution-recognition dilemma," she proposed to replace conventional "affirmative" strategies, aimed at mitigating unjust outcomes without disturbing the underlying structures that generate them, with more radical "transformative" strategies, aimed at altering the deep structures themselves. Faulting both "mainstream multiculturalism" and the liberal welfare state, she called on feuding left-wing currents to unite in a broader integrated struggle for "socialism in the economy" plus "deconstruction in the culture."

Fraser's proposal to "add insult to injury" provoked varied and often heated responses. Engaging some of the leading left-wing thinkers of the age, the debate took up the pressing questions of theory and practice raised by her essay. But the argument raged well beyond that initial provocation. As Fraser went on to refine her views in the subsequent decade, the problematic of "redistribution and recognition" continued to command attention and spark disagreement. Even today, in a vastly changed political landscape, the relation between "insult and injury" remains a focus of lively debate.

The present volume charts the unfolding of this extended, ongoing debate. Starting with Fraser's 1995 essay and ending with a 2007 exchange, it includes most of the major high points along the way. (An exception is Fraser's debate with Axel Honneth, which is the subject of another book.) Driven by concerns that are as much systematic as chronological, Adding Insult to Injury delineates four distinct rounds of discussion, each centered on a different set of issues. In the first round, the central issue is Fraser's diagnosis of the rift between redistribution and recognition. In the second round, that proposition is taken as a given, and the focus is how, exactly, to integrate the two approaches to social justice—in theory and practice. In the third round, the key question is whether redistribution and recognition really exhaust the full meaning of justice or whether it is necessary to incorporate a third, political dimension. In the fourth round, finally, the core concern is the philosophical underpinnings of Fraser's theory, especially its normative foundations and social ontology. Let me elaborate.

The volume's first section maps the initial debate over "From Redistribution to Recognition?" Comprising that essay, some early critiques, and Fraser's rejoinders, it focuses largely on her diagnosis of the uncoupling of recognition from redistribution. As if to confirm that she struck a raw nerve, the reactions run the full gamut of left-wing opinion. Judith Butler writes to defend the cultural Left against "neoconservative Marxism." Contending that heterosexism is just as material and essential to capitalism as class exploitation, she claims to deconstruct Fraser's distinction between cultural and economic injustices. Conversely, Richard Rorty intervenes on behalf of the social Left. Criticizing the focus on cultural recognition as a political dead end, he pleads for a return to social democracy, including the priority of class and distributive justice. By contrast, Iris Young enters the fray to defend the overall pattern of progressive struggle in the post–New Left era. Denying the existence of a redistribution/recognition split within the Left, she contends that Fraser's diagnosis is an artifact of her own "dichotomous" thinking. Meanwhile, Anne Phillips proposes to mediate that last dispute. Claiming to split the difference between them, she seconds Fraser's worry that recognition is displacing redistribution, while rejecting her deconstructive preference in cultural politics in favor of Young's identity-friendly orientation. Finally, in a series of spirited rejoinders, Fraser seeks not only to rebut her critics' objections but also to elaborate the quasi-Weberian, "perspectival-dualist" social theory that underpins her views.

That theory constitutes the bone of contention in Section Two. In this second round of debate, the split between proponents of redistribution and recognition is taken as given, as is the need to overcome it. Here, accordingly, the dispute is not about whether, but rather *how* to integrate redistribution and recognition in theory and practice. Opening with Fraser's 2000 amplification of that project, the section continues with four further critical essays, two centered largely on recognition and two focused primarily on redistribution. The mood here is darker, however, shadowed by the increasing virulence of identity politics, on the one hand, and the growing hegemony of neoliberalism, on the other, at the turn of the century. Against this backdrop, Fraser proposes "Rethinking Recognition" to dissociate it from repressive chauvinism and connect it with egalitarian redistribution. Seeking to shift the focus from identities to institutions, she analyzes misrecognition as status subordination, rooted in institutionalized patterns of cultural value that violate the requirements of justice by depriving some social actors of the possibility of participating fully, as peers, in social life. Linked to her view of *justice as parity of participation*, this "status model" of recognition avoids the reifying tendencies of identity politics. Linked, too, to a view of capitalist society as doubly ordered, by culture and economy, and doubly stratified, by status and class, it foregrounds the imbrication of misrecognition with maldistribution. Or so Fraser claims.

The other contributors to this section doubt that her approach is fully satisfactory. Here, too, the objections come from a variety of different directions: some doubt Fraser's view of recognition, others dispute her view of redistribution, and some reject her account of their interrelation. Christopher Zurn criticizes Fraser's status model of recognition. From his perspective, her account focuses too single-mindedly on institutions at the expense of individual psychology. In contrast, Elizabeth Anderson faults Fraser's critique of affirmative recognition. Denying that such recognition necessarily stands in tension with redistribution, Anderson proposes a counterexample: the anti-racist policy of affirmative action, as she reconceives it. From the redistribution side, meanwhile, Ingrid Robeyns disputes Fraser's claim that no existing theory of distributive justice adequately addresses misrecognition. In her view, Amartya Sen's capability model already does so—more successfully than Fraser's own model. Joseph Heath, too, rehabilitates a theory of redistribution criticized by Fraser. In his case, however, the preferred approach is Ronald Dworkin's account of justice as equality of resources, which Heath proposes to ground in a deliberative-democratic politics of recognition. Although Fraser does not reply directly to these critics here, readers can find relevant passages in her exchanges with Axel Honneth (2003) and other critics (2007).

If the second round of debate assumes a two-dimensional conception of justice, the third round calls that assumption into question. Far from accepting Fraser's view that the conjunction of redistribution and recognition exhausts the full substance of justice, the essays comprising this round reflect an emerging consensus that a third, political dimension is also necessary. Leonard Feldman first made the case, in a 2002 article, that political injustices are analytically distinct from, and cannot be reduced to, inequities of economy or culture. Here, in a new essay, he extends that argument to cases in which the state itself produces subordinate political statuses while claiming merely to recognize pre-existing differences. My own essay takes the further step of prioritizing the political dimension of justice over redistribution and recognition. Contending that political participation is not only analytically distinct from, but also normatively and conceptually prior to other forms of social participation, I assign it a privileged place in Fraser's theory. On this basis I outline a politically richer conception of participatory parity.

Fraser's "Reframing Justice in a Globalizing World" constitutes a reply of sorts to her third-round critics. Although not written expressly for that purpose, this 2005 essay adopts the critics' idea of a distinctively political dimension of justice. Adding "representation" to redistribution and recognition, Fraser now elaborates a three-dimensional conception, effectively updating Weber's triad of class, status, and party. Directed at clarifying struggles over globalization, the new dimension is not exhausted by what she calls "ordinary-political injustices," which arise internally, within a bounded political community, when skewed decision rules entrench disparities of political voice among fellow citizens. In addition, Fraser's conception encompasses "meta-political injustices" that arise when the division of political space into bounded polities frames what are actually transnational injustices as national matters. In that case, affected non-citizens are wrongly excluded from consideration —as, for example, when the claims of the global poor are shunted into the domestic political arenas of weak or failed states and diverted from the offshore sources of their dispossession. It is this second, meta-political level of misrepresentation that is Fraser's primary concern in the present essay. Naming the injustice in question "misframing," she argues here for a theory of "post-Westphalian democratic justice" that problematizes unjust frames. The result is a major revision of her theory, aimed at addressing transborder inequities in a globalizing world.

This volume's fourth and final round of debate concerns the philosophical underpinnings of Fraser's theorizing. At issue here are the basic aims of critical theory, as well as its normative foundations and social ontology. Whereas such matters went largely without saying in the earlier rounds, they now become subject to explicit dispute. Nikolas Kompridis questions two key pillars of Fraser's approach: the harnessing of recognition to a theory of justice and the focus on public-sphere claimsmaking. Contending that their effect is to occlude harms experienced by vulnerable subjects who have not yet acquired a political voice, he defends an alternative model of critical theorizing: an agonistic, disclosive model, grounded in freedom instead of justice and oriented to the search for new expressive forms that can articulate inchoate suffering. Rainer Forst, in contrast, largely endorses Fraser's conception of critical theory while disputing her decision to cast participatory parity as the fundamental principle of justice. Assigning that role, instead, to "the right to justification," Forst joins me in conceiving politics as the primary dimension of justice, and hence in rejecting Fraser's account of representation as but one of three equally basic dimensions.

Fraser, however, is not convinced by these objections. Replying in the volume's concluding essay to her fourth-round critics, she defends both her general understanding of critical theory and the specific form in which she proposes to reconstruct it. Responding to Kompridis, she argues that theorists of recognition merit the title of *critical* theorists only if they make the unmasking of institutionalized domination their first priority. Absent a justice-theoretic account of recognition, they can never establish the *emancipatory* force of agonistic contestation or linguistic innovation. Responding to Forst, she maintains that a theory of justice as participatory parity can better unmask power asymmetries than one centered on the right to justification. Whereas the latter succumbs to a "reductive politicism" that reduces all injustice to misrepresentation, the former respects the relative autonomy of maldistribution and misrecognition, which typically subtend and distort representation.

If the present volume accords Fraser the last word, the argument over her theory by no means ends here. On the contrary, the project of adding insult to injury continues to command attention and spark disagreement. It is thus worth considering why this work resonates so widely in a time when there is no shortage of theorizing about justice. One reason is Fraser's success in shifting the terms of debate away from sterile either/or arguments that counterpose "cultural politics" and "social democracy" as mutually antithetical, to the difficult but more productive question of how to integrate those two orientations while acknowledging the tensions between them. A second reason is her keen ability to make the presently chaotic scene surveyable and intelligible. Affording a synoptic view of the political landscape, her framework connects the dots among apparently discrete injustices, enabling us to consider how we might relate otherwise disparate, fragmentary struggles to the larger picture—and to one another. Finally and perhaps most importantly, Fraser's theorizing continues to deepen with time. An eminently dialogical thinker, she treats every critical exchange as an opportunity to extend her framework in new directions, most recently to clarify global injustices. The present volume provides a unique window on this process of dialogical theorizing.

I. REDISTRIBUTION OR RECOGNITION? A FALSE ANTITHESIS

FROM REDISTRIBUTION TO RECOGNITION? DILEMMAS OF JUSTICE IN A "POSTSOCIALIST" AGE

Nancy Fraser

The "struggle for recognition" is fast becoming the paradigmatic form of political conflict in the late twentieth century. Demands for "recognition of difference" fuel the struggles of groups mobilized under the banners of nationality, ethnicity, "race," gender, and sexuality. In these "postsocialist" conflicts, group identity supplants class interest as the chief medium of political mobilization. Cultural domination supplants exploitation as the fundamental injustice. And cultural recognition displaces socioeconomic redistribution as the remedy for injustice and the goal of political struggle.

That, of course, is not the whole story. Struggles for recognition occur in a world of exacerbated material inequality—in income and property ownership; in access to paid work, education, health care and leisure time; but also more starkly in caloric intake and exposure to environmental toxicity, hence in life expectancy and rates of morbidity and mortality. Material inequality is on the rise in most of the world's countries—in the United States and in Haiti, in Sweden and in India, in Russia and in Brazil. It is also increasing globally, most dramatically across the line that divides North from South. How, then, should we view the eclipse of a socialist imaginary centered on terms such as "interest," "exploitation," and "redistribution"? And what should we make of the rise of a new political imaginary centered on notions of "identity," "difference," "cultural domination," and "recognition"? Does this shift represent a lapse into "false consciousness"? Or does it, rather, redress the culture-blindness of a materialist paradigm rightfully discredited by the collapse of Soviet Communism?

Neither of those two stances is adequate, in my view. Both are too wholesale and un-nuanced. Instead of simply endorsing or rejecting all of identity politics *simpliciter*, we should see ourselves as presented with a new intellectual and practical task: that of developing a *critical* theory of recognition, one which identifies and defends only those versions of the cultural politics of difference that can be coherently combined with the social politics of equality.

In formulating this project, I assume that justice today requires *both* redistribution *and* recognition. And I propose to examine the relation between them. In part, this means figuring out how to conceptualize cultural recognition and social equality in forms that support rather than undermine one another. (For there are many competing conceptions of both!) It also means theorizing the ways in which economic disadvantage and cultural disrespect are currently entwined with and support one another. Then, too, it requires clarifying the political dilemmas that arise when we try to combat both those injustices simultaneously.

My larger aim is to connect two political problematics that are currently dissociated from one another. For only by articulating recognition and redistribution can we arrive at a critical-theoretical framework that is adequate to the demands of our age. That, however, is far too much to take on here. In what follows, I shall consider only one aspect of the problem. Under what circumstances can a politics of recognition help support a politics of redistribution? And when is it more likely to undermine it? Which of the many varieties of identity politics best synergize with struggles for social equality? And which tend to interfere with the latter?

In addressing these questions, I shall focus on axes of injustice that are simultaneously cultural and socioeconomic, paradigmatically gender and "race." (I shall not say much, in contrast, about ethnicity or nationality.)[1] And I must enter one crucial preliminary caveat: in proposing to assess recognition claims from the standpoint of social equality, I assume that varieties of recognition politics that fail to

---

1 This omission is dictated by reasons of space. I believe that the framework elaborated below can fruitfully address both ethnicity and nationality. Insofar as groups mobilized on these lines do not define themselves as sharing a situation of socioeconomic disadvantage and do not make redistributive claims, they can be understood as struggling primarily for recognition. National struggles are peculiar, however, in that the form of recognition they seek is political autonomy, whether in the form of a sovereign state of their own (e.g., the Palestinians) or in the form of more limited provincial sovereignty within a multinational state (e.g., the majority of Québécois). Struggles for ethnic recognition, in contrast, often seek rights of cultural expression within polyethnic nation-states. These distinctions are insightfully discussed in Will Kymlicka, *Multicultural Citizenship*, Oxford: Oxford University Press, 1996.

respect human rights are unacceptable even if they promote social equality.[2]

Finally, a word about method: in what follows, I shall propose a set of analytical distinctions—for example, cultural injustices versus economic injustices, recognition versus redistribution. In the real world, of course, culture and political economy are always imbricated with one another; and virtually every struggle against injustice, when properly understood, implies demands for both redistribution and recognition. Nevertheless, for heuristic purposes, analytical distinctions are indispensable. Only by abstracting from the complexities of the real world can we devise a conceptual schema that can illuminate it. Thus, by distinguishing redistribution and recognition analytically, and by exposing their distinctive logics, I aim to clarify —and begin to resolve—some of the central political dilemmas of our age.

My discussion proceeds in four parts. In section one, I conceptualize redistribution and recognition as two analytically distinct paradigms of justice, and I formulate "the redistribution-recognition dilemma." In section two, I distinguish three ideal-typical modes of social collectivity in order to identify those vulnerable to the dilemma. In section three, I distinguish between "affirmative" and "transformative" remedies for injustice, and I examine their respective logics of collectivity. Lastly, I use these distinctions, in section four, to propose a political strategy for integrating recognition claims with redistribution claims with a minimum of mutual interference.

I. The redistribution-recognition dilemma

Let me begin by noting some complexities of contemporary "post-socialist" political life. With the decentering of class, diverse social movements are mobilized around crosscutting axes of difference. Contesting a range of injustices, their claims overlap and at times conflict. Demands for cultural change intermingle with demands for economic change, both within and among social movements. Increasingly, however, identity-based claims tend to predominate, as prospects for redistribution appear to recede. The result is a complex political field with little programmatic coherence.

---

2 My principal concern in this essay is the relation between the recognition of cultural difference and social equality. I am not directly concerned, therefore, with the relation between recognition of cultural difference and liberalism. However, I assume that no identity politics is acceptable that fails to respect fundamental human rights of the sort usually championed by left-wing liberals.

To help clarify this situation and the political prospects it presents, I propose to distinguish two broadly conceived, analytically distinct understandings of injustice. The first is socioeconomic injustice, which is rooted in the political-economic structure of society. Examples include exploitation (having the fruits of one's labor appropriated for the benefit of others); economic marginalization (being confined to undesirable or poorly paid work or being denied access to income-generating labor altogether), and deprivation (being denied an adequate material standard of living).

Egalitarian theorists have long sought to conceptualize the nature of these socioeconomic injustices. Their accounts include Marx's theory of capitalist exploitation, John Rawls's account of justice as fairness in the distribution of "primary goods," Amartya Sen's view that justice requires ensuring that people have equal "capabilities to function," and Ronald Dworkin's view that it requires "equality of resources."[3] For my purposes here, however, we need not commit ourselves to any one particular theoretical account. We need only subscribe to a rough and general understanding of socioeconomic injustice informed by a commitment to egalitarianism.

The second kind of injustice is cultural or symbolic. It is rooted in social patterns of representation, interpretation, and communication. Examples include cultural domination (being subjected to patterns of interpretation and communication that are associated with another culture and are alien and/or hostile to one's own); nonrecognition (being rendered invisible via the authoritative representational, communicative, and interpretative practices of one's culture); and disrespect (being routinely maligned or disparaged in stereotypic public cultural representations and/or in everyday life interactions).

---

3 Karl Marx, *Capital*, vol. 1; John Rawls, *A Theory of Justice*, Cambridge, MA: Harvard University Press, 1971, and subsequent papers; Amartya Sen, *Commodities and Capabilities*, Amsterdam: North-Holland, 1985; and Ronald Dworkin, "What is Equality? Part 2: Equality of Resources," *Philosophy and Public Affairs* 10: 4, fall 1981, pp. 283–345. Although I here classify all these writers as theorists of distributive economic justice, it is also true that most of them have some resources for dealing with issues of cultural justice as well. Rawls, for example, treats "the social bases of self-respect" as a primary good to be fairly distributed, while Sen considers a "sense of self" to be relevant to the capability to function. (I am indebted to Mika Manty for this point.) Nevertheless, as Iris Marion Young has suggested, the primary thrust of their thought leads in the direction of distributive economic justice. See her *Justice and the Politics of Difference*, Princeton: Princeton University Press, 1990.

Some political theorists have recently sought to conceptualize the nature of these cultural or symbolic injustices. Charles Taylor, for example, has drawn on Hegelian notions to argue the following:

> Nonrecognition or misrecognition . . . can be a form of oppression, imprisoning someone in a false, distorted, reduced mode of being. Beyond simple lack of respect, it can inflict a grievous wound, saddling people with crippling self-hatred. Due recognition is not just a courtesy but a vital human need.[4]

Likewise, Axel Honneth has argued that

> we owe our integrity . . . to the receipt of approval or recognition from other persons. [Negative concepts such as "insult" or "degradation"] are related to forms of disrespect, to the denial of recognition. [They] are used to characterize a form of behavior that does not represent an injustice solely because it constrains the subjects in their freedom for action or does them harm. Rather, such behavior is injurious because it impairs these persons in their positive understanding of self—an understanding acquired by intersubjective means.[5]

Similar conceptions inform the work of many other critical theorists who do not use the term "recognition."[6] Once again, however, it is not necessary here to settle on a particular theoretical account. We need only subscribe to a general and rough understanding of cultural injustice, as distinct from socioeconomic injustice.

Despite the differences between them, both socioeconomic injustice and cultural injustice are pervasive in contemporary societies. Both are rooted in processes and practices that systematically disadvantage

---

4 Charles Taylor, *Multiculturalism and "The Politics of Recognition,"* Princeton: Princeton University Press, 1992, p. 25.

5 Axel Honneth, "Integrity and Disrespect: Principles of a Conception of Morality Based on the Theory of Recognition," *Political Theory* 20: 2, May 1992, pp. 188–9. See also his *Kampf um Anerkennung*, Frankfurt: Suhrkamp, 1992, translated into English by Joel Anderson as *Struggle for Recognition*, Cambridge, MA: MIT Press, 1995. It is no accident that both of the major contemporary theorists of recognition, Honneth and Taylor, are Hegelians.

6 See, for example, Patricia J. Williams, *The Alchemy of Race and Rights,* Cambridge, MA: Harvard University Press, 1991, and Young, *Justice and the Politics of Difference.*

some groups of people vis-à-vis others. Both, consequently, should be remedied.[7]

Of course, this distinction between economic injustice and cultural injustice is analytical. In practice, the two are intertwined. Even the most material economic institutions have a constitutive, irreducible cultural dimension; they are shot through with significations and norms. Conversely, even the most discursive cultural practices have a constitutive, irreducible political-economic dimension; they are underpinned by material supports. Thus, far from occupying two airtight separate spheres, economic injustice and cultural injustice are usually interimbricated so as to reinforce one another dialectically. Cultural norms that are unfairly biased against some are institutionalized in the state and the economy; meanwhile, economic disadvantage impedes equal participation in the making of culture, in public spheres and in everyday life. The result is often a vicious circle of cultural and economic subordination.[8]

Despite these mutual entwinements, I shall continue to distinguish economic injustice and cultural injustice analytically. And I shall also distinguish two correspondingly distinct kinds of remedy. The remedy

---

7 Responding to an earlier draft of this paper, Mika Manty posed the question of whether and how a schema focused on classifying justice issues as either cultural or political-economic could accommodate "primary political concerns" such as citizenship and political participation ("Comments on Fraser," unpublished typescript presented at the Michigan symposium on "Political Liberalism"). My inclination is to follow Jürgen Habermas in viewing such issues bifocally. From one perspective, political institutions (in state-regulated capitalist societies) belong with the economy as part of the "system" that produces distributive socioeconomic injustices; in Rawlsian terms, they are part of "the basic structure" of society. From another perspective, however, such institutions belong with "the lifeworld" as part of the cultural structure that produces injustices of recognition; for example, the array of citizenship entitlements and participation rights conveys powerful implicit and explicit messages about the relative moral worth of various persons. Thus, "primary political concerns" could be treated as matters either of economic justice or cultural justice, depending on the context and perspective in play.

8 For the interimbrication of culture and political economy, see my "What's Critical About Critical Theory? The Case of Habermas and Gender" in Nancy Fraser, *Unruly Practices: Power, Discourse and Gender in Contemporary Social Theory*, Cambridge: Polity Press, 1989; "Rethinking the Public Sphere" in Fraser, *Justice Interruptus: Critical Reflections on the "Postsocialist" Condition*, New York, Routledge, 1977; and Fraser, "Pragmatism, Feminism, and the Linguistic Turn," in Benhabib, Butler, Cornell and Fraser, *Feminist Contentions: A Philosophical Exchange*, New York: Routledge, 1995. See also Pierre Bourdieu, *Outline of a Theory of Practice*, trans. Richard Nice, Cambridge: Cambridge University Press, 1977. For critiques of the cultural meanings implicit in the current US political-economy of work and social welfare, see the last two chapters of *Unruly Practices* and Nancy Fraser and Linda Gordon, 'A Genealogy of Dependency': Tracing a Keyword of the US Welfare State," in *Justice Interruptus*.

for economic injustice is political-economic restructuring of some sort. This might involve redistributing income, reorganizing the division of labor, subjecting investment to democratic decision-making, or transforming other basic economic structures. Although these various remedies differ importantly from one another, I shall henceforth refer to the whole group of them by the generic term "redistribution."[9] The remedy for cultural injustice, in contrast, is some sort of cultural or symbolic change. This could involve upwardly revaluing disrespected identities and the cultural products of maligned groups. It could also involve recognizing and positively valorizing cultural diversity. More radically still, it could involve the wholesale transformation of societal patterns of representation, interpretation and communication in ways that would change *everybody's* sense of self. Although these remedies differ importantly from one another, I shall henceforth refer to the whole group of them by the generic term "recognition."[10]

Once again, this distinction between redistributive remedies and recognition remedies is analytical. Redistributive remedies generally presuppose an underlying conception of recognition. For example, some proponents of egalitarian socioeconomic redistribution ground their claims on the "equal moral worth of persons"; thus, they treat economic redistribution as an expression of recognition.[11] Conversely, recognition remedies sometimes presuppose an underlying conception of redistribution. For example, some proponents of multicultural recognition ground their claims on the imperative of a just distribution of the "primary good" of an "intact cultural structure"; they therefore treat cultural recognition as a species of redistribution.[12] Such conceptual entwinements not withstanding, however, I shall leave to one side questions such as, do redistribution and recognition constitute two distinct, irreducible, *sui generis* concepts of justice, or alternatively,

---

9 In fact, these remedies stand in some tension with one another, a problem I shall explore in a subsequent section of this paper.

10 These various cultural remedies also stand in some tension with one another. It is one thing to accord recognition to existing identities that are currently undervalued; it is another to transform symbolic structures and thereby alter people's identities. I shall explore the tensions among the various remedies in a subsequent section of the paper.

11 For a good example of this approach, see Ronald Dworkin, "Liberalism," in his *A Matter of Principle*, Cambridge, MA: Harvard University Press, 1985, pp. 181–204.

12 For a good example of this approach, see Will Kymlicka, *Liberalism, Community and Culture*, Oxford: Oxford University Press, 1989. The case of Kymlicka suggests that the distinction between socioeconomic justice and cultural justice need not always map onto the distinction between distributive justice and relational or communicative justice.

can either one of them be reduced to the other?[13] Rather, I shall assume that however we account for it metatheoretically, it will be useful to maintain a working, first-order distinction between socioeconomic injustices and their remedies, on the one hand, and cultural injustices and their remedies, on the other.[14]

With these distinctions in place, I can now pose the following questions: what is the relation between claims for recognition, aimed at remedying cultural injustice, and claims for redistribution, aimed at redressing economic injustice? And what sorts of mutual interferences can arise when both kinds of claims are made simultaneously?

There are good reasons to worry about such mutual interferences. Recognition claims often take the form of calling attention to, if not performatively creating, the putative specificity of some group, and then of affirming the value of that specificity. Thus, they tend to promote group differentiation. Redistribution claims, in contrast, often call for abolishing economic arrangements that underpin group specificity. (An example would be feminist demands to abolish the gender division of labor.) Thus, they tend to promote group de-differentiation. The upshot is that the politics of recognition and the politics of redistribution appear to have mutually contradictory aims. Whereas the first tends to promote group differentiation, the second tends to undermine it. Thus, the two kinds of claim stand in tension with one another; they can interfere with, or even work against, one another.

Here, then, is a difficult dilemma. I shall henceforth call it the redistribution-recognition dilemma. People who are subject to both cultural injustice and economic injustice need both recognition and redistribution. They need both to claim and to deny their specificity. How, if at all, is this possible?

Before taking up this question, let us consider precisely who faces the recognition-redistribution dilemma.

II. Exploited classes, despised sexualities, and bivalent collectivities

Imagine a conceptual spectrum of different kinds of social collectivities. At one extreme are modes of collectivity that fit the redistribution model of justice. At the other extreme are modes of collectivity that

---

13 Axel Honneth's *Kampf um Anerkennung* represents the most thorough and sophisticated attempt at such a reduction. Honneth argues that recognition is the fundamental concept of justice and can encompass distribution.

14 Absent such a distinction, we foreclose the possibility of examining conflicts between them. We miss the chance to spot mutual interferences that could arise when redistribution claims and recognition claims are pursued simultaneously.

fit the recognition model. In between are cases that prove difficult because they fit both models of justice simultaneously.

Consider, first, the redistribution end of the spectrum. At this end let us posit an ideal-typical mode of collectivity whose existence is rooted wholly in the political economy. It will be differentiated as a collectivity, in other words, by virtue of the economic structure, as opposed to the cultural order, of society. Thus, any structural injustices its members suffer will be traceable ultimately to the political economy. The root of the injustice, as well as its core, will be socioeconomic maldistribution, while any attendant cultural injustices will derive ultimately from that economic root. At bottom, therefore, the remedy required to redress the injustice will be polit-ical-economic redistribution, as opposed to cultural recognition.

In the real world, to be sure, political-economy and culture are mutually intertwined, as are injustices of distribution and recognition. Thus, we may doubt whether there exist any pure collectivities of this sort. For heuristic purposes, however, it is useful to examine their properties. To do so, let us consider a familiar example that can be interpreted as approximating the ideal type: the Marxian conception of the exploited class, understood in an orthodox and theoretical way.[15] And let us bracket the question of whether this view of class fits the actual historical collectivities that have struggled for justice in the real world in the name of the working class.[16]

---

15 In what follows, I conceive class in a highly stylized, orthodox, and theoretical way in order to sharpen the contrast to the other ideal-typical kinds of collectivity discussed below. Of course, this is hardly the only interpretation of the Marxian conception of class. In other contexts and for other purposes, I myself would prefer a less economistic interpretation, one that gives more weight to the cultural, historical and discursive dimensions of class emphasized by such writers as E. P. Thompson and Joan Wallach Scott. See Thompson, *The Making of the English Working Class*, New York: Random House, 1963; and Scott, *Gender and the Politics of History*, New York: Columbia University Press, 1988.

16 It is doubtful that any collectivities mobilized in the real world today correspond to the notion of class presented below. Certainly, the history of social movements mobilized under the banner of class is more complex than this conception would suggest. Those movements have elaborated class not only as a structural category of political economy but also as a cultural-valuational category of identity—often in forms problematic for women and blacks. Thus, most varieties of socialism have asserted the dignity of labor and the worth of working people, mingling demands for redistribution with demands for recognition. Sometimes, moreover, having failed to abolish capitalism, class movements have adopted reformist strategies of seeking recog-nition of their "difference" within the system in order to augment their power and support demands for what I below call "affirmative redistribution." In general, then, historical class-based movements may be closer to what I below call "bivalent modes of collectivity" than to the interpretation of class sketched here.

In the conception assumed here, class is a mode of social differentiation that is rooted in the political-economic structure of society. A
class only exists as a collectivity in virtue of its position in that structure
and of its relation to other classes. Thus, the Marxian working class
is the body of persons in a capitalist society who must sell their labor
power under arrangements that authorize the capitalist class to
appropriate surplus productivity for its private benefit. The injustice
of these arrangements, moreover, is quintessentially a matter of
distribution. In the capitalist scheme of social reproduction, the
proletariat receives an unjustly large share of the burdens and an
unjustly small share of the rewards. To be sure, its members also suffer
serious cultural injustices, the "hidden (and not so hidden) injuries of
class." But far from being rooted directly in an autonomously unjust
cultural structure, these derive from the political economy, as ideologies
of class inferiority proliferate to justify exploitation.[17] The remedy
for the injustice, consequently, is redistribution, not recognition.
Overcoming class exploitation requires restructuring the political
economy so as to alter the class distribution of social burdens and
social benefits. In the Marxian conception, such restructuring takes
the radical form of abolishing the class structure as such. The task of
the proletariat, therefore, is not simply to cut itself a better deal, but
"to abolish itself as a class." The last thing it needs is recognition of
its difference. On the contrary, the only way to remedy the injustice
is to put the proletariat out of business as a group.

Now consider the other end of the conceptual spectrum. At this
end we may posit an ideal-typical mode of collectivity that fits the
recognition model of justice. A collectivity of this type is rooted
wholly in culture, as opposed to in political economy. It only exists
as a collectivity by virtue of the reigning social patterns of interpretation and evaluation, not by virtue of the division of labor. Thus,
any structural injustices its members suffer will be traceable ultimately
to the cultural-valuational structure. The root of the injustice, as well
as its core, will be cultural misrecognition, while any attendant
economic injustices will derive ultimately from that cultural root. At
bottom, therefore, the remedy required to redress the injustice will be
cultural recognition, as opposed to political-economic redistribution.

---

17 This assumption does not require us to reject the view that distributive deficits
are often (perhaps even always) accompanied by recognition deficits. But it does entail
that the recognition deficits of class, in the sense elaborated here, derive from the political
economy. Later, I shall consider other sorts of cases in which collectivities suffer from
recognition deficits whose roots are not directly political-economic in this way.

Once again, we may doubt whether there exist any pure collectivities of this sort, but it is useful to examine their properties for heuristic purposes. An example that can be interpreted as approximating the ideal type is the conception of a despised sexuality, understood in a specific stylized and theoretical way.[18] Let us consider this conception, while leaving aside the question of whether this view of sexuality fits the actual historical homosexual collectivities that are struggling for justice in the real world.

Sexuality in this conception is a mode of social differentiation whose roots do not lie in the political economy, as homosexuals are distributed throughout the entire class structure of capitalist society, occupy no distinctive position in the division of labor, and do not constitute an exploited class. Rather, their mode of collectivity is that of a despised sexuality, rooted in the cultural-valuational structure of society. From this perspective, the injustice they suffer is quintessentially a matter of recognition. Gays and lesbians suffer from heterosexism: the authoritative construction of norms that privilege heterosexuality. Along with this goes homophobia: the cultural devaluation of homosexuality. Their sexuality thus disparaged, homo-sexuals are subject to shaming, harassment, discrimination, and violence, while being denied legal rights and equal protections—all fundamentally denials of recognition. To be sure, gays and lesbians also suffer serious economic injustices; they can be summarily dismissed from work and are denied family-based social-welfare benefits. But far from being rooted directly in the economic structure, these derive instead from an unjust cultural-valuational structure.[19] The remedy

---

18 In what follows, I conceive sexuality in a highly stylized theoretical way in order to sharpen the contrast to the other ideal-typical kinds of collectivity discussed here. I treat sexual differentiation as rooted wholly in the cultural structure, as opposed to in the political economy. Of course, this is not the only interpretation of sexuality. Judith Butler (personal communication) has suggested that one might hold that sexuality is inextricable from gender, which, as I argue below, is as much a matter of the division of labor as of the cultural-valuational structure. In that case, sexuality itself might be viewed as a "bivalent" collectivity, rooted simultane-ously in culture and political economy. Then, the economic harms encountered by homosexuals might appear economically rooted rather than culturally rooted, as they are in the account I offer here. While this bivalent analysis is certainly possible, to my mind it has serious drawbacks. Yoking gender and sexuality together too tightly, it covers over the important distinction between a group that occupies a distinct position in the division of labor (and that owes its existence in large part to this fact), on the one hand, and one that occupies no such distinct position, on the other hand. I discuss this distinction below.

for the injustice, consequently, is recognition, not redistribution. Overcoming homophobia and heterosexism requires changing the cultural valuations (as well as their legal and practical expressions) that privilege heterosexuality, deny equal respect to gays and lesbians, and refuse to recognize homosexuality as a legitimate way of being sexual. It is to revalue a despised sexuality, to accord positive recognition to gay and lesbian sexual specificity.

Matters are thus fairly straightforward at the two extremes of our conceptual spectrum. When we deal with collectivities that approach the ideal type of the exploited working class, we face distributive injustices requiring redistributive remedies. When we deal with collectivities that approach the ideal type of the despised sexuality, in contrast, we face injustices of misrecognition requiring remedies of recognition. In the first case, the logic of the remedy is to put the group out of business as a group. In the second case, on the contrary, it is to valorize the group's "groupness" by recognizing its specificity.

Matters become murkier, however, once we move away from these extremes. When we consider collectivities located in the middle of the

---

19 An example of an economic injustice rooted directly in the economic structure would be a division of labor that relegates homosexuals to a designated disadvantaged position and exploits them as homosexuals. To deny that this is the situation of homosexuals today is not to deny that they face economic injustices. But it is to trace these to another root. In general, I assume that recognition deficits are often (perhaps even always) accompanied by distribution deficits. But I nevertheless hold that the distribution deficits of sexuality, in the sense elaborated here, derive ultimately from the cultural structure. Later, I shall consider other sorts of cases in which collectivities suffer from distribution deficits whose roots are not (only) directly cultural in this sense. I can perhaps further clarify the point by invoking Oliver Cromwell Cox's contrast between anti-Semitism and white supremacy. Cox suggested that for the anti-Semite, the very existence of the Jew is an abomination; hence the aim is not to exploit Jews but to eliminate them, whether by expulsion, forced conversion, or extermination. For the white supremacist, in contrast, "Negroes" are just fine—in their place as an exploitable supply of cheap, menial labor power. Here the preferred aim is exploitation, not elimination. (See Cox's unjustly neglected masterwork, *Caste, Class, and Race,* New York: Monthly Review Press, 1970.) Contemporary homophobia appears in this respect to be more like anti-Semitism than white supremacy: it seeks to eliminate, not exploit, homosexuals. Thus, the economic disadvantages of homosexuality are derived effects of the more fundamental denial of cultural recognition. This makes it the mirror image of class, as just discussed, where the "hidden (and not so hidden) injuries" of misrecognition are derived effects of the more fundamental injustice of exploitation. White supremacy, in contrast, as I shall suggest shortly, is "bivalent," rooted simultaneously in political economy and culture, inflicting co-original and equally fundamental injustices of distribution and recognition. (On this last point, incidentally, I differ from Cox, who treats white supremacy as effectively reducible to class.)

conceptual spectrum, we encounter hybrid modes that combine features of the exploited class with features of the despised sexuality. These collectivities are "bivalent." They are differentiated as collectivities by virtue of *both* the political-economic structure *and* the cultural-valuational structure of society. When disadvantaged, therefore, they suffer injustices that are traceable to both political economy and culture simultaneously. Bivalent collectivities, in sum, may suffer both socioeconomic maldistribution and cultural misrecognition in forms where neither of these injustices is an indirect effect of the other, but where both are primary and co-original. In that case, neither redistributive remedies alone nor recognition remedies alone will suffice. Bivalent collectivities need both.

Both gender and "race" are paradigmatic bivalent collectivities. Although each has peculiarities not shared by the other, both encompass political-economic dimensions and cultural-valuational dimensions. Gender and "race," therefore, implicate both redistribution and recognition.

Gender, for example, has political-economic dimensions. It is a basic structuring principle of the political economy. On the one hand, gender structures the fundamental division between paid "productive" labor and unpaid "reproductive" and domestic labor, assigning women primary responsibility for the latter. On the other hand, gender also structures the division within paid labor between higher-paid, male-dominated, manufacturing and professional occupations and lower-paid, female-dominated "pink collar" and domestic service occupations. The result is a political-economic structure that generates gender-specific modes of exploitation, marginalization, and deprivation. This structure constitutes gender as a political-economic differentiation endowed with certain class-like characteristics. When viewed under this aspect, gender injustice appears as a species of distributive injustice that cries out for redistributive redress. Much like class, gender justice requires transforming the political economy so as to eliminate its gender structuring. Eliminating gender-specific exploitation, marginalization, and deprivation requires abolishing the gender division of labor—both the gendered division between paid and unpaid labor and the gender division within paid labor. The logic of the remedy is akin to the logic with respect to class: it is to put gender out of business as such. If gender were nothing but a political-economic differentiation, in sum, justice would require its abolition.

That, however, is only half the story. In fact, gender is not only a political-economic differentiation, but a cultural-valuational differentiation as well. As such, it also encompasses elements that are more

like sexuality than class and that bring it squarely within the problematic of recognition. Certainly, a major feature of gender injustice
is androcentrism: the authoritative construction of norms that privilege
traits associated with masculinity. Along with this goes cultural sexism:
the pervasive devaluation and disparagement of things coded as
"feminine," paradigmatically—but not only—women.[20] This devaluation is expressed in a range of harms suffered by women, including
sexual assault, sexual exploitation, and pervasive domestic violence;
trivializing, objectifying, and demeaning stereotypical depictions in
the media; harassment and disparagement in all spheres of everyday
life; subjection to androcentric norms in relation to which women
appear lesser or deviant and which work to disadvantage them, even
in the absence of any intention to discriminate; attitudinal discrimination; exclusion or marginalization in public spheres and deliberative
bodies; and denial of full legal rights and equal protections. These
harms are injustices of recognition. They are relatively independent
of political economy and are not merely "superstructural." Thus, they
cannot be remedied by political-economic redistribution alone but
require additional independent remedies of recognition. Overcoming
androcentrism and sexism requires changing the cultural valuations
(as well as their legal and practical expressions) that privilege masculinity and deny equal respect to women. It requires decentering
androcentric norms and revaluing a despised gender. The logic of the
remedy is akin to the logic with respect to sexuality: it is to accord
positive recognition to a devalued group specificity.

Gender, in sum, is a bivalent mode of collectivity. It contains a
political-economic face that brings it within the ambit of redistribution.
Yet it also contains a cultural-valuational face that brings it simultaneously within the ambit of recognition. Of course, the two faces
are not neatly separated from one another. Rather, they intertwine
to reinforce one another dialectically, as sexist and androcentric
cultural norms are institutionalized in the state and the economy, while
women's economic disadvantage restricts women's "voice," impeding
equal participation in the making of culture, in public spheres, and
in everyday life. The result is a vicious circle of cultural and economic
subordination. Redressing gender injustice, therefore, requires changing
both political economy and culture.

But the bivalent character of gender is the source of a dilemma.

---

20 Gender disparagement can take many forms, of course, including conservative
stereotypes that appear to celebrate, rather than demean, "femininity."

Insofar as women suffer at least two analytically distinct kinds of injustice, they necessarily require at least two analytically distinct kinds of remedy—both redistribution and recognition. The two remedies pull in opposite directions, however. They are not easily pursued simultaneously. Whereas the logic of redistribution is to put gender out of business as such, the logic of recognition is to valorize gender specificity.[21] Here, then, is the feminist version of the redistribution-recognition dilemma: how can feminists fight simultaneously to abolish gender differentiation and to valorize gender specificity?

An analogous dilemma arises in the struggle against racism. "Race," like gender, is a bivalent mode of collectivity. On the one hand, it resembles class in being a structural principle of political economy. In this aspect, "race" structures the capitalist division of labor. It structures the division within paid work between low-paid, low-status, menial, dirty, and domestic occupations held disproportionately by people of color, and higher-paid, higher-status, white-collar, professional, technical, and managerial occupations, held disproportionately by "whites."[22] Today's racial division of paid labor is part of the historical legacy of colonialism and slavery, which elaborated racial categorization to justify brutal new forms of appropriation and exploitation, effectively constituting "blacks" as a political-economic caste. Currently, moreover, "race" also structures access to official labor markets, constituting large segments of the population of color as a "superfluous," degraded subproletariat or underclass, unworthy

---

21 This helps explain why the history of women's movements records a pattern of oscillation between integrationist equal-rights feminisms and "difference"-oriented "social" and "cultural" feminisms. It would be useful to specify the precise temporal logic that leads bivalent collectivities to shift their principal focus back and forth between redistribution and recognition. For a first attempt, see my "Multiculturalism, Antiessentialism, and Radical Democracy: A Genealogy of the Present Impasse in Feminist Theory" in *Justice Interruptus*.

22 In addition, "race" is implicitly implicated in the gender division between paid and unpaid labor. That division relies on a normative contrast between a domestic sphere and a sphere of paid work, associated with women and men respectively. Yet the division in the United States (and elsewhere) has always also been racialized in that domesticity has been implicitly a "white" prerogative. African-Americans especially were never permitted the privilege of domesticity either as a (male) private "haven" or a (female) primary or exclusive focus on nurturing one's own kin. See Jacqueline Jones, *Labor of Love, Labor of Sorrow: Black Women, Work, and the Family from Slavery to the Present*, New York: Basic Books, 1985, and Evelyn Nakano Glenn, "From Servitude to Service Work: Historical Continuities in the Racial Division of Reproductive Labor," *Signs: Journal of Women in Culture and Society* 18: 1, Autumn 1992, pp. 1–43.

even of exploitation and excluded from the productive system altogether. The result is a political-economic structure that generates "race"-specific modes of exploitation, marginalization, and deprivation. This structure constitutes "race" as a political-economic differentiation endowed with certain class-like characteristics. When viewed under this aspect, racial injustice appears as a species of distributive injustice that cries out for redistributive redress. Much like class, racial justice requires transforming the political economy so as to eliminate its racialization. Eliminating "race"-specific exploitation, marginalization, and deprivation requires abolishing the racial division of labor—both the racial division between exploitable and superfluous labor and the racial division within paid labor. The logic of the remedy is like the logic with respect to class: it is to put "race" out of business as such. If "race" were nothing but a political-economic differentiation, in sum, justice would require its abolition.

However, "race," like gender, is not only political-economic. It also has cultural-valuational dimensions, which bring it into the universe of recognition. Thus, "race" too encompasses elements that are more like sexuality than class. A major aspect of racism is Eurocentrism: the authoritative construction of norms that privilege traits associated with "whiteness." Along with this goes cultural racism: the pervasive devaluation and disparagement[23] of things coded as "black," "brown," and "yellow," paradigmatically—but not only—people of color.[24] This depreciation is expressed in a range of harms suffered by people of color, including demeaning stereotypical depictions in the media as criminal, bestial, primitive, stupid, etc.; violence, harassment, and disrespect in all spheres of everyday life; subjection to Eurocentric norms in relation to which people of color appear lesser or deviant and which work to disadvantage them, even in the absence of any intention to discriminate; attitudinal discrimination; exclusion from and/or marginalization in public spheres and deliberative bodies; and denial of full legal rights and equal protections. As in the case of

---

23 In a previous draft of this paper I used the term "denigration." The ironic consequence was that I unintentionally perpetrated the exact sort of harm I aimed to criticize—in the very act of describing it. "Denigration," from the Latin *nigrare* (to blacken), figures disparagement as blackening, a racist valuation. I am grateful to the Saint Louis University student who called my attention to this point.

24 Racial disparagement can take many forms, of course, ranging from the stereotypical depiction of African-Americans as intellectually inferior, but musically and athletically gifted, to the stereotypical depiction of Asian-Americans as a "model minority."

gender, these harms are injustices of recognition. Thus, the logic of their remedy, too, is to accord positive recognition to devalued group specificity.

"Race," too, therefore, is a bivalent mode of collectivity with both a political-economic face and a cultural-valuational face. Its two faces intertwine to reinforce one another dialectically, moreover, as racist and Eurocentric cultural norms are institutionalized in the state and the economy, while the economic disadvantage suffered by people of color restricts their "voice." Redressing racial injustice, therefore, requires changing both political economy and culture. And as with gender, the bivalent character of "race" is the source of a dilemma. Insofar as people of color suffer at least two analytically distinct kinds of injustice, they necessarily require at least two analytically distinct kinds of remedy, which are not easily pursued simultaneously. Whereas the logic of redistribution is to put "race" out of business as such, the logic of recognition is to valorize group specificity.[25] Here, then, is the anti-racist version of the redistribution-recognition dilemma: how can anti-racists fight simultaneously to abolish "race" and to valorize racialized group specificity?

Both gender and "race," in sum, are dilemmatic modes of collectivity. Unlike class, which occupies one end of the conceptual spectrum, and unlike sexuality, which occupies the other, gender and "race" are bivalent, implicated simultaneously in both the politics of redistribution and the politics of recognition. Both, consequently, face the redistribution-recognition dilemma. Feminists must pursue political-economic remedies that would undermine gender differentiation, while also pursuing cultural-valuational remedies that valorize the specificity of a despised collectivity. Anti-racists, likewise, must pursue political-economic remedies that would undermine "racial" differentiation, while also pursuing cultural-valuational remedies that valorize the specificity of despised collectivities. How can they do both things at once?

---

25 This helps explain why the history of black liberation struggle in the United States records a pattern of oscillation between integration and separatism (or black nationalism). As with gender, it would be useful to specify the dynamics of these alternations.

III. *Affirmation or transformation?*
Revisiting the question of remedy

So far I have posed the redistribution-recognition dilemma in a form
that appears quite intractable. I have assumed that redistributive
remedies for political-economic injustice always dedifferentiate
social groups. Likewise, I have assumed that recognition remedies
for cultural-valuational injustice always enhance social group
differentiation. Given these assumptions, it is difficult to see how
feminists and anti-racists can pursue redistribution and recognition
simultaneously.

Now, however, I want to complicate these assumptions. In this
section, I shall examine alternative conceptions of redistribution, on
the one hand, and alternative conceptions of recognition, on the other.
My aim is to distinguish two broad approaches to remedying injustice
that cut across the redistribution-recognition divide. I shall call them
"affirmation" and "transformation" respectively. After sketching each
of them generically, I shall show how each operates in regard to both
redistribution and recognition. On this basis, finally, I shall reformulate
the redistribution-recognition dilemma in a form that is more amenable
to resolution.

Let me begin by briefly distinguishing affirmation and transformation. By affirmative remedies for injustice I mean remedies aimed
at correcting inequitable outcomes of social arrangements without
disturbing the underlying framework that generates them. By transformative remedies, in contrast, I mean remedies aimed at correcting
inequitable outcomes precisely by restructuring the underlying gener-
ative framework. The nub of the contrast is end-state outcomes versus
the processes that produce them. It is *not* gradual versus apocalyptic
change.

This distinction can be applied, first of all, to remedies for cultural
injustice. Affirmative remedies for such injustices are currently associated
with mainstream multiculturalism.[26] This proposes to redress disrespect
by revaluing unjustly devalued group identities, while leaving intact both

---

26 Not all versions of multiculturalism fit the model I describe here. The latter is
an ideal-typical reconstruction of what I take to be the majority understanding of
multiculturalism. It is also the version that is usually debated in mainstream public
spheres. Other versions are discussed in Linda Nicholson, "To Be or Not to Be: Charles
Taylor on the Politics of Recognition," *Constellations* 3: 1, 1996, pp. 1–16; and in
Michael Warner, et al., "Critical Multiculturalism," *Critical Inquiry* 18: 3, Spring
1992, pp. 530–56.

the contents of those identities and the group differentiations that underlie them. Transformative remedies, by contrast, are currently associated with deconstruction. They would redress disrespect by transforming the underlying cultural-valuational structure. By destabilizing existing group identities and differentiations, these remedies would not only raise the self-esteem of members of currently disrespected groups. They would change *everyone's* sense of belonging, affiliation, and self.

To illustrate the distinction, let us consider, once again, the case of the despised sexuality.[27] Affirmative remedies for homophobia and heterosexism are currently associated with gay-identity politics, which aims to revalue gay and lesbian identity.[28] Transformative remedies, in contrast, include the approach of "queer theory," which would deconstruct the homo-hetero dichotomy. Gay-identity politics treats homosexuality as a substantive, cultural, identificatory positivity, much like an ethnicity.[29] This positivity is assumed to subsist in and of itself and to need only additional recognition. "Queer theory," in contrast, treats homosexuality as the constructed and devalued correlate of heterosexuality; both are reifications of sexual ambiguity and are co-defined only in respect to one another.[30] The transformative aim is not to solidify a gay identity, but to deconstruct the homo-hetero dichotomy so as to destabilize all fixed sexual identities. The point is not to dissolve all sexual difference in a single, universal human identity; it is rather to sustain a sexual field of multiple, debinarized, fluid, ever-shifting differences.

Both these approaches have considerable interest as remedies for misrecognition. But there is one crucial difference between them. Whereas gay-identity politics tends to enhance existing sexual group differentiation, queer-theory politics tends to destabilize it—at least

---

27 Recall that sexuality is here assumed to be a collectivity rooted wholly in the cultural-valuational structure of society; thus, the issues here are unclouded by issues of political-economic structure, and the need is for recognition, not redistribution.

28 An alternative affirmative approach is gay-rights humanism, which would privatize existing sexualities. For reasons of space, I shall not discuss it here.

29 For a critical discussion of the tendency in gay-identity politics to tacitly cast sexuality in the mold of ethnicity, see Steven Epstein, "Gay Politics, Ethnic Identity: The Limits of Social Constructionism," *Socialist Review* no. 93/94, May–August 1987, pp. 9–54.

30 The technical term for this in Jacques Derrida's deconstructive philosophy is *supplement*.

ostensibly and in the long run.[31] The point holds for recognition remedies more generally. Whereas affirmative recognition remedies tend to promote existing group differentiations, transformative recognition remedies tend, in the long run, to destabilize them so as to make room for future regroupments. I shall return to this point shortly.

Analogous distinctions hold for the remedies for economic injustice. Affirmative remedies for such injustices have been associated historically with the liberal welfare state.[32] They seek to redress end-state maldistribution, while leaving intact much of the underlying political-economic structure. Thus, they would increase the consumption share of economically disadvantaged groups, without otherwise restructuring the system of production. Transformative remedies, in contrast, have been historically associated with socialism. They would redress unjust distribution by transforming the underlying political-economic structure. By restructuring the relations of production, these remedies would not only alter the end-state distribution of consumption shares;

---

31 Despite its professed long-term deconstructive goal, queer theory's practical effects may be more ambiguous. Like gay-identity politics, it, too, seems likely to promote group solidarity in the here and now, even as it sets its sights on the promised land of deconstruction. Perhaps, then, we should distinguish what I below call its "official recognition commitment" of group dedifferentiation from its "practical recognition effect" of (transitional) group solidarity and even group solidification. The queer theory recognition strategy thus contains an internal tension: in order eventually to destabilize the homo-hetero dichotomy, it must first mobilize "queers." Whether this tension becomes fruitful or debilitating depends on factors too complex to discuss here. In either case, however, the recognition politics of queer theory remains distinct from that of gay identity. Whereas gay-identity politics simply and straightforwardly underlines group differentiation, queer theory does so only indirectly, in the undertow of its principal dedifferentiating thrust. Accordingly, the two approaches construct qualitatively different kinds of groups. Whereas gay-identity politics mobilizes self-identified homosexuals qua homosexuals to vindicate a putatively determinate sexuality, queer theory mobilizes "queers" to demand liberation from determinate sexual identity. "Queers," of course, are not an identity group in the same sense as gays; they are better understood as an anti-identity group, one that can encompass the entire spectrum of sexual behaviors, from gay to straight to bi. (For a hilarious —and insightful—account of the difference, as well as for a sophisticated rendition of queer politics, see Lisa Duggan, "Queering the State," Social Text, 39, Summer 1994, pp. 1–14.) Complications aside, then, we can and should distinguish the (directly) differentiating effects of affirmative gay recognition from the (more) dedifferentiating (albeit complex) effects of transformative queer recognition.

32 By "liberal welfare state," I mean the sort of regime established in the US following the New Deal. It has been usefully distinguished from the social-democratic welfare state and the conservative-corporatist welfare state by Gøsta Esping-Andersen in The Three Worlds of Welfare Capitalism, Princeton: Princeton University Press, 1990.

they would also change the social division of labor and thus the conditions of existence for everyone.[33]

Let us consider, once again, the case of the exploited class.[34] Affirmative redistributive remedies for class injustices typically include income transfers of two distinct kinds: social insurance programs share some of the costs of social reproduction for the stably employed, the so-called primary sectors of the working class; public assistance programs provide means-tested, "targeted" aid to the "reserve army" of the unemployed and underemployed. Far from abolishing class differentiation per se, these affirmative remedies support it and shape it. Their general effect is to shift attention from the class division between workers and capitalists to the division between employed and nonemployed fractions of the working class. Public assistance programs "target" the poor, not only for aid but for hostility. Such remedies, to be sure, provide needed material aid. But they also create strongly cathected, antagonistic group differentiations.

The logic here applies to affirmative redistribution in general. Although this approach aims to redress economic injustice, it leaves intact the deep structures that generate class disadvantage. Thus, it must make surface reallocations again and again. The result is to mark the most disadvantaged class as inherently deficient and insatiable, as always needing more and more. In time such a class can even come to appear privileged, the recipient of special treatment and undeserved largesse. Thus, an approach aimed at redressing injustices of distribution can end up creating injustices of recognition.

In a sense, this approach is self-contradictory. Affirmative redistribution generally presupposes a universalist conception of recognition,

---

33 Today, of course, many specific features of socialism of the "really existing" variety appear problematic. Virtually no one continues to defend a pure "command" economy in which there is little place for markets. Nor is there agreement concerning the place and extent of public ownership in a democratic socialist society. For my purposes here, however, it is not necessary to assign a precise content to the socialist idea. It is sufficient, rather, to invoke the general conception of redressing distributive injustice by deep political-economic restructuring, as opposed to surface reallocations. In this light, incidentally, social democracy appears as a hybrid case that combines affirmative and transformative remedies; it can also be seen as a "middle position," which involves a moderate extent of economic restructuring, more than in the liberal welfare state but less than in socialism.

34 Recall that class, in the sense defined above, is a collectivity wholly rooted in the political-economic structure of society; the issues here are thus unclouded by issues of cultural-valuational structure; and the remedies required are those of redistribution, not recognition.

the equal moral worth of persons. Let us call this its "official recognition commitment." Yet the practice of affirmative redistribution, as
iterated over time, tends to set in motion a second—stigmatizing—
recognition dynamic, which contradicts universalism. This second
dynamic can be understood as the "practical recognition-effect" of
affirmative redistribution.[35] It conflicts with its official recognition
commitment.[36]

Now contrast this logic with transformative remedies for distributive
injustices of class. Transformative remedies typically combine universalist   social-welfare   programs,   steeply   progressive   taxation,
macroeconomic policies aimed at creating full employment, a large
non-market public sector, significant public and/or collective ownership, and democratic decision-making about basic socioeconomic
priorities. They try to ensure access to employment for all, while also
tending to de-link basic consumption shares from employment. Hence
their tendency is to undermine class differentiation. Transformative
remedies reduce social inequality without, however, creating stigmatized classes of vulnerable people perceived as beneficiaries of special
largesse.[37] They tend therefore to promote reciprocity and solidarity
in the relations of recognition. Thus, an approach aimed at redressing
injustices of distribution can help redress (some) injustices of
recognition as well.[38]

This approach is self-consistent. Like affirmative redistribution, transformative redistribution generally presupposes a universalist conception
of recognition, the equal moral worth of persons. Unlike affirmative
redistribution, however, its practice tends not to undermine this

---

35 In some contexts, such as the United States today, the practical recognition-
effect of affirmative redistribution can utterly swamp its official recognition
commitment.

36 My terminology here is inspired by Pierre Bourdieu's distinction, in *Outline of
a Theory of Practice*, between "official kinship" and "practical kinship."

37 I have deliberately sketched a picture that is ambiguous between socialism and
robust social democracy. The classic account of the latter remains T. H. Marshall's
"Citizenship and Social Class," in *Class, Citizenship, and Social Development: Essays
by T. H. Marshall*, ed. Seymour Martin Lipset, Chicago: University of Chicago Press,
1964. There Marshall argues that a universalist social-democratic regime of "social
citizenship" undermines class differentiation, even in the absence of full-scale socialism.

38 To be more precise: transformative redistribution can help redress those forms
of misrecognition that derive from the political-economic structure. Redressing
misrecognition rooted in the cultural structure, in contrast, requires additional independent recognition remedies.

conception. Thus, the two approaches generate different logics of group differentiation. Whereas affirmative remedies can have the perverse effect of promoting class differentiation, transformative remedies tend to blur it. In addition, the two approaches generate different subliminal dynamics of recognition. Affirmative redistribution can stigmatize the disadvantaged, adding the insult of misrecognition to the injury of deprivation. Transformative redistribution, in contrast, can promote solidarity, helping to redress some forms of misrecognition.

What, then, should we conclude from this discussion? In this section, we have considered only the "pure" ideal-typical cases at the two extremes of the conceptual spectrum. We have contrasted the divergent effects of affirmative and transformative remedies for the economically rooted distributive injustices of class, on the one hand, and for the culturally rooted recognition injustices of sexuality, on the other. We saw that affirmative remedies tend generally to promote group differentiation, while transformative remedies tend to destabilize or blur it. We also saw that affirmative redistribution remedies can generate a backlash of misrecognition, while transformative redistribution remedies can help redress some forms of misrecognition.

All this suggests a way of reformulating the redistribution-recognition dilemma. We might ask: for groups who are subject to injustices of both types, what combinations of remedies work best to minimize, if not altogether to eliminate, the mutual interferences that can arise when both redistribution and recognition are pursued simultaneously?

IV. Finessing the dilemma: revisiting gender and "race"

Imagine a four-celled matrix. The horizontal axis comprises the two general kinds of remedies we have just examined, namely, affirmation and transformation. The vertical axis comprises the two aspects of justice we have been considering, namely, redistribution and recognition. On this matrix we can locate the four political orientations just discussed. In the first cell, where redistribution and affirmation intersect, is the project of the liberal welfare state; centered on surface reallocations of distributive shares among existing groups, it tends to support group differentiation; it can also generate backlash misrecognition. In the second cell, where redistribution and transformation intersect, is the project of socialism; aimed at deep restructuring of the relations of production, it tends to blur group differentiation; it can also help redress some forms of misrecognition. In the third cell, where recognition and affirmation intersect, is the project of mainstream multiculturalism; focused on surface reallocations of respect among existing groups, it tends to support group differentiation. In the fourth cell, where recognition and transformation intersect, is the project of deconstruction; aimed at deep restructuring of the relations of recognition, it tends to destabilize group differentiations.

	Affirmation	Transformation
Redistribution	the liberal welfare state surface reallocations of existing goods to existing groups; supports group differentiation; can generate misrecognition	socialism deep restructuring of relations of production; blurs group differentitation; can help remedy some forms of misrecognition.
Recognition	mainstream multiculturalism surface reallocations of respect to existing identities of existing groups; supports group differentiation	deconstruction deep restructuring of relations of recognition; destabilizes group differentiation

This matrix casts mainstream multiculturalism as the cultural analogue of the liberal welfare state, while casting deconstruction as the cultural analogue of socialism. It thereby allows us to make some preliminary assessments of the mutual compatibility of various remedial strategies. We can gauge the extent to which pairs of remedies would work at cross-purposes with one another if they were pursued simultaneously. We can identify pairs that seem to land us squarely on the horns of the redistribution-recognition dilemma. We can also identify pairs that hold out the promise of enabling us to finesse it.

Prima facie at least, two pairs of remedies seem especially *un*promising. The affirmative redistribution politics of the liberal welfare state seems at odds with the transformative recognition politics of deconstruction; whereas the first tends to promote group differentiation, the second tends rather to destabilize it. Similarly, the transformative redistribution politics of socialism seems at odds with the affirmative recognition politics of mainstream multiculturalism; whereas the first tends to undermine group differentiation, the second tends rather to promote it.

Conversely, two pairs of remedies seem comparatively promising. The affirmative redistribution politics of the liberal welfare state seems compatible with the affirmative recognition politics of mainstream multiculturalism; both tend to promote group differentiation, although the former can generate backlash misrecognition. Similarly, the transformative redistribution politics of socialism seems compatible with the transformative recognition politics of deconstruction; both tend to undermine existing group differentiations.

To test these hypotheses, let us revisit gender and "race." Recall that these are bivalent differentiations, axes of both economic and cultural injustice. Thus, people subordinated by gender and/or "race" need both redistribution and recognition. They are the paradigmatic subjects of the redistribution-recognition dilemma. What happens in their cases, then, when various pairs of injustice remedies are pursued simultaneously? Are there pairs of remedies that permit feminists and anti-racists to finesse, if not wholly to dispel, the redistribution-recognition dilemma?

Consider, first, the case of gender.[39] Recall that redressing gender injustice requires changing both political economy and culture, so as to undo the vicious circle of economic and cultural subordination. As we saw, the changes in question can take either of two forms, affirmation or transformation.[40] Let us consider, first, the prima facie promising

---

39 Recall that gender, qua political-economic differentiation, structures the division of labor in ways that give rise to gender-specific forms of exploitation, marginalization, and deprivation. Recall, moreover, that qua cultural-valuational differentiation, gender also structures the relations of recognition in ways that give rise to androcentrism and cultural sexism. Recall, too, that for gender, as for all bivalent group differentiations, economic injustices and cultural injustices are not neatly separated from one another; rather they intertwine to reinforce one another dialectically, as sexist and androcentric cultural norms are institutionalized in the economy, while economic disadvantage impedes equal participation in the making of culture, both in everyday life and in public spheres.

40 I shall leave aside the prima facie unpromising cases. Let me simply stipulate that a cultural-feminist recognition politics aimed at revaluing femininity is hard to combine with a socialist-feminist redistributive politics aimed at degendering the political economy. The incompatibility is overt when we treat the recognition of "women's difference" as a long-term feminist goal. Of course, some feminists conceive the struggle for such recognition not as end in itself but as a stage in a process they envision as leading eventually to degenderization. Here, perhaps, there is no formal contradiction with socialism. At the same time, however, there remains a practical contradiction, or at least a practical difficulty: can a stress on women's difference in the here and now really end up dissolving gender difference in the by-and-by? The converse argument holds for the case of the liberal-feminist welfare state plus deconstructive feminism. Affirmative action for women is usually seen as a transitional remedy aimed at achieving the long-term goal of "a sex-blind society." Here, again, there is perhaps no formal contradiction with deconstruction. But there remains nevertheless a practical contradiction, or at least a practical difficulty: can liberal-feminist affirmative action in the here and now really help lead us to deconstruction in the by-and-by?

case in which affirmative redistribution is combined with affirmative recognition. As the name suggests, affirmative redistribution to redress gender injustice in the economy includes affirmative action, the effort to ensure women their fair share of existing jobs and educational places, while leaving unchanged the nature and number of those jobs and places. Affirmative recognition to redress gender injustice in the culture includes cultural feminism, the effort to ensure women respect by revaluing femininity, while leaving unchanged the binary gender code that gives the latter its sense. Thus, the scenario in question combines the socioeconomic politics of liberal feminism with the cultural politics of cultural feminism. Does this combination really finesse the redistribution-recognition dilemma?

Despite its initial appearance of promise, this scenario is problematic. Affirmative redistribution fails to engage the deep level at which the political economy is gendered. Aimed primarily at combating attitudinal discrimination, it does not attack the gendered division of paid and unpaid labor, or the gendered division of masculine and feminine occupations within paid labor. Leaving intact the deep structures that generate gender disadvantage, it must make surface reallocations again and again. The result is not only to underline gender differentiation. It is also to mark women as deficient and insatiable, as always needing more and more. In time women can even come to appear privileged, recipients of special treatment and undeserved largesse. Thus, an approach aimed at redressing injustices of distribution can end up fueling backlash injustices of recognition.

This problem is exacerbated when we add the affirmative recognition strategy of cultural feminism. That approach insistently calls attention to, if it does not performatively create, women's putative cultural specificity or difference. In some contexts, such an approach can make progress toward decentering androcentric norms. In this context, however, it is more likely to have the effect of pouring oil onto the flames of resentment against affirmative action. Read through that lens, the cultural politics of affirming women's difference appears as an affront to the liberal welfare state's official commitment to the equal moral worth of persons.

The other route with a prima facie promise is that which combines transformative redistribution with transformative recognition. Transformative redistribution to redress gender injustice in the economy consists in some form of socialist feminism or feminist social democracy. And transformative recognition to redress gender injustice in the culture consists in feminist deconstruction aimed at dismantling androcentrism by destabilizing gender dichotomies. Thus, the scenario in question combines the socioeconomic politics of socialist feminism with the cultural politics of deconstructive feminism. Does this combination really finesse the redistribution-recognition dilemma?

This scenario is far less problematic. The long-term goal of deconstructive feminism is a culture in which hierarchical gender dichotomies are replaced by networks of multiple intersecting differences that are demassified and shifting. This goal is consistent with transformative socialist-feminist redistribution. Deconstruction opposes the sort of sedimentation or congealing of gender difference that occurs in an unjustly gendered political economy. Its utopian image of a culture in which ever new constructions of identity and difference are freely elaborated and then swiftly deconstructed is only possible, after all, on the basis of rough social equality.

As a transitional strategy, moreover, this combination avoids fanning the flames of resentment.[41] If it has a drawback, it is rather that both deconstructive-feminist cultural politics and socialist-feminist economic politics are far removed from the immediate interests and identities of most women, as these are currently culturally constructed.

Analogous results arise for "race," where the changes can again take either of two forms, affirmation or transformation.[42] In the first prima facie promising case, affirmative redistribution is paired with affirmative recognition. Affirmative redistribution to redress racial injustice in the economy includes affirmative action, the effort to assure people of color their fair share of existing jobs and educational places, while leaving unchanged the nature and number of those jobs and places. Affirmative recognition to redress racial injustice in the culture includes cultural nationalism, the effort to assure people of color respect by revaluing "blackness," while leaving unchanged the binary black-white code that gives the latter its sense. The scenario in question thus combines the socioeconomic politics of liberal anti-racism with the cultural politics of black nationalism or black power. Does this combination really finesse the redistribution-recognition dilemma?

---

41 Here I am assuming that the internal complexities of transformative recognition remedies, as discussed in note 31 above, do not generate perverse effects. If, however, the practical recognition effect of deconstructive feminist cultural politics is strongly gender-differentiating, despite the latter's official recognition commitment to gender dedifferentiation, perverse effects could indeed arise. In that case, there could be interferences between socialist-feminist redistribution and deconstructive-feminist recognition. But these would probably be less debilitating than those associated with the other scenarios examined here.

42 The same can be said about "race" here as about gender in notes 39 and 40.

Such a scenario is again problematic. As in the case of gender, affirmative redistribution here fails to engage the deep level at which the political economy is racialized. It does not attack the racialized division of exploitable and surplus labor, nor the racialized division of menial and non-menial occupations within paid labor. Leaving intact the deep structures that generate racial disadvantage, it must make surface reallocations again and again. The result is not only to underline racial differentiation. It is also to mark people of color as deficient and insatiable, as always needing more and more. Thus, they too can be cast as privileged recipients of special treatment. The problem is exacerbated when we add the affirmative recognition strategy of cultural nationalism. In some contexts, such an approach can make progress toward decentering Eurocentric norms, but in this context, the cultural politics of affirming black difference appears as an affront to the liberal welfare state. Fueling the resentment against affirmative action, it can elicit intense backlash misrecognition.

In the alternative route, transformative redistribution is combined with transformative recognition. Transformative redistribution to redress racial injustice in the economy consists in some form of anti-racist democratic socialism or anti-racist social democracy. And transformative recognition to redress racial injustice in the culture consists in anti-racist deconstruction aimed at dismantling Eurocentrism by destabilizing racial dichotomies. Thus, the scenario in question combines the socioeconomic politics of socialist anti-racism with the cultural politics of deconstructive anti-racism. As with the analogous approach to gender, this scenario is far less problematic. The long-term goal of deconstructive anti-racism is a culture in which hierarchical racial dichotomies are replaced by networks of multiple intersecting differences that are demassified and shifting. This goal, once again, is consistent with transformative socialist redistribution. Even as a transitional strategy, this combination, too, avoids fanning the flames of resentment.[43] Its principal drawback, again, is that both deconstructive-anti-racist cultural politics and socialist-anti-racist

---

43 Once again, I am assuming that the internal complexities of transformative recognition remedies, as discussed in note 31 above, do not generate perverse effects. If, however, the practical recognition effect of deconstructive anti-racist cultural politics is strongly color-differentiating, despite the latter's official recognition commitment to racial dedifferentiation, perverse effects could indeed arise. The result could be some mutual interferences between anti-racist socialist redistribution and anti-racist deconstructive recognition. But again, these would probably be less debilitating than those accompanying the other scenarios examined here.

economic politics are far removed from the immediate interests and identities of most people of color, as these are currently culturally constructed.[44]

What, then, should we conclude from this discussion? For both gender and "race," the scenario that best finesses the redistribution-recognition dilemma is socialism in the economy plus deconstruction in the culture.[45] But for this scenario to be psychologically and politically feasible requires that all people be weaned from their attachment to current cultural constructions of their interests and identities.[46]

V. Conclusion

The redistribution-recognition dilemma is real. There is no neat theoretical move by which it can be wholly dissolved or resolved. The best we can do is to try to soften the dilemma by finding approaches that minimize conflicts between redistribution and recognition in cases where both must be pursued simultaneously.

I have argued here that socialist economics combined with deconstructive cultural politics works best to finesse the dilemma for the bivalent collectivities of gender and "race"—at least when they are considered separately. The next step would be to show that this combination also works for our larger sociocultural configuration. After all, gender and "race" are not neatly cordoned off from one another. Nor are they neatly cordoned off from sexuality and class. Rather, all these

---

44 Ted Koditschek (personal communication) has suggested to me that this scenario may have another serious drawback: "The deconstructive option may be less available to African-Americans in the current situation. Where the structural exclusion of [many] black people from full economic citizenship pushes 'race' more and more into the forefront as a cultural category through which one is attacked, self-respecting people cannot help but aggressively affirm and embrace it as a source of pride." Koditschek goes on to suggest that Jews, in contrast, "have much more elbowroom for negotiating a healthier balance between ethnic affirmation, self-criticism, and cosmopolitan universalism—not because we are better deconstructionists (or more inherently disposed toward socialism) but because we have more space to make these moves."

45 Whether this conclusion holds as well for nationality and ethnicity remains a question. Certainly bivalent collectivities of indigenous peoples do not seek to put themselves out of business as groups.

46 This has always been the problem with socialism. Although cognitively compelling, it is experientially remote. The addition of deconstruction seems to exacerbate the problem. It could turn out to be too negative and reactive, that is, too *deconstructive*, to inspire struggles on behalf of subordinated collectivities attached to their existing identities.

axes of injustice intersect one another in ways that affect everyone's interests and identities. No one is a member of only one such collectivity.
And people who are subordinated along one axis of social division
may well be dominant along another.[47]

The task then is to figure out how to finesse the redistribution-
recognition dilemma when we situate the problem in this larger field
of multiple, intersecting struggles against multiple, intersecting injustices. Although I cannot make the full argument here, I will venture
three reasons for expecting that the combination of socialism and
deconstruction will again prove superior to the other alternatives.

First, the arguments pursued here for gender and "race" hold for
all bivalent collectivities. Thus, insofar as real-world collectivities mobilized under the banners of sexuality and class turn out to be more
bivalent than the ideal-typical constructs posited above, they too should
prefer socialism plus deconstruction. And that doubly transformative
approach should become the orientation of choice for a broad range
of disadvantaged groups.

Second, the redistribution-recognition dilemma does not only arise
endogenously, as it were, within a single bivalent collectivity. It also
arises exogenously, so to speak, across intersecting collectivities. Thus,
anyone who is both gay and working-class will face a version of the
dilemma, regardless of whether or not we interpret sexuality and class
as bivalent. And anyone who is also female and black will encounter
it in a multilayered and acute form. In general, then, as soon as we
acknowledge that axes of injustice cut across one another, we must
acknowledge crosscutting forms of the redistribution-recognition

---

47 Much recent work has been devoted to the "intersection" of the various axes
of subordination that I have treated separately in this essay for heuristic purposes. A
lot of this work concerns the dimension of recognition; it aims to demonstrate that
various collective identifications and identity categories have been mutually co-consti-
tuted or co-constructed. Joan Scott, for example, has argued (in *Gender and the
Politics of History*) that French working-class identities have been discursively
constructed through gender-coded symbolization; and David R. Roediger has argued
(in *The Wages of Whiteness: Race and the Making of the American Working Class*,
London: Verso, 1991) that US working-class identities have been racially coded.
Meanwhile, many feminists of color have argued both that gender identities have been
racially coded and that racialized identities have been gender coded. I myself have
argued, with Linda Gordon, that gender, "race," and class ideologies have intersected
to construct current US understandings of "welfare dependency" and "the underclass."
(See Fraser and Gordon, "A Genealogy of 'Dependency': Tracing a Keyword of the
US Welfare State.")

dilemma. And these forms are, if anything, even more re istant to resolution by combinations of affirmative remedies than the forms we considered above. For affirmative remedies work additively and are often at cross-purposes with one another. Thus, the intersection of class, "race," gender, and sexuality intensifies the need for transformative solutions, making the combination of socialism and deconstruction more attractive still.

Third, that combination best promotes coalition building. Coalition building is especially pressing today, given the multiplication of social antagonisms, the fissuring of social movements, and the growing appeal of the Right in the United States. In this context, the project of transforming the deep structures of both political economy and culture appears to be the one overarching programmatic orientation capable of doing justice to *all* current struggles against injustice. It alone does not assume a zero-sum game.

If that is right, then, we can begin to see how badly off track is the current US political scene. We are currently stuck in the vicious circles of mutually reinforcing cultural and economic subordination. Our best efforts to redress these injustices via the combination of the liberal welfare state plus mainstream multiculturalism are generating perverse effects. Only by looking to alternative conceptions of redistribution and recognition can we meet the requirements of justice for all.

MERELY CULTURAL
Judith Butler

I propose to consider two different kinds of claims that have circulated recently, representing a culmination of sentiment that has been building for some time. One has to do with an explicitly Marxist objection to the reduction of Marxist scholarship and activism to the study of culture, sometimes understood as the reduction of Marxism to cultural studies. The second has to do with the tendency to relegate new social movements to the sphere of the cultural, indeed, to dismiss them as being preoccupied with what is called the "merely" cultural, and then to construe this cultural politics as factionalizing, identitarian, and particularistic. If I fail to give the names of those I take to hold these views, I hope that I will be forgiven. The active cultural presumption of this essay is that we utter and hear such views, that they form some part of the debates that populate the intellectual landscape within progressive intellectual circles. I presume as well that to link individuals to such views runs the risk of deflecting attention from the meaning and effect of such views to the pettier politics of who said what, and who said what back—a form of cultural politics that, for the moment, I want to resist.

These are some of the forms that this kind of argument has taken in the last year: that the cultural focus of left politics has abandoned the materialist project of Marxism, that it fails to address questions of economic equity and redistribution, that it fails as well to situate culture in terms of a systematic understanding of social and economic modes of production; that the cultural focus of left politics has splintered the Left into identitarian sects, that we have lost a set of common ideals and goals, a sense of a common history, a common set of values, a common language and even an objective and universal mode of rationality; that the cultural focus of left politics substitutes a self-centered and trivial form of politics that focuses on transient events, practices, and objects rather than offering a more robust, serious and comprehensive vision of the systematic interrelatedness of social and economic conditions.

Clearly, one more or less implicit presumption in some of these arguments is the notion that poststructuralism has thwarted Marxism, and that any ability to offer *systematic* accounts of social life or to assert norms of rationality—whether objective, universal, or both—is now seriously hampered by a poststructuralism that has entered the field of cultural politics, where that poststructuralism is construed as destructive, relativistic and politically paralyzing.

Parody as a form of identification

Perhaps you are already wondering how it is that I might take the time to rehearse these arguments in this way, giving them airtime, as it were, and perhaps you are also wondering whether or not I am already parodying these positions. Do I think that they are worthless, or do I think that they are important, deserving of a response? If I were parodying these positions, that might imply that I think that they are ridiculous, hollow, formulaic, that they have a generalizability and currency as discourse that allows for them to be taken up by almost anyone and to sound convincing, even if delivered by the most improbable person.

But what if my rehearsal involves a temporary identification with them, even as I myself participate in the cultural politics under attack? Is that temporary identification that I perform, the one that raises the question of whether I am involved in a parody of these positions, not precisely a moment in which, for better or worse, they become my position?

It is, I would argue, impossible to perform a convincing parody of an intellectual position without having a prior affiliation with what one parodies, without having and wanting an intimacy with the position one takes in or on as the object of parody. Parody requires a certain ability to identify, approximate, and draw near; it engages an intimacy with the position it appropriates that troubles the voice, the bearing, the performativity of the subject such that the audience or the reader does not quite know where it is you stand, whether you have gone over to the other side, whether you remain on your side, whether you can rehearse that other position without falling prey to it in the midst of the performance. You might conclude, she is not being serious at all, or you might conclude that this is some sort of deconstructive play, and resolve to look elsewhere to find a serious discussion. But I would invite you to enter into this apparent wavering of mine, if you will, because I think that it actually serves the purposes of overcoming unnecessary divisions on the Left, and that is part of my purpose here.

I want to suggest that the recent efforts to parody the cultural Left could not have happened if there were not this prior affiliation and intimacy, and that to enter into parody is to enter into a relationship of both desire and ambivalence. In the hoax of last year, we saw a peculiar form of identification at work, one in which the one who performs the parody aspires, quite literally, to occupy the place of the one parodied, not only to expose the cultural icons of the cultural Left, *but to acquire and appropriate that very iconicity*, and, hence, to open oneself happily to public exposure as the one who performed the exposure, thus occupying both positions in the parody, territorial- izing the position of that other and acquiring temporary cultural fame.[1] Thus, it cannot be said that the purpose of the parody is not to denounce the way in which left politics had become media-driven or media- centered, degraded by the popular and the cultural, but, rather, precisely to enter into and drive the media, to become popular, and to triumph in the very cultural terms that have been acquired by those one seeks to demean, thus reconfirming and embodying the values of popularity and media success that goad the critique to begin with. Consider the thrilling sadism, the release of pent-up *ressentiment* at the moment of occupying the popular field that is apparently deplored as an object of analysis, paying tribute to the power of one's opponent, thus rein- vigorating the very idealization that one sought to dismantle.

Thus, the result of parody is paradoxical: the gleeful sense of triumph indulged by the avatars of an ostensibly more serious Marxism about their moment in the cultural limelight exemplifies and sympto- matizes precisely the cultural object of critique they oppose; the sense of triumph over this enemy, which cannot take place without in some eerie way taking the very place of the enemy, raises the question of whether the aims and goals of this more serious Marxism have not become hopelessly displaced onto a cultural domain, producing a *transient* object of media attention in the place of a more systematic analysis of economic and social relations. This sense of triumph rein- scribes a *factionalization* within the Left at the very moment in which welfare rights are being abolished in this country, class differentials are intensifying across the globe, and the right wing in this country

---

1 The hoax referred to is Alan D. Sokal, "Transgressing the Boundaries: Towards a Transformative Hermeneutics of Quantum Gravity," *Social Text* 46–7, 1996, pp. 217–52.

has successfully gained the ground of the "middle," effectively making the Left itself invisible within the media. When does it appear on the front page of the *New York Times*, except on that rare occasion in which one part of the Left swipes at another, producing a spectacle of the Left for mainstream liberal and conservative press consumption which is all too happy to discount every and any faction of the Left within the political process, much less honor the Left of any kind as a strong force in the service of radical social change?

Is the attempt to separate Marxism from the study of culture and to rescue critical knowledge from the shoals of cultural specificity simply a turf war between left cultural studies and more orthodox forms of Marxism? How is this attempted separation related to the claim that new social movements have split the Left, deprived us of common ideals, factionalized the field of knowledge and political activism, reducing the latter to the mere assertion and affirmation of cultural identity? The charge that new social movements are "merely cultural," that a unified and progressive Marxism must return to a materialism based in an objective analysis of class, itself presumes that the distinction between material and cultural life is a stable one. And this recourse to an apparently stable distinction between material and cultural life is clearly the resurgence of a theoretical anachronism, one that discounts the contributions to Marxist theory since Althusser's displacement of the base-superstructure model, as well as various forms of cultural materialism—for instance, Raymond Williams, Stuart Hall and Gayatri Chakravorty Spivak. Indeed, the untimely resurgence of that distinction is in the service of a tactic that seeks to identify new social movements with the merely cultural, and the cultural with the derivative and secondary, thus embracing an anachronistic materialism as the banner for a new orthodoxy.

Orthodox unity

This resurgence of left orthodoxy calls for a "unity" that would, paradoxically, redivide the Left in precisely the way that orthodoxy purports to lament. Indeed, one way of producing this division becomes clear when we ask which movements, and for what reasons, get relegated to the sphere of the merely cultural, and how that very division between the material and the cultural becomes tactically invoked for the purposes of marginalizing certain forms of political activism? And how does the new orthodoxy on the Left work in tandem with a social and sexual conservativism that seeks to make questions of race and sexuality secondary to the "real" business of politics, producing a new and eerie political formation of neoconservative Marxisms.

On what principles of exclusion or subordination has this ostensible unity been erected? How quickly we forget that new social movements based on democratic principles became articulated against a hegemonic Left as well as a complicitous liberal center and a truly threatening right wing? Have the historical reasons for the development of semi-autonomous new social movements ever really been taken into account by those who now lament their emergence and credit them with narrow identitarian interests? Is this situation not simply reproduced in the recent efforts to restore the universal by fiat, whether through the imaginary finesse of Habermasian rationality or notions of the common good that prioritize a racially cleansed notion of class? Is the point of the new rhetorics of unity not simply to "include" through domestication and subordination precisely those movements that formed in part in opposition to such domestication and subordination, showing that the proponents of the "common good" have failed to read the history that has made this conflict possible?

What the resurgent orthodoxy may resent about new social movements is precisely the vitality that such movements are enjoying. Paradoxically, the very movements that continue to keep the Left alive are credited with its paralysis. Although I would agree that a narrowly identitarian construal of such movements leads to a narrowing of the political field, *there is no reason to assume that such social movements are reducible to their identitarian formations.* The problem of unity or, more modestly, of solidarity cannot be resolved through the transcendence or obliteration of this field, and certainly not through the vain promise of retrieving a unity wrought through exclusions, one that reinstitutes subordination as the condition of its own possibility. The only possible unity will not be the synthesis of a set of conflicts, but will be *a mode of sustaining conflict in politically productive ways*, a practice of contestation that demands that these movements articulate their goals under the pressure of each other without therefore exactly becoming each other.

This is not quite the chain of equivalence proposed by Laclau and Mouffe, although it does sustain important relations to it.[2] New political formations do not stand in an analogical relation with one another, as if they were discrete and differentiated entities. They are overlapping, mutually determining, and convergent fields of politicization. In fact, most promising are those moments in which one social movement

---

2 See my dialogue on equality with Ernesto Laclau in *Diacritics* 27, spring 1997, pp. 3–12.

comes to find its condition of possibility in another. Here difference is not simply the *external* differences between movements, understood as that which differentiates them from one another but, rather, *the self-difference of movement itself*, a constitutive rupture that makes movements possible on non-identitarian grounds, that installs a certain mobilizing conflict as the basis of politicization. Factionalization, understood as the process whereby one identity excludes another in order to fortify its own unity and coherence, makes the mistake of locating the problem of difference as that which emerges *between* one identity and another; but difference is the condition of possibility of identity or, rather, its constitutive limit: what makes its articulation possible is at the same time what makes any final or closed articulation possible.

Within the academy, the effort to separate race studies from sexuality studies from gender studies marks various needs for autonomous articulation, but it also invariably produces a set of important, painful, and promising confrontations that expose the ultimate limits to any such autonomy: the politics of sexuality within African-American studies, the politics of race within queer studies, within the study of class, within feminism, the question of misogyny within any of the above, the question of homophobia within feminism, to name a few. This may seem to be precisely the tedium of identitarian struggles that a new, more inclusive Left hopes to transcend. And yet, for a politics of "inclusion" to mean something other than the redomestication and resubordination of such differences, it will have to develop a sense of alliance in the course of a new form of conflictual encounter. When new social movements are cast as so many "particularisms" in search of an overarching universal, it will be necessary to ask how the rubric of a universal itself only became possible through the erasure of the prior workings of social power. This is not to say that universals are impossible, but rather that they become possible only through an abstraction from its location in power that will always be falsifying and territorializing, and calls to be resisted at every level. Whatever universal becomes possible—and it may be that universals only become possible for a time, "flashing up" in Benjamin's sense—will be the result of a difficult labor of translation in which social movements offer up their points of convergence against a background of ongoing social contestation.

To fault new social movements for their vitality, as some have done, is precisely to refuse to understand that any future for the Left will have to build on the basis of movements that compel democratic participation, and that any effort to impose unity upon such

movements from the outside will be rejected once again as a form
of vanguardism dedicated to the production of hierarchy and dissen-
sion, producing the very factionalization that it asserts is coming
from outside itself.

Queer politics and the disparagement of the cultural

The nostalgia for a false and exclusionary unity is linked to the disparagement of the cultural, and with a renewed sexual and social
conservatism on the Left. Sometimes this takes the form of trying to
resubordinate race to class, failing to consider what Paul Gilroy and
Stuart Hall have argued, that race may be one modality in which class
is lived. In this way, race and class are rendered distinct analytically
only to realize that the analysis of the one cannot proceed without
the analysis of the other. A different dynamic is at work in relation
to sexuality, and I propose to concentrate on that issue for the rest of
this essay. Considered inessential to what is most pressing in material
life, *queer politics is regularly figured by the orthodoxy as the cultural
extreme of politicization.*

Whereas class and race struggles are understood as pervasively
economic, and feminist struggles to be sometimes economic and sometimes cultural, queer struggles are understood not only to be cultural
struggles, but to typify the "merely cultural" form that contemporary
social movements have assumed. Consider the recent work of a
colleague, Nancy Fraser, whose views are in no way orthodox, and
who has, on the contrary, sought to find ways to offer a comprehensive
framework for understanding the interlocking relationship of emancipatory struggles of various kinds. I turn to her work in part because
the assumption I worry about can be found there, and because she
and I have a history of friendly argumentation, one which I trust will
continue from here as a productive exchange—which is also the reason
why she remains the only person I agree to name in this essay.[3]

In Fraser's recent book, *Justice Interruptus,* she rightly notes that
"in the United States today, the expression 'identity politics' is increasingly used as a derogatory term for feminism, anti-racism, and
anti-heterosexism."[4] She insists that such movements have everything
to do with social justice, and argues that any left movement must

---

3 See Seyla Benhabib, Judith Butler, Drucilla Cornell and Nancy Fraser, eds.,
Feminist Contentions: A Philosophical Exchange, New York: Routledge, 1994.
4 Nancy Fraser, *Justice Interruptus: Critical Reflections on the "Postsocialist"
Condition,* New York: Routledge, 1997, p. 17.

respond to their challenges. Nevertheless, she reproduces the division
that locates certain oppressions as part of political economy, and relegates others to the exclusively cultural sphere. Positing a spectrum that
spans political economy and culture, she situates lesbian and gay
struggles at the cultural end of this political spectrum. Homophobia,
she argues, has no roots in political economy, because homosexuals
occupy no distinctive position in the division of labor, are distributed
throughout the class structure, and do not constitute an exploited
class: "the injustice they suffer is quintessentially a matter of recognition,"
thus making their struggles into a matter of cultural recognition, rather
than a material oppression.[5]

Why would a movement concerned to criticize and transform the
ways in which sexuality is socially regulated not be understood as
central to the functioning of political economy? Indeed, that this
critique and transformation is central to the project of materialism
was the trenchant point made by socialist feminists and those interested
in the convergence of Marxism and psychoanalysis in the 1970s and
1980s, and was clearly inaugurated by Engels and Marx with their
own insistence that "mode of production" needed to include forms of
social association. In *The German Ideology* (1846), Marx famously
wrote, "men, who daily remake their own life, begin to make other
men, to propagate their kind: the relation between man and woman,
parents and children, the *family*."[6] Although Marx vacillates between
regarding procreation as a natural and a social relationship, he makes
clear not only that a mode of production is always combined with a
mode of cooperation, but that, importantly, "a mode of production
is itself a 'productive force.'"[7] Engels clearly expands upon this
argument in *The Origin of Family, Private Property, and the State*
(1884), and offers there a formulation that became, for a time, perhaps
the most widely cited quotation in socialist-feminist scholarship:

> According to the materialist conception, the determining factor
> in history is, in the final instance, the production and reproduc-
> tion of immediate life. This, again, is of a twofold character: on
> the one side, the production of the means of existence, of food,

---

5 Ibid., pp. 17–18; for another statement of these views, see Fraser, "From
Redistribution to Recognition? Dilemmas of Justice in a 'Postsocialist' Age," in this
volume.

6 Robert C. Tucker, ed., *The Marx-Engels Reader*, New York: Norton, 1978,
p. 157.

7 Ibid.

clothing, and shelter and the tools necessary for that production; on the other side, the production of human beings themselves, the propagation of the species.[8]

Indeed, many of the feminist arguments during that time sought not only to identify the family as part of the mode of production, but to show how the very production of gender had to be understood as part of the "production of human beings themselves," according to norms that reproduced the heterosexually normative family. Thus, psycho-analysis entered as one way of showing how kinship operated to reproduce persons in social forms that served the interest of capital. Although some participants in those debates ceded the territory of kinship to Lévi-Strauss and to that theory's Lacanian successors, still others maintained that a specifically social account of the family was needed to explain the sexual division of labor and the gendered reproduction of the worker. Essential to the socialist-feminist position of the time was precisely the view that the family is not a natural given, and that as a specific social arrangement of kin functions, it remained historically contingent and, in principle, transformable. The scholarship in the 1970s and 1980s sought to establish the sphere of sexual reproduction as part of the material conditions of life, a proper and constitutive feature of political economy. It also sought to show how the reproduction of gendered persons, of "men" and "women," depended on the social regulation of the family and, indeed, on the reproduction of the heterosexual family as a site for the reproduction of heterosexual persons, fit for entry into the family as social form. Indeed, the presumption became, in the work of Gayle Rubin and

---

8 Frederick Engels, "Preface to the First Edition," *The Origin of the Family, Private Property and the State*, ed. Eleanor Burke Leacock, New York: International Publishers, 1972, pp. 71–2. Engels continues in this paragraph to note how societies develop from a stage in which they are dominated by kinship to ones in which they are dominated by the state, and in this latter development, kinship becomes subsumed by the state. It is interesting to note the convergence of this argument with Foucault's remarks in Volume 1 of *The History of Sexuality*, trans. Robert Hurley, New York: Norton, 1978, where he argues the following: "Particularly from the eighteenth century onwards, Western societies created and deployed a new apparatus which was superimposed upon the previous one" (p. 106). Kinship determines sexuality in the ostensibly earlier form, one which Foucault characterizes as "a system of alliance" (p. 107), and continues to support a newer organization of "sexuality" even as the latter maintains some autonomy from that earlier one. For an extended discussion of this relation, see the interview I conducted with Gayle Rubin, "Sexual Traffic," in *differences* 6: 2–3, summer–fall 1994, pp. 62–97.

others, that the normative reproduction of gender was essential to the reproduction of heterosexuality and the family. Thus, the sexual division of labor could not be understood apart from the reproduction of gendered persons, and psychoanalysis usually entered as a way of understanding the psychic trace of that social organization, and the ways in which that regulation appeared in sexual desires. Thus, the regulation of sexuality was systematically tied to *the mode of production* proper to the functioning of political economy.

Material exclusion

Note that both "gender" and "sexuality" become part of "material life" not only because of the way in which it serves the sexual division of labor, but also because normative gender serves the reproduction of the normative family. The point here is that, contra Fraser, struggles to transform the social field of sexuality do not become central to political economy to the extent that they can be directly tied to questions of unpaid and exploited labor, but also because they cannot be understood without an expansion of the "economic" sphere itself to include both the reproduction of goods as well as the social reproduction of persons.

Given the socialist-feminist effort to understand how the reproduction of persons and the social regulation of sexuality were part of the very process of production and, hence, part of the "materialist conception" of political economy, how is it that suddenly when the focus of critical analysis turns from the question of how normative sexuality is reproduced to the queer question of how that very normativity is confounded by the non-normative sexualities it harbors within its own terms—as well as the sexualities that thrive and suffer outside those terms—that the link between such an analysis and the mode of production is suddenly dropped? Is it only a matter of cultural recognition when non-normative sexualities are marginalized and debased? And is it possible to distinguish, even analytically, between a lack of cultural recognition and a material oppression, when the very definition of legal "personhood" is rigorously circumscribed by cultural norms that are indissociable from their material effects? For example, in those instances in which lesbians and gays are excluded from state-sanctioned notions of the family (which is, according to both tax and property law, an economic unit); stopped at the border, deemed inadmissible to citizenship; selectively denied the status of freedom of speech and freedom of assembly; are denied the right (as members of the military) to speak his or her desire; or are deauthorized by law to make emergency medical decisions about one's dying lover, to receive the property of one's dead lover, to receive from the hospital the body of one's dead lover—do not these examples mark the "holy family" once again constraining the routes by which property interests are regulated and distributed? Is this simply the circulation of vilifying cultural attitudes or do such disenfranchisements mark a specific operation of the sexual and gendered distribution of legal and economic entitlements?

If one continues to take the mode of production as the defining structure of political economy, then surely it would make no sense for feminists to dismiss the hard-won insight that sexuality must be understood as part of that mode of production. But even if one takes the "redistribution" of rights and goods as the defining moment of political economy, as Fraser does, how is it we might fail to recognize how these operations of homophobia are central to the functioning of political economy? Given the distribution of health care in this country, is it really possible to say that gay people do not constitute a differential "class," considering how the profit-driven organization of health care and pharmaceuticals impose differential burdens on those who live with HIV and AIDS? How are we to understand the production of the HIV population as a class of permanent debtors? Do poverty rates among lesbians not call to be thought of in relation to the normative heterosexuality of the economy?

The mode of sexual production

In *Justice Interruptus*, although Fraser acknowledges that "gender" is "a basic structuring principle of the political economy," the reason she offers is that it structures unpaid reproductive work.[9] Although she makes very clear her support for lesbian and gay emancipatory struggles and her opposition to homophobia, she does not pursue radically enough the implications of this support for the conceptualization she offers. She does not ask how the sphere of reproduction that guarantees the place of "gender" within political economy is circumscribed by sexual regulation, that is, through what mandatory exclusions the sphere of reproduction becomes delineated and naturalized. Is there any way to analyze how normative heterosexuality and its "genders" are produced within the sphere of reproduction without noting the compulsory ways in which homosexuality and bisexuality, as well as transgender, are *produced* as the sexually "abject," and extending the mode of production to account for precisely this social mechanism of regulation? It would be a mistake to understand such productions as "merely

---

9 Fraser, *Justice Interruptus*, p. 19.

cultural" if they are essential to the functioning of the sexual order of political economy, that is, constituting a fundamental threat to its very workability. The economic, tied to the reproductive, is necessarily linked to the reproduction of heterosexuality. It is not that non-heterosexual forms of sexuality are simply left out, but that their suppression is essential to the operation of that prior normativity. This is not simply a question of certain people suffering a lack of cultural recognition by others but, rather, a specific mode of sexual production and exchange that works to maintain the stability of gender, the hetero-sexuality of desire, and the naturalization of the family.[10]

Why, then, considering this fundamental place for sexuality in the thinking of production and distribution, would sexuality emerge as the exemplary figure for the "cultural" within recent forms of Marxist and neo-Marxist argument?[11] How quickly—and sometimes unwit-tingly—the distinction between the material and the cultural is remanufactured when it assists in the drawing of the lines that jettison sexuality from the sphere of fundamental political structure! This suggests that the distinction is not a conceptual foundation, for it rests on a selective amnesia of the history of Marxism itself. After all, in addition to the structuralist supplementation of Marx, one finds the distinction between culture and material life entered into crisis from any number of different quarters. Marx himself argued that pre-capitalist economic formations could not be fully extricated from the cultural and symbolic worlds in which they were embedded, and this thesis has driven the important work in economic anthropology—Marshall Sahlins, Karl Polanyi, Harry Pearson. This work expands and refines Marx's thesis in *Precapitalist Economic Formations* that seeks to explain how the cultural and the economic themselves became established as separable spheres—indeed, how the institution of the economic as a separate sphere is the consequence of an operation of abstraction initiated by capital. Marx himself was aware that such distinctions are the effect and culmination of the division of labor, and cannot, therefore, be excluded from its structure: in *The German*

---

10 Moreover, although Fraser distinguishes between matters of cultural recognition and political economy, it is important to remember that only by entering into exchange does one become "recognizable" and that recognition itself is a form and precondition of exchange.

11 The place of sexuality in "exchange" has been the focus of much of the work that sought to reconcile Lévi-Strauss's notion of kinship, based on normative accounts of heterosexual exchange within exogamic social structure, with Marxist notions of exchange.

Ideology, he writes, for example, that "the division of labor only becomes truly such from the moment when a division of material and mental labor appears."[12] This in part drives Althusser's effort to rethink the division of labor in "Ideology and Ideological State Apparatuses" in terms of the reproduction of labor power and, most saliently, "the forms of ideological subjection that [provide] for the reproduction of the skills of labor power."[13] This salience of the ideological in the reproduction of persons culminates in Althusser's groundbreaking argument that "an ideology always exists in an apparatus, and its practice, or practices. This existence is material."[14] Thus, even if homophobia were conceived only as a cultural attitude, that attitude should still be located in the apparatus and practice of its institutionalization.

Cultural and material gifts

Within feminist theory, the turn to Lévi-Strauss imported the analysis of the exchange of women into the Marxist critique of the family, and assumed for a time a paradigmatic status for the thinking of both gender and sexuality. Moreover, it was this important and problematic move that unsettled the stability of the distinction between cultural and material life. If women were a "gift," according to Lévi-Strauss, then they entered into the process of exchange in ways that could be reduced to neither a cultural or a material sphere. According to Marcel Mauss, whose theory of the gift was appropriated by Lévi-Strauss, the gift establishes the limits of materialism. For Mauss, the economic is only one part of an exchange that assumes various cultural forms, and the relation between economic and cultural spheres is not as distinct as they have come to be. Although Mauss does not credit capitalism with the distinction between cultural and material life, he does offer an analysis that faults current forms of exchange for forms of brute materialism: "originally the *res* need not have been the crude, merely tangible thing, the simple, passive object of transaction that it has become."[15] On the contrary, the *res* is understood to be the site for the convergence of a set of relationships. Similarly, the "person" is not primarily separable from his or her "objects": exchange consolidates or threatens social bonds.

---

12 Tucker, ed., *The Marx-Engels Reader*, p. 51.

13 Louis Althusser, *Lenin and Philosophy, and Other Essays*, trans. Ben Brewster, New York: Monthly Review Press, 1971, p. 133.

14 Ibid., p. 166.

15 Marcel Mauss, *An Essay on the Gift*, trans. W.D. Halls, New York: Norton, 1990, p. 50.

Lévi-Strauss showed that this relation of exchange was not only cultural and economic at once, but also made the distinction inappropriate and unstable: exchange produces a set of social relations, communicates a cultural or symbolic value—the coupling of which becomes salient for Lacanian departures from Lévi-Strauss—and secures routes of distribution and consumption. If the regulation of sexual exchange makes the distinction between the cultural and the economic difficult, if not impossible, to draw, then what are the consequences for a radical transformation of the lines of those exchange as they exceed and confound the ostensibly elementary structures of kinship? Would the distinction between the economic and the cultural become any easier to make if non-normative and counter-normative sexual exchange came to constitute the excessive circuitry of the gift in relation to kinship? The question is not whether sexual politics thus belong to the cultural or to the economic, but how the very practices of sexual exchange confound the distinction between the two spheres.

Indeed, queer studies and lesbian and gay studies in their overlapping efforts have sought to challenge the presumed link between kinship and sexual reproduction, as well as the link between sexual reproduction and sexuality. One might see in queer studies an important return to the Marxist critique of the family, based on a mobilizing insight into a *socially contingent and socially transformable account of kinship*, which takes its distance from the universalizing pathos of the Lévi-Straussian and Lacanian schemes that become paradigmatic for some forms of feminist theorizing. Although Lévi-Strauss's theory helped to show how heterosexual normativity produced gender in the service of its own self-augmentation, it could not provide the critical tools to show a way out of its impasses. The compulsory model of sexual exchange reproduces not only a sexuality constrained by reproduction, but a naturalized notion of "sex" for which the role in reproduction is central. To the extent that naturalized sexes function to secure the heterosexual dyad as the holy structure of sexuality, they continue to underwrite kinship, legal and economic entitlement, and those practices that delimit what will be a socially recognizable person. To insist that the social forms of sexuality cannot only exceed but confound heterosexual kinship arrangements as well as reproduction is also to argue that what qualifies as a person and a sex will be radically altered—an argument that is not merely cultural, but which confirms the place of sexual regulation as a mode of producing the subject.

Are we perhaps witnessing a scholarly effort to ameliorate the political force of queer struggles by refusing to see the fundamental

shift in the conceptualizing and institutionalizing of social relations
that they demand? Is the association of the sexual with the cultural,
and the concomitant effort to render autonomous and degrade the
cultural sphere, the unthinking response to a sexual degradation
perceived to be happening within the cultural sphere, an effort to
colonize and contain homosexuality in and as the cultural itself?

The neoconservativism within the Left that seeks to discount the
cultural can only always be another cultural intervention, whatever
else it is. And yet the tactical manipulation of the distinction between
cultural and economic to reinstitute the discredited notion of secondary
oppression will only reprovoke the resistance to the imposition of
unity, strengthening the suspicion that unity is only purchased through
violent excision. Indeed, I would add that the understanding of this
violence has compelled the affiliation with poststructuralism on the
Left, that is, a way of reading that lets us understand what must be
cut out from a concept of unity in order for it to gain the appearance
of necessity and coherence, and to insist that difference remain
constitutive of any struggle. This refusal to become resubordinated
to a unity that caricatures, demeans, and domesticates difference
becomes the basis for a more expansive and dynamic political impulse.
This resistance to "unity" carries with it the cipher of democratic
promise on the Left.

HETEROSEXISM, MISRECOGNITION, AND CAPITALISM: A RESPONSE TO JUDITH BUTLER

Nancy Fraser

Judith Butler's essay is welcome on several counts. It returns us to deep and important questions in social theory that have gone undiscussed for some time. And it links a reflection on such questions to a diagnosis of the troubled state of the Left in the current political conjuncture. Most important, however, is Butler's commitment in this essay to identifying, and retrieving, the genuinely valuable aspects of Marxism and the socialist-feminism of the 1970s, which current intellectual and political fashions conspire to repress. Also exemplary is her interest in integrating the best insights of those paradigms with defensible strands of more recent paradigms, including discourse analysis, cultural studies, and poststructuralism, in order to understand contemporary capitalism. These are commitments I wholeheartedly share.

Nevertheless, Butler and I disagree. Our most important disagreements, and the most fruitful for discussion, turn on how precisely to realize this shared project of reclamation and integration. We hold divergent views of what precisely constitutes the enduring legacy of Marxism and the still-relevant insights of socialist-feminism. We also diverge in our respective assessments of the merits of various poststructuralist currents and in our respective views of how these can best inform social theorizing that retains a materialist dimension. Finally, we disagree about the nature of contemporary capitalism.

In order to clear the way for a fruitful discussion of these issues, I want to begin by disposing quickly of what I take to be the red herrings. Butler conjoins her discussion of my book *Justice Interruptus* to a critique of a group of unnamed interlocutors whom she calls "neoconservative Marxists." Whatever the merits of her critique of this group —a question I shall return to later—her strategy of using it to frame a discussion of me is unfortunate. Despite her disclaimers to the contrary, readers could draw the erroneous conclusion that I share the "neoconservative Marxist" dismissal of the oppression of gays and lesbians as "merely" cultural, hence as secondary, derivative, even trivial. They might assume that I see sexual oppression as less fundamental, material, and real than class oppression and that I wish to subordinate struggles against heterosexism to struggles against workers' exploitation. Finding me thus lumped together with "sexually conservative orthodox" Marxists, readers could even conclude that I view gay and lesbian movements as unjustified particularisms that have split the Left and on whom I wish forcibly to impose left unity.

I, of course, believe nothing of the sort. On the contrary, in *Justice Interruptus* I have analyzed the current decoupling of so-called identity politics from class politics, the cultural Left from the social Left, as a constitutive feature of the "postsocialist" condition.[1] Seeking to overcome these splits and to articulate the basis for a united front of the Left, I have proposed a theoretical framework that eschews orthodox distinctions between "base" and "superstructure," "primary" and "secondary" oppressions, and the primacy of the economic. In the process, I have posited both the conceptual irreducibility of heterosexist oppression and the moral legitimacy of gay and lesbian claims.

Central to my framework is a normative distinction between injustices of distribution and injustices of recognition. Far from derogating the latter as "merely cultural," the point is to conceptualize two equally primary, serious, and real kinds of harm that any morally defensible social order must eradicate. To be misrecognized, in my view, is not simply to be thought ill of, looked down on, or devalued in others' conscious attitudes or mental beliefs. It is rather to be denied the status of a *full partner* in social interaction and prevented from *participating as a peer* in social life—not as a consequence of a distributive inequity (such as failing to receive one's fair share of resources or "primary goods") but rather as a consequence of *institutionalized* patterns of interpretation and evaluation that constitute one as comparatively unworthy of respect or esteem. When such patterns of disrespect and disesteem are institutionalized, for example, in law, social welfare, medicine, and/or popular culture, they impede parity of participation, just as surely as do distributive inequities. The resulting harm is in either case all too real.

---

1 See especially the introduction to my *Justice Interruptus: Critical Reflections on the "Postsocialist" Condition*, New York: Routledge, 1997; and my "From Redistribution to Recognition? Dilemmas of Justice in a 'Postsocialist' Age," in this volume.

In my conception, therefore, misrecognition is an institutionalized social relation, not a psychological state. In essence a status injury, it is analytically distinct from, and conceptually irreducible to, the injustice of maldistribution, although it *may* be accompanied by the latter. Whether misrecognition converts into maldistribution, and vice versa, depends on the nature of the social formation in question. In precapitalist, pre-state societies, for example, where status simply *is* the overarching principle of distribution, and where the status order and the class hierarchy are therefore fused, misrecognition simply entails maldistribution. In capitalist societies, in contrast, where the institutionalization of specialized economic relations permits the relative uncoupling of economic distribution from structures of prestige, and where status and class can therefore diverge, misrecognition and maldistribution are not fully mutually convertible. Whether and to what extent they coincide today is a question I shall take up anon.

Normatively, however, the key point is this: misrecognition constitutes a fundamental injustice, whether accompanied by maldistribution or not. And the point has political consequences. It is not necessary to show that a given instance of misrecognition brings with it maldistribution in order to certify the claim to redress it as a genuine claim for social justice. The point holds for heterosexist misrecognition, which involves the institutionalization of sexual norms and interpretations that deny participatory parity to gays and lesbians. Opponents of heterosexism need not labor to translate claims of sexual status injury into claims of class deprivation in order to vindicate the former. Nor need they show that their struggles threaten capitalism in order to prove they are just.

On my account, then, injustices of misrecognition are fully as serious as distributive injustices. And they cannot be reduced to the latter. Thus, far from claiming that cultural harms are superstructural reflections of economic harms, I have proposed an analysis in which the two sorts of harms are co-fundamental and conceptually irreducible. From my perspective, therefore, it makes no sense to say that heterosexist misrecognition is "merely" cultural. That locution presupposes the very sort of base-superstructure model, the very sort of economistic monism, that my framework aims to displace.

Butler, in sum, has mistaken what is actually a quasi-Weberian dualism of status and class for an orthodox Marxian economistic monism. Erroneously assuming that to distinguish redistribution from recognition is necessarily to devalue recognition, she treats my normative distinction as a "tactic" aimed at derogating gay and lesbian struggles and imposing a new "orthodoxy." Contra Butler, I mean to

defend the distinction while disclaiming the tactic. To get at the real
issues between us, therefore, requires decoupling two questions that
are too closely identified in her discussion. The first is a political
question concerning the depth and seriousness of heterosexist oppression; on this, I have argued, we do not disagree. The second is a
theoretical question concerning the conceptual status of what Butler
misleadingly calls "the material/cultural distinction" as it relates to
the analysis of heterosexism and the nature of capitalist society; here
lie our real disagreements.[2]

Let me begin unpacking these real disagreements by schematically
recapping Butler's critique. As I read it, she offers three principal
theoretical arguments against my redistribution/recognition framework. First, she contends that because gays and lesbians suffer material,
economic harms, their oppression is not properly categorized as
misrecognition. Second, invoking the important 1970s socialist-feminist

---

2 In what follows I shall leave aside a problem with Butler's rendition of the argument
of *Justice Interruptus*. She presents me as arguing categorically that heterosexism is a
pure injustice of misrecognition, unalloyed by maldistribution. In fact, I discussed the
issue hypothetically in the mode of a thought experiment. Aiming to disclose the distinctive logics of redistribution claims and recognition claims respectively, I invited readers
to imagine a conceptual spectrum of oppressed collectivities, ranging from ideal-typical
victims of pure maldistribution at one end to ideal-typical victims of pure misrecognition
at the other end, with hybrid or "bivalent" cases in the middle. In this hypothetical
spirit, I sketched a conception of a "despised sexuality" as a concrete approximation
of the ideal type at the misrecognition end of the spectrum, while explicitly noting that
this conception of sexuality was controversial and while leaving open the question of
whether and how closely it corresponded to the actually existing homosexual collectivities
struggling for justice in the real world. Thus, my "misrecognition" analysis of heterosexism in *Justice Interruptus* is far more qualified than Butler lets on. Recently, moreover,
I have argued that for practical purposes virtually all real-world oppressed collectivities
are "bivalent." Virtually all, that is, have both an economic and a status component;
virtually all, therefore, suffer both maldistribution and misrecognition *in forms where
neither of those injustices is a mere indirect effect of the other but where each has some
independent weight.* Nevertheless, not all are bivalent in the same way, nor to the same
degree. Some axes of oppression tilt more heavily toward the distribution end of the
spectrum, others incline more to the recognition end, while still others cluster closer to
the center. On this account, heterosexism, while consisting in part in maldistribution,
consists primarily in injustices of misrecognition and is rooted predominantly in a status
order that constructs homosexuality as devalued and that institutes it as a despised
sexuality. For the original argument, see "From Redistribution to Recognition?" in this
volume. For the subsequent refinement, see Nancy Fraser, "Social Justice in the Age of
Identity Politics: Redistribution, Recognition, and Participation," in Nancy Fraser and
Axel Honneth, *Redistribution or Recognition: A Political-Philosophical Exchange*, trans.
Joel Golb, James Ingram and Christiane Wilke, London: Verso, 2003..

insight that the family is part of the mode of production, she contends that the heteronormative regulation of sexuality is "central to the functioning of the political economy" and that contemporary struggles against that regulation "threaten the workability" of the capitalist system. Third, after revisiting anthropological accounts of pre-capitalist exchange, she contends that the distinction between the material and the cultural is "unstable," a "theoretical anachronism" to be eschewed in social theory. None of these arguments is persuasive, in my view, largely because none affords an adequately differentiated and historically situated view of modern capitalist society. Let me consider the three arguments in turn.

Butler's first argument appeals to some indisputable facts about the harms currently suffered by gays and lesbians. Far from being "merely symbolic," these harms include serious economic disadvantages with undeniable material effects. In the United States today, for example, gays and lesbians can be summarily dismissed from civilian employment and military service, are denied a broad range of family-based social-welfare benefits, are disproportionately burdened with medical costs, and are disadvantaged in tax and inheritance law. Equally material are the effects of the fact that homosexuals lack the full range of constitutional rights and protections enjoyed by heterosexuals. In many jurisdictions, they can be prosecuted for consensual sex; and in many more, they can be assaulted with impunity. It follows, claims Butler, from the economic and material character of these liabilities, that the "misrecognition" analysis of heterosexism is mistaken.

Butler's premise is true, of course, but her conclusion does not follow. She assumes that injustices of misrecognition must be immaterial and non-economic. Leaving aside for the moment her conflation of the material with the economic, the assumption is on both counts mistaken. Consider first the issue of materiality. In my conception, injustices of misrecognition are just as material as injustices of maldistribution. To be sure, the first are rooted in social patterns of interpretation, evaluation, and communication, hence, if you like, in the symbolic order. But this does not mean they are "merely" symbolic. On the contrary, the norms, significations, and constructions of personhood that impede women, racialized peoples, and/or gays and lesbians from parity of participation in social life are materially instantiated—in institutions and social practices, in social action and embodied habitus, and yes, in ideological state apparatuses. Far from occupying some wispy, ethereal realm, they are material in their existence and effects.

From my perspective, therefore, the material harms cited by Butler

constitute paradigm cases of misrecognition. They reflect the institutionalization of heterosexist meanings, norms, and constructions of
personhood in such arenas as constitutional law, medicine, immigration
and naturalization policy, federal and state tax codes, social welfare
and employment policy, equal opportunity legislation, and the like.
What is institutionalized, moreover, as Butler herself notes, are cultural
constructions of entitlement and personhood that produce homosexual
subjects as abjects. This, to repeat, is the essence of misrecognition:
the *material* construction through the institutionalization of cultural
norms of a class of devalued persons who are impeded from participatory parity.

If the harms arising from misrecognition can thus be material, can
they also be economic? It is true, as Butler notes, and as I myself
expressly noted in *Justice Interruptus*, that some forms of heterosexism
inflict economic harms on gays and lesbians. The question is how to
interpret them.[3] One possibility is to see these economic harms as
direct expressions of the economic structure of society, much like
Marxists see the exploitation of workers. On this interpretation, which
Butler appears to endorse, the economic liabilities of homosexuals
would be hard-wired in the relations of production. To remedy them
would require transforming those relations. Another possibility,
favored by me, is to see the economic harms of heterosexism as
indirect (mal)distributive consequences of the more fundamental
injustice of misrecognition. On this interpretation, which I defended
in *Justice Interruptus*, the roots of economic heterosexism would be
the "relations of recognition": an institutionalized pattern of interpretation and valuation that constructs heterosexuality as normative
and homosexuality as deviant, thereby denying participatory parity
to gays and lesbians. Change the relations of recognition and the maldistribution would disappear.

This conflict of interpretations raises deep and difficult questions.
Is it necessary to transform the economic structure of contemporary
capitalism in order to redress the economic liabilities of homosexuals?
What precisely is meant by the "economic structure"? Should one
conceive the heteronormative regulation of sexuality as belonging
directly to the capitalist economy? Or is it better seen as belonging to

---

3 In general, one should distinguish several questions here: 1) the nature of the
injustices in question; 2) their ultimate causes; 3) the contemporary causal mechanisms
that reproduce them; and 4) their remedies. I am grateful to Erik Olin Wright for this
point (private communication, 1997).

a status order that is differentiated from, and complexly related to, the economic structure? More generally, do the relations of recognition in late-capitalist society coincide with economic relations? Or do the institutional differentiations of modern capitalism introduce gaps between status and class?

To pursue these questions, let us examine Butler's second argument. Here she invokes the 1970s socialist-feminist insight that the family is part of the mode of production to support the thesis that the hetero-normative regulation of sexuality is "central to the functioning of the political economy." It follows, claims Butler, that contemporary struggles against that regulation "threaten the workability" of the capitalist system.

Actually, two different variants of the argument are discernible here, one definitional, the other functionalist. According to the first variant, (hetero)sexual regulation belongs by definition to the economic structure. The economic structure simply *is* the entire set of social mechanisms and institutions that (re)produce persons and goods. By definition, then, the family is part of this structure, as the primary site for the reproduction of persons. So, by extension, is the gender order, which standardizes the family's "products" to conform to one of two, and only two, mutually exclusive, seemingly natural kinds of persons: men and women. The gender order, in turn, is held to presuppose a mode of sexual regulation that produces and naturalizes heterosexuality, while simultaneously producing homosexuality as abject. The conclusion drawn by Butler is that the heteronormative regulation of sexuality is a part of the economic structure by definition, *despite the fact that it structures neither the social division of labor nor the mode of exploitation of labor power in capitalist society.*

This definitional argument has an air of Olympian indifference to history. As a result, it risks accomplishing too much. Stipulating that the mode of sexual regulation belongs to the economic structure by definition, even in the absence of any impact on the division of labor or the mode of exploitation, threatens to dehistoricize the idea of the economic structure and drain it of conceptual force. What gets lost is the specificity of capitalist society as a distinctive and highly peculiar form of social organization. This organization creates an order of specialized economic relations that are relatively decoupled from relations of kinship and political authority. Thus, in capitalist society, the link between the mode of sexual regulation, on the one hand, and an order of specialized economic relations whose raison d'être is the accumulation of surplus value, on the other, is attenuated. It is far more attenuated, certainly, than in pre-capitalist, pre-state societies, where economic relations are largely adumbrated through the mechanisms of kinship and directly imbricated with sexuality. In the late capitalist society of the twentieth century, moreover, the links between sexuality and surplus value accumulation have been still further attenuated by the rise of what Eli Zaretsky has called "personal life": a space of intimate relations, including sexuality, friendship, and love, that can no longer be identified with the family and that are lived as disconnected from the imperatives of production and reproduction.[4] In general, then, contemporary capitalist society contains "gaps": between the economic order and the kinship order; between the family and personal life; between the status order and the class hierarchy. In this sort of highly differentiated society, it does not make sense to me to conceive the mode of sexual regulation as simply a part of the economic structure. Nor to conceive queer demands for the recognition of difference as misplaced demands for redistribution.

In another sense, moreover, the definitional argument accomplishes very little. Butler wants to conclude that struggles over sexuality are economic, but that conclusion has been rendered tautologous. If sexual struggles are economic by definition, then they are not economic in the same sense as are struggles over the rate of exploitation. Simply calling both sorts of struggles "economic" risks collapsing the differences, creating the misleading impression that they will synergize automatically, and blunting our capacity to pose, and answer, hard but pressing political questions as to how they can be *made* to synergize when in fact they diverge or conflict.[5]

This brings me to the functionalist variant of Butler's second argument. Here the claim is that the heteronormative regulation of sexuality is economic, not by definition, but because it is functional to the expansion of surplus value. Capitalism, in other words, "needs" or benefits from compulsory heterosexuality. It follows, according to Butler, that gay and lesbian struggles against heterosexism threaten the "workability" of the capitalist system.

---

4 Eli Zaretsky, *Capitalism, the Family, and Personal Life*, New York: Harper & Row, 1976.

5 Thus, the definitional argument simply pushes the need for distinctions to another level. One *might* of course say that a political claim can be economic in either of two ways: first, by contesting the production and distribution of economic value, including surplus value; and second, by contesting the production and reproduction of norms, significations, and constructions of personhood, including those concerning sexuality. But I fail to see how this improves on my simpler strategy of restricting the term "economic" to its capitalist meaning and distinguishing claims for recognition from claims for redistribution.

Like all functionalist arguments, this one stands or falls with the empirical relations of cause and effect. Empirically, however, it is highly implausible that gay and lesbian struggles threaten capitalism in its actually existing historical form. That might be the case if homosexuals were constructed as an inferior but useful class of menial laborers whose exploitation were central to the workings of the economy, as African-Americans, for example, have been. Then one could say that capital's interests are served by keeping them "in their place." In fact, however, homosexuals are more often constructed as a group whose very existence is an abomination, much like the Nazi construction of Jews; they should have no "place" in society at all. No wonder, then, that the principal opponents of gay and lesbian rights today are not multinational corporations, but religious and cultural conservatives, whose obsession is status, not profits. In fact, some multinationals, notably American Airlines, Apple Computer, and Disney, have elicited the wrath of such conservatives by instituting gay-friendly policies, such as domestic partnership benefits. They apparently see advantages in accommodating gays, provided they are not subject to boycotts or are big enough to withstand them if they are.

Empirically, therefore, contemporary capitalism seems not to require heterosexism. With its gaps between the economic order and the kinship order, and between the family and personal life, capitalist society now permits significant numbers of individuals to live through wage labor outside of heterosexual families. It could permit many more to do so —provided the relations of recognition were changed. Thus we can now answer a question posed earlier: the economic disabilities of homosexuals are better understood as effects of heterosexism in the relations of recognition than as hard-wired in the structure of capitalism. The good news is that we do not need to overthrow capitalism in order to remedy those disabilities—although we may well need to overthrow it for other reasons. The bad news is that we need to transform the existing status order and restructure the relations of recognition.

With her functionalist argument, Butler has resurrected what is in my view one of the worst aspects of 1970s Marxism and socialist-feminism: the overtotalized view of capitalist society as a monolithic "system" of interlocking structures of oppression that seamlessly reinforce one another. This view misses the "gaps." It has been resoundingly and persuasively critiqued from many directions, including the post-structuralist paradigm that Butler endorses and the Weberian one adapted by me. Functionalist systems theory is one strand of 1970s thought that is better left forgotten.

The question of what should replace functionalism bears on Butler's third argument against my redistribution/recognition framework. This argument is deconstructive. Far from insisting that the roots of hetero-sexism are economic as opposed to "merely" cultural, its point is to deconstruct the "material/cultural distinction." That distinction, claims Butler, is "unstable." Important currents of neo-Marxian thought, ranging from Raymond Williams to Althusser, have irretriev-ably thrown it into "crisis." The knockdown argument comes from the anthropologists, however, notably Mauss and Lévi-Strauss. Their respective accounts of "the gift" and "the exchange of women" reveal that "primitive" processes of exchange cannot be assigned to one side or the other of the material/cultural divide. Being both at once, such processes "destabilize" the very distinction. Thus, in invoking the material/cultural distinction today, Butler contends, I have lapsed into a "theoretical anachronism."

This argument is unconvincing for several reasons, the first of which is that it conflates "the economic" with "the material." Butler assumes that my normative distinction between redistribution and recognition rests on an ontological distinction between the material and the cultural. She therefore assumes that to deconstruct the latter distinction is to pull the rug out from under the former. In fact, however, the assumption does not hold. As I noted earlier, injustices of misrecognition are from my perspective just as material as injustices of maldistribution. Thus, my normative distinction rests on no ground of ontological difference. What it *does* correlate with, in capitalist societies, is a distinction between the economic and the cultural. This, however, is not an ontological distinction but a social-theoretical distinction. The economic/cultural distinction, not the material/cultural distinction, is the real bone of contention between Butler and me, the distinction whose status is at issue.

What, then, is the conceptual status of the economic/cultural distinc-tion? The anthropological arguments do shed light on this matter, in my view, but not in a way that supports Butler's position. As I read them, both Mauss and Lévi-Strauss analyzed processes of exchange in pre-state, pre-capitalist societies, where the master idiom of social relations was kinship. In their accounts, kinship organized not only marriage and sexual relations, but also the labor process and the distribution of goods; relations of authority, reciprocity, and obligation; and symbolic hierarchies of status and prestige. Neither distinctively economic relations nor distinctively cultural relations existed; hence the economic/cultural distinction was presumably not available to the members of those societies. It does not follow, however, that the distinc-tion is senseless or useless. On the contrary, it can be meaningfully and usefully applied to capitalist societies, which unlike so-called primitive societies *do* contain the social-structural differentiations in question. Moreover, it can also be applied *by us* to societies that lack these differentiations in order to indicate how they differ from ours. One can say, for example, as I just did, that in such societies a single order of social relations handles both economic integration and cultural integration, matters that are relatively decoupled in capitalist society. This, moreover, is precisely the spirit in which I understand Mauss and Lévi-Strauss. Whatever their intentions regarding "the economic" and "the cultural," we gain less from reading them as having "destabilized" the distinction than from reading them as having *historicized* it. The point, in other words, is to historicize a distinction central to modern capitalism, and with it modern capitalism itself, by situating both in the larger anthropological context and thereby revealing their historical specificity.

Thus, Butler's "destabilization" argument goes astray at two crucial points. First, it illegitimately generalizes to capitalist societies a feature specific to pre-capitalist societies, namely, the absence of a social-structural economic/cultural differentiation. Second, it erroneously assumes that to historicize a distinction is to render it nugatory and useless in social theory. In fact, historicization does the contrary. Far from rendering distinctions unstable, it renders their usage more precise.

From my perspective, then, historicization represents a better approach to social theory than destabilization or deconstruction.[6] It allows us to appreciate the social-structurally differentiated and historically specific character of contemporary capitalist society. In so doing, it also enables us to locate the antifunctionalist moment, the possibilities for countersystemic "agency" and social change. These appear not in an abstract transhistorical property of language, such as "resignification" or "performativity," but rather in the actual contradictory character of specific social relations. With an historically specific, differentiated view of contemporary capitalist society, we can locate the gaps, the non-isomorphisms of status and class, the multiple

---

6 At another level, however, I mean to endorse deconstruction. It represents an approach to the politics of recognition that is often superior in my view to standard identity politics. A deconstructive politics of recognition is transformative, not affirmative, of existing group identities and differentiations. In this respect, it has affinities with socialism, which I understand as a transformative, as opposed to affirmative, approach to the politics of redistribution. (For an elaboration of this argument see "From Redistribution to Recognition?") Nevertheless, I do not find deconstruction useful at the level on which Butler invokes it here, namely, the level of social theory.

contradictory interpellations of social subjects, and the multiple complex *moral imperatives* that motivate struggles for social justice.

Seen from this sort of perspective, moreover, the current political conjuncture is not adequately grasped by a diagnosis centered on the putative resurgence of orthodox Marxism. It is better grasped, rather, by one that forthrightly acknowledges, and seeks to overcome, splits in the Left between socialist/social-democratic currents oriented to the politics of redistribution, on the one hand, and multiculturalist currents oriented to the politics of recognition, on the other. The indispensable starting point for such an analysis must be a principled acknowledgment that *both sides have legitimate claims*, which must somehow be harmonized programmatically and made to synergize politically. Social justice today, in sum, requires *both* redistribution *and* recognition; neither alone will suffice.

On this last point, I feel certain, Butler and I agree. Despite her reluctance to invoke the language of social justice, and despite our theoretical disagreements, both of us are committed to reclaiming the best elements of socialist politics and to integrating them with the best elements of the politics of the "new social movements." Likewise, we are both committed to retrieving the genuinely valuable strands of the neo-Marxian critique of capitalism and to integrating them with the most insightful strands of post-Marxian critical theorizing. It is the merit of Butler's essay, and I would hope of my own book as well, to have put this project on the agenda once again

IS "CULTURAL RECOGNITION"
A USEFUL NOTION FOR
LEFTIST POLITICS?

Richard Rorty

Judith Butler and Nancy Fraser are among the most widely read and discussed philosophers in the US. I appreciate this chance to discuss a point on which I differ from both of them—the utility of the notion of "cultural recognition." In their contributions to this volume, both of these writers take for granted that this notion is, or should be, at or near the center of leftist political thinking. I doubt this, and will use this occasion to say why.

I frequently assign articles by Butler or Fraser to my students. They read those assignments with relish and appreciation, and the ensuing class discussion is often unusually lively. The students typically find the notions of "culture" and "cultural recognition" as important as do Butler and Fraser, and are baffled by my doubts about their utility. They regard my attempts to brush these notions aside, and my skepticism about the recent vogue of "cultural studies" in departments of literature, as symptoms of blindness to the current political situation. When I suggest that the growing "cultural studies" literature does not amount to much as a form of leftist political activity, they sharply disagree. They do the same when I suggest, as I did in my book *Achieving Our Country*, that the American academic Left overestimates the utility of philosophy, and that terms like "deconstruction," "subject-position" and "power" are of little help in deliberating about what is to be done.

In discussion with students concerning these matters, I often have the feeling of just not getting it. I suspect that I am missing something, and that the rising generation may glimpse something I do not. Even if this is the case, however, it may be useful for me to lay out my persisting doubts in some detail. Setting them down might help clarify the differences between habits of mind characteristic of my generation, whose leftism is a product of the 1940s and 1950s, and those characteristic of people whose leftism took shape in the 1970s and 1980s and owed a great deal to memories of the 1960s.

A few decades ago, the term "culture" rarely came up in political discussion. The idea that we should assign "positive value" to many different cultures had not yet surfaced, except in specifically anthropological contexts. In those days, American leftists talked about the need to overcome prejudice against stigmatized groups rather than about the need to grant recognition to the cultures of these groups. The central leftist idea then was that we all share a common humanity, and that this commonality makes us fit to be citizens of the same nations, to marry each other's brothers and sisters, and so on. The notion of "respect for differences" had not yet made its appearance.

Up through the sixties, "prejudice" was the word leftists used to signify inability to acknowledge this commonality, and a consequent failure to treat other people fairly. To say that someone is prejudiced, in this sense, is to say that he or she prejudges fellow humans who are members of despised groups. Prejudiced people assume that membership in such a group trumps everything else—that no feature of intellect or character can redeem such membership, and that the stigma of membership in the despised group makes marriage, friendship, and other cherished forms of association very difficult. Such people are reluctant to think of members of despised groups as fellow citizens. They assume that people who bear a certain ineradicable stigma are not worth knowing, much less talking with about public affairs.

Many people—especially poor people—gain great benefits from being prejudiced. For they can maintain their own sense of worth by contrasting themselves with purported natural inferiors. Their prejudices are integral to their self-respect. In America, the paradigm of this phenomenon was the need of poor whites in the post-Civil War South to take pride in not being "niggers." This need drove them to maintain and defend a system in which African-Americans were treated as only semi-human.

People like these poor whites think of the members of stigmatized groups as degraded specimens of humanity, people whom they would be disgusted to think of their sister or brother marrying. The blood of such people carries pollution. Similarly, many straight men and women would feel blemished by physical proximity to a homosexual, and would regard themselves as having been permanently damaged if they should once take part in a homosexual act. These are a few among many examples of the sort of patterns of exclusion that became institutionalized in the caste systems of India, Japan, and many other places. Whole societies have been organized around ideas of purity and pollution. These are the societies the Left has always hoped may someday be replaced by a society in which no human being is regarded as anything less that a full-fledged member of both the species and the local community.

In the old days, American leftists assumed that creating a decent and civilized society was in part a matter of redistributing money and opportunity, and in part a matter of erasing stigma by eliminating prejudice. The two efforts were assumed to go hand in hand. No theoretical problems arose about how to integrate the two, though many practical problems did. In those days, the question of whether blacks, or members of lower castes, or manual workers, or women, or homosexuals, had a culture of their own—one that it behooved their oppressors to understand and appreciate—did not often arise. (The exception was the idea of "proletarian culture," a specifically Marxist phenomenon.)

All this was before the rise of second-wave feminism. That movement owed a great deal to the example set by Dr. King's Civil Rights Movement, as did the movement for gay and lesbian rights. But though gay and lesbian activists could speak of the need to eliminate prejudice and stigma, that terminology did not work well as a description of the changes for which feminists were working. The humiliation of women by men is not happily described as a result of men's *prejudice* against women. Being a woman is not exactly a matter of bearing a *stigma*. Women as a group are not scapegoated in the way blacks or Jews are. Scapegoats must be driven out or killed, whereas wives are too useful to be dispensed with. A man's connection with a woman is thought to pollute him only in occasional, special circumstances.

"Recognition," however, is a term that works equally well to describe what blacks need from whites, gays need from straights, and women need from men. They all need to be recognized as full members of the species, sharing in the common humanity that straight white males, within a given local community, typically take for granted in their dealings with one another. When the new social movements, with second-wave feminism in the vanguard, tried to bring their struggles under a common rubric, "the need for recognition" seemed more apposite than "the need to eliminate prejudice."

It is less clear, however, why "recognition" came to be thought of as recognition of *culture* or of "cultural differences," rather than as recognition of a common humanity. One reason may be that one claim frequently made about stigmatized people has been that they lacked, and would forever be unable to acquire, culture—culture in the older,

Arnoldian, sense. A similar inability was, until very recently, attributed to women by men: they might acquire a kind of lightweight culture (centered around piano-playing and novel-reading) but not the sort of heavyweight culture required to become, for example, professors or legislators. So one part of granting recognition to black Americans, manual laborers, and women was to concede that they too had the kind of dense, comforting web of associations, memories, and traditions that the ruling males had thought unique to themselves (and that they sometimes thought could be had only by people with an old-fashioned classical education). Raymond Williams's work was particularly important in changing the intellectuals' way of using the term "culture" to mean something less Arnoldian and more anthropological.

It helps, when trying to recognize a common humanity in people of another gender, class, or ethnicity, to think of them as having as rich an inner life as one does oneself. To picture such an inner life, it helps to know something about the web of memories and associations that makes it up. So one way to help eliminate prejudice and erase stigma is to point out that, for example, women have a history, that homosexuals take pride in belonging to the same stigmatized group as Socrates and Proust, and that African-Americans have detailed memories of the battles that make up what Russell Banks calls "the three hundred-year War Between the Races in America"—the sort of memories that whites are currently learning about from Toni Morrison's novels. It helps to realize that all such groups wrap a comforting blanket of memories and traditions, customs and institutions, around themselves, just as do classical scholars, old Etonians, or members of the Benevolent and Protective Order of Elks.

Yet drawing attention to this fact is hardly the only way to eliminate prejudice. Another way is to get the prejudiced to see the stigmatized as having the same tendency to bleed when pricked that they themselves possess: they too worry about their children and parents; they are possessed by the same self-doubts, and lose self-confidence when humiliated; their difficulties in moving from one stage of life to another are much like everyone else's, despite the fact that their life-chances may be minimal. These ways of emphasizing commonality rather than difference have little to do with "cultural recognition." They have to do with experiences shared by members of all cultures and all historical epochs, and which remain pretty much the same despite cultural change.

So we still need an explanation of why cultural recognition is thought so important. I think one reason it has become so important in the discourse of the American academic Left may be the result of a specifically academic set of circumstances. The only thing we academics can do, in our specifically professional capacities, to eliminate prejudice is to write women's history, celebrate black artistic achievements, and the like. This is what academics who work in such programs as Women's Studies, African-American Studies, and Gay Studies do best. These programs are the academic arms of the new social movements—the movements that, as Judith Butler rightly says, have kept the Left alive in the US in recent years—years during which the rich have consistently had the best of it in the class struggle.

When these academic programs were set up, their founders could not describe themselves as attempting to use the tax-supported resources of the higher education system to pursue political goals—the description preferred by rightist opponents of these programs. Yet the rightists' description was, as far as it went, accurate enough. These programs are, among other things, attempts to continue doing what colleges and universities have, thank God, been doing more and more in recent times: helping the societies they serve become more generous and tolerant. Still, you cannot persuade a university faculty to institute a new program by pointing out that such a program will help change the manners and morals of the citizenry for the better—that it will correct the opinions of the students, and cause them to be less prejudiced than their parents. You need to describe the projected new program as pursuing some apolitical, purely academic, purpose. So those who set up such programs often said that they would devote themselves to studying the *culture* of one or another stigmatized group, an area which previous scholarship had neglected.

I suspect that this pragmatic accommodation to the customs of academic life did a lot to insure that "cultural recognition" would replace "eliminating prejudice" as a leftist political goal. It may help explain why American leftists now talk about more recognition of difference rather about recognition of a common humanity. For the vast majority of leftists in the US now are, we must sadly admit, academics. It is tempting for any group to think that the means they have found to promote a decent and civilized society are essential means to that goal—that any program for reaching that goal must feature their own specialty.

The generation of academics whose political views were formed in the sixties became, after McGovern's defeat in 1972, distrustful of the idea of reform, and of appeals to the good judgment of an electorate that had re-elected Nixon by a landslide. Because all the campaigning for McGovern had come to nothing, it seemed unlikely that envelope-licking, leafleting, picketing, demonstrating, and similar modes of

participating in the political process would do much good. So it was
tempting for this generation to think that perhaps they could promote
a cultural, rather than a political, revolution—one that would
eventually do some political good.

As I said in *Achieving Our Country*, a kind of cultural revolution
actually took place: between 1972 and the present, the treatment of
women, African-Americans and gays by American institutions and
American straight white males improved enormously, thanks in large
measure to the generation of teachers that entered the schools, colleges
and universities between 1975 and 1990. But, as I also said in that
book, nothing much has been done by that generation to help under-
paid straight white males make more money and unemployed straight
white males get jobs. Culture pushed economics aside, in part because
the maturing sixties leftists had a lot of ideas about cultural change,
but few ideas about how to counter Reagan's soak-the-poor policies,
what to do for the unemployed in the Rust Belt, or how to make sure
that a global economy did not pauperize American wage-earners.
Because culture pushed economics aside, the straight white male
working class in America may find it tempting to think that the leftist
academy is uninterested in its problems.

Nowadays, as Nancy Fraser says, "demands for 'recognition of
difference' fuel struggles of groups mobilized under the banners of
nationality, ethnicity, 'race', gender, and sexuality." But I am not sure
that such demands add anything useful to the old demand that these
groups not be (in Fraser's words) "routinely maligned or disparaged
in stereotypic public cultural representations and/or in everyday life
interactions."[1] The difference between the old and the new demands
is the difference between asking not to be singled out for ill treatment
and asking for attention to, and respect for, one's distinctive features.
The new demand is harder to meet than the older, and I am not sure
that there is any good reason for the change from the easier to the
more stringent demand.

The only plausible explanation I can give for this change is that the
post-sixties academic Left knows a lot about these differences, and
thinks that the public as a whole ought to take an interest in them.
This phenomenon strikes me as analogous to the Marxist students of
the thirties knowing a lot about dialectical materialism, and concluding
that the members of the UAW ought to take an interest in this topic,
lest they succumb to the temptations of bourgeois, non-revolutionary

---

1 This volume, p. 14.

trade-unionism. Those students, like the present generation of leftist academics, desperately wanted to be of use to those who were getting the dirty end of the stick. So they overestimated the importance of their own expertise. The attempt to put "cultural recognition" on a par with redistribution seems to me the result of a similar overestimation: the academics are desperately eager to assure themselves that what they are doing is central, rather than marginal, to leftist politics.

Like Fraser, I quite agree with Charles Taylor that disrespect dictated by prejudice, or by the age-old assumption that women are second-rate members of the species, can "inflict a grievous wound, saddling people with crippling self-hatred." I also agree with Axel Honneth's Hegelian claim that "we owe our integrity . . . to the receipt of approval or recognition from other persons." We are crippled unless most of the people we encounter treat us as conversable and as trustworthy partners in cooperative projects. But the idea that we need recognition *as members of a particular community, rather than as individuals*, is not prominent in Hegel, and is not intuitively evident. The Hegelian dialectic of master and slave, a dialectic easily rewritten as that of husband and wife, does not take place between cultures but between individuals.

David Bromwich (in his *Politics by Other Means*) has pointed out that the change from "eliminating prejudice" to "recognizing cultural differences" has produced confusion on the Left because it runs athwart everything individualistic in recent Western ways of thinking—everything that suggests that we want, and should want, to be recognized either simply as human, or else for our individual traits and achievements. This suggestion has been central to most of the Left's rhetoric since the French Revolution. It is hard to integrate this rhetoric with an insistence on the importance of cultural differences.

Such individualistic—and, at the limit, existentialist—ways of thinking suggest that a young person should not focus on what she owes to her ancestors, her parents, or the community from which she comes, but rather on how she might break free of all those, and become who she is. We think well of someone who refuses to be stereotyped as an X, resents being thought of as an X, and tries to create a self-image for herself that escapes all the classificatory terminologies employed by those around her. If someone chooses not to break free from her roots, and instead tries to develop a self-image to which group membership is central, we think it important that this decision be fully conscious and entirely free, rather than being treated as the recognition of an evident duty.

This admiration for self-creating independence has nothing to do with a belief in the Cartesian ego, and is entirely compatible with the claim that our selves are social constructions—with the realization that our selves are contingent products of interactions with other people, and that these interactions are largely governed by what Foucault calls "power." One can agree with Foucault that all choices among alternative beliefs are made within the limits of the truth-candidates available at the time, and that these truth-candidates are available only because somebody had the power to suppress other candidates, while still retaining the individualistic, quasi-Nietzschean, ways of thinking that make us prize self-creation. (Foucault was himself, and knew himself to be, an admirable example of such self-creation.)

Nor does the recognition of our common humanity have anything to do with Kantian or Habermasian univeralism. Such recognition is not a matter of believing that our consciences can be relied upon to give us the same instructions, or that moral and political discussion will converge to agreement thanks to what Habermas and Apel call "the force of the better argument." As I said above, it is much more a matter of coming to think of previously despised people as like oneself in specific, concrete, banal ways: as bleeding when pricked, and crippled when shunned.

I think that if the Left had continued to try to eliminate prejudice by emphasizing such commonalities, rather than emphasizing cultural differences, it might have been able to effect the same cultural revolution as in fact occurred. I doubt that the term "culture" added much weight or force to efforts to get people to treat previously despised groups as fellow humans. So I would rephrase Fraser's statement that "The remedy for cultural injustice . . . is some sort of cultural or symbolic change" in old-fashioned terms as "The remedy for thinking of people as, first and foremost, members of traditionally despised groups is to emphasize what these people share with those who despise them."

Fraser goes on to say that this remedy "could involve upwardly revaluing disrespected identities and the cultural products of maligned groups. It could also involve recognizing and positively valorizing cultural diversity."[2] I agree that it *could*, but it could also involve raising kids not to think much about whether people are black or female or gay or Navajo—to raise them so that they will see little point in questions like "What must it be like to be a women (or to be gay)?" or "In what does black (or Navajo) identity consist?" or "Which cultural

---

2 This volume, p. 17.

products are preeminently associated with being African-American? Vietnamese-American? Mexican-American?"

While reading Fraser's paper, and many of the other papers in this volume, I kept asking myself what would be lost if one crossed out the word "cultural" in such contexts as homosexuals' "mode of collectivity is that of a despised sexuality, rooted in the cultural-valuational structure of society" or "homophobia: the cultural devaluation of homosexuality."[3] I kept wondering why in order to overcome homophobia we had to "accord positive recognition to gay and lesbian sexual specificity," rather than just raising children to think that being gay or lesbian is no big deal. I wondered why, in order to overcome ethnic prejudice against recent immigrants, we had to try to interest people in these immigrants' native cultures.

Such doubts made me skeptical about the need for what Fraser calls "deconstruction," thought of as "deep restructuring of relations of recognition," a process that "tends to blur group differentiation." I am not sure that in order to eliminate prejudice we need a "transformative recognition politics of deconstruction." Do we really need to replace "hierarchical racial dichotomies" with "networks of multiple intersecting differences that are demassified and shifting" rather than just, for example, trying to bring up white kids to think less about differences in skin color and more about shared pains and pleasures?[4] Doing the latter would accomplish what Fraser calls weaning white people "from their attachment to current cultural constructions of their interests and identities" insofar as it would make it unimportant for white kids to think of themselves as white.[5] Granted that white kids badly need to learn the history of the War Between the Races; that is not the same thing as learning to appreciate the merits of a distinctively black culture.

I find much to admire in Fraser's analyses of the problems confronting the contemporary Left, and I am more or less on her side in her disagreements with Iris Marion Young and with Judith Butler. Still, I think that "deconstruction" is a fancier, more sophisticated, weapon than the Left needs. Fraser's suggestion that "deconstruction" be elevated to be on a par with "socialism" among leftist aims seems to me to smell of the lamp. Spotting latent incoherence in ideas, identities, and institutions, in the Derridean manner, is something people

---

3 This volume, p. 21.
4 Ibid. pp. 33, 34, 38.
5 Ibid. p. 39.

trained in various recently founded academic programs are often good at. But I doubt that this additional skill makes them any better equipped to help our society eliminate prejudice and increase fairness than, for example, training in battered women's shelters, AIDS support groups, or Head Start programs for black kids in the ghettos.

Fraser says that "the intersection of class, 'race,' gender, and sexuality intensifies the need for transformative solutions, making the combination of socialism and deconstruction more attractive still."[6] I cannot see the relevance of this intersection to anything as philo-sophically sophisticated as deconstruction. The intersection seems to amount merely to such facts as that someone may be humiliated or discriminated against for being a woman in the morning, for being black in the afternoon, and for being a lesbian in the evening, and low-paid for any or all of these three reasons. The remedies for this situation do not seem to me to have anything to do with questions about her "identity" as any of these. I am not sure that she will be helped by attending to the construction of such an identity, or that her persecutors will be helped by recognizing it once it has been constructed.

Nor does it help to think about possible remedies when Judith Butler, describing the differences between social movements that may attempt alliances, reminds us of "the self-difference of movement itself, a constitutive rupture that makes movements possible on non-identitarian grounds, that installs a certain mobilizing conflict as the basis of politicization."[7] As a fellow student of Hegel and Derrida, I can see what she means when she says that "difference is the condition of the possibility of identity or, rather, its constitutive limit," but I do not see the relevance of this philosophical point to the problems encountered in getting movements to relieve the situation of African-Americans together with, for example, move-ments to relieve that of lesbians. It strikes me as about as *merely* philosophical as a point can get.

A bit later on, Butler says,

> When new social movements are cast as so many "particularisms" in search of an overriding universal, it will be necessary to ask how the rubric of a universal itself only became possible through the erasure of the prior workings of social power. This is not to

6 This volume, p. 78.
7 This volume, p. 47.

say that universals are impossible, but rather that they become possible only through an abstraction from its location in power that will always be falsifying and territorializing, and calls to be resisted at every level.

I doubt the "always," and I do not see the relevance of the claim. In what sense does anybody want to bring the various new social movements under "a universal"? Negotiating local and provisional alliances between these movements (as when one movement offers votes, or money, or live bodies to another) does not require finding a relevant "universal." Urging, as I have, that these new social movements need to get themselves hitched up, in the present American situation, to attempts to improve the lot of unemployed or ludicrously ill-paid straight white males, is not a matter of subsuming them under a universal. It is more like suggesting that taking several different medicines at once will have a desirable synergistic effect.

In the pages from which I have quoted, Butler is concerned to respond to people who claim that, as she puts it, "the cultural focus of leftist politics has splintered the Left into identitarian sects," with the result that we have "lost a set of common ideals and goals." Todd Gitlin, Arthur Schlesinger and I have indeed said things of this sort. But I cannot see the relevance of Butler's philosophical points to our complaints, which are about the dangerous consequences of developing a Left that neglects class and money by focusing on the elimination of prejudice and sexism. I, and probably Gitlin and Schlesinger as well, would never dream of calling the new social movements "a self-centered and trivial form of politics." Nor do we have an interest in exchanging these movements for "a more robust, serious and comprehensive vision of the systematic interrelatedness of social and economic conditions." Doubtless there are such interrelations, but getting them mapped out is not a prerequisite for undertaking leftist initiatives that would serve the purposes of both the newer social movements and the older ones.

Fraser and Kevin Olson do think it important to work out such a vision. Although I admire the philosophical acuity both bring to the production of analytical categories, I do not share their sense of priorities. Nor do I think that there is any way to put Fraser in the same box with Gitlin, Schlesinger and myself, as Butler seems to do. All that the three of us share with Fraser is that, like her, we should like to figure out a way to produce a stronger American Left, a Left that might become a voting majority of citizens. We all want to facilitate alliances between the victims of the Republicans' soak-the-poor legislation and people who are stigmatized, or deprived, for reasons other than poverty. The two groups overlap, but are not identical, and the Republicans are getting good at playing them off against each other.

Though I take it Butler too would like to help create a leftist majority among American voters, I doubt that the philosophical sophistication she brings to bear on questions of identity and difference will be of much use to the Left in its attempt to pursue majoritarian politics. I am happy to agree that this sort of philosophical sophistication has been put to good use in the process of building up the academic wings of the new movements. But I see Butler as running together problems of academic politics with larger problems, and of trying to squeeze more political utility out of philosophical sophistication than she is likely to get.

Butler says,

> Within the academy, the effort to separate race studies from sexuality studies from gender studies marks various needs for autonomous articulation, but it also invariably produces a set of important, painful, and promising confrontations that expose the ultimate limits to any such autonomy: the politics of sexuality within African American studies, the politics of race within queer studies, within the study of class, within feminism, the question of misogyny within any of the above, the question of homophobia within feminism, to name a few. This may seem to be precisely the tedium of identitarian struggles that a new, more inclusive Left hopes to transcend.[8]

As I see it, however, it is not a matter of transcending these struggles, but of broadening the horizons of those who engage in them—of producing leftist students who spend less time thinking about efforts to separate, or not to separate, these various studies from one another. My own hunch is that they need to spend more time thinking about what will happen if American wages continue to sink toward the level of the global wage market. But whether I am right in this hunch or not, the question of what our students should be thinking about if the American Left is to grow stronger is a purely practical, and presently quite urgent, question. It is a question to which Derrida and Foucault are no more relevant than are Aquinas and Leibniz.

The philosophers who seem to me most useful for leftist students

---

8 This volume, p. 47.

are the old standbys—Mill and Dewey. Mill was right to urge that the aim of social institutions should be the encouragement of the greatest possible human diversity. But we should think of this diversity as he did, as a diversity of self-creating individuals, rather than a diversity of cultures. Our utopian dreams should be of a world in which cultures are seen as transitory comings-together of individuals—expedients for increasing human happiness rather than as the principal source of a person's sense of self-worth.

WHY OVERCOMING PREJUDICE IS NOT ENOUGH: A REJOINDER TO RICHARD RORTY

Nancy Fraser

I welcome Richard Rorty's response to "From Redistribution to Recognition?" There, in what was effectively a proposal for a united front of the Left, I sought to demonstrate that social democrats and multiculturalists need not be at war with each other. Rather, it is possible, and desirable, to combine a politics of recognition with a politics of redistribution. The trick is to abandon affirmative approaches, which encourage zero-sum thinking, in favor of transformative approaches, which promote synergy. On the recognition side, this means replacing identity politics with a politics aimed at deinstitutionalizing unjust value hierarchies; on the distribution side, it means replacing neoliberal economics with democratic socialism or social democracy. By thus combining a deconstructive politics of recognition with a democratic-socialist politics of redistribution, one can do justice, I argued, to each of the two Lefts. One can also envision reforms that could redress injustices of culture and of political economy simultaneously.[1]

Rorty is skeptical of this proposal. Writing as a social-democratic critic of the cultural Left, he sees my interest in recognition as a "symptom of blindness to our current political situation." In his view, the post-Vietnam Left has already won the cultural revolution, having largely succeeded in dispelling the stigma that used to mark racial minorities, women, and gays. Preoccupied with combating "sadism," however, it neglected the fight against "selfishness," allowing the rich to win the class struggle, as "culture pushed economics aside." Equally unfortunately, the cultural Left substituted the dubious project of affirming the distinctive cultures of disadvantaged groups for the

---

1 Nancy Fraser, "From Redistribution to Recognition? Dilemmas of Justice in a 'Postsocialist' Age," in this volume.

time-honored left goal of "eliminating prejudice." What is needed now, contends Rorty, is a return to an earlier strategy, favored by the pre-Vietnam Left. Prioritizing economics over culture, shared humanity over group differences, the Left today should emphasize redistribution while continuing to oppose lingering prejudice. Instead of following my proposal to combine redistribution with recognition, it should drop the idea of "cultural recognition." That idea has nothing useful to contribute to contemporary politics.[2]

In what follows, I aim to rebut Rorty's conclusion about what the Left should be doing today. On the one hand, I shall defend a specific interpretation of recognition as an indispensable dimension of social justice. On the other, I shall argue, contra Rorty, that major injustices of misrecognition cannot be remedied by eliminating prejudice alone. In this way, I hope to demonstrate that a politics of recognition is politically useful and indeed morally required. In combination with redistribution, it remains an essential ingredient of a viable Left politics for our time.

The question, of course, is *what kind* of politics of recognition. Most of Rorty's arguments are directed against traditional identity politics. Premised on what I have called *the identity model of recognition*, such a politics aims to counter demeaning representations of a disadvantaged group by validating its purportedly distinctive cultural identity. I agree with Rorty that this kind of politics of recognition is problematic. From my perspective, the difficulties can be summarized under two counts. First, by treating misrecognition as a free-standing cultural harm, identity politics abstracts the injustice from its institutional matrix and obscures its entwinement with economic inequality. Thus, far from synergizing with struggles for redistribution, it all too easily displaces the latter. (I have called this the problem of *displacement*.) Second, by seeking to consolidate an authentic self-elaborated group culture, this approach essentializes identity, pressuring individual members to conform, denying the complexity of their lives, the multiplicity of their identifications, and the cross-pulls of their various affiliations. Thus, far from promoting interaction across differences, it reifies group identities and neglects shared humanity, promoting separatism and repressive communitarianism. (I have called this the problem of *reification*.)[3]

---

2 Richard Rorty, "Is 'Cultural Recognition' a Useful Notion for Left Politics?" in this volume.

3 Nancy Fraser, "Rethinking Recognition: Overcoming Displacement and Reification in Cultural Politics" in this volume.

In general, then, I agree with Rorty that the identity model of recognition is deeply flawed. But I draw a different conclusion as to what should be done. Whereas he proposes to jettison the politics of recognition altogether, I have proposed to reconstruct it in a form that discourages both the displacement of redistribution and the reification of group differences.

My suggestion, in brief, is to reinterpret recognition in terms of *status*. From this perspective, what requires recognition is not group-specific identity but rather the status of individual group members as full partners in social interaction. Misrecognition, accordingly, does not mean the depreciation of group identity. Rather, it means *social subordination* in the sense of being prevented from participating as a peer in social life as a result of institutionalized patterns of cultural value that constitute one as relatively unworthy of respect or esteem. To redress the injustice requires a politics of recognition, but this does not mean identity politics. On the status model, rather, it means a politics aimed at overcoming subordination by *deinstitutionalizing patterns of cultural value that impede parity of participation and replacing them with patterns that foster it.*[4]

This approach differs from Rorty's in that it takes misrecognition seriously as a species of unjust subordination. The underlying premise is that justice requires social arrangements that permit all members of society to interact with one another *as peers*. Insofar as institutionalized patterns of cultural value impede parity of participation, they violate justice and cannot be justifiably ignored. In fact, misrecognition is institutionalized throughout the world in a host of laws, government policies, administrative regulations, professional practices, and social customs that constitute some categories of persons as less than full members of society. Examples include marriage laws that exclude same-sex partnerships as illegitimate and perverse, social-welfare policies that stigmatize single mothers as sexually irresponsible scroungers, and policing practices such as racial profiling that associate racialized persons with criminality. By no means simple by-products of political economy, such instances of misrecognition cannot be redressed by a politics of redistribution alone. On the contrary, the only way to overcome the injustice is to replace institutionalized cultural patterns that subordinate people with patterns that establish them as peers.

In contrast to Rorty's rejectionism, the status model avoids throwing out the baby of recognition with the bathwater of identity politics.

---

4 For a fuller account, see Nancy Fraser, "Rethinking Recognition," ibid.

Far from displacing the politics of redistribution, this approach appreciates that institutionalized patterns of cultural value are not the only obstacles to participatory parity. Rather, equal participation is also impeded when some actors lack the necessary resources to interact with others as peers. Thus, from this perspective, maldistribution too is a serious injustice. Under capitalist conditions, moreover, it is not a mere expression of status hierarchy and so cannot be remedied by a politics of recognition alone. For the status model, therefore, claims for recognition must be linked expressly with claims for redistribution.

Likewise, the status model does not encourage reification of group identities. From its perspective, culture becomes an object of political concern only when institutionalized patterns of value deny some social actors the chance to participate fully and equally in social life. Redressing the injustice requires affirming group differences only in cases where the obstacle to parity is underacknowledgment of distinctiveness. In other cases, the remedy could be universalist recognition of denied humanity (which is Rorty's all-purpose solution), deconstruction of the terms in which group differences are currently elaborated, or some combination thereof. In all cases, the aim is to promote the broadest possible range of social interaction. In addition, the ideal of participatory parity serves as a justificatory standard for testing recognition claims in the public sphere. Inherently dialogic and democratic, this approach avoids the monologic and authoritarian propensities of identity politics, which often appeals to cultural authenticity. Thus, far from reifying group differences, the version of recognition politics that I am proposing discourages separatism and repressive communitarianism.

In general, then, the status model of recognition escapes Rorty's criticisms of identity politics. Its advantages stand out sharply, moreover, when we compare it to the approach he recommends. In fact, Rorty vacillates among several mutually contradictory claims. In some passages, he suggests that all misrecognition has already been eliminated, thanks to the cultural revolution that began in the 1960s. In others, he suggests that while some misrecognition persists, it can be redressed by a politics of redistribution. In still other passages, he suggests that while redistribution alone may not suffice to dispel all lingering misrecognition, that result can be achieved by familiar liberal reforms aimed at eliminating prejudice.

Of these claims, only the third requires sustained attention. (The first extrapolates one set of positive cultural trends to the point of utopian fancy, overlooking their uneven institutionalization and the

powerful countervailing tendencies; the second rests on a vulgar
economic determinism that is belied by the highly differentiated character
of contemporary capitalist society.)[5] Thus, the question is: Does a
politics focused exclusively on redistributing resources and eliminating
prejudice constitute an adequate left politics for today? Can such a
politics mount a credible challenge to the full range of contemporary
injustices, which includes misrecognition as well as maldistribution?

In my view, the answer is no. The problem is that not all misrecognition can be dispelled by eliminating prejudice, even in
combination with redistribution. For one thing, misrecognition is not
purveyed primarily through prejudice, if by that we mean derogatory
attitudes and beliefs. Rather, it is relayed through institutions and
practices that regulate social interaction according to norms that
impede parity. Since these often operate below the threshold of
consciousness, only an effort aimed at changing such institutions and
practices can remedy the injustice. (And of course only such an effort
can avoid the illiberal temptation to substitute the re-engineering of
consciousness for social change.)

In addition, not all misrecognition takes the form of denying
common humanity. In some cases, the injustice arises from a failure
to acknowledge group differences. Examples include US court rulings
holding that employers' failure to provide pregnancy leave does not
constitute sex discrimination because it does not deny women a benefit
provided to men; firefighter job application procedures that test climb-
ing speed on ladders designed for persons whose height falls in the
normal range for men, thus disadvantaging many women; and regulations mandating uniform headgear for Canadian mounted police,
effectively closing that occupation to observant Sikhs. In these cases,
the problem is not prejudice in Rorty's sense of disregard for shared
humanity. Rather, parity of participation is impeded because norms
tailored to the situation of dominant or majority groups are applied
across the board, to the detriment of those situated differently. Thus,
the nub of the injustice is failure to recognize, and accommodate,
differences. Contra Rorty, therefore, it cannot be remedied by stressing
what everyone shares. On the contrary, the only way to establish parity

---

5 For an extended critique of economic determinism, see Nancy Fraser, "Social
Justice in the Age of Identity Politics: Redistribution, Recognition and Participation,"
in *The Tanner Lectures on Human Values*, vol. 19, ed. Grethe B. Peterson, The
University of Utah Press, 1998, pp. 1–67. A revised and expanded version is reprinted
in Nancy Fraser and Axel Honneth, *Redistribution or Recognition? A Political-
Philosophical Exchange*, London: Verso, 2003.

of participation is to replace problematic difference-disregarding norms with alternatives that are difference-accommodating. The latter must convey more than that women and Sikhs, too, bleed when pricked. They must convey, for example, that persons who can give birth have as much legitimacy in the workplace as those who cannot; and that being a Mountie does not exclude being a Sikh.

Pace Rorty, then, justice sometimes requires recognition of differences. But such recognition neither contradicts nor supersedes respect for what everyone shares. If anything, it deepens the latter, providing the means to realize universalism more fully. The rationale runs roughly like this: the universalist norm of the equal moral worth of human beings requires ensuring all members of society the possibility of participating on a par with others. This in turn requires removing obstacles to participatory parity in whatever form they arise, including failure to recognize group difference. Thus, recognition of group difference is sometimes necessary to assure respect for common humanity.

Nevertheless, Rorty is right to worry that difference-regarding recognition carries risks. What begins as a means for assuring participatory parity can easily take on a life its own. Readily reified, such recognition can end up freezing group differences, stifling individuals, and fueling the very antagonisms one intended to regulate. The solution, however, is not to retreat to inadequate forms of difference-blind universalism. Rather, one must add yet another—deconstructive—layer of recognition that helps counteract tendencies to reification. In part this means engaging in cultural agitation aimed at propounding a lively sense of the constructedness and contingency of all group classifications. Stressing the fundamental openness to historical change of identifications, such a deconstructive cultural politics can help defuse the risks associated with the politics of recognizing difference.

Sometimes, moreover, deconstruction has more straightforward institutional implications. This is so in cases where misrecognition arises from compulsory systems of classification, which force individuals to identify with one side or the other of a conceptual polarity. In the United States, for example, citizens are sometimes compelled to identify as gay or straight, black or white, in ways that violate the complexity of their sexual and/or ethnic identifications. Here the appropriate redress is neither abstract universalism nor simple affirmation of difference but rather deconstruction of current classifications. Contra Rorty, therefore, deconstruction *can* be politically useful—provided that it is understood not as an esoteric academic philosophy but as one element among others of a multifaceted strategy for remedying status subordination.

The moral here is that no one-size-fits-all approach can suffice. Because misrecognition comes in several different forms and guises, a multi-pronged effort is required. The aim should be to tailor recognition remedies to misrecognition harms, supplementing universal respect with difference-regarding esteem where necessary, and adding a healthy dose of deconstructive skepticism about all classificatory systems that claim more than contingent validity. More consistently pragmatic than Rorty's, such an approach is the only one that can hope to remove the full range of obstacles that now stand in the way of participatory parity.

For all these reasons, I conclude that the Left should reject Rorty's proposal to turn back the clock. Instead of returning to the strategy of the pre-Vietnam Left, it should build on the gains of the last forty years, which have expanded and deepened the meaning of social justice. Thus, far from dropping the politics of recognition, the Left should adopt a version of the latter aimed at overcoming status subordination and fostering parity of participation. In this way, it can succeed in avoiding the traps of identity politics, including the reification of group identities and the displacement of struggles for redistribution. Equally important, it can redirect energy now being wasted on internecine polemics and begin to focus on the difficult task at hand: integrating recognition with redistribution in a coherent left vision that can guide the fight against injustice in the coming period of accelerating globalization.

UNRULY CATEGORIES:

A CRITIQUE OF NANCY FRASER'S

DUAL SYSTEMS THEORY

Iris Marion Young

Have theorists of justice forgotten about political economy? Have we traced the most important injustices to cultural roots? Is it time for critical social theory to reassert a basic distinction between the material processes of political economy and the symbolic processes of culture? In two recent essays, Nancy Fraser answers these questions in the affirmative.[1] She claims that some recent political theory and practice privilege the recognition of social groups, and that they tend to ignore the distribution of goods and the division of labor.

> Demands for "recognition of difference" fuel struggles of groups mobilized under the banners of nationality, ethnicity, "race," gender, and sexuality. In these "postsocialist" conflicts, group identity supplants class interest as the chief medium of political mobilization. Cultural domination supplants exploitation as the fundamental injustice. And cultural recognition displaces socioeconomic redistribution as the remedy for injustice and the goal of political struggle.[2]

Fraser proposes to correct these problems by constructing an analytic framework that conceptually opposes culture and political economy, and then locates the oppressions of various groups on a continuum between them. With a clear distinction between those issues of justice

---

1 Nancy Fraser, "Recognition or Redistribution? A Critical Reading of Iris Young's *Justice and the Politics of Difference*," *Journal of Political Philosophy* 3: 2, 1995, pp. 166–80, reprinted in Fraser, *Justice Interruptus*, Chapter 8; "From Redistribution to Recognition? Dilemmas of Justice in a 'Postsocialist' Age," in this volume.

2 In this volume, p. 11.

that concern economic issues and those that concern cultural issues, she suggests, we can restore political economy to its rightful place in critical theory, and evaluate which politics of recognition are compatible with transformative responses to economically based injustice.

Fraser's essays call our attention to an important issue. Certain recent political theories of multiculturalism and nationalism do indeed highlight respect for distinct cultural values as primary questions of justice, and many seem to ignore questions of the distribution of wealth and resources and the organization of labor. Fraser cites Charles Taylor's much discussed work *Multiculturalism and the Politics of Recognition* as an example of this one-sided attention to recognition at the expense of redistribution, and I think she is right.[3] Even the paradigmatic theorist of distributive justice, John Rawls, now emphasizes cultural and value differences and plays down conflict over scarce resources.[4] Some activist expressions of multiculturalism, moreover, especially in schools and universities, tend to focus on the representation of groups in books and curricula as an end in itself, losing sight of the issues of equality and disadvantage that have generated these movements.[5] Some recent theoretical writing by feminists, gay men, and lesbians has pondered questions of group identity abstracted from social relations of economic privilege and oppression.

Nevertheless, I think that Fraser, like some other recent left critics of multiculturalism, exaggerates the degree to which a politics of recognition retreats from economic struggles. The so-called culture wars have been fought on the primarily cultural turf of schools and universities. I see little evidence, however, that feminist or anti-racist activists, as a rule, ignore issues of economic disadvantage and control. Many who promote the cultivation of African-American identity, for example, do so on the grounds that self-organization and solidarity in predominantly African-American neighborhoods will improve the material lives of those who live there by providing services and jobs.

---

3 Charles Taylor, *Multiculturalism and the Politics of Recognition*, Princeton: Princeton University Press, 1992.

4 See John Rawls, *Political Liberalism*, New York: Columbia University Press, 1993; I have commented on this shift in a review-essay of this book in *Journal of Political Philosophy* 3: 2, 1995, pp. 181–90.

5 Todd Gitlin tells stories of such a focus on recognition as an end itself in school board battles in California. See *Twilight of Common Dreams*, New York: Metropolitan Books, 1995. I do not think that such stories of excess in the politics of difference warrant his blanket inference that all attention to group difference has been destructive of left politics in the US.

To the degree they exist, Fraser is right to be critical of tendencies for a politics of recognition to supplant concerns for economic justice. But her proposed solution, namely to reassert a category of political economy entirely opposed to culture, is worse than the disease. Her dichotomy between political economy and culture leads her to misrepresent feminist, anti-racist and gay liberation movements as calling for recognition as an end in itself, when they are better understood as conceiving cultural recognition as a means to economic and political justice. She suggests that feminist and anti-racist movements in particular are caught in self-defeating dilemmas that I find to be a construction of her abstract framework rather than concrete problems of political strategies. The same framework makes working-class or queer politics appear more one-dimensional than they actually are.

Fraser's opposition of redistribution and recognition, moreover, constitutes a retreat from the New Left theorizing that has insisted that the material effects of political economy are inextricably bound to culture. Some of Nancy Fraser's own earlier essays stand as significant contributions to this insistence that Marxism is also cultural studies. Rather than oppose political economy to culture, I shall argue, it is both theoretically and politically more productive to pluralize categories and understand them as differently related to particular social groups and issues. Thus the purpose of this essay is primarily to raise questions about what theoretical strategies are most useful to politics, and to criticize Fraser for adopting a polarizing strategy. The goal of strong coalitions of resistance to dominant economic forces and political rhetoric, I suggest, is not well served by an analysis that opposes cultural politics to economic politics. Specifying political struggles and issues in more fine-tuned and potentially compatible terms better identifies issues of possible conflict and alliance.

1. Redistribution versus recognition

According to Fraser, there are two primary kinds of injustice. The first, socioeconomic injustice, is "rooted" in the political and economic structure of society. Exploitation, economic marginalization, and deprivation of basic goods are the primary forms of such injustice. The second kind of injustice is cultural or symbolic. It is "rooted" in social patterns of representation, interpretation, and communication. Such injustice includes being subject to an alien culture, being rendered invisible in one's cultural specificity, and being subject to deprecating stereotypes and cultural representations. Corresponding to these two irreducible roots of injustice are two different remedies. Redistribution produces political and economic changes that result in greater economic equality. Recognition redresses the harms of disrespect, stereotyping and cultural imperialism.

Fraser asserts that in the real world the structures of political economy and the meanings of cultural representation are inseparable: "Even the most material economic institutions have a constitutive, irreducible cultural dimension; they are shot through with significations and norms. Conversely, even the most discursive cultural practices have a constitutive, irreducible political-economic dimension; they are underpinned by material supports."[6] The distinction between redistribution and recognition is, therefore, entirely theoretical, an analytical distinction necessary for the construction of an account. Fraser claims that this categorical opposition is useful and even necessary in order to understand how the political aims of oppressed groups are sometimes contradictory.

To demonstrate this tension, Fraser constructs a continuum for classifying the forms of injustice that groups suffer. At one end of the continuum are groups that suffer a "pure" form of political economic injustice. Since the redistribution-recognition distinction is ideal and not real, such a group must also be an ideal type. Class oppression considered by itself approximates this ideal type. On the other end of the continuum are groups that suffer "pure" cultural oppression. Injustice suffered by gay men and lesbians approximates this ideal type, inasmuch as their oppression, considered by itself, has its roots only in cultural values that despise their sexual practices.

Remedies for injustice at each of these extremes come in reformist and revolutionary varieties, which Fraser respectively terms "affirmative" and "transformative." The affirmative remedy for class oppression is a welfare-state liberalism that redistributes goods, services and income while leaving the underlying economic structure undisturbed. A transformative remedy for class injustice, on the other hand, changes the basic economic structure and thereby eliminates the proletariat. An affirmative remedy for sexual oppression seeks to solidify a specific gay or lesbian identity in the face of deprecating stereotypes, whereas a transformative cultural politics deconstructs the very categories of sexual identity.

The main trouble comes with groups that lie in the middle of the continuum, subject both to political-economic and cultural injustices. The oppressions of gender and race lie here, according to Fraser. As subject to two different and potentially opposing forms of injustice, the political struggles of women and people of color are also potentially

---

6 In this volume, p. 16.

contradictory. From the point of view of political economy, the radically transformative struggles of women and people of color ought to have the aim of eliminating the gender or racial group as a distinct position in the division of labor. This goal of eliminating the structured position of the group, however, comes into conflict with a "politics of identity." In the latter, women or people of color wish to affirm the group's specific values and affinity with one another in the face of deprecating stereotypes and cultural representation. Affirmative politics of recognition, according to Fraser, conflicts with transformative politics of redistribution because the latter requires eliminating the group as a group while the former affirms the group identity. This conflict shows the error of such an affirmative politics of recognition, and the need instead for a transformative cultural politics that deconstructs identities.

2. Why theorize with a dichotomy?

Fraser recommends a "deconstructive" approach to a politics of recognition, which unsettles clear and oppositional categories of identity. Yet her theorizing in these essays is brazenly dichotomous. Injustices to all groups are reducible to two, and only two, mutually exclusive categories. The remedies for these injustices also come in two mutually exclusive categories, with each further divisible into a reformist and radical version. All social processes that impact on oppression can be conceptualized on one or the other side of this dichotomy or as a product of their intersection. Thus redistribution and recognition are not only exclusive categories, but together they comprehend everything relevant to oppression and justice.

As I have already noted, Fraser denies that this dichotomy describes reality. What, then, justifies its use in theory? Fraser answers that an analytical framework requires concepts through which to analyze reality, and it must be able to distinguish among these concepts. This is certainly true. Such a justification does not explain, however, why a critical social theory should rely on only two categories. Why adopt an analytical strategy, furthermore, that aims to reduce more plural categorizations of social phenomena to this "bifocal" categorization?

In *Justice and the Politics of Difference*, I explicate a plural categorization of oppression. I distinguish five "faces" of oppression— exploitation, marginalization, powerlessness, cultural imperialism, and violence.[7] Many concrete instances of oppression should be described

---

7 Iris M. Young, *Justice and the Politics of Difference*, Princeton: Princeton University Press, 1990, Chapter 2.

using several of these categories, though most descriptions will not use all. The purpose of elaborating a plural but limited categorization of oppression is to accommodate the variations in oppressive structures that position individuals and groups, and thus to resist the tendency to reduce oppression to one or two structures with "primacy."

In her essay criticizing this book, Fraser performs just such a reduction.[8] These five forms of oppression are "really" reducible to two: a political-economic injustice of maldistribution (exploitation, marginalization, and powerlessness) and a cultural injustice of misrecognition (cultural imperialism and violence). Fraser neither justifies this reduction of five to two, nor does she notice that the description of at least one of the categories she allocates to the "redistributive" side— namely powerlessness—is explicitly described *both* in terms of the division of labor and in terms of norms of respect. My point is not to argue for the particular framework I have developed, but to ask why the imposition of two categories is not arbitrary.

In her later essay "From Redistribution to Recognition?" Fraser considers an objection to her claim that the categories of political economy and culture exhaust description of social structures and injustice: this categorization appears to have no place for a third, political aspect of social reality, concerning institutions and practices of law, citizenship, administration, and political participation. Rather than taking this objection seriously, Fraser sets to work reducing these political phenomena to the dichotomous framework of political economy and culture. She appeals to Habermas to do so:

> My inclination is to follow Jürgen Habermas in viewing such issues bifocally. From one perspective, political institutions (in state-regulated capitalist societies) belong with the economy as part of the "system" that produces distributive socioeconomic injustices; in Rawlsian terms, they are part of the "basic structure" of society. From another perspective, however, such institutions belong with "the lifeworld" as part of the cultural structure that produces injustices of recognition; for example, the array of citizenship entitlements and participation rights conveys powerful implicit and explicit messages about the relative moral worth of various persons.[9]

---

8 Fraser, "Recognition or Redistribution?"
9 In this volume, p. 16, note 7.

In an earlier essay, "What's Critical about Critical Theory? The Case of Habermas and Gender," Fraser fashioned an important and persuasive critique of dichotomous thinking in general, and of this particular dichotomy between "system" and "lifeworld."[10] She argued that Habermas's categorical opposition between system and lifeworld eclipses more nuanced concepts in his theory. She showed how this dichotomy obscures the contribution of women's domestic labor to a reproduction of state and economic systems, while reinforcing a gendered opposition between public (system) and private (the lifeworld in which people appear as cared-for individuals). She argued that Habermas's dichotomy wrongly separates cultural norms from the social processes that reproduce bureaucratic and corporate institutions. For this reason, she suggested, Habermas's dichotomous theory cannot ground the conditions for the possibility of communicative democratization within those state and corporate institutions. Contrary to her reduction of the political to system and lifeworld in the above quotation, in "What's Critical about Critical Theory?" Fraser invoked a category of political action and struggle as additional to, and upsetting, the neat dichotomy of system and lifeworld. While in that essay Fraser suggested that dichotomous theorizing tends to devalue and obscure the phenomena that do not easily fit the categories, and to distort those that are conceptualized in its terms, a similar argument can be applied to her own theoretical strategy in these more recent essays.

3. Distinctions in theory and reality

Fraser's stated reason for constructing a dichotomy is that a mutually exclusive opposition best enables the theorist to identify contradictions in reality. With the dichotomy between political economy and culture, redistribution and recognition, Fraser wants to highlight the contradiction between various political goals. Feminist and anti-racist movements, she aims to show, cannot take as ends both the affirmation of their group identities and the elimination of their gender- or race-specific positions in the division of labor. Because she conceptualizes transformative redistribution as incompatible with affirmative recognition, Fraser succeeds in constructing an account in which the goals of feminist and anti-racist movements appear internally contradictory. If the dichotomous categorization of redistribution and recognition does not correspond to reality, however, but is merely

---

10 Nancy Fraser, *Unruly Practices: Power, Discourse and Gender in Contemporary Social Theory*, Minneapolis: University of Minnesota Press, 1989.

heuristic, how do we know that the tension is not merely an artifact of the theoretical dichotomy? Why should we accept Fraser's claim that the dichotomy reveals a fundamental political tension, rather than a superficial or even imagined one? Shortly I will argue that this categorization fails to understand that, for most social movements, what Fraser calls "recognition" is a means to the economic and social equality and freedom that she brings under the category of redistribution.

The injustices of political economy, according to Fraser's account, include exploitation, marginalization and deprivation. The remedy for any economic injustice is some sort of political-economic restructuring:

> This might involve redistributing income, reorganizing the division of labor, subjecting investment to democratic decision-making, or transforming other basic economic structures. Although these various remedies differ importantly from one another, I shall henceforth refer to the whole group of them by the generic term "redistribution."[11]

But one can surely ask why such diverse social processes should all be categorized as redistribution, especially since Fraser herself wishes to reintroduce distinctions into that category. Fraser believes, and I agree with her, that redistributive remedies for economic injustice, typical of the public provision of goods and services for needy people, do not change the conditions that produce this injustice and, in some ways, tend to reinforce those conditions. She thus recommends those remedies that transform the basic economic structure: "By restructuring the relations of production, these remedies would not only alter the end-state distribution of consumption shares; they would also change the social division of labor and thus the conditions of existence for everyone."[12] Fraser calls these remedies "transformative redistribution," as distinct from the "affirmative redistributive" remedies that leave the basic structure intact. But why bring them both under the same general category at all? Why not choose plural categories to distinguish and reflect those issues of justice that concern the patterns of the distribution of goods from those that concern the division of labor or the organization of decision-making power?

In earlier work, I proposed just such distinctions in order to show that many theories of justice wrongly collapse all issues of justice into

---

11 In this volume, p. 17.
12 Ibid. p. 30–31.

those of distribution, and thereby often wrongly identify the remedies for injustice with the redistribution of goods. I criticize this distributive paradigm for just the reasons that Fraser distinguishes affirmative and transformative redistributive remedies: to emphasize that end-state distributions are usually rooted in social and economic structures that organize the division of labor and decision-making power about investment, the organization of production, pricing, and so on. For evaluating the justice of social institutions, I propose a four-fold categorization. Societies and institutions should certainly be evaluated according to the patterns of distribution of resources and goods they exhibit; but, no less important, they should be evaluated according to their division of labor, the way they organize decision-making power, and whether their cultural meanings enhance the self-respect and self-expression of all society's members.[13] Structures of the division of labor and decision-making power are no more reducible to the distribution of goods than are cultural meanings. They both involve practices that condition actions and the relations among actors in different social locations; these serve as the context within which income, goods, services, and resources are distributed. If we begin with distinctions among distribution, division of labor, and decision-making power in our analytic framework, then we do not need later to uncover a confusion between remedies that "merely" redistribute and those that transform the basic structure.

Fraser's desire to dichotomize issues of justice between economy and culture produces categories that are too stark. A more plural categorization better guides action because it shows how struggles can be directed at different kinds of goals or policies. For example, distinguishing issues of justice about decision-making power from those concerning distribution can show that struggles about environmental justice cannot simply be about the placement of hazardous sites, a distributive issue, but must more importantly be about the processes through which such placements are decided.[14] Changes in the division of labor, furthermore, do not amount merely to "redistributing" tasks, as Fraser's dichotomy suggests, but often in redefining the cultural meaning and value of different kinds of work. The gender division of labor that allocates primary responsibility for care work to women outside the paid economy, for example, will not change without greater recognition of the nature and value of this work.

---

13 Young, *Justice and the Politics of Difference*, Chapter 1.

14 Christian Hunold and Iris Marion Young, "Justice, Democracy and Hazardous Siting," *Political Studies* 46: 1, 1998, pp. 82–95.

With a more plural categorization of issues of justice, furthermore, we can more clearly see the variables that must come together to constitute just institutions, as well as the tensions among them that can occur. Just as a plural categorization diffuses the starkness of redistribution, moreover, it demotes culture to one among several of such variables to be combined with others in analysis of social justice.

4. An alternative: Fraser's materialist cultural theorizing

Fraser introduces the dichotomy between redistribution and recognition to correct what she perceives as a tendency in multiculturalism and identity politics to ignore issues of political economy. While I agree that this characterization is sometimes accurate, the remedy for such a failing does not consist in setting up a category of political economy alongside, and in opposition to, culture. A more appropriate theoretical remedy would be to conceptualize issues of justice involving recognition and identity as having inevitably material economic sources and consequences, without thereby being reducible to market dynamics or economic exploitation and deprivation.

As I understand it, this has been the project of the best of what is called "cultural studies": to demonstrate that political economy, as Marxists think of it, is through and through cultural without ceasing to be material, and to demonstrate that what students of literature and art call "culture" is economic, not as base to superstructure, but in its production, distribution and effects, including effects on reproducing class relations. Political economy is cultural, and culture is economic.

The work of Pierre Bourdieu well exemplifies this mutual effect of culture and political economy. In several of his works, Bourdieu demonstrates that acquiring or maintaining positions in privileged economic strata depends partly on cultural factors of education, taste and social connection. Access to such enculturation processes, however, crucially depends on having economic resources and the relative leisure that accompanies economic comfort.[15] In his remarkable book *Encountering Development*, Arturo Escobar similarly argues for the mutual effect of cultural and material survival issues of access to resources in the

---

15 See Pierre Bourdieu, *Distinction: A Social Critique of the Judgement of Taste*, Cambridge, MA: Harvard University Press, 1979. Also "What makes a Social Class?" *Berkeley Journal of Sociology* 32, 1988, pp. 1–18; Craig Calhoun, *Critical Social Theory: Culture, History and the Challenge of Difference*, Oxford: Blackwell, 1995, Chapter 5.

struggles of oppressed peasants. Many Latin American peasants, who often come from indigenous cultures that have been neither eliminated nor assimilated by the dominant Latin culture, are struggling against repressive governments and international finance giants to obtain a barely decent life. Such peasant resistance, says Escobar, "reflects more than the struggle for land and living conditions; it is above all a struggle for symbols and meaning, a cultural struggle."[16] Latin American peasants struggle with World Bank representatives, local government officials and well-intentioned NGO leaders over the cultural interpretation of the most basic terms of political economy: land, natural resources, property, tools, labor, health, food. We should not mistake this claim for a "reduction" of political economy to culture. On the contrary, in this case, struggle about cultural meaning and identity has life and death consequences.

> The struggle over representation and for cultural affirmation must be carried out in conjunction with the struggle against the exploitation and domination over the conditions of local, regional, and global political economies. The two projects are one and the same. Capitalist regimes undermine the reproduction of socially valued forms of identity; by destroying existing cultural practices, development projects destroy elements necessary for cultural affirmation.[17]

With such a materialist cultural-political theory one can, for example, problematize the apparently simple call for an economic system that meets needs. With Amartya Sen, we can ask just *what* is to be equalized when we call for equality.[18] A materialist cultural approach understands that needs are contextualized in political struggle over who gets to define whose needs for what purpose. This is the approach that Nancy Fraser herself takes in an earlier paper, "Struggle Over Needs," where she argues that needs are always subject to struggle and interpretation, and that the inequalities in the struggling parties are structured

---

16 Arturo Escobar, *Encountering Development*, Princeton: Princeton University Press, 1995, p. 168.

17 Ibid., pp. 170–1.

18 In "From Redistribution to Recognition?" Fraser incorrectly identifies Sen as a pure theorist of political economy. In fact, Sen is acutely sensitive to variations in cultural meaning and the implications of human needs and the cultural meaning of goods and social networks within which needs are to be met. See *Inequality Reexamined*, Cambridge, MA: Harvard University Press, 1992.

simultaneously by access to material resources and discursive resources: "Needs talk appears as a site of struggle where groups with unequal discursive and non-discursive resources compete to establish as hegemonic their respective interpretations of legitimate social needs."[19] With a materialist cultural analysis, we can notice that, under circumstances of unjust social and economic inequality, the mobilization of communication in official publics often reflects and reproduces social and economic inequalities. In another earlier essay, Nancy Fraser argues that the best recourse that economically subordinated groups have is to form subaltern counter-publics as "discursive arenas where members of subordinated social groups invent and circulate counter-discourses to formulate oppositional interpretations of identities, interests and needs."[20] Any struggle against oppression, Fraser suggests in that essay, is simultaneously a struggle against cultural and economic domination, because the cultural styles of subordinated groups are devalued and silenced, and the political economy of the bourgeois public sphere ensures that subordinated groups lack equal access to the material means of equal participation.

Thus the Nancy Fraser of "From Redistribution to Recognition" appears as nearly the contrary of the Nancy Fraser of at least three earlier papers I have cited. Where the earlier Nancy Fraser theorized discursive cultural processes of group identification and of needs and interests from its own point of view, as a process of political context to produce change in economic structures, the more recent Fraser separates culture from economy, and argues that they tend to pull against each other in movements against injustice. I recommend the position of the earlier Fraser over the later. The earlier articles consider a politics of recognition as a means of struggle toward the end of material, social and economic equality and well-being. In the most recent work, however, Fraser takes recognition as an end in itself, politically disconnected from redistribution.

5. Recognition for the sake of redistribution

In her critique of multiculturalism and the politics of identity, Fraser writes as though the politics of recognition is an end in itself for movements of subordinated groups. Sometimes it is. The separatist

---

19 Fraser, "Struggle over Needs: Outline of a Socialist-Feminist Critical Theory of Late Capitalist Political Culture," in *Unruly Practices*, p. 116.

20 "Rethinking the Public Sphere: A Contribution to the Critique of Actually Existing Democracy," in Craig Calhoun, ed., *Habermas and the Public Sphere*, Cambridge, MA: MIT Press, 1992, p. 123.

movement of the Québécois, on which Taylor models his politics of difference, arguably takes recognition of the Québécois as a distinct people as a political end in itself, and the same is sometimes true of other nationalist movements. Interest in multiculturalism in education, to take a different sort of example, sometimes considers attention to and recognition of previously excluded groups as an end in itself.

When recognition is taken as a political end in itself, it is usually disconnected from economic issues of distribution and division of labor. I agree with Fraser that a political focus on recognition disconnected from injustices of exploitation, deprivation or control over work is a problem. The remedy, however, is to reconnect issues of political economy with issues of recognition. We should show how recognition is a means to, or an element in, economic and political equality.

In "From Redistribution to Recognition" Fraser does just the reverse of this. She treats all instances of group-based claims to cultural specificity and recognition as though recognition is an end in itself. For the movements that Fraser is most concerned with, however—namely, women's movements, movements of people of color, gay and lesbian movements, movements of poor and working-class people—a politics of recognition functions more as a means to, or element in, broader ends of social and economic equality, rather than as a distinct goal of justice.

Fraser constructs gay and lesbian liberation as a "pure" case of the politics of recognition. In this ideal type, the "root" of injustice to gay men and lesbians is entirely cultural. Gays and lesbians suffer injustice because of the cultural construction of heterosexism and homophobia. Although the images of gays and lesbians as despicable and unnatural has distributive consequences, because the root of the oppression is culture, the remedy must also be cultural: the recognition of gay and lesbian lifestyles and practices as normal and valuable, and the giving of equal respect to persons identified with those practices.

Although arguments could be mounted that historically marriage is largely an economic institution, I will not quarrel here with the claim that heterosexism and homophobia are cultural. Nevertheless, the claim that, even as an ideal type, oppression through sexuality is purely cultural trivializes the politics of those oppressed because of sexuality. Whatever the "roots" of heterosexism, and I would theorize them as multiple, this harm matters because those on the wrong side of the heterosexual matrix experience systematic limits to their freedom, constant risk of abuse, violence and death, and unjustly limited access to resources and opportunities. Among the primary political goals of gay, lesbian, bisexual, transsexual or queer activists are material, economic and political equality: an end to discrimination in employment, housing, health care; equal protection by police and courts; equal freedom to partner and raise children. Precisely because the source of inequality in this case is cultural imagery that demonizes those who transgress heterosexual norms, a politics of difference is a crucial means for achieving the material goals of equal protection and equal opportunity. For example, positive and playful images of the possibilities of sexuality aim to undermine the monolithic construction of norm and deviant, which is a necessary condition of respect and freedom.

The polarization of political economy and culture, redistribution and recognition, I have argued, distorts the plurality and complexity of social reality and politics. Fraser's account of anti-racist and feminist politics reveals such distortions. Race and gender, Fraser argues, are "dilemmatic" modes of collectivity. The injustices of race and gender consist in a dialectical combination of two analytically distinct modes of oppression, distributive injustice and lack of recognition, for which there are two distinct kinds of remedy, redistribution and recognition. But these two forms of remedy are often contradictory, according to Fraser. The radical, transformative goal of redistributive justice for women or people of color should consist in eliminating the structures in the division of labor that allocate certain kinds of devalued work to white women and women of color, and which keep them—especially people of color—in a marginalized underclass "reserve army." Insofar as gender and race are defined by this division of labor and structural marginalization, the goal of redistribution should be to eliminate the oppressed gender or race as a group, just as the goal of working-class movements must be the elimination of the proletariat as a group.

According to Fraser, however, the politics of recognition when applied to gender or race pulls the other way. The goal of such cultural politics is to affirm the specific difference of women or African-Americans or Chicanos or Navajos, to develop pride in women's relational orientation, or the moral qualities generated by musical, religious and storytelling legacies. Thus a politics of recognition seeks to affirm the group as a good, which contradicts and undermines the transformative goal of redistribution:

> Insofar as people of color suffer at least two analytically distinct
> kinds of injustice, they necessarily require at least two analytically
> distinct kinds of remedy, which are not easily pursued simulta-
> neously. Whereas the logic of redistribution is to put "race" out

of business as such, the logic of recognition is to valorize group
specificity . . . How can anti-racists fight simultaneously to
abolish "race" and to valorize racialized group specificity?[21]

Here Fraser imposes dichotomous categories on a more complex reality
and, by doing so, finds contradiction where none exists. She suggests
that culturally affirming movements of people of color aim to abolish
"race" by affirming "race." But this is a distortion of, for example,
most black cultural politics. The purpose of affirming the cultural and
social specificity of African-Americans or First Nations or North
African Muslim immigrants is precisely to puncture the naturalized
construction of these groups as "raced." These groups affirm cultural
specificity in order to deny the essentialism of "race" and encourage
the solidarity of the members of the group against deprecating stereotypes. Fraser's position seems similar to that of conservative opponents
of anti-racist politics who refuse to distinguish the affirmation of
specific economic, political and cultural institutions of solidarity and
empowerment for oppressed people of color from the discriminatory
and racist institutions of white exclusion.

6. The material and the cultural entwined
Fraser finds these movements internally contradictory, moreover,
because she assumes that their politics of recognition is an end in
itself. It may be true that some activities and writings of culturally
affirming movements of people of color treat cultural empowerment
and recognition as itself the substance of liberation. More often,
however, those affirming cultural pride and identity for people of color
understand such recognition as a means of economic justice and social
equality. Most African Americans who support culturally based
African-American schools and universities, for example, believe that
the schools will best enable African-American young people to develop
the skills and self-confidence to confront white society, and collectively
help transform it to be more hospitable to African-American success.

Movements of indigenous peoples, to take another example,
certainly consider recognition of their cultural distinctness an end in
itself. They also see it as a crucial means to economic development.
They assert claims to land for the sake of building an economic base
for collective development and for achieving the effective redistribution
of the fruits of white colonial exploitation. Many also believe that the

---

21 In this volume, p. 27.

recovery of traditional indigenous cultural values provides vision for forms of economic interaction and the protection of nature whose wider institutionalization would confront capitalism with transformative possibilities.

Fraser's claim of internal contradiction may have a bit more force in respect to struggles against gender oppression. The infamous "equality versus difference" debate poses a genuine dilemma for feminist politics. Ought feminists to affirm gender blindness in the policies of employers, for example, in the allocation of health benefits, leave, promotion criteria, and working hours? Or should they demand that employers explicitly take into account the position of many women as primary caretakers of children or elderly relatives in deliberations about just allocations? Opting for the latter strategy risks solidifying a sexual division of labor that most feminists agree is unjust and ought to be eliminated. Opting for the former, however, allows employers to continue privileging men under the banner of equality.

Notice, however, that this feminist dilemma is not between a redistributive strategy and a strategy of recognition, but rather between two different redistributive strategies. By Fraser's own criteria, moreover, it could be argued that the second strategy has more transformative possibilities, because it takes the gender division of labor explicitly into account, whereas the first ignores this basic structure. Be that as it may, it is difficult to see how a feminist politics of recognition "pulls against" a feminist politics of redistribution. To the extent that undermining the misogyny that makes women victims of violence and degradation entails affirming the specific gendered humanity of women, this would seem also to contribution to women's economic revaluation. To affirm the normative and human value of the work that women do outside the labor force, moreover, is to contribute to a redistributive restructuring that takes account of the hidden social costs of markets and social policies.

Feminists discuss these issues in counter-publics where they encourage one another to speak for themselves, from their own experience. In these counter-publics, they form images and interests with which to speak to a larger public that ignores or distorts women's concerns. Such solidarity-forming identity politics need not reduce women to some common culture or set of concerns. While some feminist discourse constructs and celebrates a "women's culture" for its own sake, more often claims to attention for gender-specific experience and position occur in the context of struggles about economic and political opportunity.

I conclude, then, that Fraser is wrong to conceptualize struggles for recognition of cultural specificity as contradicting struggles for radical transformation of economic structures. So long as the cultural denigration of groups produces or reinforces structural economic oppressions, the two struggles are continuous. If a politics of difference disconnects culture from its role in producing material oppressions and deprivations, and asserts cultural expression as an end in itself, then such politics may obscure complex social connections of oppression and liberation. If Muslims were to focus only on their freedom to send their girls to school in headscarves, or Native Americans were to limit their struggles to religious freedom and the recovery of cultural property, then their politics would be superficial. Set in the context of a larger claim that people should not suffer material disadvantage and deprivation because they are culturally different, however, even such issues as these become radical.

Conclusion

Fraser is right to insist that radicals renew attention to material issues of the division of labor, access to resources, the meeting of needs, and the social transformations required to bring about a society in which everyone can be free to develop and exercise their capacities, associate with others and express themselves under conditions of material comfort. Her polarization of redistribution versus recognition, however, leads her to exaggerate the extent to which some groups and movements claiming recognition ignore such issues. To the degree such a tendency exists, I have argued, the cure is to reconnect issues of symbols and discourse to their consequences in the material organization of labor, access to resources, and decision-making power, rather than to solidify a dichotomy between them. I have suggested that a better theoretical approach is to pluralize concepts of injustice and oppression so that culture becomes one of several sites of struggle interacting with others.

Despite Fraser's claim to value recognition as much as redistribution, her criticisms of what she calls an affirmative politics of recognition seem pragmatically similar to other recent left critiques of the so-called politics of identity. On these accounts, the politics of difference influential among progressives in the last twenty years has been a big mistake. Feminist, gay and lesbian, African-American, Native American, and other such movements have only produced divisiveness and backlash, and have diverted radical politics from confronting economic power.[22]

---

22 See James Weinstein, report on independent politics, *In These Times*, February 18, 1996, pp. 18–21; Gitlin, *Twilight of Common Dreams*.

Yet, when capitalist hegemony is served by a discourse of "family values," when affirmative action, reproductive rights, voting rights for people of color, and indigenous sovereignty are all seriously under attack, suggesting that gender- or race-specific struggles are divisive or merely reformist does not promote solidarity. Instead, it helps fuel a right-wing agenda and further marginalizes some of the most economically disadvantaged people. A strong anti-capitalist progressive movement requires a coalition politics that recognizes the differing modalities of oppression that people experience and affirms their culturally specific networks and organizations.

The world of political ends and principles Fraser presents is eerily empty of action. She calls for a "deconstructive" rather than an "affirmative" approach to culture and identity, but I do not know what this means for the conduct of activism on the ground. From Zapatista challengers to the Mexican government, to Ojibwa defenders of fishing rights, to African-American leaders demanding that banks invest in their neighborhoods, to unions trying to organize a Labor Party, to those sheltering battered women, resistance has many sites and is often specific to a group without naming or affirming a group essence. Most of these struggles self-consciously involve issues of cultural recognition and economic deprivation, but not constituted as totalizing ends. None of them alone is "transformative," but, if linked together, they can be deeply subversive. Coalition politics can only be built and sustained if each grouping recognizes and respects the specific perspective and circumstances of the others, and works with them in fluid counterpublics. I do not think that such a coalition politics is promoted by a theoretical framework that opposes culture and economy.

AGAINST POLLYANNA-ISM:
A REPLY TO IRIS YOUNG

Nancy Fraser

Iris Young and I seem to inhabit different worlds. In her world, there are no divisions between the social Left and the cultural Left. Proponents of cultural politics work cooperatively with proponents of social politics, linking claims for the recognition of difference with claims for the redistribution of wealth. Virtually no practitioners of identity politics are essentialist, moreover, let alone authoritarian or chauvinist. Claims for the recognition of difference are only rarely advanced, finally, as ends in themselves; nearly all are put forward as transitional socialist demands. According to Young, therefore, the divisions that inspired my article are artifacts of my "dichotomous framework," figments of my imagination.

In fact, of course, it was not I but "postsocialist" political culture that has conjured up these divisions. I did not fantasize a march on Washington of a million black men in which not a single socioeconomic demand was raised. Nor did I imagine the widespread gloating on the US social Left over the *Social Text* hoax, which was thought to discredit the "phony leftism" of cultural studies. What I *did* do was construct a framework for analyzing existing splits between class politics and identity politics, socialist or social-democratic politics and multiculturalist politics. My aim was to show that these splits rest on false antitheses. "Postsocialist" ideology notwithstanding, we do not in reality face an either/or choice between social politics and cultural politics, redistribution and recognition. It is possible in principle to have both.

Recall the context my essay addressed: increased marketization and sharply rising inequality worldwide; the apparent delegitimation of socialist ideals; the growing salience of claims for the recognition of difference and the relative eclipse of claims for egalitarian redistribution; the decoupling of the cultural Left from the social Left; and the

seeming absence of any credible vision of a comprehensive alternative
to the present order. In my diagnosis, unlike that of Todd Gitlin and
James Weinstein, and unlike that of Young, who is on this point their
mirror opposite, the split in the Left is *not* between class struggles,
on the one hand, and gender, "race," and sex struggles, on the other.
Rather, it cuts across those movements, each of which is internally
divided between cultural currents and social currents, between currents
oriented to redistribution and currents oriented to recognition. In my
diagnosis, moreover, the split does not reflect a genuine antithesis.
Rather, it is possible in principle to combine an egalitarian politics of
redistribution with an emancipatory politics of recognition.

Thus, far from dichotomizing culture and political economy, I
diagnosed their current decoupling in "postsocialist" ideology. Far
from championing class politics against identity politics, I refuted the
view that we must make an either/or choice between them. Far from
manufacturing nonexistent contradictions, I provided a framework for
transcending political divisions that exist. Far from trashing movements
against sexism, racism, and heterosexism, I distinguished affirmative
from transformative currents within those movements in order to show
how claims for redistribution and recognition could be integrated with
one another in a comprehensive political project.

Young, however, systematically distorts my argument. In a discussion
that is more tendentious than analytical, she conflates three different
levels of analysis: the philosophical, the social-theoretical, and the
political.

On the philosophical level, my starting point was the current dissociation of two distinct paradigms of justice. One of these, the distributive
paradigm, has supplied the chief approach for analyzing justice claims
for at least 150 years; in the 1970s and '80s especially, it was subject to
intense and often brilliant philosophical elaboration. The other paradigm
is, in contrast, much newer; centered on the normative concept of recognition, it is currently being developed by philosophers such as Axel
Honneth and Charles Taylor, largely in response to the recognition
politics of the 1980s and '90s. Both paradigms are normatively powerful;
each succeeds in identifying an important set of justice claims and in
accounting for their moral force. Yet the two paradigms of justice don't
communicate. They are mutually dissociated in moral philosophy today
and need to be articulated with one another.

Contra Young, I did not invent these paradigms, nor did I contrive
their dissociation. Still less did I advocate a theory of justice divided
into "two mutually exclusive categories." On the contrary, I posed the
philosophical question of how we should understand their relation to

one another. One possibility is that one of the paradigms can be conceptually reduced to the other; but no one has managed to do this, and I doubt that in fact it can be done. Short of that, the most philosophically satisfying approach is to develop a more general overarching conception of justice that can encompass both distribution and recognition. This is the approach pursued in my *New Left Review* essay.[1]

On the social-theoretical level, I did not describe the material processes of political economy as "entirely opposed" to the symbolic processes of culture. Rather, I began where capitalism has placed us, in a social formation that differentiates specialized economic arenas and institutions from other arenas and institutions, including some that are designated as cultural, and from the larger background that Karl Polanyi called "society." To illuminate this social formation, one must account both for the historical fact of capitalist economic/cultural differentiation and also for the underlying reality of their thorough interpenetration. To that end, I invoked the culture/economy distinction in a specific—analytical—guise. Contra Young, I did not mark out two substantive institutional domains, economy and culture, assigning redistribution to the first and recognition to the second. Rather, I distinguished two analytical perspectives that can be trained upon any domain. Refuting the view that culture and economy constitute two separate mutually insulated spheres, I revealed their interpenetration by tracing the unintended effects of cultural and economic claims. The entire thrust of my essay was to demonstrate that cultural claims have distributive implications, that economic claims carry recognition subtexts, and that we ignore their mutual impingement at our peril. Thus, what Young labels a "dichotomy" is actually a *perspectival duality*.[2]

This approach is consistent, moreover, with my earlier work, including my 1985 essay on Habermas. There, I took what had been presented as a substantive institutional distinction (system and lifeworld) and reinterpreted it as an analytical distinction of perspectives (the system perspective and the lifeworld perspective). Contra Young, I did not simply reject the distinction; nor did I criticize dichotomous thinking in general. Rather, I criticized the conflation of an important analytical methodological distinction with a substantive institutional distinction.

---

1 For a further elaboration of this approach, see my "Social Justice in the Age of Identity Politics," in Nancy Fraser and Axel Honneth, *Redistribution or Recognition: A Political-Philosophical Exchange*, trans. Joel Golb, James Ingram, and Christiane Wilke, London: Verso, 2003.

2 For further elaboration, see "Social Justice in the Age of Identity Politics."

(The identical perspectival dualist view is clearly stated, incidentally, in the passage on politics Young cites from page 72 of my *New Left Review* essay; there I claim that political phenomena can be viewed from both the lifeworld and the system perspectives.) Thus, the two Nancy Frasers are really one.

Throughout her discussion, Young erroneously assumes that to draw a twofold distinction is to dichotomize. Hence her insistence, at odds with scientific parsimony, that five is better than two. (One is tempted to say that she is "brazenly" pentagonist, an ominously militarist stance.) The real issue, of course, is not the number of categories but their epistemic status and explanatory power.[3] But here Young's objections to my distinctions are unpersuasive. She gives us no good reasons to reject, for example, my contrast between affirmative and transformative remedies for injustice, a contrast that is illuminating in two respects. First, it permits us to preserve the formal essence of the idea of socialism, as distinct from the liberal welfare state, even when we are no longer clear about how to fill in socialism's substantive content. Second, it reveals otherwise hidden connections between socialism and deconstruction, on the one hand, and the liberal welfare state and mainstream multiculturalism, on the other.

This brings me, finally, to the level of politics. Contra Young, the existing splits between proponents of recognition and proponents of redistribution are not simply a matter of false consciousness. Rather, they give expression in distorted form to genuine tensions among multiple aims that must be pursued simultaneously in struggles for social justice. Theorists can help illuminate these tensions, provided that they eschew cheerleading and think critically about the social movements they support. To deny or minimize the difficulties is to bury one's head in the sand. Nor does it suffice to point out that some who press claims for the recognition of cultural differences hope thereby to promote economic restructuring; rather, one must go on to ask whether such hopes are well-founded or whether, rather, they are likely to run aground. Nor, finally, is it helpful to adopt the Pollyanna-ish view that the tensions within and among progressive social movements will

---

3 Here Young's own approach is deficient. The fivefold "plural" schema she proposes to characterize "group oppressions" is ad hoc and undertheorized. Indiscriminately mixing items from different regions of conceptual space, it contains nothing that cannot be analyzed from the standpoints of redistribution, recognition, or both. See my "Culture, Political Economy, and Difference: On Iris Young's Justice and the Politics of Difference," in Nancy Fraser, *Justice Interruptus: Critical Reflections on the "Postsocialist" Condition*, New York: Routledge, 1997.

somehow be automatically resolved in some all-encompassing "coalition" whose basis and content need not be specified.

My essay defended the project of integrating the best of socialist politics with the best of multicultural politics, while frankly acknowledging its genuine difficulties. I did not claim, contra Young, that redistribution conflicts with recognition. I argued, rather, that in the current historical context, the tensions between various group-differentiating and group de-differentiating claims assume the guise of a single contradiction, which I called "the redistribution/recognition dilemma." In this context, demands for economic justice seem to conflict necessarily with demands for cultural justice. But the appearance, I sought to demonstrate, is misleading. Once we distinguish affirmative approaches from transformative approaches, what looked like an ineluctable contradiction gives way to a plurality of possible strategies from which we must reflectively choose. Some kinds of recognition claims, especially the "deconstructive" kind, are better suited than others to synergizing with claims for socioeconomic equality.

Young rejects this last conclusion, of course, having written what is in essence a brief for the politics of affirmative recognition. In the end, however, she offers no good reasons for thinking that such a politics can promote transformative redistribution. I continue to believe it cannot.

FROM INEQUALITY TO DIFFERENCE:
A SEVERE CASE OF DISPLACEMENT?
Anne Phillips

When considering the shifts in left thinking over the past fifteen years, it is hard to avoid some notion of displacement: the cultural displacing the material; identity politics displacing class; the politics of constitutional reform displacing the economics of equality. Difference, in particular, seems to have displaced inequality as the central concern of political and social theory. We ask ourselves how we can achieve equality while still recognizing difference, rather than how we can eliminate inequality. This rephrasing of the questions can be traced to a variety of sources, but one undoubted element is the shift from exclusively class analyses of inequality to alternatives that consider class on a continuum with inequalities of gender, ethnicity or race. Class inequality lent itself to a strategy of elimination: a notion that the inequalities will disappear when the differences have finally gone. Once attention shifted to other forms of group difference that were not so amenable to erasure, it became inappropriate to regard difference as always and inevitably a problem. Why should sexual equality depend on abolishing the distinction between women and men? Why should equality between ethnic cultures depend on each losing its distinctive features? The idea that equality is antithetical to difference has been extensively criticized by feminists, as well as by those theorizing the conditions for equal citizenship in societies that are multicultural and multi-ethnic.[1] For some, this remains a strategic point: that we cannot hope to achieve equality by ignoring differences, for all attempts to pretend difference away—not noticing whether someone is male or

---

1 For an example of the feminist critique see Iris Marion Young, *Justice and the Politics of Difference*, Princeton: Princeton University Press, 1990. For the latter, see Will Kymlicka, *Multicultural Citizenship*, Oxford: Oxford University Press, 1996.

female, not noticing whether she is white or black— will end up reinforcing the dominance of already dominant groups. For others, it has
a more celebratory dimension: that diversity should be regarded as a
positive feature and actively embraced in our political initiatives. In
either case, the emphasis is on heterogeneity rather than homogeneity,
diversity rather than sameness, with the prior recognition of difference
a crucial stage in the achievement of equality.

One example of this is the questioning of universal models of citizenship that expect all individuals to enjoy identical sets of rights or
all groups to conform to the same constitutional arrangements.[2]
Another is the increasingly influential tradition of deliberative
democracy, which starts from the presumption of radical difference:
not the differences of opinion that lead one person to vote Labour
and another Conservative, nor indeed the differences of class location
that place one group in conflict with another, but the seemingly
intractable differences of experience, values or cultural practices that
get in the way of our mutual comprehension.[3]

Inequalities in power have figured prominently in this tradition, and
those who favor a more deliberative democracy often present it as a
way of eliminating the power of vested interests or redressing the
exclusion of minority perspectives. Yet here, too, there is a discernible
shift from the economic to the cultural, a movement away from the
economic conditions that have been considered necessary to democratic
equality and toward the discursive interaction between groups that
differ in their cultural values or moral beliefs. Marxism, par excellence,
tended to see political equality as a deceptive achievement unless

---

2 For example, Kymlicka argues for group-differentiated citizenship, and Young
for additional forms of group representation for those who are marginalized and
oppressed: what is being proposed in both cases is a notion of equality through difference rather than equality as identical treatment. One might also think of the current
arguments about devolution in Scotland and Wales. When people ask whether it is
fair for Scots to have their own national assembly and also be able to influence legislative
decisions for the rest of the United Kingdom, they are working within a universal
model of citizenship that would require all citizens to have exactly the same rights
and all areas of a country exactly the same constitutional arrangements. Those who
argue for asymmetrical arrangements are challenging this.

3 For example, Joshua Cohen, "Deliberation and Democratic Legitimacy," in A.
Hamlin and P. Pettit, eds., *The Good Polity: Normative Analysis of the State*, Oxford:
Blackwell, 1989; Iris Marion Young, "Justice and Communicative Democracy," in R.
Gottlieb, ed., *Tradition, Counter-Tradition, Politics: Dimensions of Radical
Philosophy*, Philadelphia: Temple University Press, 1994; Amy Gutmann and Dennis
Thompson, *Democracy and Disagreement*, Harvard: Harvard University Press, 1996.

combined with substantive equalities in social and economic life. Indeed, even in the paradigm of equal citizenship that developed from T.H. Marshall's essay on civil, political and social rights, we were encouraged to see political equality as requiring substantive social rights such as the right to education or employment. Contemporary debates, by contrast, focus more on securing political inclusion to groups that differ in their cultural or moral norms. In her introduction to a recent collection, *Democracy and Difference*, Seyla Benhabib notes that one or two of the contributors continue to stress economic and social rights as part of the substantive precondition for a successful deliberative democracy. But the main line of division is between those who defend a proceduralist or deliberative model that anticipates the possibility of political consensus, and those who develop an "agonistic model of democratic politics" that views difference as inescapable and resolution an impossible dream.[4] The shift from inequality to difference is typically framed by the unequal power relations that have denied recognition to minority groups, but it often seems to divert attention away from economic aspects of inequality—and has remarkably little to say about specifically class inequality. In a recent article on the relationship between class and discourses of difference, Diana Coole argues that "economic inequality is bracketed out of discussion of difference."[5] In extending the range of relevant differences to include those associated with gender, ethnicity or race, we may have left economic inequalities out of the picture.

Much of the impetus for this exclusion derived from well-rehearsed weaknesses in left politics: the deployment of class analysis against any politics associated with gender or ethnicity; the disdain for democracy that so often developed out of the stand-off between liberalism and socialism; the tendency to disparage the "merely" cultural as of negligible significance in a world structured by economic exploitation. The primacy once accorded to class is no longer defensible. It is now all too apparent that the practice of an exclusively class politics overrode crucial differences of experience associated with gender, ethnicity, or race; in doing so, it left "class" as an empty category, bereft of historical meaning, or else elided it with the experiences and interests of the dominant sex or dominant ethnic group. But where

---

4 Seyla Benhabib, ed., *Democracy and Difference: Contesting the Boundaries of the Political*, Princeton: Princeton University Press, 1996, p. 7.

5 Diana Coole, "Is Class a Difference that Makes a Difference?" *Radical Philosophy* 77, 1996, p. 19.

the first formulations of this critique still seemed compatible with a broadly materialist analysis of exploitation and oppression, later versions have proved more challenging. Much feminist work in the 1970s, for example, continued to work within a framework derived from Marx, building on his insights even while addressing his blind spots about women's oppression. Class was not so much "displaced" as retheorized in its racialized and gendered complexity, while those who adopted a "dual systems" approach to sexual and class oppression typically developed their theories of patriarchal relations on a model derived from the analysis of class. Such initiatives proved rather short-lived, however, and rapidly developed into a deeper questioning of the primacy attached to political economy per se. It was not just the dominance of class that had to be questioned. It was also the underlying hierarchy of causation that had distinguished an economic base from a political and cultural superstructure, or defined "real" interests through location in economic relations.

One element in this rethinking was epistemological: the incoherence of conceiving of interests outside the discourses within which these are generated. Much of it was more directly political, for many of the struggles of the last twenty years have addressed forms of domination that cannot be captured by "material interest": the viciousness of domestic violence or racial assaults, the demonization of Islam, the persistent devaluing of "deviant" sexualities, the "crippling self-hatred" that can be imposed on people whose cultural values are socially despised.[6] Despite valiant efforts over the years, these phenomena have continued to escape redescription as effects of economic inequality. None of them is entirely detached from relations of subordination in the economy: it would be perverse to seek to explain violence against women without any reference to women's positioning in the social division of labor; or to explain racism in contemporary America without any reference to the legacy of a slave-owning economy. But neither the problems nor their solutions have fitted neatly into what has passed for materialist analysis, for the primacy attached to economic relations played down what was "merely" cultural, while the invocation of "real" or "essential" interests seemed to query the authenticity of what people perceived as their most urgent concerns. It is only in dislodging the economic from its earlier theoretical dominance—what Ernesto Laclau has described as the "arbitrary dogma" that attached a determining

---

6 Charles Taylor et al., *Multiculturalism and the Politics of Recognition*, Princeton: Princeton University Press, 1992, p. 25.

role to the development of the productive forces—that we have been
better able to address the corrosive impact of cultural subordination
or the crucial role of political and cultural struggle in contesting
relations of exclusion.[7]

The anxiety now voiced by a number of theorists is that this
dislodging becomes a displacement, and that what promised to be an
enlargement of the political terrain ends up excising the economic. In
a series of recent articles, now collected together under the title *Justice
Interruptus: Critical Reflections on the "Postsocialist" Condition*,
Nancy Fraser identifies what she sees as a major shift in the political
imaginary:

> Many actors appear to be moving away from a socialist political
> imaginary, in which the central problem of justice is redistribu-
> tion, to a "postsocialist" political imaginary, in which the central
> problem of justice is recognition. With this shift, the most salient
> social movements are no longer economically defined "classes"
> who are struggling to defend their "interests," end "exploitation,"
> and win "redistribution." Instead, they are culturally defined
> "groups" or "communities of value" who are struggling to defend
> their "identities," end "cultural domination," and win "recognition."
> The result is a decoupling of cultural politics from social politics,
> and the relative eclipse of the latter by the former.[8]

For many of those associated with this shift, the initial expectation
was that the old and the new would be brought together in a more
satisfactory combination. The question Fraser raises is whether this
more satisfactory combination ends up as mere displacement. She talks
of group identity as "supplanting" class interest, cultural domination
as "supplanting" economic exploitation, cultural recognition as
"displacing" socioeconomic redistribution, and this language of
displacement conveys her perception that earlier preoccupations have
been pushed to one side, not so much built on as discarded.[9]

Fraser's description of the new politics of recognition is in many
ways specific to contemporary politics in North America. It conjures
up the so-called culture wars on American campuses, which have

---

7 Ernesto Laclau, *New Reflections on the Revolution of Our Time*, London: Verso,
1990, p. 7.

8 Nancy Fraser, *Justice Interruptus: Critical Reflections on the "Postsocialist"
Condition*, London: Routledge, 1997, p. 2.

9 Ibid., p. 11.

centered on the representation in the teaching curriculum of women or African-Americans, and do indeed seem to fit within a discourse of cultural domination; and it employs a language of recognition that has been particularly associated with Charles Taylor's writings on the politics of Quebec. Political developments in Britain are less evidently preoccupied with battles to defend identities or end cultural domination or win recognition for culturally despised groups: we might cite a few episodes relating to the claims of Muslim minorities or of gay and lesbian groups, but we could not seriously contend that politics has been transformed into a politics of identity or struggles for group recognition. In other ways, however, this displacement of the economic is precisely what worries so many on the Left in Britain. The radicalism of the new Labour government is far more evident in its program for constitutional reform than in any policies for the redistribution of income or wealth; and however much we may welcome this belated attention to questions of democratic accountability, the enlargement of horizons could mean that economic equality drops out of view.

This is the issue at stake in the recent interchange between Nancy Fraser and Iris Marion Young.[10] Both theorists have been notable for their persistent attention to issues of socioeconomic equality, and both have rung the alarm bell at various stages when colleagues have lost interest in matters of economic privilege and economic oppression. Both are also—if to varying degrees—attached to what Fraser calls the politics of recognition and Young the politics of difference; both, that is, see contemporary societies as characterized by a combination of economic *and* cultural injustices, and neither makes any explicit claim about one being more "fundamental" than the other. But where Young stresses the continuity and mutual reinforcement between what might be deemed "economic" and what might be deemed "cultural," Fraser insists on an analytic distinction in order to highlight tensions between these two. For Young, the risk of displacement is just one of those perennial risks that faces any progressive movement: there will always be theorists or activists who lose sight of issues of inequality and disadvantage, and the others have to be vigilant in arguing against such retreats. For Fraser, by contrast, the risk of displacement is significantly heightened by the failure to make distinctions. Some ways of

---

10 Nancy Fraser, "Recognition or Redistribution? A Critical Reading of Iris Young's *Justice and the Politics of Difference*," *Journal of Political Philosophy* 3: 2, 1995; see also Fraser, *Justice Interruptus*, Chapter 8; Iris Marion Young, "Unruly Categories," in this volume; Nancy Fraser, "Against Pollyanna-ism," in this volume.

battling against cultural injustice make it harder to fight economic injustice. If we do not admit the potential areas of conflict, we will be unable to move forward on both fronts at once.

The economic injustices Fraser refers to are rooted in the political-economic structure of society: exploitation, economic marginalization, and the starker deprivation that deprives people of an adequate standard of living. The remedy for these lies in what (despite Marx's strictures!) Fraser terms "redistribution"—a redistribution of income, a reorganization of the division of labor, a democratization of investment decisions, a transformation of basic economic structures. The cultural injustices, by contrast, are rooted in the cultural or symbolic order: the domination that subjects members of one cultural group to patterns of interpretation and communication that are associated with an alien and/or hostile culture; the misrecognition of one's own cultural understandings so often associated with this; the routine malignment, disparagement and disrespect that is dealt out to people because of their sexuality, gender or race. It is hard to see any remedy for these short of recognizing and revaluing what have been despised or marginalized identities. Reforms in the field of employment could weed out overt discrimination—could ensure that homosexuals, for example, are given equal access to employment in the armed forces or the equal right to work with children. But as long as people continue to regard homosexuals with distaste—treat them, in Fraser's phrase, as a "despised sexuality"—they will still be subject to shaming, harassment, and violence. The remedy for this lies in recognition, not redistribution, in changing the cultural valuations that have denied gays and lesbians equal respect.

Fraser does not claim one form of injustice as more fundamental than the other: "I assume," she says, "that justice today requires both redistribution and recognition," and she makes it clear that battling on one front alone will not automatically deliver results on the other.[11] We might then conclude that we should just buckle down to both tasks, for each of them matters and neither is more fundamental than the other. Fraser's main concern is that this easy eclecticism does not work in relation to groups that suffer both forms of injustice: women, for example, or people defined by their "race." The socioeconomic injustices associated with gender and race are best remedied by putting race and gender out of business as categories: restructuring the division of labor and income so that people's position in social and economic

---

11 in this volume, p. 12.

relations is no longer dictated by their gender or race. But the cultural injustices—"the pervasive devaluation and disparagement of things coded as 'feminine'," and of "things coded as 'black', 'brown', and 'yellow' "—seem to require a positive revaluation of the characteristics of the despised groups, a stronger affirmation of their group identity.[12] Hence, Fraser suggests, the familiar tension that arises in the politics of gender and race, that seemingly intractable dilemma between strategies that seek to eliminate the significance of gender or race, and strategies that insist on the intrinsic worth of one's sex or race. This is, she argues, a real dilemma, but it is one we can soften by the approaches we adopt. Notions of a continuum—or, in more dynamic language, of multiple interlocking sites of struggle—are not particularly helpful here, for they encourage us to see all advances as mutually reinforcing. They then draw our attention away from what might be important questions of strategic choice.

This, effectively, is the charge Nancy Fraser levels at Iris Young. She sees Young's work in *Justice and the Politics of Difference* as unusual in seeking to encompass claims of both recognition and redistribution, but argues that Young does not sufficiently recognize the tensions between these two. Because she has not thought through the relationship between the two paradigms, she inadvertently ends up with "a wholesale, undifferentiated and uncritical endorsement of the politics of difference," an endorsement that "is at odds with her own professed commitment to the politics of redistribution."[13] Fraser argues that Iris Young collapses what are different forms of group oppression into a single category of "the social group," marked by any one of five faces of oppression—exploitation, marginalization, powerlessness, cultural imperialism, violence. In the process, Fraser argues, she "implicitly privileges the culture-based social group," failing to perceive that in other contexts, the politics of difference might prove counterproductive.[14] What, she asks, of manual workers, a group that suffers from powerlessness and exploitation, and that may develop cultural affinities out of these conditions that identify them as a distinct social group? Does this group really need the cultural affirmation associated with a politics of difference? Or does it need, on the contrary, a reorganization of work that would abolish the gap between mental and manual labor and thereby undermine those cultural affinities that have

---

12 In this volume, p. 26.
13 Fraser, *Justice Interruptus*, p. 190.
14 Ibid., p. 196.

separated manual from professional workers? In Young's analysis, anything that destroys cultural specificity smacks of cultural imperialism. In Fraser's analysis, there are some cultural specificities that should wither away in the face of a successful politics of redistribution.

There are two issues here: whether it is theoretically and/or politically appropriate to make this distinction between redistribution and recognition; and whether Fraser's analysis ends up reinstating economic injustices as her central concern. Fraser presents the shift from a language of exploitation to a language of cultural oppression and recognition as a shift from economic to cultural concerns, a movement from one sphere to another—and a movement that then threatens to leave the former behind. Young notes that this ignores the extensive literature—to which Fraser herself has contributed—that has challenged dichotomous distinctions between the economic and the cultural, and has explored the power of cultural representations in defining the so-called economic. Iris Young sums this up in her description of the project of the best of what is called cultural studies:

> to demonstrate that political economy, as Marxists think of it, is through and through cultural without ceasing to be material, and to demonstrate that what students of literature and art call "culture" is economic, not as base to superstructure, but in its production, distribution and effects, including effects on reproducing class relations. Political economy is cultural, and culture is economic.[15]

At one level, one might note, this is also what Fraser claims. She talks of "even the most material economic institutions" as having "a constitutive, irreducible cultural dimension," and "even the most discursive cultural practices" having "a constitutive, irreducible political-economic dimension."[16] If Fraser continues to use the term "economic" as if it can be distinguished from "cultural," so too does Iris Young when she refers to the way they produce or reinforce one another. Indeed, it hard to see how we can operate without some kind of distinction, for even if we describe political economy as cultural, and culture as economic, we will still want to be able to talk of the economic resources that sustain cultural identity or the cultural resources that enable people to press their economic claims. (To make an obvious parallel, we might want to say that everything is political, but this

---

15 In this volume, p. 98.
16 In this volume, p. 16.

does not commit us to the view that there is no difference between private and public life, nor to the conclusion that political equality simply means economic equality, as if there were no distinction between these two.) The key point is not whether we make an analytical separation, but whether we regard the things we have separated as having an independent life of their own. Fraser stresses the potential conflicts that can arise between one form of struggle and another; Young is far more struck by their interconnection. When African-Americans, for example, support culturally based African-American schools or universities, they are not just pursuing some notion of cultural pride or identity; they are also anticipating that such schools will help young African-Americans to achieve economic justice and social equality. When women affirm the normative value of the care-work they do outside the labor force, they are not just claiming a pride in women's difference; they are also calling for a restructuring of the social division of labor so as to redress the balance between paid and unpaid work. Young positions herself, in other words, within a mutually reinforcing plurality of struggles. She sees this as what already happens, and she favors a form of analysis that continues to strengthen the interconnections. We need "to pluralize concepts of injustice and oppression so that culture becomes one of several sites of struggle interacting with others."[17] It does not help to pit one of these against the others.

At this point I find myself in the familiar position of agreeing with both. The great contribution of Nancy Fraser's work is that it enables us to think more precisely about political dilemmas: to consider how one desirable objective might come into conflict with another equally desirable one; and whether there are alternative ways of approaching our objectives that might—to use her term—"finesse" the dilemma. The distinction between economic and cultural injustices is indeed shaky— what exactly goes into one camp or the other?—but I find the underlying point about recognizing the importance of different kinds of struggle while also identifying their potential conflicts and tensions extremely illuminating. The split between class politics and identity politics is not, as Fraser observes, a mere figment of her imagination, and even if some of those who press claims for recognition see this as contributing to economic restructuring, one is still obliged to consider whether the route they have chosen makes it harder for them to achieve both aims.[18] In the political division of labor, no one can hope to do everything at once, but if the

17 In this volume, p. 105.
18 See Fraser, "Against Pollyanna-ism," in this volume.

choices we make block out other issues, it does not help just to say that everything is interconnected.

Consider, in this context, the widely voiced claims for equality of political representation for women and people from ethnic and racial minorities. In the older socialist paradigm that saw political equalities as a reflex of socioeconomic equalities, it would hardly be appropriate to make this an independent matter of political contestation: the under-representation of women or black people is self-evidently a consequence of their positioning in the social division of labor, and best addressed by tackling the relations of economic subordination. No need to bother, then, with troubling initiatives like the Labour Party's all-woman short lists, or the redrawing of constituency boundaries in the US so as to generate voting districts in which minority groups can form a voting majority; equality in political representation will come readily enough when we have equality in economic relations. This response strikes me as deeply inadequate. It presents socioeconomic transformation as the condition for challenging patterns of political and cultural dominance, even though our chances of the first remain minimal until we make some headway on the second. It also plays down the independent importance of a political—in Fraser's term, a "cultural"—injustice, as if the marginalization of whole segments of the population had no independent claims on our attention. Increasing the political represen-tation of women or black people matters. It matters in itself, as a way of contesting the exclusion—almost infantilization—of a majority of the population; it also matters as a way of transforming the political agenda so as to enable economic change.

But if this is self-evident to me, so too are the risks. When the battle for parity of representation is conducted in the name of "women's interests" or "black interests," this can generate essentialist notions of a unified voice that have neither theoretical nor empirical validity. In encouraging the view that any woman is representative of all women, or any black person of all black people, it can also obscure the economic differentiation within each category and displace into a distant limbo any remaining issues of economic equality. Hence the arguments devel-oped in the US for mechanisms of cumulative voting and proportional representation that can increase the political representation of minority groups while detaching the claim for racial group representation from its dangerous grounding in racial authenticity.[19] Hence, also, the arguments

---

19 Especially Lani Guinier, *The Tyranny of the Majority: Fundamental Fairness in Representative Democracy*, New York: Free Press, 1995.

for changing the gender composition of elected assemblies that detach the claim for parity of representation from essentialist definitions of "women" or "men."[20] The choice of arguments, like the choice of mechanisms, makes a difference, for while some threaten to bracket out issues of economic privilege or inequality, others make it easier to sustain the connections. Our chances of achieving the latter are much improved if we recognize that there can be real dilemmas. Failing this, we may end up displacing what we desperately needed to find.

On this point, I am in close agreement with Nancy Fraser. But lurking below the surface is a more troubling element that seems to reassert the priority of "the economic." Fraser does not employ socioeconomic injustice as a way of downgrading cultural injustice, and she explicitly argues that justice requires both of these together. The questions she poses, however, suggest that the struggles for redistribution take priority in her overall vision: "Under what circumstances can a politics of recognition help support a politics of redistribution? And when is it more likely to undermine it?"[21] The answers she gives reaffirm the importance of cultural struggles, but it could be said that they do this while refusing to accept the importance of culture per se.

Her preferred solution is a deconstructive politics that plays on the instabilities of gender or racial identity, blurs the sharp male/female, white/black distinctions, and weans people away from their rigid constructions. Such a politics "would redress disrespect by transforming the underlying cultural-valuational structure." But instead of simply reversing the old order of priorities in categorizations that otherwise remain the same, this approach would destabilize all our identities, changing "*everyone's* sense of belonging, affiliation, and self."[22] It would require us to challenge fixed notions of cultural identity, question our attachment to current cultural constructions of our interests and identities, undermine the binary oppositions between male/female, white/black, and replace these "by networks of multiple intersecting differences that are demassified and shifting."[23] I have considerable sympathy with this in relation to gender identities, but it still sounds to me like a strategy for demystifying the importance of culture: challenging notions of femininity or masculinity, for example, by stressing the many ways in which individuals cross the border between what

---

20 I develop these arguments in *The Politics of Presence*, Oxford: Oxford University Press, 1995.

21 In this volume, p. 12.

22 In this volume, p. 29.

23 In this volume, p. 37.

is conceived as masculine and feminine; or challenging notions of ethnic identity by stressing the many ways in which individuals evade definition by their so-called culture. From one perspective, this promises a much desired liberation from tightly coded notions of gender or ethnic or racial identity. From another perspective, it looks like an assimilationist project that ultimately expects all barriers and divisions to dissolve. The weight attached to transformation inevitably suggests a process of convergence between what are currently distinct values or identities, a cultural "melting pot" out of which new—but then no longer "cultural"—identities will be forged.

This is a cultural politics without the culture. It is symptomatic, perhaps, that while she charges Young with deriving her politics of difference from the model of the ethnic group, Fraser herself leaves the question of ethnic identity to the occasional footnote, and does not address those further struggles for recognition that revolve around religious or linguistic identities. Culture is not only analytically distinguished from the economic; it is also turned into something rather insubstantial. We are to battle on the terrain of cultural construction —we should not ignore cultural injustices as if they had no salience in the world of gross material inequality—but we are to do this without attaching real weight to the notion of cultural recognition. Fraser's argument then threatens to reintroduce that prioritization of the economic that has so much bedeviled left thinking over the years: measuring the validity of cultural struggles by whether they reinforce or disrupt economic struggles; attaching authenticity to demands for economic equality but no parallel authenticity to demands for cultural recognition. So perhaps Young is right. It seems that the separation between the economic and the cultural—even if it is pursued as an analytical device, with no claims about their "real" separation—has emptied the cultural of much of its meaning. Despite Fraser's declared objective, redistribution emerges as the central site of political struggle, with a rather cursory nod in the direction of recognition.

Fraser has commented that theorists of distributive justice tend simply to ignore identity politics, while theorists of recognition tend to ignore questions of social equality—and I agree with her that this either/or choice is unacceptable. Fraser's reintegration is, however, considerably less evenhanded than she intends, partly for the reasons that Iris Young suggests—that she employs an overly stark dichotomy between economic and cultural—and partly because the effect of this dichotomy is to make economic claims seem more real than cultural ones. Yet the underlying point surely remains that there is something deeply unsatisfactory about simply placing everything on a continuum of mutually reinforcing concerns, or incorporating all existing problems of inequality and injustice under a single rubric of "difference." In her parallel assessment of discourses of difference, Diana Coole has also made the point that these discourses work better for some groups than for others—they work particularly badly, she suggests, for that rough category of "underclass," defined through unemployment or employment insecurity. Changing the focus from problems of inequality to questions of difference has, in my view, been immensely fruitful, but when difference becomes the hegemonic language through which we approach all problems of inequality, it can indeed lead to displacement. In Coole's assessment, discourses of difference "convey an erroneous impression that they have a capacity to accommodate diversities of all kinds."[24] All too often, the result of this is that economic difference is silenced as a significant form.

What we need, as Fraser argues, is to recognize that there are different kinds of differences, and that the strategies appropriate to one kind may not be so appropriate to another. We need an analysis that can acknowledge potential conflicts, tensions and dilemmas, but we have to pursue this without presuming in advance that one set of initiatives always takes priority over another. When Fraser asks (admittedly as "only one aspect of the problem") under what circumstances a politics of recognition helps support a politics of redistribution, and when it is more likely to undermine it, she gives the impression that we should measure the importance of the former by what we have already decided as the importance of the latter.[25] This edges dangerously close to an older socialist paradigm that accommodated identity struggles only when they were demonstrably in tune with the "real" struggles around economic conditions, and in the process undermines her own official endorsement of the politics of recognition. I remain convinced, however, that we can build on Nancy Fraser's analysis of strategic choices to ensure that the newer politics around the recognition of difference does not displace an older politics around economic inequality. Acknowledging the possibility of conflicts is the first crucial stage in this.

---

24 Coole, "Is Class a Difference that Makes a Difference?" p. 24.
25 In this volume, p. 12.

II. RECONCILING REDISTRIBUTION AND RECOGNITION: JUSTICE IN TWO DIMENSIONS

RETHINKING RECOGNITION: OVERCOMING DISPLACEMENT AND REIFICATION IN CULTURAL POLITICS

Nancy Fraser

In the seventies and eighties, struggles for the "recognition of difference" seemed charged with emancipatory promise. Many who rallied to the banners of sexuality, gender, ethnicity and "race" aspired not only to assert hitherto denied identities but to bring a richer, lateral dimension to battles over the redistribution of wealth and power as well. With the turn of the century, issues of recognition and identity have become even more central, yet many now bear a different charge: from Rwanda to the Balkans, questions of "identity" have fueled campaigns for ethnic cleansing and even genocide—as well as movements that have mobilized to resist them.

It is not just the character but the scale of these struggles that has changed. Claims for the recognition of difference now drive many of the world's social conflicts, from campaigns for national sovereignty and subnational autonomy, to battles around multiculturalism, to the newly energized movements for international human rights, which seek to promote both universal respect for shared humanity and esteem for cultural distinctiveness. They have also become predominant within social movements such as feminism, which had previously foregrounded the redistribution of resources. To be sure, such struggles cover a wide range of aspirations, from the patently emancipatory to the downright reprehensible (with most probably falling somewhere in between). Nevertheless, the recourse to a common grammar is worth considering. Why today, after the demise of Soviet-style Communism and the acceleration of globalization, do so many conflicts take this form? Why do so many movements couch their claims in the idiom of recognition?

To pose this question is also to note the relative decline in claims for egalitarian redistribution. Once the hegemonic grammar of political contestation, the language of distribution is less salient today. The movements that not long ago boldly demanded an equitable share of

resources and wealth have not, to be sure, wholly disappeared. But
thanks to the sustained neoliberal rhetorical assault on egalitarianism,
to the absence of any credible model of "feasible socialism" and to
widespread doubts about the viability of state-Keynesian social democracy in the face of globalization, their role has been greatly reduced.

We are facing, then, a new constellation in the grammar of political
claims-making—and one that is disturbing on two counts. First, this
move from redistribution to recognition is occurring despite—or
because of—an acceleration of economic globalization, at a time when
an aggressively expanding capitalism is radically exacerbating
economic inequality. In this context, questions of recognition are
serving less to supplement, complicate and enrich redistributive
struggles than to marginalize, eclipse and displace them. I shall call
this *the problem of displacement*. Second, today's recognition struggles
are occurring at a moment of hugely increasing transcultural interaction and communication, when accelerated migration and global
media flows are hybridizing and pluralizing cultural forms. Yet the
routes such struggles take often serve not to promote respectful interaction within increasingly multicultural contexts, but to drastically
simplify and reify group identities. They tend, rather, to encourage
separatism, intolerance and chauvinism, patriarchalism and authori-
tarianism. I shall call this *the problem of reification*.

Both problems—displacement and reification—are extremely
serious: insofar as the politics of recognition displaces the politics of
redistribution, it may actually promote economic inequality; insofar
as it reifies group identities, it risks sanctioning violations of human
rights and freezing the very antagonisms it purports to mediate. No
wonder, then, that many have simply washed their hands of "identity
politics"—or proposed jettisoning cultural struggles altogether. For
some, this may mean reprioritizing class over gender, sexuality, "race"
and ethnicity. For others, it means resurrecting economism. For others
still, it may mean rejecting all "minoritarian" claims out of hand
and insisting upon assimilation to majority norms—in the name of
secularism, universalism or republicanism.

Such reactions are understandable; they are also deeply misguided.
Not all forms of recognition politics are equally pernicious: some represent genuinely emancipatory responses to serious injustices that cannot
be remedied by redistribution alone. Culture, moreover, is a legitimate,
even necessary, terrain of struggle, a site of injustice in its own right
and deeply imbricated with economic inequality. Properly conceived,
struggles for recognition can aid the redistribution of power and wealth
and can promote interaction and cooperation across gulfs of difference.

Everything depends on how recognition is approached. I want to argue here that we need to rethink the politics of recognition in a way that can help to solve, or at least mitigate, the problems of displacement and reification. This means conceptualizing struggles for recognition so that they can be integrated with struggles for redistribution, rather than displacing and undermining them. It also means developing an account of recognition that can accommodate the full complexity of social identities, instead of one that promotes reification and separatism. Here, I propose such a rethinking of recognition.

Misrecognition as identity distortion?

The usual approach to the politics of recognition—what I shall call the "identity model"—starts from the Hegelian idea that identity is constructed dialogically, through a process of mutual recognition. According to Hegel, recognition designates an ideal reciprocal relation between subjects, in which each sees the other both as its equal and also as separate from it. This relation is constitutive for subjectivity: one becomes an individual subject only by virtue of recognizing, and being recognized by, another subject. Recognition from others is thus essential to the development of a sense of self. To be denied recognition—or to be "misrecognized"—is to suffer both a distortion of one's relation to one's self and an injury to one's identity.

Proponents of the identity model transpose the Hegelian recognition schema onto the cultural and political terrain. They contend that to belong to a group that is devalued by the dominant culture is to be misrecognized, to suffer a distortion in one's relation to one's self. As a result of repeated encounters with the stigmatizing gaze of a culturally dominant other, the members of disesteemed groups internalize negative self-images and are prevented from developing a healthy cultural identity of their own. In this perspective, the politics of recognition aims to repair internal self-dislocation by contesting the dominant culture's demeaning picture of the group. It proposes that members of misrecognized groups reject such images in favor of new self-representations of their own making, jettisoning internalized, negative identities and joining collectively to produce a self-affirming culture of their own—which, publicly asserted, will gain the respect and esteem of society at large. The result, when successful, is "recognition": an undistorted relation to oneself.

Without doubt, this identity model contains some genuine insights into the psychological effects of racism, sexism, colonization and cultural imperialism. Yet it is theoretically and politically problematic. By equating the politics of recognition with identity politics, it encourages both the reification of group identities and the displacement of redistribution.

Let us consider first the ways in which identity politics tend to displace struggles for redistribution. Largely silent on the subject of economic inequality, the identity model treats misrecognition as a free-standing cultural harm: many of its proponents simply ignore distributive injustice altogether and focus exclusively on efforts to change culture; others, in contrast, appreciate the seriousness of maldistribution and genuinely wish to redress it. Yet both currents end by displacing redistributive claims.

The first current casts misrecognition as a problem of cultural depreciation. The roots of injustice are located in demeaning representations, but these are not seen as socially grounded. For this current, the nub of the problem is free-floating discourses, not *institutionalized* significations and norms. Hypostatizing culture, they both abstract misrecognition from its institutional matrix and obscure its entwinement with distributive injustice. They may miss, for example, the links (institutionalized in labor markets) between androcentric norms that devalue activities coded as "feminine," on the one hand, and the low wages of female workers on the other. Likewise, they overlook the links institutionalized within social-welfare systems between heterosexist norms which delegitimate homosexuality, on the one hand, and the denial of resources and benefits to gays and lesbians on the other. Obfuscating such connections, they strip misrecognition of its social-structural underpinnings and equate it with distorted identity. With the politics of recognition thus reduced to identity politics, the politics of redistribution is displaced.

A second current of identity politics does not simply ignore maldistribution in this way. It appreciates that cultural injustices are often linked to economic ones, but misunderstands the character of the links. Subscribing effectively to a "culturalist" theory of contemporary society, proponents of this perspective suppose that maldistribution is merely a secondary effect of misrecognition. For them, economic inequalities are simple expressions of cultural hierarchies—thus, class oppression is a superstructural effect of the cultural devaluation of proletarian identity (or, as one says in the United States, of "classism"). It follows from this view that all maldistribution can be remedied indirectly, by a politics of recognition: to revalue unjustly devalued identities is simultaneously to attack the deep sources of economic inequality; no explicit politics of redistribution is needed.

In this way, culturalist proponents of identity politics simply reverse the claims of an earlier form of vulgar Marxist economism: they allow the politics of recognition to displace the politics of redistribution, just as vulgar Marxism once allowed the politics of redistribution to displace the politics of recognition. In fact, vulgar culturalism is no more adequate for understanding contemporary society than vulgar economism was.

Granted, culturalism might make sense if one lived in a society in which there were no relatively autonomous markets, one in which cultural value patterns regulated not only the relations of recognition but those of distribution as well. In such a society, economic inequality and cultural hierarchy would be seamlessly fused; identity depreciation would translate perfectly and immediately into economic injustice, and misrecognition would directly entail maldistribution. Consequently, both forms of injustice could be remedied at a single stroke, and a politics of recognition that successfully redressed misrecognition would counter maldistribution as well. But the idea of a purely "cultural" society with no economic relations—fascinating to generations of anthropologists—is far removed from the current reality, in which marketization has pervaded all societies to some degree, at least partially decoupling economic mechanisms of distribution from cultural patterns of value and prestige. Partially independent of such patterns, markets follow a logic of their own, neither wholly constrained by culture nor subordinated to it; as a result they generate economic inequalities that are not mere expressions of identity hierarchies. Under these conditions, the idea that one could remedy all maldistribution by means of a politics of recognition is deeply deluded: its net result can only be to displace struggles for economic justice.

Displacement, however, is not the only problem: the identity politics model of recognition tends also to reify identity. Stressing the need to elaborate and display an authentic, self-affirming and self-generated collective identity, it puts moral pressure on individual members to conform to a given group culture. Cultural dissidence and experimentation are accordingly discouraged, when they are not simply equated with disloyalty. So, too, is cultural criticism, including efforts to explore intragroup divisions, such as those of gender, sexuality and class. Thus, far from welcoming scrutiny of, for example, the patriarchal strands within a subordinated culture, the tendency of the identity model is to brand such critique as "inauthentic." The overall effect is to impose a single, drastically simplified group identity that denies the complexity of people's lives, the multiplicity of their identifications and the cross-pulls of their various affiliations. Ironically, then, the identity model serves as a vehicle for misrecognition: in reifying group identity, it ends by obscuring the politics of cultural identification, the struggles *within* the group for the authority—and the power—to represent it. By shielding such struggles from view, this approach masks the power of dominant fractions and reinforces intragroup domination. The identity model thus lends itself all too easily to repressive forms of communitarianism, promoting conformism, intolerance and patriarchalism.

Paradoxically, moreover, the identity model tends to deny its own Hegelian premises. Having begun by assuming that identity is dialogical, constructed via interaction with another subject, it ends by valorizing monologism—supposing that misrecognized people can and should construct their identity on their own. It supposes, further, that a group has the right to be understood solely in its own terms—that no one is ever justified in viewing another subject from an external perspective or in dissenting from another's self-interpretation. But again, this runs counter to the dialogical view, making cultural identity an auto-generated auto-description, which one presents to others as an obiter dictum. Seeking to exempt "authentic" collective self-representations from all possible challenges in the public sphere, this sort of identity politics scarcely fosters social interaction across differences: on the contrary, it encourages separatism and group enclaves.

The identity model of recognition, then, is deeply flawed. Both theoretically deficient and politically problematic, it equates the politics of recognition with identity politics and, in doing so, encourages both the reification of group identities and the displacement of the politics of redistribution.

Misrecognition as status subordination

I shall consequently propose an alternative approach: that of treating recognition as a question of social status. From this perspective, what requires recognition is not group-specific identity but the status of individual group members as full partners in social interaction. Misrecognition, accordingly, does not mean the depreciation and deformation of group identity, but social subordination—in the sense of being prevented from participating as a peer in social life. To redress this injustice still requires a politics of recognition, but in the "status model" this is no longer reduced to a question of identity: rather, it means a politics aimed at overcoming subordination by establishing the misrecognized party as a full member of society, capable of participating on a par with the rest.

Let me explain. To view recognition as a matter of status means examining institutionalized patterns of cultural value for their effects on the relative standing of social actors. If and when such patterns constitute actors as peers, capable of participating on a par with one another in social life, then we can speak of reciprocal recognition and status equality. When, in contrast, they constitute some actors as inferior, excluded, wholly other, or simply invisible—in other words, as less than full partners in social interaction—then we can speak of misrecognition and status subordination. From this perspective, misrecognition is neither a psychic deformation nor a free-standing cultural harm but an institutionalized relation of social subordination. To be misrecognized, accordingly, is not simply to be thought ill of, looked down upon or devalued in others' attitudes, beliefs or representations. It is rather to be denied the status of a full partner in social interaction, as a consequence of institutionalized patterns of cultural value that constitute one as comparatively unworthy of respect or esteem.

On the status model, moreover, misrecognition is not relayed through free-floating cultural representations or discourses. It is perpetrated, as we have seen, through institutionalized patterns—in other words, through the workings of social institutions that regulate interaction according to parity-impeding cultural norms. Examples might include marriage laws that exclude same-sex partnerships as illegitimate and perverse; social-welfare policies that stigmatize single mothers as sexually irresponsible scroungers; and policing practices, such as "racial profiling," that associate racialized persons with criminality. In each of these cases, interaction is regulated by an institutionalized pattern of cultural value that constitutes some categories of social actors as normative and others as deficient or inferior: "straight" is normal, "gay" is perverse; "male-headed households" are proper, "female-headed households" are not; "whites" are law-abiding, "blacks" are dangerous. In each case, the result is to deny some members of society the status of full partners in interaction, capable of participating on a par with the rest.

As these examples suggest, misrecognition can assume a variety of forms. In today's complex, differentiated societies, parity-impeding values are institutionalized at a plurality of institutional sites, and in qualitatively different modes. In some cases, misrecognition is juridified, expressly codified in formal law; in other cases, it is institutionalized via government policies, administrative codes or professional practice. It can also be institutionalized informally—in associational patterns, longstanding customs or sedimented social practices of civil society. But whatever the differences in form, the core of the injustice remains the same: in each case, an institutionalized pattern of cultural value constitutes some social actors as less than full members of society and prevents them from participating as peers.

On the status model, then, misrecognition constitutes a form of institutionalized subordination, and thus a serious violation of justice. Wherever and however it occurs, a claim for recognition is in order. But note precisely what this means: aimed not at valorizing group identity but rather at overcoming subordination, in this approach claims for recognition seek to establish the subordinated party as a full partner in social life, able to interact with others as a peer. They aim, in other words, to de-institutionalize patterns of cultural value that impede parity of participation and to replace them with patterns that foster it. Redressing misrecognition now means changing social institutions—or, more specifically, changing the interaction-regulating values that impede parity of participation at all relevant institutional sites. Exactly how this should be done depends in each case on the mode in which misrecognition is institutionalized. Juridified forms require legal change, policy-entrenched forms require policy change, associational forms require associational change, and so on: the mode and agency of redress vary, as does the institutional site. But in every case, the goal is the same: redressing misrecognition means replacing institutionalized value patterns that impede parity of participation with ones that enable or foster it.

Consider again the case of marriage laws that deny participatory parity to gays and lesbians. As we saw, the root of the injustice is the institutionalization in law of a heterosexist pattern of cultural value that constitutes heterosexuals as normal and homosexuals as perverse. Redressing the injustice requires de-institutionalizing that value pattern and replacing it with an alternative that promotes parity. This, however, might be done in various ways: one way would be to grant the same recognition to gay and lesbian unions as heterosexual unions currently enjoy, by legalizing same-sex marriage; another would be to de-institutionalize heterosexual marriage, decoupling entitlements such as health insurance from marital status and assigning them on some other basis, such as citizenship. Although there may be good reasons for preferring one of these approaches to the other, in principle both of them would promote sexual parity and redress this instance of misrecognition.

In general, then, the status model is not committed a priori to any one type of remedy for misrecognition; rather, it allows for a range of possibilities, depending on what precisely the subordinated parties need in order to be able to participate as peers in social life. In some cases, they may need to be unburdened of excessive ascribed or constructed distinctiveness; in others, to have hitherto under-acknowledged distinctiveness taken into account. In still other cases, they may need to shift the focus onto dominant or advantaged groups, outing the latter's distinctiveness, which has been falsely parading as universal; alternatively, they may need to deconstruct the very terms in which attributed differences are currently elaborated. In every case, the status model tailors the remedy to the concrete arrangements that impede parity. Thus, unlike the identity model, it does not accord an a priori privilege to approaches that valorize group specificity. Rather, it allows in principle for what we might call universalist recognition, and deconstructive recognition, as well as for the affirmative recognition of difference. The crucial point, once again, is that on the status model the politics of recognition does not stop at identity but seeks institutional remedies for institutionalized harms. Focused on culture in its socially grounded (as opposed to free-floating) forms, *this* politics seeks to overcome status subordination by changing the values that regulate interaction, entrenching new value patterns that will promote parity of participation in social life.

There is a further important difference between the status and identity models. For the status model, institutionalized patterns of cultural value are not the only obstacles to participatory parity. On the contrary, equal participation is also impeded when some actors lack the necessary resources to interact with others as peers. In such cases, maldistribution constitutes an impediment to parity of participation in social life, and thus a form of social subordination and injustice. Unlike the identity model, then, the status model understands social justice as encompassing two analytically distinct dimensions: a dimension of recognition, which concerns the effects of institutionalized meanings and norms on the relative standing of social actors; and a dimension of distribution, which involves the allocation of disposable resources to social actors.[1] Thus, each dimension is associated with an analytically distinct aspect of social order. The recognition

---

1 Actually, I should say "*at least* two analytically distinct dimensions" in order to allow for the possibility of more. I have in mind specifically a possible third class of obstacles to participatory parity that could be called *political*, as opposed to economic or cultural. Such obstacles would include decision-making procedures that systematically marginalize some people even in the absence of maldistribution and misrecognition, for example, single-district winner-take-all electoral rules that deny voice to quasi-permanent minorities. (For an insightful account of this example, see Lani Guinier, *The Tyranny of the Majority*, New York: Free Press, 1994). The possibility of a third class of political obstacles to participatory parity brings out the extent of my debt to Max Weber, especially

dimension corresponds to the status order of society, hence to the
constitution, by socially entrenched patterns of cultural value, of
culturally defined categories of social actors—status groups—each
distinguished by the relative honor, prestige and esteem it enjoys vis-
à-vis the others. The distributive dimension, in contrast, corresponds
to the economic structure of society, hence to the constitution, by
property regimes and labor markets, of economically defined categories
of actors, or classes, distinguished by their differential endowments
of resources.[2]

Each dimension, moreover, is associated with an analytically distinct
form of injustice. For the recognition dimension, as we saw, the
associated injustice is misrecognition. For the distributive dimension,
in contrast, the corresponding injustice is maldistribution, in which
economic structures, property regimes or labor markets deprive actors
of the resources needed for full participation. Each dimension, finally,
corresponds to an analytically distinct form of subordination: the
recognition dimension corresponds, as we saw, to status subordination,
rooted in institutionalized patterns of cultural value; the distributive
dimension, in contrast, corresponds to economic subordination, rooted
in structural features of the economic system.

In general, then, the status model situates the problem of recognition
within a larger social frame. From this perspective, societies appear
as complex fields that encompass not only cultural forms of social
ordering but economic forms of ordering as well. In all societies, these

to his "Class, Status, Party," in *From Max Weber: Essays in Sociology*, eds. Hans H.
Gerth and C. Wright Mills, Oxford: Oxford University Press, 1958. In the present essay,
I align a version of Weber's distinction between class and status with the distinction
between distribution and recognition. Yet Weber's own distinction was tripartite, not
bipartite: "class, status, and party." Thus, he effectively prepared a place for theorizing
a third, political kind of obstacle to participatory parity, which might be called *political
marginalization or exclusion.* I do not develop this possibility here, however, but confine
myself to maldistribution and misrecognition, while leaving the analysis of political
obstacles to participatory parity for another occasion.

2 In this essay, I deliberately use a Weberian conception of class, not a Marxian
one. Thus, I understand an actor's class position in terms of her or his relation to
the market, not in terms of her or his relation to the means of production. This
Weberian conception of class as an *economic* category suits my interest in
distribution as a normative dimension of justice better than the Marxian conception
of class as a *social* category. Nevertheless, I do not mean to reject the Marxian idea
of the "capitalist mode of production" as a social totality. On the contrary, I find that
idea useful as an overarching frame within which one can situate Weberian
understandings of both status and class. Thus, I reject the standard view of Marx
and Weber as antithetical and irreconcilable thinkers. For the Weberian definition of
class, see Max Weber, "Class, Status, Party."

two forms of ordering are interimbricated. Under capitalist conditions, however, neither is wholly reducible to the other. On the contrary, the economic dimension becomes relatively decoupled from the cultural dimension, as marketized arenas, in which strategic action predominates, are differentiated from non-marketized arenas, in which value-regulated interaction predominates. The result is a partial uncoupling of economic distribution from structures of prestige. In capitalist societies, therefore, cultural value patterns do not strictly dictate economic allocations (contra the culturalist theory of society), nor do economic class inequalities simply reflect status hierarchies; rather, maldistribution becomes partially uncoupled from misrecognition. For the status model, therefore, not all distributive injustice can be overcome by recognition alone. A politics of redistribution is also necessary.[3]

Nevertheless, distribution and recognition are not neatly separated from each other in capitalist societies. For the status model, the two dimensions are interimbricated and interact causally with each other. Economic issues such as income distribution have recognition subtexts: value patterns institutionalized in labor markets may privilege activities coded "masculine," "white" and so on over those coded "feminine" and "black." Conversely, recognition issues—judgments of aesthetic value, for instance—have distributive subtexts: diminished access to economic resources may impede equal participation in the making of art.[4] The result can be a vicious circle of subordination, as the status order and the economic structure interpenetrate and reinforce each other.

Unlike the identity model, then, the status model views misrecognition in the context of a broader understanding of contemporary society. From this perspective, status subordination cannot be understood in isolation from economic arrangements, nor can recognition be abstracted from distribution. On the contrary, only by considering both dimensions together can one determine what is impeding participatory parity in any particular instance; only by teasing out the complex imbrications

---

3 For fuller discussions of the mutual irreducibility of maldistribution and misrecognition, class and status in contemporary capitalist societies, see Nancy Fraser, "Heterosexism, Misrecognition, and Capitalism: A Response to Judith Butler," in this volume; and "Social Justice in the Age of Identity Politics: Redistribution, Recognition and Participation," in Nancy Fraser and Axel Honneth, *Redistribution or Recognition: A Political-Philosophical Exchange*, trans. Joel Golb, James Ingram, and Christiane Wilke, London: Verso, 20003.

4 For a comprehensive, if somewhat reductive, account of this issue, see Pierre Bourdieu, *Distinction: A Social Critique of the Judgement of Taste*, trans. Richard Nice, Cambridge, MA: Harvard University Press, 1984.

of status with economic class can one determine how best to redress the injustice. The status model thus works against tendencies to displace struggles for redistribution. Rejecting the view that misrecognition is a free-standing cultural harm, it understands that status subordination is often linked to distributive injustice. Unlike the culturalist theory of society, however, it avoids short-circuiting the complexity of these links: appreciating that not all economic injustice can be overcome by recognition alone, it advocates an approach that expressly integrates claims for recognition with claims for redistribution, and thus mitigates the problem of displacement.

The status model also avoids reifying group identities: as we saw, what requires recognition in this account is not group-specific identity but the status of individuals as full partners in social interaction. This orientation offers several advantages. By focusing on the effects of institutionalized norms on capacities for interaction, the model avoids hypostatizing culture and substituting identity-engineering for social change. Likewise, by refusing to privilege remedies for misrecognition that valorize existing group identities, it avoids essentializing current configurations and foreclosing historical change. Finally, by establishing participatory parity as a normative standard, the status model submits claims for recognition to democratic processes of public justification, thus avoiding the authoritarian monologism of the politics of authenticity and valorizing transcultural interaction, as opposed to separatism and group enclaves. Far from encouraging repressive communitarianism, then, the status model militates against it.

Conclusion

To sum up: today's struggles for recognition often assume the guise of identity politics. Aimed at countering demeaning cultural representations of subordinated groups, they abstract misrecognition from its institutional matrix and sever its links with political economy and, insofar as they propound "authentic" collective identities, serve less to foster interaction across differences than to enforce separatism, conformism and intolerance. The results tend to be doubly unfortunate: in many cases, struggles for recognition simultaneously displace struggles for economic justice and promote repressive forms of communitarianism.

The solution, however, is not to reject the politics of recognition tout court. That would be to condemn millions of people to suffer grave injustices that can only be redressed through recognition of some kind. What is needed, rather, is an alternative politics of recognition, a non-identitarian politics that can remedy misrecognition without encouraging displacement and reification. The status model, I have argued, provides the basis for this. By understanding recognition as a question of status, and by examining its relation to economic class, one can take steps to mitigate, if not fully solve, the displacement of struggles for redistribution; and by avoiding the identity model, one can begin to diminish, if not fully dispel, the dangerous tendency to reify collective identities.

ARGUING OVER PARTICIPATORY PARITY: ON NANCY FRASER'S CONCEPTION OF SOCIAL JUSTICE

Christopher F. Zurn

I. Introduction: The tasks of a critical social theory

Over the last decade, Nancy Fraser has been developing a comprehensive and incisive critical social theory, one that, to use Marx's phrase, can further the "the work of our time to clarify to itself (critical philosophy) the meaning of its own struggles and its own desires" or, to use Max Horkheimer's conception, would count as an adequate interdisciplinary social theory with emancipatory intent.[1] What then are the requirements for an interdisciplinary social theory, one critically oriented towards emancipation? First and foremost it must offer a theory of society, that is, some description and/or explanation of why social and institutional structures, cultural understandings, personality structures and the like have taken the particular shape they have today. More than a mere sociology or social psychology or combination of their results, however, a critical social theory also needs some kind of account of what emancipation means. Or, at the very least, some kind of account of the normative standards it evokes in denouncing various institutional formations, social expectations, cultural understandings, and the rest as non-emancipatory, oppressive, repressive, subordinating or whatever terms of negative assessment are going to be used. Finally, of course, as anyone who is familiar with reading critical social theory from Germany in the last thirty years will be well aware, a critical social theory also requires a fair amount of philosophical reflexivity

---

1 Karl Marx, "For a Ruthless Criticism of Everything Existing [Letter to Arnold Ruge, September 1843]," in *The Marx-Engels Reader*, ed. Robert C. Tucker, New York: W. W. Norton & Company, 1978, p. 15; Max Horkheimer, "The Social Function of Philosophy" and "Traditional and Critical Theory," in *Critical Theory: Selected Essays*, New York: Continuum, 1992.

about the standards of evidence it uses, the procedures it uses to investigate contemporary society, the ways it goes about justifying its
normative standpoints, and so on. In other words, an interdisciplinary
theory with emancipatory intent is supported by at least three kinds
of reflection. First is the more or less comprehensive social theory that
gives us an empirically accurate picture of our contemporary situation,
of "the meaning of our time's struggles," as it were. Second is some
account of why certain of "our time's desires" are worthwhile desires,
desires that point us toward the right struggles—we need an account
of the normative standards employed in comprehending contemporary
society. Third are the requirements of "critical philosophy clarifying
our time to itself": critical social theory needs a philosophically reflective account of its own methodological procedures and standards of
rationality.

There is, however, a fourth desideratum any critical social theory
must meet. We might call this, for lack of a better word, "perspicacity."
That is to say, the struggles and wishes of the age that the theory
picks out as important, the way in which it analyzes contemporary
social formations, its particular analytic lens on the present, have to
somehow insightfully illuminate the important social conditions, social
changes, and social actors that we ought to be attending to. To put
the perspicacity requirement in another way, the social-theoretic,
normative, and methodological tasks of critical social theory cannot
become so overwhelming and hyper-reflexive that they overshadow, in
the end, the question of whether that critical social theory picks out
important practical issues. No matter how accurate the empirical social
theory, no matter how unassailable the normative framework, no matter
how cogent the methodological self-understanding of the theory, if,
at the end of the day, that critical social theory doesn't tell us something
insightful and practically useful about the actual struggles and wishes
of our age, then it has missed its target.

I believe that Nancy Fraser's critical social theory fulfills the first
three tasks as well as other contemporary social theories, and I would
contend that it better fulfills the requirement for perspicacity than
most others, giving a more insightful theory of the social world we
find ourselves in and of the prospects and avenues for progressive
change of that world. As is clear from her recently co-authored book
with Axel Honneth, Fraser has several interesting things to say about
many different aspects of contemporary social reality, new social movements, and ongoing struggles to increase social justice in an ever more
globalized, interconnected, and culturally pluralistic world, one that
in certain ways perpetuates and intensifies the social subordination

and oppression of some in favor of others.[2] However, rather than broadly vindicating the significance of her critical social theory, the following more limited reflections fall into two parts. In the first part, I will sketch out a few of the main features of Fraser's view with an eye toward trying to highlight how those features contribute to the power of her critical social theory. Then, in the second half of the essay, I would like to explore some more critical reflections—in particular, concerning the normative standard of "parity of participation" which she proposes as the overarching normative framework for her theory. As I have elsewhere focused critical attention on the methodological and socio-theoretic aspects of her claims—especially concerning the use of Weberian categories for understanding social struggles for recognition—I will only attend to such issues as a brief lead-in to the critical reflections on parity of participation.[3]

2. Fraser's distinctive claims

Let me briefly highlight three distinctive features of the theory that greatly contribute to its increased capacity to comprehend the present in comparison with other theories: 1) a bivalent social theory focusing on both maldistribution and misrecognition, 2) an account of misrecognition as status subordination rather than harm to personal identity, and 3) a normative standard of justice in terms of parity of participation.

First, and perhaps most famously, Fraser argues that the most prominent injustices in contemporary society cannot be comprehended by a social theory that focuses exclusively on either maldistribution or misrecognition. We need, rather, a theory that is (at least) bivalent or bifocal: one simultaneously attentive to those injustices causally rooted in the class structures of the political economy and those causally rooted in institutionally anchored status hierarchies, without, however, reducing either dimension of injustice to the other.[4] She argues that

---

2 Nancy Fraser and Axel Honneth, *Redistribution or Recognition? A Political-Philosophical Exchange*, trans. Joel Golb, James Ingram, and Christiane Wilke, New York: Verso, 2003.

3 Christopher F. Zurn, "Identity or Status? Struggles over 'Recognition' in Fraser, Honneth, and Taylor," *Constellations* 10: 4, 2003, pp. 519–37; "Group Balkanization or Societal Homogenization: Is There a Dilemma Between Recognition and Distribution Struggles?" *Public Affairs Quarterly* 18: 2, 2004, pp. 159–86.

4 Her original construction of a bivalent social theory, in Nancy Fraser, "Recognition or Redistribution? A Critical Reading of Iris Young's *Justice and the Politics of Difference*," *The Journal of Political Philosophy* 3: 2, 1995, and Nancy Fraser, *Justice Interruptus: Critical Reflections on the "Postsocialist" Condition*, New York: Routledge, 1997, has been updated and somewhat modified in Fraser and Honneth, *Redistribution or Recognition?*

social theories that attempt to explain all injustices in terms of one or the other dimension of social ordering inevitably end up distorting the phenomena they are trying to capture and, perhaps more worrying, end up recommending strategies of political action that may be ineffective or even counterproductive in fighting injustice. Thus theories that attempt to reduce all social struggles and injustices to their political-economic roots—purveyors of the "it's the economy, stupid" analysis—will simply not have the conceptual resources needed to capture the important cultural, symbolic, and evaluative dimensions of social struggles to overcome demeaning, denigrating, and hate-based evaluative patterns aimed at certain groups and which function to deny their members an equal role in social life. Worse, such economistic theories may recommend remedies to rectify maldistributions that in fact have the unintended consequence of actually intensifying the patterns of misrecognition members of the oppressed group are already subject to: witness the backlash stigmatization suffered by the recipients of means-targeted redistributive welfare programs. As theorists of recognition such as Axel Honneth, Charles Taylor, and Iris Young have repeatedly pointed out, however, purely distributive theories of justice, in focusing exclusively on the uneven allocation of the material benefits and burdens of social cooperation, systematically overlook the asymmetrical structures of cultural evaluation and social recognition that underlie new social movements focused on identity-constitutive group membership.[5]

However, many theorists of the politics of recognition have oversold such insights and made the complementary errors of either overlooking economic injustices or of reducing all social injustices to matters of misrecognition—Axel Honneth's account of recognition struggles represents the most articulate account of such a reductionist, "mono-focal" recognition theory. As Fraser convincingly argues, it is simply implausible to think that many of the injustices apparently caused by political-economic structures can be captured theoretically in terms of problematic patterns of comparative evaluation of the worth or dignity of persons. Consider, for instance, the problems of de-industrialization under conditions of globalization, or of the transfer from one nation-state to another of quality wage labor jobs, or of the instabilities

---

5 Axel Honneth, *The Struggle for Recognition: The Moral Grammar of Social Conflicts*, trans. Joel Anderson, Cambridge, MA: Polity Press, 1995; Charles Taylor, "The Politics of Recognition," in *Multiculturalism and "The Politics of Recognition,"* Princeton, NJ: Princeton University Press, 1992; Iris Marion Young, *Justice and the Politics of Difference*, Princeton, NJ: Princeton University Press, 1990.

caused by rapid and unpredictable global capital flows, or of the massively asymmetrical ecological burdens externalized by the developed nations onto underdeveloped nations. These and like injustices arise from a different kind of social ordering than that captured in theories of recognition, one whose effects are analytically independent of the structures of institutionalized patterns of cultural evaluation and esteem. Of course there will be important relations of mutual reinforcement and mutual interference between the political-economic and the cultural-symbolic orderings of society, but we need a theory that analytically distinguishes them in the first place in order to perceptively analyze such interrelations.[6]

Fraser's singular contribution is to have constructed a careful bifocal theory that can attend simultaneously to the recognition and distribution dimensions of social institutions, without inaccurately reducing either one to the other. Only such a theory can be sufficiently attentive to the interconnections, the interferences, the mutual reinforcements, and the negative and positive feedback loops that occur between economic and cultural forms of injustice. To put it briefly, Fraser's bivalent critical theory is opposed on the one hand to theories that say, "It's the culture, stupid" and, on the other hand, to those insisting "It's the economy, stupid." If misrecognition and maldistribution have different causal roots and follow different logics, then we should not expect that changing institutionalized patterns of cultural value will itself overcome maldistribution, nor that changing economic mechanisms of material distribution will itself overcome systematic misrecognition. Social injustice involves at least two analytically distinct forms of social ordering, and an adequate critical social theory needs to attend at least to both.

Now, I said "at least two" different forms because Fraser has consistently left open the possibility for a further development of her theory in order to embrace a third analytically distinct form of social ordering: namely, political forms of exclusion.[7] For here we seem to find a form of injustice that is not the causal result directly of either distributive structures or patterns of cultural value, but rather of state-centered political and legal forms of exclusion from democratic political practices,

---

6 For an extended set of arguments that Honneth's theory suffers socio-theoretic deficits due to its attempt to integrate distributive injustices within a monofocal theory of recognition, see my "Recognition, Redistribution, and Democracy: Dilemmas of Honneth's Critical Social Theory," *European Journal of Philosophy* 13: 1, 2005.

7 See, inter alia, pages 67–69, and note 40 on p. 101 of Fraser and Honneth, *Redistribution or Recognition?*

which result in the institutional subordination of some groups vis-à-vis others. Fraser hasn't developed this third analytically distinct axis of social subordination, but I, with others, would encourage her to do so.[8] I look forward to the results, for we should expect the same sorts of advantages to accrue to such a "trivalent" social theory. I take it that there is no going back behind Fraser's insight into the need for at least a bivalent social theory. It seems incontrovertible that a critical social theory cannot hope to accurately or perspicaciously describe contemporary social reality if it either reduces misrecognition to maldistribution, or maldistribution to misrecognition. But it also seems that critical social theory needs an account of legal institutions and formal political structures, as independent causal sources of injustice, if it is to adequately diagnose the struggles and wishes of our age.

Let me now turn to a second, more recent innovation that Fraser has introduced in the context of her critical social theory. Within the last five years or so Fraser has been trying to analyze misrecognition not in terms of what she calls an "identity" model of recognition but, rather, in terms of a "status" model of recognition.[9]

According to Fraser, identity models of recognition, such as those put forward by Honneth and Taylor, start from psychological premises about the intersubjective conditions for the development of a sense of personal identity, identify various cultural and symbolic patterns of disrespect and denigration that may impede the development of personal integrity, and then assess these demeaning patterns as an injustice, since they harm individuals' capacity to form healthy self-respect and self-esteem. In contrast to the identity model's focus on psychological and ideational factors, Fraser's status model is sociological from the get-go: it treats recognition from the external perspective of a sociological observer rather than the internal perspective of individuals engaged in intersubjective relations of recognition and identity-formation. Thus, although it does not deny the multiplicity of kinds of social affinity groups, collectivities, associations, coalitions, and so on found in complex societies, it focuses only on those groups that owe their existence as a group to being placed in a subordinate social

---

8 An elegant argument for the need to extend Fraser's bivalent social theory in the direction of politics, along with a fascinating application of such a trivalent theory to homeless policy in the United States can be found in Leonard C. Feldman, "Redistribution, Recognition, and the State: The Irreducibly Political Dimension of Injustice," *Political Theory* 30: 3, 2002, pp. 410–40.

9 See especially Nancy Fraser, "Rethinking Recognition," in this volume, and "Recognition without Ethics?" *Theory, Culture & Society* 18: 2–3, 2001.

position because of entrenched patterns of cultural value. According to the status model, then, misrecognition arises not merely from cultural and symbolic slights, but only from those that are anchored in social institutions and that systematically deny the members of denigrated groups equal opportunities for participation in social life. Thus, legitimate recognition struggles are seen as those aimed at changing institutionalized patterns of cultural value that subordinate certain persons and groups in such a way that they are denied the opportunity to participate in social life on an equal basis. Misrecognition proper occurs not in a purely cultural realm of stigmatizing symbolic patterns or a psychological realm of demeaning evaluative attitudes, as implied by identity models of recognition, but rather in cultural value patterns that are *institutionally anchored* and *systematically subordinating*.

For example, while we can clearly identify a set of cultural values and symbolic meanings that differentiate Italian-Americans as a group in contemporary America, and these values may be demeaning and stigmatizing, it is (perhaps) no longer the case that these cultural and symbolic stereotypes are anchored in asymmetric social structures that systematically deny parity of social participation to Italian-Americans; in this respect, Italian-Americans no longer constitute a *status* group. In short, on the status model, there can be no misrecognition through culture alone: misrecognition occurs only through institutionally anchored, status-denying patterns of cultural value, not through "free-floating" attitudes and symbolic patterns.

The third distinctive feature of Fraser's theory is its clear articulation of a normative framework—one using the yardstick of "parity of participation"—for assessing both the relative merits of various claims made by citizens to more just distributional and recognition structures, and the relative prospects of success for proposed remedies for over-coming social injustice.[10]

The basic idea is that we should call unjust precisely those social structures that deny some members of society the opportunity to participate in social life on a par with others. Fraser explicates the norm of participatory parity in terms of two sets of necessary conditions for justice:

---

10 Nancy Fraser, "Social Justice in the Age of Identity Politics: Redistribution, Recognition, and Participation," in *The Tanner Lectures on Human Values*, vol. 19, ed. Grethe B. Peterson, Salt Lake City: University of Utah Press, 1998; Fraser, "Recognition Without Ethics?"; Fraser and Honneth, *Redistribution or Recognition?*

Justice requires social arrangements that permit all (adult) members of society to interact with one another as peers. For participatory parity to be possible, I claim, at least two conditions must be satisfied. First the distribution of material resources must be such as to ensure participants' independence and "voice." . . . The second condition requires that institutionalized patterns of cultural value express equal respect for all participants and ensure equal opportunity for achieving social esteem.[11]

According to the first "objective" condition, participatory parity is impeded by economic structures such as the gendered division of unpaid reproductive labor that systematically makes wives more dependent on husbands than husbands are on wives, and no-fault divorce laws which have reinforced the asymmetries of exit options open to husbands and wives in such as way as to deny equal voice to women. According to the second "intersubjective" condition, participatory parity is impeded by institutionalized cultural value patterns such as those evinced in the legal remnants of coverture that deny wives both equal respect as persons and equal opportunities for achieving social esteem. Under coverture, equal respect is denied, for example, by the so-called marital exemption to rape laws whereby the act of marriage is taken as full consent to any and all future sexual acts performed by the husband, while equal opportunities for self-esteem are denied by the inability of wives to participate in the contestatory definition of their roles in the sex-based division of labor and so to participate in defining the evaluative schemas that code their contributions as of much less worth than husbands' and other adult males'.

I would like to briefly consider now three advantages promised by this normative framework of participatory parity. The first advantage is that participatory parity revitalizes an older tradition in normative social theory that attempted to get a handle on social justice, broadly construed. That is, it is not a theory restricted to the formal conditions of justice as evinced in ideal legal and political structures modeled on the equal rights of all, the kind of theory epitomized by Rawls's *A Theory of Justice* and developed by liberal political theorists since.[12] Recall that for Rawls, his two principles of justice are designed to apply to a "well-ordered" society, that is, one whose major social

---

11 Fraser and Honneth, *Redistribution or Recognition?* p. 36.

12 John Rawls, *A Theory of Justice*, revised edition, Cambridge, MA: Harvard University Press, 1999.

institutions are not themselves guilty of major injustices and problematic internal structures. But, of course, we know from everyday
life that that is simply not our situation. It is precisely because our
basic social institutions, across a wide spectrum—not just political or
legal institutions, but also educational institutions, familial structures,
socialization practices, mass-communications institutions, civil society
organizations, economic relations of production and distribution,
major cultural discourses, and so on—seem *not* to be well-ordered
that social theory is spurred to develop interdisciplinary theories with
emancipatory intent. That means that we need more expansive and
incisive normative standards for evaluating a much broader range of
social phenomena than have been provided by deontological, Kantian-
inspired theories of justice, which typically focus only on ideal
distributions of rights and responsibilities according to formal definitions of fairness. Rather, Fraser's normative framework, as a capacious
ideal of social justice writ large, holds out the promise of fulfilling
older ambitions of critical social theory to think seriously about the
prospects and deficiencies of contemporary society as it is. And, of
course, the capaciousness of the norm of parity of participation is
written into its formulation: it requires the widespread democratization
of social institutions, broadly understood, in order to allow for each
to participate in *social life* as a peer with others, not simply to be
treated as an equal before the law with some equal chance of voter
input into governmental policies.

The second advantage of Fraser's framework is that it can underwrite
this capacious normative ideal without, however, taking on the traditional argumentative burdens associated with deep and broad utopian
thinking about social relations. It achieves this by a sort of *via negativa*:
rather than painting a detailed canvas delineating the features of a
fully just society or of a well-ordered society, the participatory parity
framework specifies what count as *injustices* in current social relations.
There is thus no need to take on the significant—perhaps unbearable
—burdens of argument for a utopian specification: there is no immediate theoretical demand for arguments about the empirical plausibility
of the proposed utopia, no need for complex assessments of the inertia
of traditional social structures, no requirement for bridging principles
for connecting the principles of ideal theory with non-ideal reality
on the model of "partial compliance theory,"[13] no methodological

---

13 The phrase is Rawls's, and is illuminatingly introduced in the context of
somewhat ad hoc discussions of "the several parts of nonideal theory," p. 216; see
sections 38, 39, and 53 of Ibid.

obligation to account for why others have not been able or willing to envision such utopian ideals, and so on.[14] Furthermore, such a *via negativa* tracks much more closely the public language of assessment actually used by citizens and social movements. We as everyday members of the social world tend to gauge phenomena in terms of concrete harms, violations, disruptions, injustices, distortions, pathologies, and so on. We tend not to abstractly compare our entire political and social institutions, structures, and procedures against an ideal standard of the good and just society.

In addition, the *via negativa* standard of participatory parity is more ecumenical and less contestable than a grand theory specifying the necessary and sufficient conditions for justice and the good life. Here the benefits are, not the least, practical benefits. We can spend less time arguing about the rightness of basic normative principles and more time and effort identifying and remedying concrete violations. This ecumenical character follows not only from the starting point of identifying impediments to parity, but also from the fact that parity is a deontological standard of justice, not a teleological specification of the good life. Therefore it can respect the conditions of reasonable pluralism we find in the world today, acknowledging that different persons and groups have different and incommensurable understandings of what makes a worthwhile life, while at the same time making substantial normative judgments concerning what we owe any person simply as a person. It is precisely by focusing only on the requirements of justice that all people ought to recognize as binding on them that the theory promises to avoid the philosophical disputation that comes from the reliance of utopian and ideal theories on contestable anthropological and teleological premises concerning who we are and who we want to be. Thus, surprisingly, it is the thinness and negative character of the framework of parity of participation that secures its ecumenical character and so makes it able to do so much actual work in assessing contemporary social formations.

The third advantage of Fraser's normative framework is that it fosters a truly *critical* attitude towards the welter of competing claims evinced in the public sphere of modern, complex, and pluralistic democratic societies. Rather than simply taking all claims to maldistribution and

---

14 A sensitive account of the systematic problems of utopian forms of thinking as they plagued the development of Western or Hegelian Marxism, an account that, however, refuses to surrender the promise of utopia ideals, can be found in Seyla Benhabib, *Critique, Norm, and Utopia: A Study of the Foundations of Critical Theory*, New York: Columbia University Press, 1986.

misrecognition as justified on their face, the framework of parity of participation helps us to sort out worthy from unworthy claims. Take for instance the claims made by various hate groups and fascist minorities that they suffer from misrecognition in the broader society. Here, while it may be true that existing social structures impede their members' capacity to develop full self-esteem in the light of their xenophobic vision of a worthy life, and precisely because that vision is denigrated by the larger society, Fraser insists that we should not acknowledge their claims for expanded recognition as justifiable. While it is certainly true that their attempt to develop an integral identity is impeded, and so they appear to suffer a form of misrecognition, on Fraser's model the crucial question is one of social relations of subordination, not psychological experiences of identity deformation. Precisely because their xenophobic vision of a worthy life is aimed at the denial of equal respect and an equal opportunity for the development of self-esteem for other social group members, such groups violate the intersubjective conditions of participatory parity; their claims for expanded recognition should therefore be denied.

Likewise, some claimants to have suffered distributive injustices fail prima facie in the light of the objective conditions for participatory parity. Thus, for example, a system that funded public schools only by means of local property taxes may be couched as an issue of justice and liberty, even though such systems demonstrably limit the equal independence and voice of those students who grow up in class-segregated school districts, and so deny them the objective conditions of parity of participation.

This capacity for a critical assessment of claims is particularly useful with respect to some forms of identity politics that mobilize the jargon of authentic group meaning and membership in order to further their aims. Here Fraser is particularly sensitive to the ways such an understanding of group membership can be used to reify contingently constructed group identities as quasi-natural states of affairs that all group members are held accountable to. However, not only is such a reification of group identity empirically and historically false, it also often functions to mask the specific forms of power and control that have been mobilized in constructing and policing that group identity. Thus the jargon of authenticity is often used within groups to structure internal relations of status subordination by coding some as less authentic than others or of incorrectly realizing the putatively natural, "authentic" identity. Fraser's normative framework provides an insightful way of spelling out why merely invoking some heretofore misrecognized distinctiveness is not sufficient to carry legitimate claims

to redress. For once we couch misrecognition in terms of status subordination, it becomes clear that misrecognition can occur not only
across groups, but within groups as well. This is particularly clear in
the case of multiply intersecting differences, where different group
members may suffer from various forms of status subordination
depending on their sex, sexuality, race, ethnicity, and so on. Any claims
to redress of misrecognition and proposed remedies must themselves
be scrutinized for their expected effects in terms of other forms of
misrecognition, and maldistribution—and for such tasks, we need a
clear, persuasive, and compelling normative framework such as Fraser
has provided us.

3. Arguing over participatory parity

This third section turns from exposition to some more reflective and
critical comments about Fraser's normative framework of participatory
parity. First I briefly raise three general areas of concern, before turning
to a more extended development of some socio-theoretic worries about
the status model of recognition; worries that, however, can only be
answered by clarifications concerning the character of the normative
theory Fraser has proposed.

   Is it true that the substantive evaluations she proposes as examples
of her theory can really be carried on fully at the deontological level,
and without a "premature" turn to ethical evaluations, as she claims?
Take, for instance, what she considers to be an easy case of unjustifiable
status subordination: the denial of the right to marry to same-sex
partners. Here, Fraser argues that since the denial of same-sex marriage
constitutes a status subordination that denies gays and lesbians the
intersubjective conditions for parity of participation, we can remain
at the deontological level of justice, "without recourse to ethical evaluation—without, that is, assuming the substantive judgment that
homosexual relationships are ethically valuable."[15] It is not so clear
to me, however, how the requisite distinctions between who can and
who cannot marry can be made while remaining at the supposedly
ecumenical level of justice claims. For instance, it is unclear how, simply
on the basis of the norm of participatory parity, we can deny the
substantial benefits and entitlements of marriage to groups larger than
the dyadic pair of traditional marriage. On its face, this would seem
to be a denial of parity to some, and by means of institutionalized
cultural patterns that devalue non-dyadic romantic relationships. It

15 Fraser and Honneth, *Redistribution or Recognition?*, p. 40.

may well be that for some other reasons, we would nevertheless want to deny such parity to non-dyadic relationships, but it is hard to imagine what kinds of reasons these could be beyond those kinds of historically specific and particularistic ethical reasons the deontological framework was invoked to avoid in the first place.

In general, I am not as confident as she is that, for instance, issues about same-sex marriage, sex-segregated primary schools, or duties to future generations for environmental stewardship, or even what the "objective" conditions of independence and voice require in terms of material distributions, can be decided wholly independently of assumptions about particularistic ideals of the good life.[16] Considering that debates about the intersubjective conditions of parity will necessarily involve differing interpretations of cultural values, symbols, and representations, it seems particularly unlikely that these can be carried out without reference to thick hermeneutical judgments, judgments which seem to be ineliminably bound up with context-specific horizons of value. I share the hope for a non-sectarian language for adjudicating recognition and distribution claims; I am skeptical of its practical possibility for many of the most important issues facing us today.

Secondly, does the focus on status equality, and the deontological framework of justice generally, even as it delimits an important normative baseline of minimally acceptable social structures, nevertheless tend to flatten out the radicalism of many social movement claims? Many current struggles appear to aim not primarily at securing a society free of injustices, but more fundamentally at restructuring our ways of life, our practices of self-realization, our notions of the good life. For example, queer politics aims for much more than the mere overcoming of status subordinations currently inflicted on some because minority sexualities are denigrated and despised in the broader culture. Rather, such politics may aim, for instance, to liberate all forms of sexuality—normal and queer, majority and minority, celebrated and despised—from the debilitating ethical framework of sexual shame. Here the idea is to mobilize not so much to correct an injustice visited on some, but basically to reconstruct all of our social practices of sexual shaming in such a way as to promote all forms of sexual autonomy. The point here is not to get straight society to tolerate certain forms of queerness as acceptably small deviations from normal,

---

16 For Fraser's more detailed consideration of these issues see especially pp. 33–8 of Fraser, "Recognition without Ethics?" and pp. 38–42 of Fraser and Honneth, *Redistribution or Recognition?*

but fundamentally to remake the ethical self-understanding of society towards, as Michael Warner puts it, "a frank embrace of queer sex in all its apparent indignity, together with a frank challenge to the damaging hierarchies of respectability."[17] Consider also how much of the content of recent anti-globalization and anti-capitalist protests is missed by focusing only on the objective, material conditions needed for each person's independence and voice. Here the deep critique of, say, the careerism, competitiveness, and egoistic individualism embedded in the anonymous imperatives of capitalist economic structures may simply fly under the radar of a theory focused solely on economic injustices to individuals.

One way to put this worry is to say that, although a deontological focus on justice has clear philosophical and methodological advantages over competing normative frameworks, it may cause us to foreshorten theoretically the semantics and grammar of many social movements, and so may lead to a diminution of the ambitions of a critical social theory looking to comprehend the struggles and wishes of the age. I am not suggesting that we ignore issues of economic and cultural injustice, nor that we cede the priority of the right over the good that is the cornerstone of a justice-based normative framework. My worry is rather whether such a framework alone is sufficient to fulfill the aspirations of many important social movements, and of a radical critique of the present that is the hallmark of critical social theories. Said in terms of the tasks of critical social theory I introduced at the beginning, the worry is whether the gains in methodological astuteness come at the cost of a less accurate and perspicuous account of the struggles and wishes of the age.

A third area of concern is highlighted by the fact that normative theories of justice have usually been concerned to adumbrate distinct priority relationships between the different principles they advance. For instance, Ronald Dworkin insists that questions of principle— roughly, considerations of individual liberty rights—trump questions of policy—roughly, considerations of the collective goals of a society, while John Rawls carefully delineates the priority relations between the commutative and distributive aspects of justice as fairness.[18] Fraser, however, has not said much about how she envisions the principle of

---

17 Michael Warner, *The Trouble with Normal: Sex, Politics, and the Ethics of Queer Life*, Cambridge, MA: Harvard University Press, 2000, p. 74.

18 See, inter alia, Ronald Dworkin, *Taking Rights Seriously*, Cambridge, MA: Harvard University Press, 1978, and Rawls.

participatory parity working in those cases where we must decide
between adequate redistribution and sufficient recognition. Such
questions are even more pressing if we follow her suggestions and
posit a third analytically independent axis of social ordering in terms
of political decision-making processes, and then analyze political
marginalization and exclusion as a third analytically distinct form of
the denial of participatory parity. Fraser does suggest many ways to
finesse various tensions between redistribution and recognition in
actual practice, and perhaps such practical solutions are the best that
can be hoped for here. But it seems it would tell us something important
about the shape of a critical social theory to know how it proposes
to prioritize claims in those situations where we cannot completely
satisfy all of our normative principles simultaneously.

I would like now to turn, at a bit greater length, to certain confusions
I have about the character of the normative framework Fraser has
advanced, and in particular about how she conceives of the relationship
between normative theory and social practice. Rather than turning
directly to this framework, however, the issues will be approached
obliquely, by considering a set of prima facie objections to Fraser's socio-
theoretic proposal to uncouple the theory of misrecognition from
theories of personal identity formation, and to reconceptualize misrecognition in terms of status subordination. Since I have elsewhere considered
at length the advantages and disadvantages of the status model of recognition in comparison with Honneth's and Taylor's identity-based
models,[19] here I will present my reservations about Fraser's model in
terms of a set of examples that problematize her claim that the status
model can pick out all and only those harms that we intuitively understand as recognition harms. In other words, these examples are meant
to raise prima facie objections to her claim that status subordination is
the best frame for conceiving of and diagnosing misrecognition. However,
it seems that the only adequate way to assess the socio-theoretic import
of these problematic examples is by turning to the normative framework,
and this in turn will open some important questions about exactly how
the standards of parity of participation are to be understood and
employed by both social theorists and participants.

Consider first the possibility of a status violation that is not actually
connected to one's identity, to one's sense of self—it surely may be a
wrong, but I think we should not call it a case of misrecognition. Yet
Fraser's social theory would seem to force us to accept it as a case of

---

19 Zurn, "Identity or Status?"

misrecognition. Imagine a mid-level manager in a corporation. She may not achieve participatory parity precisely because she is excluded from decision-making procedures, and she is so excluded because of a set of institutionalized cultural value patterns, a set of patterns that define her group—mid-level managers—as to be excluded from participation. Yet, it would be strange to say that she had suffered a harm of misrecognition, since the exclusion in no way attacks or threatens her sense of self, her fundamental identity, that with which she strongly identifies.[20] At a different level of institutionally anchored norms, imagine a national procedure for weighting the political influence of individual citizens such that citizens in some communities were accorded more influence than in other communities. This situation obtains, for example, in the US constitutional scheme of federalism with respect to (at least) Senate representation and presidential representation, by means of the Electoral College. Here we have an apparently clear violation of participatory parity with respect to formal democratic institutions, one that reflects an institutionalized set of cultural values that codes urbanites as of less political trustworthiness and patriotic zeal than rural persons—in short, as of lower status as a group. And yet, I think we should hesitate to call this form of status subordination a case of misrecognition. Isn't the hesitation here precisely that the injustice seems unconnected to the social bases of one's sense of self, and does not seem to arise from an attack on one's identity?

Consider now the possibilities for identity-based harms that are independent of status subordination: here the idea is that some individuals may suffer harms because of cultural patterns of contempt or stigmatization that attack their fundamental sense of self, but where those symbolic patterns are not anchored in socially subordinating institutions. Imagine a gay man who lives in a progressive, cosmopolitan and tolerant city, yet remains in the closet about his sexuality because his self-esteem is undermined by stereotypes in the mass media and culture portraying gay men as licentious libertines.[21] Alternatively,

---

21 My example assumes that persons do not usually perceive a strong connection between their sense of self and being a mid-level manager. One might object here that one's personal identity is frequently tied to one's place in the division of labor. But in my example, the status subordination does not accrue to the person because she works in a corporation, or in a specific kind of business, or has a white collar job, or does particular kinds of labor. Rather the subordination is caused by her membership in the class of mid-level managers, a membership I doubt is strongly connected to her sense of self.

21 My thanks to Jon Mandle for this example and discussion of it.

consider a physically disabled person whose interests in removing barriers to mobility is in fact secured by a high level of compliance with anti-discrimination legislation, but who is regularly subject to overly solicitous attempts to help her with physical tasks, attempts that tend to infantilize her because of her physical disability. In this case, she feels a violation of the social bases for her self-respect, as she is treated as incapable of full individual autonomy and hence as lacking full human dignity. Yet this harm to her sense of self is not institutionally anchored in ways that violate her capacity to operate as an equal in the major activities of social life. In both cases, it seems that we have cases of misrecognition rooted in harms to the social bases required for the healthy development of a person's identity, but harms that are "free-floating" in cultural value hierarchies and merely attitudinal patterns, and so do not constitute institutionally anchored obstacles to participatory parity. Hence they are cases of misrecognition without status subordination.

If one can suffer a status subordination that is unconnected to misrecognition, and one can suffer misrecognition without status subordination—contrary to the analysis of Fraser's model—then it seems that the status model is in some ways strikingly unsuited to an analysis of recognition politics, and precisely because it sidesteps consideration of the social psychology of identity formation and main-tenance. Surely many forms of culturally elaborated misrecognition do in fact lead to institutionalized status subordination, and many forms of culturally unelaborated status subordination may later develop demeaning and stigmatizing images as a kind of false legiti-mation of unjustifiable social arrangements. Nevertheless, it appears that a theory of social justice oriented to the struggles and wishes of the age cannot avoid an account of the internal connection between individual identity formation and the intersubjective conditions of recognition that make it possible. Otherwise it will over-diagnose all forms of status subordination as unjustifiable forms of misrecognition, and yet be unable to diagnose institutionally unanchored identity-based harms as the misrecognitions they appear to be.

Now, the key questions in handling these prima facie objections concern whether a critical social theory should in fact be worried about, on the one hand, any and all forms of status hierarchy and, on the other, all forms of cultural and attitudinal disrespect. These questions cannot, however, be addressed purely at the level of empirical social theory, for they clearly involve normative issues about what kinds of social structures and processes are truly deleterious to justice and which are comparatively harmless; or so I shall now argue.

Consider how one might respond to the examples of managerial hierarchies, unequal voting powers, the self-closeting of sexual minorities, and disrespectful infantilization of the disabled: "Well," one might say, "those simply aren't the kinds of social interactions and structures critical social theory needs to be worried about. Since they are not significant, persistent, and truly harmful forms of status subordination that actually deny equal respect and equal opportunities for self-esteem, we need not account for them in our theory. And further, it is precisely a liability of identity-based theories of recognition that they identify any and all harms to identity as worrisome forms of misrecognition. Finally, it is this deference on the part of identity-based theories to any and all claimants for expanded recognition that leads such models down the road to an unreflective endorsement of the claims of both intolerant hate groups and illiberal purveyors of the reifying jargon of authenticity." This response boils down to the claims that these cases simply are not examples of significant or real injustice, and so we need not worry about the inability of our social theory to identify them.

However, it is not clear how persuasive this response can be, especially given the fact that Fraser appears to be committed to democracy at both the first order of social relations, and at the second order of adjudicating claims about those relations.[22] Let me explain. The most natural way to understand the response above is as a denial, from the point of view of one who has insight into what justice is and what it truly requires, that ordinary social participants have a satisfactory grasp on what justice is and requires. On this understanding of the response—let me call it the expertocratic understanding—the counterexamples do not have traction against the theory of status subordination, since critical social theory articulates clear and justified normative standards that theorists can use to substantively evaluate whether the first-order claims of social actors are warranted. The theory thus reserves the appellation "misrecognition" only for those examples of status subordination that it means to condemn and never for those institutionalized hierarchies it takes as justifiable, and it never uses "misrecognition" in reference to those instances where individuals experience some identity-based disrespect or denigration that the theorist doesn't countenance as real

---

22 My thinking about these two levels of claims adjudication, and about the relationships between social theorists and social movement participants with respect to these two levels is indebted to the interesting analysis in Kevin Olson, "Participatory Parity and Democratic Justice," in this volume.

or significant injustices. This expertocratic approach has the advantage of being able to clearly adjudicate conflicts over recognition claims, while simultaneously saving the socio-theoretic account of misrecognition as status subordination. The problem is that it seems to violate our democratic scruples by treating social participants as comparatively incapable and undeserving of performing the delicate task of distinguishing between justifiable and unjustifiable social structures.

Fraser clearly recognizes the participatory and egalitarian deficits of this expertocratic understanding, and rejects it, insisting that

> the norm of participatory parity must be applied dialogically and discursively, through democratic processes of public debate. In such debates, participants argue about whether existing institutionalized patterns of cultural value impede parity of participation and about whether proposed alternatives would foster it . . . For the status model, then, participatory parity serves as an idiom of public contestation and deliberation about questions of justice. More strongly, it represents *the principal idiom of public reason*, the preferred language for conducting democratic political argumentation on issues of both distribution and recognition.[23]

Here we seem to be invited toward an alternative, let us say, populist understanding of the response to the prima facie objections. In the case of slights to personal integrity experienced by persons as instances of violations of the intersubjective structures of expectable recognition, the theory must take them seriously as examples of misrecognition. But then Fraser's insistence on the difference between institutionally anchored and merely free-floating cultural value patterns and attitudes collapses. What then counts as misrecognition is just what the identity theorists seem to claim: those social conditions that persons in fact experience as impeding their equal opportunity to achieve an intact and integral personal identity. In the case of those institutionalized status subordinations, such as managerial hierarchies and unequal voting power, that aren't registered in the everyday public sphere as caused by disrespectful patterns of cultural evaluation, critical social theory on the populist interpretation need not worry about them. They are simply status hierarchies that we theorists must acknowledge as justified, since

---

23 Fraser and Honneth, *Redistribution or Recognition?*, p. 43 (italics in original).

there is no democratic debate and contestation over them as examples of possible misrecognition. So, the populist understanding of the response apparently saves the everyday sense of what the difference is between pressing recognition harms and unimportant differences in status, but in doing so, it undercuts the response to the prima facie socio-theoretic objections. Status subordination turns out to be just a theoretical way of talking about what social participants experience and thematize as identity deformations. The status model of recognition then collapses into a populist interpretation of the identity model, and social theory is no longer fully critical vis-à-vis existing forms of hate groups and the politics of authenticity.

Given that the expertocratic understanding of the response saves the theory from the counterexamples at the price of an unattractive Platonist understanding of the theory, and that the populist response concedes the objection, and so saves our democratic scruples at the price of giving up the theoretical advantages of the status model of recognition, it is perhaps not surprising that Fraser has endorsed a more subtle division of labor between everyday social participants and critical social theorists. She suggests we employ a "rule of thumb" for the intellectual division of labor when assessing proposed remedies to injustice: "when we consider institutional questions, the task of theory is to circumscribe the range of policies and programs that are compatible with the requirements of justice; weighing the choices within that range, in contrast, is a matter for citizen deliberation."[24] Although in the context of her argument, this division is suggested as appropriate for the evaluation of proposed remedies for injustice, perhaps we could extend it here to the initial diagnosis of justice violations as well. Thus, to return to my counterexamples, the theorist would delimit the range of what are to count as injustices—including only those status hierarchies that are unjustifiable and excluding all those identity-based slights that are seen as unimportant—and then allow democratic participation to investigate and determine which amongst that range of phenomena are to be counted as significant enough to deserve remedy. The problem in this understanding— perhaps we could call it the agenda-setting understanding—however, seems to me the same as that which follows from the expertocratic understanding: it presupposes that only the theorist has the best insight into social reality and the requirements of justice; public dialogue and participation is needed merely to add a patina of legitimacy through

---

24 Ibid., p. 72.

the democratic choice between the options pre-selected by superior moral insight.[25]

Perhaps Fraser could reply to the prima facie counterexamples at the level of social theory, without getting involved here with normative judgments about whether the examples should be included in the category status subordination. One response along these lines might be to rely upon a more thorough account of exactly what it means for patterns of cultural interpretations, social norms, and attitudinal dispositions to be "institutionally anchored." On further analysis, for example, it might turn out that we should consider both those mass cultural interpretations that lead to the self-closeting of the urban gay man and those widely expressed solicitous attitudes that infantilize the physically disabled woman as patterns of interpretation, behavior, and attitudes that are, in fact, institutionally anchored. In this case, then, what looked like forms of identity-based misrecognition would turn out to be true forms of status subordination; the theory could maintain its account of status subordination by means of refinement in the social theory rather than recourse to a normative analysis.[26]

The question then becomes how to make the socio-theoretic judgments that would enable social theory to steer a healthy middle course between unacceptably formal accounts of institutional anchoring that would focus narrowly, say, on extant legal restrictions and unacceptably thick accounts of institutional anchoring that would have license, say, to investigate all types of inner psychological beliefs and attitudes. I think Fraser would want a social theory that could say more about the diversity of sites of institutional anchoring than legalistic political theories are able to, while avoiding the need to delve too deeply into the psychological states of social actors, a need she critiques in competing identity-based theories of misrecognition. The hope would be for a purely socio-theoretic distinction between unacceptably

---

25 In oral response to an earlier version of this paper at the 42nd Annual SPEP conference, Boston, MA, November 6, 2003, Fraser indicated that she no longer supports what I have called the agenda-setting model of a division of labor between theorists and citizens that she had suggested in *Redistribution or Recognition?* Indicating that both Jeremy Waldron and I had rightly taken her theory to task for the unacceptably elitist and expertocratic tendencies of this proposal, she reasserted her fundamental commitment to a fully democratic understanding of the norm of participatory parity, at both the first and second orders. While I welcome this clarification, I am still unclear about how the theory can remain sufficiently critical vis-à-vis various extant recognition claims to generate the advantages promised by the status model.

26 Fraser suggested a move along these lines in her response to my paper at SPEP.

institutionalized and acceptably episodic and "free-floating" patterns of misrecognition. Not surprisingly, however, at this point I would wonder how this discrimination between acceptable and unacceptable interpretive, behavioral, and attitudinal patterns could be done without invoking distinctly normative considerations. And here the problem I identified above would return once again: Who makes these judgments on both specific cases and on general criteria for sets of cases? If theorists do, then how do we avoid an anti-democratic perspicacity; if social participants do, then how do we avoid a loss of diagnostic and critical acumen that nevertheless assuages our worries about democratic legitimacy?

I am not sure that I have adequately portrayed Fraser's position here, nor that I fully understand how she intends to finesse the tensions between theoretical perspicacity and the first- and second-order requirements of democratic legitimacy. It appears to me that there is a real conflict between the desire to admit democratic deliberation "all the way up" into theory, as it were, and the critical aspirations of a theory that attempts to make substantive distinctions between warranted and unwarranted social justice claims and remedies.

Said another way, there appear to be significant conflicts between the various tasks required to critically clarify the struggles and wishes of the age: between the need for an empirically accurate assessment of those present struggles, the normative requirements for a defensible account of the evaluative standards employed both by theorists and activists, the methodological requirements for reflexive clarity of theory, and the aspirations toward a perspicuous lens that can insightfully illuminate our present in a new, revealing, and practically effective way. Perhaps these are, ultimately, irreconcilable tasks. It is to Nancy Fraser's credit that she has provided us with an important and powerful conception of critical social theory that promises, nevertheless, to fulfill these various tasks.

AFFIRMATIVE ACTION AND FRASER'S REDISTRIBUTION-RECOGNITION DILEMMA

Elizabeth Anderson

Affirmative action in higher education has suffered from rollbacks in California, Texas, Maryland, and Washington, and is threatened by legal challenges in Michigan. These challenges have put its advocates on the defensive. If affirmative action is to survive, advocates need to articulate more clearly than they have before why such programs are justified. In this context, it is worth considering how Nancy Fraser's account of the redistribution-recognition dilemma helps us understand its problems and potentials.

Arguments for race-conscious affirmative action in higher education have generally fallen into two categories: "compensatory" and "diversity" rationales. These correspond respectively, in Fraser's classifications, to "redistributive" and "recognition" strategies for overcoming racism. Both represent what she calls "affirmative" rather than "transformative" remedies. Affirmative action that aims to open up educational and hence career opportunities to subordinated racial groups neither challenges the hierarchy of economic classes under capitalism nor the hierarchy of elite educational institutions.[1] According to Fraser's

---

1 Affirmative action is practiced only in the small segment of elite colleges and universities that practice selective admissions. The vast majority of schools accept all applicants with a high school diploma. Thus, the point of affirmative action in higher education is not to enable subordinated racial groups to attend some college, but to give them access to elite education. So-called class-based affirmative action is no more transformative of the class structure than is race-based affirmative action. Both versions practice redistribution only within the middle class, not between the poor and the middle class. There is no serious prospect of using affirmative action to advance the prospects of those whom William Julius Wilson has called "the truly disadvantaged," because these individuals have received such inadequate K-12 education that most are not prepared to meet the challenges of any four-year college, much less the challenges posed by elite schools.

analysis, then, we should expect the two types of remedy to be individually inadequate and contradictory in combination.

The contradiction is easy to see, at least in the long run. The compensatory rationale for affirmative action aims to "use race to get beyond race," and thus envisions race-consciousness in higher education as a temporary way station toward a color-blind society. The diversity rationale, as embodied in mainstream multiculturalism, casts racial differences as valued cultural differences, and thus envisions race-consciousness as a permanent feature of higher education.

What is somewhat harder to see is the individual inadequacy of both rationales. To be sure, Fraser accurately diagnoses a fundamental weakness of purely compensatory race-based affirmative action: by failing to challenge the underlying mechanisms and structures that generate racial disadvantage, it must always put its thumb on the scale, thereby marking people of color as "deficient and insatiable" and as "privileged recipients of special treatment," fueling white resentment and "backlash misrecognition." Here affirmative redistribution undermines affirmative recognition.

But what, exactly, is the problem with taking up "diversity" as the *exclusive* rationale for race-conscious affirmative action in higher education? Fraser does not identify a problem with affirmative recognitional remedies that is parallel to that from which affirmative redistributive remedies suffer. She does not claim that the former exacerbate distributive inequality, the way redistributive remedies exacerbate recognitional inequality. Perhaps she assumes that purely recognitional remedies must ignore distribution. But in the case of diversity-based affirmative action, this assumption is doubly mistaken. First, whether affirmative action is rationalized by redistributive or recognitional rationales, it has first-order redistributive effects: it gives disadvantaged racial groups access to elite education, and to the networks of connections that lead to elite careers upon graduation. Second, mainstream multiculturalism's advocacy of race as a dimension of merit has helped to transform American business culture, which now to a surprising extent embraces "diversity" as a productivity-enhancing feature of organizations rather than as a demand of justice (or of a meddling state) that interferes with efficiency and competitiveness. This has the second-order redistributive effect of shifting criteria of merit to favor disadvantaged racial groups, while defusing backlash misrecognition. Thus, redistribution gets a free ride on an overtly recognitional remedy.

I want to suggest that this *appearance* of a reconciliation between recognition and redistribution within an affirmative strategic framework goes very far in explaining why diversity has come to dominate compensation as the leading justification for race-conscious affirmative action in higher education. Positing a pure diversity rationale for affirmative action has additional advantages. From a legal point of view, the Supreme Court in *Bakke* imposed conditions on compensatory affirmative action that are difficult for many public universities to meet, while leaving open the door to diversity rationales.[2] A pure diversity rationale widens the coalition in favor of affirmative action in two ways: first, by giving groups such as Chinese-, Japanese- and Cuban-Americans, who are not economically disadvantaged on average, a stake in these policies; and second, by reuniting liberals and ethno-racial nationalists on the Left under a seemingly common banner. Finally, the resort to diversity has enabled liberals to evade some uncomfortable challenges that arise when issues of racial justice are on the table: explaining why "preferential treatment" is still needed thirty-five years after racial discrimination was supposedly extinguished by the civil rights laws; why the relatively most privileged African-Americans (the proverbial child of two black professionals) need and deserve special consideration over the innocent children of poor and working-class white parents who scored higher on standardized exams; why the principle of merit should be compromised at all. The point is not that these challenges cannot be met by advocates of purely compensatory affirmative action. It is that meeting them on purely distributive grounds makes people uncomfortable. Confronted with distributive arguments, whites tend either to feel guilty or (if they hate to admit that their relative privilege was unjustly acquired) resentful.

There is trouble in Diversity University, however. I shall argue that understanding why this is so requires us to distinguish two kinds of recognition that Fraser does not clearly separate. One is recognition of a group as legitimately culturally distinct. This kind of recognition is the appropriate remedy for groups who suffer from invisibility or cultural stigmatization. The second kind of recognition is recognition of a group as unjustly constituted by subordination to counterpart groups. This kind of recognition is the appropriate remedy for groups whose very existence is the product of injustice. Each form of recognition tells a different story about the relationship of difference to dominance. The first represents dominance as an unjust ordering of a pre-existing cultural difference. The second represents cultural difference as the product of a pre-existing dominance. Neither story

---

2 *Bakke* forbade public schools from implementing race-conscious affirmative action to remedy "societal discrimination," thus confining compensatory schemes to those schools that could prove that they had practiced racial discrimination in the recent past.

is completely true of any nonwhite American racial group. However, the second story is closer to the mark for African-Americans. And African-Americans are properly taken as the principal beneficiaries of affirmative action in the United States.

I shall argue that the trouble with a pure diversity rationale for affirmative action in higher education is that it offers a recognitional remedy of the first kind, and thereby undermines and misrepresents the rationale for affirmative action's special focus on African-Americans. The result is a systematic misrecognition of the meanings of American racial differences. What passes for a recognitional remedy —"diversity," or mainstream multiculturalism—fails in its own terms if it fails to acknowledge the ways race is a continuing, unjust feature of the political-economic class structure. In the end, I shall argue that there is no way a pure diversity rationale for affirmative action can effectively advance either the recognitional or the redistributive goals of race-conscious affirmative action. It must be combined with a redistributive rationale to make sense at all.

For analytical purposes, let us consider the features of diversity rationales for affirmative action when they are stripped of any redistributive component. At once we notice that the diversity coalition in higher education between liberals and ethno-racial nationalists is held together by a reluctance to articulate precisely what is the point of diversity. Is it to break racial stereotypes or to highlight racial differences? To expose students to the wider world or to secure their identities in their "own" internally bounded communities of ancestry? To learn that insights and creativity come from all quarters or to celebrate one's "own" culture? These questions illustrate that the multiculturalist tent houses at least two contradictory ideologies: humanism and ethnocentric identity politics. For the humanists, the point of stressing racial diversity in admissions is to break false and demeaning stereotypes about despised racial groups, by highlighting their *internal* diversity. Once we recognize that differences within racial groups swamp differences between groups, we will no longer regard "race" as a meaningful classification and be able move on to a color-blind society. Diversity enables the recognition in each individual of the common humanity we share.[3] For the practitioners of identity politics, the point of racial

---

3 Humanism illustrates how, contrary to Fraser's typology, the demand for recognition can underwrite the effacement of group difference. It is not the case that the remedy for all recognitional injustices is to revalue perceived differences. To the extent that African-Americans are viewed as distinctively "criminal, bestial [and] stupid," the remedy is not to try to cast criminality, bestiality, and stupidity in a favorable light but to attack the view as false.

diversity is to highlight racial differences—and not so much for the edification of members of other races as for the collective valorization of each group for itself. Identity politics stresses the *internal homogeneity* of racial groups, transforming what commonalities it finds or imagines into valorized identities and hence into cultural markers of the group.

The infirmities of each view are well known. Liberal humanism, to the extent that it assumes that racial prejudice resides mainly in the heads of whites, implicitly adopts a "white utility baseline" for measuring the value of nonwhite presence in elite universities. The question is "how valuable is the presence of this person of color for breaking racial stereotypes?" This perspective ignores the costs and benefits of college admission to the students of color themselves, and thereby treats them as mere instruments of white institutional purposes, as object lessons for others.[4] Moreover, it tempts admissions officers to engineer race-conscious admissions so as to select the "right" people of color—those who are in the best position to break racial stereotypes. Such counter-stereotypical students would ideally share enough similarities to the white majority student body that they would fit in rather than stand out. The "right" conclusion to draw, that we all share a common humanity, is rigged by implicitly accepting a white middle-class norm as the standard for recognizing who counts as fully human. Because it denies the reality of racial differences (races, on this view, do not exist), there can be no recognition of common humanity *across* openly acknowledged differences. At the same time, because it recognizes the reality of racial stereotyping, it sees the need to teach the lesson of sameness, and must therefore select the "right" representatives of nonwhite races to perform this task. On this model, racial difference is officially denied, covertly recognized, and everywhere misrecognized.

Ethno-racial identity politics hardly scores better than liberal humanism on the recognition front. As postmodernists have tirelessly and rightly stressed, the key problem is that of specifying the racial differences that supposedly constitute the common basis for collective identification and self-affirmation. No matter what specific cultural or physical attribute is named, some members of the group will be excluded, and an internal hierarchy of relatively esteemed and despised

---

4 This of course is an unfair characterization of actual liberal humanists, who accept the independent demands of distributive justice. Here I am considering the implications of a pure humanist diversity rationale for affirmative action, abstracting from distributive concerns.

members will be established. In the realm of college admissions, this manifests itself in the quest to admit the "authentic" African-American, Chicano, etc. Moreover, as the history of every nationalist movement testifies, the politics of identity generates an overwhelming temptation to myth-making: in claiming group differences where none exist, in fetishizing minute differences among neighboring groups, in misrepresenting group differences as primordial, sui generis, and original to the group, rather than imported adaptations or the products of interaction among groups. On this model, racial difference is also systematically misrecognized. Moreover, the goals of identity politics clash with the goals of liberal arts education. It reinforces parochialism rather than opening students up to the wider world. And it presumes to teach that racial group differences are more important than commonalities across groups, when students should be left free to draw their own conclusions about such matters.

In practice, mainstream mild-mannered multiculturalists have avoided the problems of both humanism and identity politics by keeping their conceptualizations of and rationales for diversity deliberately vague. "Diversity" has something to do with "cultural differences" and is valuable for promoting the cosmopolitan interest of the liberal arts in exposing students to a variety of cultures. But let us not say what those cultural differences are! This strategy at least has the huge advantage of not presuming to teach specific "politically correct" conclusions or to rig admissions to supply students with a predetermined range of peer experiences from which they are supposed to draw the "right" conclusions. Because it presumes no particular answer to what differences, if any, exist and which are important, it does not commit the gross recognitional injustice of selecting, from among nonwhite applicants, the "right" or "authentic" representatives of their respective races.

Mild-mannered race-conscious multiculturalism faces a serious difficulty, however. It needs to explain why identifying applicants by race is a good way to secure an important range of cultural differences. On the one hand, American racial classifications are far too crude, in that they efface genuine cultural differences within racial groups.[5] "Asians" include people who can trace their ancestry to China, Japan, India, Malaysia, Afghanistan . . . perhaps even Turkey. Common continental origins hardly testify to a common culture: So why classify these groups together? On the other hand, American racial classifications,

---

5 See David Hollinger, *Postethnic America*, New York: Basic Books, 1995.

as applied to American citizens, are far too parochial. As the African philosopher Anthony Appiah has pointed out, if you think American racial diversity makes the United States a multicultural society, try comparing it with Ghana.[6] From a distance (that is, anywhere outside North America), African-Americans seem as American as apple pie. If mild-mannered multiculturalists want a really culturally diverse campus, they should seek out first-generation immigrants and non-American citizens for admission in preference to African-Americans and even second-generation Hispanics for whom English is their first language.

I conclude that if race-conscious policies must pay their way in the currency of pure diversity, they will never get out of debt. They are doomed to a fatal series of misrecognitions that hardly do justice to their supposed beneficiaries. Pure "recognition" strategies don't even secure adequate recognition for the victims of recognitional injustice. And if they are kept vague enough to avoid recognitional injustices, they won't be able to perform their covert redistributive function, because they will not favor the admission of African-Americans. Race-conscious policies in higher education cannot work when a diversity rationale is divorced from a redistributive one.

What is missing from the pure multiculturalist picture? A clear recognition of race as a continuing structural feature of the American class system. American racial classification constitutes a quasi-caste system, in which socioeconomic hierarchy is based on ancestral origins in the various continents. People who can trace all of their ancestors back to Europe enjoy systematic socioeconomic advantages over those who have some ancestors born in Africa or pre-Columbian North and South America. This remains true today despite the abolition of formal, state-sponsored white supremacy and the institution of antidiscrimination law.[7] The primary form of recognition that African-Americans need is a recognition of the continuing unjust socioeconomic disadvantages from which they suffer, simply on account of their being constituted as a subordinate racial class.

Suppose African-Americans got this kind of recognition. Would Fraser's redistribution-recognition dilemma continue to apply to affirmative action in higher education? She is right to point out that because

---

6 Kwame Anthony Appiah, "The Multiculturalist Misunderstanding," *New York Review of Books* 44: 15, October 9, 1997, pp. 30–36.

7 For comprehensive documentation of this fact, see Douglas Massey and Nancy Denton, *American Apartheid*, Cambridge, MA: Harvard University Press, 1993.

it does not change the structures that continue to generate systematic racial disadvantage, affirmative action in higher education would have to engage in constant redistribution. But, if this point were widely understood, as we are supposing, then the need for such constant redistribution would no longer mark African Americans as "deficient and insatiable." Rather, it would mark American society as continuously offering deficient opportunities to African Americans in K-12 education. African-Americans would no longer be seen as "privileged recipients of special treatment." Instead, affirmative action would mark distinctions in the timing of investments in the education of different racial groups. White students enjoy a massive front-loading of educational investments in the K-12 years, compared to African-American students. Affirmative action back-loads investment in African-American education in the post high school years. For whites to lash back at the policy framed in this way, they would have to argue that, because African-Americans have been relatively deprived of public investment in their K-12 educations, they should be further denied investments at the collegiate level. For whites to think they are disadvantaged by these differences in the timing of educational investment, they would have to be willing to trade places with African-Americans, not just at the point of college admission, but for K-12 education as well. Only fools would accept that bargain.

If whites recognized the continuing socioeconomic significance of race, they would no longer wonder why antidiscrimination law wasn't sufficient to eliminate systematic racial disadvantage. They would understand that even upper-middle-class African-Americans still cannot convert income and wealth into power, status, access to public goods and economically valuable social connections as effectively as lower-class whites can. (Crucially, they lack access to majority white neighborhoods.) They would learn to distinguish merit from unequally distributed external advantages (for example, access to Advanced Placement courses in high school).

This thought experiment suggests that we can dissolve Fraser's redistribution-recognition dilemma by establishing a form of recognition that allows people to grasp the redistributive rationale for affirmative action. Backlash misrecognition is not the product of redistribution in itself, but of a failure to recognize that American racial distinctions do not track culture or biology but rather constitute a caste-like dimension of economic class.

This is not to deny that African-Americans also suffer from cultural misrecognition. As Fraser rightly stresses, race is a "bivalent collectivity," subject to both distributive and recognitional injustices. But even the cultural misrecognitions of African-Americans are not purely "cultural"—if "culture" is understood in the old-fashioned anthropological sense, as encompassing primordial differences of insular groups. To be sure, there are significant traces of African cultural forms in African American cultures.[8] And African-Americans have created cultural forms, such as a distinctive dialect, distinct Christian churches, and diverse family structures, that few whites share. None of these phenomena can be understood on the model of primordial black/white difference, however. There are significant traces of African cultural forms in mainstream American culture—for instance, in jazz, which is not exclusively African-American, but the product of white and black artists working together. Black English vernacular is, of course, a version of English, and owes much of its grammar and vocabulary to Scots-Irish dialect. Black Christian churches grew out of the legacy of slavery, Jim Crow, and civil rights struggles. The diverse family structures of contemporary African-Americans are largely adaptations to systematic race-based socioeconomic disadvantage. In other words, what is today put forth as distinctively African-American culture is unimaginable apart from the history of African-American interactions with whites, a history defined by socioeconomic injustice and the struggles against it. White stigmatization of African American culture represents an attempt to rationalize a racial caste-like hierarchy, not a prejudiced reaction to primordial cultural differences. Thus, there is no way to achieve even the specifically cultural recognition (destigmatization) that African Americans need without understanding it in the context of distributive injustices.

What, then, are the meanings and uses of racial diversity in higher education? Far from suggesting that we should return to a pure redistributive rationale for affirmative action, I am arguing for a reconstruction of the diversity rationale, one that stresses the central place of distributive justice in recognitional remedies. Consider three missions of elite colleges and universities: (1) to educate the future business and political leaders of a democratic society; (2) to advance the self-understanding of human beings generally through research in the humanities and human sciences; (3) to enable students to critically reflect on their own lives and identities, with the aim of enhancing their personal freedom and self-knowledge. None of these missions can be adequately fulfilled in the US without squarely confronting the

---

8 See Lawrence Levine, *Black Culture and Black Consciousness*, Oxford: Oxford University Press, 1977.

structural reality of race in America—the ways that one's race profoundly affects one's access to power and opportunities, how one is viewed and judged by others, and the terms on which one can participate in the major public institutions of American life. Racial diversity of membership in elite colleges and universities is indispensable to confronting these realities.

The task of promoting a democratic society involves promoting a democratic *culture*. This is a culture in which dialogue about matters of public concern can proceed fluently across the political-economic divisions that mark our society. It is one in which participants recognize the need to justify their proposals in terms acceptable to those who occupy different positions in the social order, and have the ability to appreciate what those terms would be. This requires skills of imaginative projection, taking up the points of view of those differently positioned and considering the merits and deficiencies of policies from those points of view. But imaginative projection in the absence of real consultation with those whose shoes one thinks one is trying on invites paternalism, arrogance, self-flattery, bigotry, and worse on the part of the privileged when they contemplate the perspectives of the disadvantaged. It invites a kind of narcissistic paranoia (conspiracy theories and ascriptions of malice to the privileged where negligence and ignorance are more often in play) on the part of the disadvantaged when they contemplate the perspectives of the privileged. Only actual dialogue with those who occupy diverse structural positions in society can remedy these ills. The prospects of such dialogue occurring among the future leaders of society outside colleges and universities are virtually nil. This is because colleges and universities constitute the only large-scale adult social sphere in US society that is both racially integrated and that enables participants (students) to meet as formal status equals, entitled to set their own agendas. The private spheres of family, friendship, neighborhood, and church are almost completely racially segregated. The world of paid work is also sharply segregated, marked by racialized and gendered hierarchies of office that impede frank talk between superiors and subordinates, and limited in conversational subject matter to issues of concern to the business enterprise. If, to fulfill the promise of democracy, citizens are to learn to engage in constructive dialogue across racial divisions, to take up the perspectives of others, universities are the only currently feasible setting where this can happen.[9]

---

9 See Robert Post, "Introduction: After Bakke," in Robert Post and Michael Rogin, eds., *Race and Representation*, New York: Zone Books, 1998, pp. 13–27.

Consider next a central internal mission of universities, to advance knowledge of human affairs through research in the humanities and social sciences. When can we be confident that the theories and stories we tell about ourselves are not mere reflections of ideology, of the interest of the powerful in legitimating their positions? Only when they have been subjected to searching critique from various points of view. In any society in which power relations are partially constituted by race, one's racial identity influences one's circumstances and hence one's experiences. Barriers to entry of disadvantaged racial groups into the academy therefore insulate knowledge claims from criticism by people with different ranges of experience than those possessed by dominant groups. Dominant groups may conduct inquiry informed by questionable unarticulated background assumptions, which, because they are taken for granted by inquirers with common experiences, escape critical scrutiny. Members of subordinate racial groups are often in a better position to detect the ways that theories developed by dominant groups ignore or misrepresent them, and usually have a greater interest in correcting these biases as well. In addition, they can advance research into human affairs by setting new research agendas, asking new questions, and formulating new theories designed to address the specific concerns of those placed in subordinated racialized positions. Ensuring the racial diversity of researchers in the academy thus advances the internal epistemic mission of universities.[10]

Finally, consider the role of higher education in stimulating critical self-reflection and identity-formation by students themselves. Questions of personal identity, particularly as they relate to the conditions of one's birth, ancestry, and unchosen group affiliations, are particularly vexed in US society. Group identification, particularly along racial lines, is a powerful force in America. But white racial identification is doubly invisible to whites: first, because whiteness is the unmarked racial identity, and second, because the ideology of individualism encourages self-ignorant denial of any kind of group identification. Patterns of white racial identification (as manifested, for example, in white flight) have obvious implications for the perpetuation of distributive injustice that need to be exposed. But they also affect the ability of white students to come to terms with themselves. White participation

---

10 See James Brown, "Affirmative Action and Epistemology," in Post and Rogin, pp. 333–37; Helen Longino, "Essential Tensions—Phase Two: Feminist, Philosophical, and Social Studies of Science," in Louise Antony and Charlotte Witt, eds., *A Mind of One's Own*, Boulder, CO: Westview Press, 1993.

in a racially diverse, integrated setting, where students can learn from the variety of ways others have subjectively dealt with their ascribed racial identities, and debate the merits of different constructions of identity, offers a unique opportunity to white students to advance their self-awareness so that they can confront otherwise unacknowledged identity conflicts. Students of color also benefit from racially diverse settings in which questions of identity are a subject matter for discussion. Diversity, on this view, is not a way of teaching students their fixed identities, but of enabling them to critically engage the varieties of ways people have coped with socially ascribed identities. True to the mission of the liberal arts, the aim of diversity on this view is not to dictate answers to identity debates, but to open students up to experiences, arguments, and modes of self-understanding by which they can decide for themselves what to make of their identities.[11]

Racial diversity in higher education thus serves democratic, epistemic, and personal ends. These ends require several varieties of recognition: of structural injustices based on race; of the racialized conflicts of interest, experience, and perspective these produce; of cultural responses to these injustices produced by racialized groups, struggling against and working with one another; of previously unacknowledged subjective racial identification; of the variety of ways people can make sense of their racial identities. Not all of these forms of recognition involve recognition of the disadvantaged by the advantaged. Some involve self-recognition by the advantaged themselves, others a recognition of a common democratic community.

This analysis vindicates Fraser's claim that justice requires an integration of the claims of redistribution and recognition. But it calls into question her construction of the redistribution-recognition dilemma, as well as her despair over the prospects of merely affirmative remedies. In the case of affirmative action for African-Americans in higher education, I argued that Fraser's account represents recognition too simplistically. Acknowledging the variety of recognitional remedies called for in this special case enables us to see how her dilemma might be escaped or at least ameliorated. At the same time, such acknowledgment enables us to enrich our understandings of the reasons for seeking racial diversity in higher education, beyond the contradictory visions of liberal humanist stereotype-breaking and racial nationalist identity-affirmation.

---

11 See Judith Butler, "An Affirmative View," in *Race and Representation*, pp. 155–73.

IS NANCY FRASER'S CRITIQUE
OF THEORIES OF DISTRIBUTIVE
JUSTICE JUSTIFIED?
Ingrid Robeyns

1. Introduction

To what extent are theories of distributive justice able to accommodate issues of recognition? According to Nancy Fraser, standard theories of distributive justice ignore issues of recognition, and cannot adequately subsume such issues. Theoretical accounts of recognition suffer from the reverse shortcoming: at present they do not pay sufficient attention to economic inequalities and redistribution, and they are also unsuited to incorporating questions of distributive justice. As most types of actual social injustice are a mixture of economic and cultural injustices, Fraser proposes a new normative framework that integrates both redistributive policies and a politics of recognition of difference. This social justice framework evaluates injustices by the degree to which they enable parity of participation in society.

I start by briefly summarizing Fraser's main contribution to the theoretical literature on social justice. Although Fraser does not provide arguments for her claim that theories of distributive justice cannot accommodate recognition, I agree that this critique is to some extent valid. However, Fraser ignores the differences between different theories of distributive justice. More specifically, while her critique holds for some theories of distributive justice, such as Ronald Dworkin's or Philippe Van Parijs's, it seems to be an oversimplified judgment of Rawls's theory and it certainly does not hold for Amartya Sen's capability approach. The case of gender is used to illustrate how these theories differ, and how Sen's capability approach can accommodate both issues of redistribution and recognition. Finally, I contrast Fraser's norm of participatory parity with Sen's capability approach, and argue that while both approaches are remarkably similar, Sen's capability approach can account for some morally relevant inequalities which do not find a place in Fraser's participatory parity.

2. Fraser on redistribution, recognition and social justice

Nancy Fraser is widely known for her claim that there has been an increase in demands for recognition of differences based on nationality, ethnicity, race, gender and sexual orientation, at the expense of claims of economic redistribution.[1] Fraser's general thesis is that "justice today requires both redistribution and recognition, as neither alone is sufficient."[2] We ought to resist the claims presenting the politics of redistribution and the politics of recognition as mutually exclusive alternatives. Instead we should concentrate our efforts to search for an alternative framework that can accommodate both demands of redistribution and recognition.

Fraser helpfully introduces the notion of *bivalent collectivity* to demonstrate why social justice has socioeconomic and cultural dimensions that cannot be separated and that are intrinsically inter-twined.[3] A bivalent collectivity is a group of people that suffers both socioeconomic maldistribution and cultural misrecognition, whereby neither of these can be reduced to an effect of the other. The injustice that such a collectivity faces is caused in the economic sphere and in the cultural sphere simultaneously. An example of such a bivalent collectivity is gender, as the causes of gender inequality are partly rooted in economic arrangements, and in part in a society's culture. While gender and race are paradigmatic examples of bivalent collectivities, all groups, such as those of class, sexuality and ethnicity, are bivalent collectivities. Of course, the relative importance of the economic and the cultural dimensions will differ between these collec-tivities. In the case of class, the economic sources of social injustice may be more pervasive than the cultural, and in the case of sexual orientation, the cultural causes of injustices may outweigh the economic, but the economic and the cultural order impinge on all of these collectivities, to a greater or lesser extent.

Acknowledging that the economic and the cultural are playing some non-reducible role in virtually all cases of social justice has some important theoretical and political implications. It implies that a critical

---

1 Nancy Fraser, "From Redistribution to Recognition?" in this volume; "Social Justice in the Age of Identity Politics: Redistribution, Recognition and Participation," in Grethe Peterson, ed., *The Tanner Lectures on Human Values* 19, Salt Lake City: University of Utah Press, 1998, pp. 3–5; "Recognition without Ethics?" *Theory, Culture and Society* 18: 2–3, 2001, p. 21.

2 Fraser, "Social Justice in the Age of Identity Politics," p. 5.

3 Ibid., p. 15.

approach to social justice should integrate "the social and the cultural, the economic and the discursive . . . It means connecting the theory of cultural justice with the theory of distributive justice."[4]

Fraser argues that both at the political and the theoretical level, one observes precisely the opposite tendency. "Increasingly . . . the politics of redistribution and the politics of recognition are posed as mutually exclusive alternatives."[5] At the theoretical level, so Fraser claims, one sees an analogous problem, wherein theories of distributive justice do not pay any attention to the cultural dimensions of injustice, whereas theories of recognition ignore the economic inequalities and claims of redistribution. In addition, Fraser holds that neither can the theories of distributive justice be modified to incorporate claims of recognition, nor are theories of recognition able to handle claims of redistribution. We therefore need a *bivalent conception of justice* that "encompasses both distribution and recognition without reducing either of them to the other."[6] Fraser suggests that arrangements and institutions should be judged by the degree to which people have *participatory parity*, that is, whether they can participate on a par with others in social life.[7] "Justice requires social arrangements that permit all (adult) members of society to interact with one another as peers."[8] Participatory parity requires that two conditions be met: an objective precondition of just redistribution, and an intersubjective precondition of reciprocal recognition.

I find Fraser's conceptualization of bivalent collectivities helpful, and agree with her general claim that for most collectivities, but especially for those that have a high degree of bivalence (such as gender), justice requires a politics of redistribution and recognition simultaneously. However, I am not convinced that in order to arrive at such a bivalent theory of justice, we have to throw away existing theories of distributive justice and start all over from scratch. In the remainder of this paper I will analyze Fraser's work on social justice from the point of view of theories of distributive justice. I will argue that Fraser has too easily dismissed all theories of distributive justice, and that it is unfair to these theories to treat them as if they are all equally unable to incorporate issues of recognition. Indeed, I will argue that in contrast

---

4 Nancy Fraser, *Justice Interruptus: Critical Reflections on the "Postsocialist" Condition*, New York: Routledge, 1997, p. 5.

5 Fraser, "Social Justice in the Age of Identity Politics," p. 10.

6 Ibid., p. 30.

7 Ibid., p. 36.

8 Ibid., p, 30.

to many other theories of distributive justice, Amartya Sen's capability approach stands out as a social justice framework that can encompass both redistribution and recognition.[9]

3. Fraser's critique of theories of distributive justice re-examined

Fraser's critique of theories of distributive justice consists of two claims. First, she claims that theories of distributive justice focus exclusively on economic inequalities, thereby ignoring issues of recognition of difference. Second, she claims that standard theories of distributive justice cannot adequately subsume problems of recognition. For neither of these two claims does she provide a detailed analysis: she simply states the claims without much supporting evidence or arguments.[10] While the theorists of distributive justice that are criticized are not listed, we can deduce from footnotes that these theorists in any case include John Rawls, Ronald Dworkin and Amartya Sen.[11]

It is unfortunate that it is implicitly suggested those three theorists would all advocate similar theories. Such generalizations are not conducive to stimulating debate with scholars working on distributive justice in the Anglo-American liberal tradition, which is building on the work of Rawls, Dworkin and Sen. In addition, if it can be shown that one of these theorists *can* accommodate issues of recognition in his theory of distributive justice, then one would expect that Fraser has to argue why this theory needs to be rejected, and a comparison between that theory and Fraser's own normative proposal would be called for.

John Rawls's "Justice as Fairness" advocates that two principles of justice should be met.[12] His first principle postulates that each person should have an equal right to a set of basic liberties. His second principle has two parts, and postulates that all offices and positions should be open to all, and social and economic inequalities should be arranged so that they are to everyone's advantage. Inequalities are only permitted

---

9 The claim that Sen's capability approach provides an attractive normative theoretical framework that can incorporate both claims of redistribution and recognition of difference has recently also been defended by Kevin Olson, "Distributive Justice and the Politics of Difference," *Critical Horizons* 2: 1, 2001, pp. 5–32.

10 Fraser, "Social Justice in the Age of Identity Politics," pp. 4, 10, 27.

11 Fraser, In this volume, p. 14, note 3; "Social Justice in the Age of Identity Politics," note 26; "Recognition without Ethics?" note 8.

12 John Rawls, *A Theory of Justice*, revised edition, Cambridge, MA: Harvard University Press, 1971/1999, pp. 52–56, 266.

if they are to the advantage of the worst-off. These inequalities are to be judged in terms of social primary goods, which are those goods that every rational person is assumed to want such as rights, liberties, opportunities, income, wealth and self-respect.[13]

Fraser has rightly argued against a view that postulates that a just distribution of rights and resources is sufficient to preclude misrecognition.[14] However, when directed against Rawls, this critique seems somewhat misplaced for the following reason. Rawls's theory of justice was developed in the US in the 1950s and 1960s, an era with pervasive discrimination against black people, women and gays. In that specific social climate and context, the political task was to advocate genuine equal rights. Rawls's work gave a moral and theoretical underpinning and support for the civil rights movement. In the context of the US in the 1950s and 1960s, the agenda of progressive political philosophy was not to debate *how* the welfare state should be designed so as to be just, but to defend and justify its very existence. In the time and place when Rawls's theory was written, this seemed to be a defensible priority and an effective normative strategy. The relevant question, then, is whether contemporary Rawlsians are still contented with equal rights and liberties. There is in Fraser's work no evidence or arguments to support such a claim. In addition, we should also note that Rawls's theory is not in the first place about redistributing resources, but about how in an ideal-utopian world *social institutions* could be designed so as to create a just society, which would include the elimination of the subordination of oppressed groups. As such, its scope and agenda for social change are much broader than other distributive theories, such as Dworkin's.

Ronald Dworkin's "Equality of Resources" advocates that impersonal resources (such as financial resources) should be divided in such a manner that people are compensated for their weaker personal resources (such as talents and handicaps).[15] Inequalities in impersonal resources due to differences in people's ambitions are justified, whereas inequalities that are due to reasons beyond people's control are not justified. An in-depth investigation of Dworkin's complex egalitarian theory shows that it has great difficulties incorporating issues of recognition and the cultural aspects of social injustices. For example,

13 Rawls, *A Theory of Justice*, revised edition, p. 54.

14 Fraser, "Social Justice in the Age of Identity Politics," p. 28.

15 Ronald Dworkin, "What is Equality? Part 2: Equality of Resources," *Philosophy and Public Affairs* 10: 3, 1981, pp. 283–345.

Dworkin's theory cannot detect an injustice in the current gender division of labor and care.[16] More generally, it has been argued that Dworkin's egalitarian theory is structurally unable to account for the cultural aspects of gender, race, and other dimensions of human diversity that create unjust inequalities between people, as his theory would by design assume that such inequalities would be caused by people's choices for which they are personally held responsible and for which no redistribution or recognition should take place.[17] When pressed on how his theory would deal with gender inequalities, Dworkin has replied that his envy test can take care of this: if a woman is willing to take a pill that would transform her into a man, then she needs to be compensated for being a woman; if she would not take such a pill, this implies that she does not envy the "package deal" of being a man and needs not be compensated for being a woman.[18] While a Dworkinian would stress that this is only an analytical device, many difference-sensitive theorists of justice find this an insulting and highly unhelpful way to think about the cultural causes of social injustice. Receiving financial compensation for not receiving recognition of one's identity and differences is not restoring injustice but only making things worse. Dworkin seems to be completely blind to the intrinsic importance of being respected for who one is. Dworkin's egalitarian theory does not allow for the possibility that injustice based on disrespect cannot be compensated for, but instead needs rectificatory strategies.

Why is it that cultural injustices find no place in equality of resources? Dworkin's theory is an ideal theory. Such theories ask how one could establish a just distribution *assuming* that one lives in a society where a number of liberties are safeguarded, that is, a society where there are no unjust gender hierarchies, no discrimination or prejudices based on gender, race, ethnicity or sexual orientation. In other words, cultural injustices are in some sense assumed away in Dworkin's theory, in that he assumes that certain liberties and legal rights are effectively protected. This makes it by design impossible to incorporate issues of recognition in Dworkin's theory of distributive justice. Dworkin belongs to a group of theorists of distributive justice

---

16 Andrew Williams, "Dworkin on Capability," *Ethics* 113, 2002, pp. 23–39; Roland Pierik and Ingrid Robeyns, "Resources or Capabilities? Social Endowments in Egalitarian Theory," mimeo, n.d.

17 Pierik and Robeyns, "Resources or Capabilities?"

18 Dworkin's reply to a question from the audience at the seminar on his work at University College London, March 2001. See also Dworkin, *Sovereign Virtue: The Theory and Practice of Equality*, Cambridge, MA: Harvard University Press, 2000, p. 292.

who hold that as long as we are able to eliminate discrimination and prejudice, cultural justice is done and we can concentrate on economic justice. Fraser has rightly argued in response to a similar suggestion by Richard Rorty that overcoming prejudice is not enough.[19] I think this is an important point that not all theorists of justice have sufficiently appreciated. A clarifying example, which supports Fraser's response to Rorty, can be taken from the activism of a group of women academics at the University of Leuven in Belgium. This group was formed in 1997 to improve women's position at this university, and advocate the introduction of gender studies. One of their very first demands was that no faculty meetings would be held after 5 PM, as the university nursery (and most other nurseries) close some time between 5:30 and 6 PM. It is clear that such a demand had nothing to do with combating prejudice, but with the recognition of their difference in being parents who are responsible for picking up their children from the nurseries—these parents more often being mothers than fathers. This group demanded recognition of the fact that not all (aspiring) university staff members are childless or have a partner at home to take care of the kids, certainly not if they are women.

In general, then, I agree with Fraser's critique that Dworkin's theory ignores issues of recognition. It should be noted that Dworkin is certainly not an exception in the Anglo-American literature on theories of distributive justice to ignore recognition of difference. For example, Philippe Van Parijs's basic income proposal, which builds to some degree on Dworkin's and Rawls's work, only looks at economic inequalities, and fails to analyze the recognition effects of his redistributive proposals.[20] I have made this argument elsewhere for the case of gender injustice.[21] While many women who currently have no income of their own will fare better in economic terms if an unconditional basic income were implemented, the gendered nature of decision-making within families will induce some employed women to reduce their labor supply, and in addition a basic income will not help at all to destabilize the traditional gender division of labor. Hence, from a feminist perspective a basic income should only be advocated if it is simultaneously introduced

---

19 Nancy Fraser, "Why Overcoming Prejudice Is Not Enough: A Rejoinder to Richard Rorty"; Richard Rorty, "Is 'Cultural Recognition' a Useful Concept for Leftist Politics?" —both in this volume.

20 Philippe Van Parijs, *Real Freedom for All: What (if Anything) Can Justify Capitalism?*, Oxford: Oxford University Press, 1995.

21 Ingrid Robeyns, "Will a Basic Income Do Justice to Women?" *Analyse und Kritik* 23: 1, 2001, pp. 88–105.

with a politics that combats gender inequities and changes gender roles —that is, deconstructs gender as we know it. Such an analysis thus provides additional support for Fraser's argument that redistribution and recognition should be considered simultaneously, that we need integrative thinking on issues of justice.

It is remarkable that since Fraser published her critique of theories of distributive justice and theories of the politics of recognition, there have been several debates and dialogues with the latter, whereas—to my knowledge—there have not been any debates with theorists of distributive justice. In my opinion, the reason why so few theorists of distributive justice have engaged with Fraser's critique is because it is an oversimplification of the literature on distributive justice. Indeed, several theorists of justice have taken liberal theories of distributive justice further to integrate issues of ethnicity, cultural difference and gender. Fraser herself points at the "exception" of Will Kymlicka's work.[22] Kymlicka's work has initiated a vast literature that analyzes issues of ethnicity and minority groups starting from the tradition of liberal theories of distributive justice. Similarly, other justice theorists have started from theories of distributive justice to analyze cultural injustices related to gender,[23] and the work of Anne Phillips pays a lot of attention to cultural differences while remaining within an (admittedly expanded) liberal theoretical framework that advocates socioeconomic equality.[24]

Fraser's project is to advance an integrative framework that can incorporate both economic and cultural inequalities and injustices for all these groups. I agree that this is a much needed and interesting project. However, we do not need to throw out the baby with the bathwater. Instead of constructing a new normative theoretical framework from scratch, we might better first look carefully at whether there is a theory of distributive justice that can do justice to human diversity and can incorporate claims of recognition. I will argue that Amartya Sen's capability approach provides such a framework. A similar argument has been made by Kevin Olson, and the egalitarian proposal by Elizabeth Anderson also provides support for the same general line of thought.[25]

---

22 Fraser, "Social Justice in the Age of Identity Politics"; Will Kymlicka, *Liberalism, Community and Culture*, Oxford: Oxford University Press, 1989; *Multicultural Citizenship*, Oxford: Oxford University Press, 1995.

23 Susan Okin, *Justice, Gender and the Family*, New York: Basic Books, 1989.

24 Anne Phillips, *Which Equalities Matter?*, Cambridge: Polity Press, 1999.

25 Olson, "Distributive Justice and the Politics of Difference"; Elizabeth Anderson, "What Is the Point of Equality?" *Ethics* 109, 1999, pp. 287–337.

4. Redistribution, recognition and Amartya Sen's capability approach

So far I have provided support for Fraser's critique of Dworkin, I questioned the fairness and reasonableness of her critique of Rawls, and I extended her critique to Van Parijs's theory of distributive justice. In what follows I want to argue that Fraser's critique is not justified with respect to Sen's capability approach, as the capability approach is, more than any other normative approach to social justice, able to accommodate both issues of redistribution and recognition.[26]

4.1. Sen's capability approach

What is the capability approach?[27] The capability approach is a general normative framework (some call it a paradigm). It advocates that the design of social policies and institutions, and the evaluation of well-being, inequality, poverty and justice, should focus primarily on people's capabilities to function. Functionings are the "beings and doings" of a person, such as working, reading, being politically active, being psychologically and physiologically healthy, being well educated, being safe, being sheltered, being part of a community and so on. The list of possible functionings is indeed endless. Some of these functionings will be more relevant to judge distributive justice in its most mainstream sense, such as being well educated, being healthy, being well sheltered. Other functionings will be more relevant to studying recognition, especially the functioning of being respected.

Sen holds that it is not so much the achieved functionings that are important, but the real opportunities that one has to achieve those

---

26 In addition, it seems that Amartya Sen has an increasing interest in issues of identity and recognition; witness his lecture *Reason Before Identity*, Oxford: Oxford University Press, 1998, and his forthcoming book on identity, as announced in Sen, "Continuing the Conversation," talks with Bina Agarwal, Jane Humphries, and Ingrid Robeyns, *Feminist Economics* 9: 2–3, 2003, pp. 319–32. He seems to be mainly concerned with how people with dominant identities might abuse these to oppress other groups in society, which is a problem that is also discussed by Fraser, "Rethinking Recognition," in this volume.

27 See Sen, "Equality of What?", The Tanner Lectures on Human Values, in Sen, *Choice, Welfare and Measurement*, Oxford: Blackwell, 1982; "Rights and Capabilities," in Sen, *Resources, Values and Development*, Cambridge: Harvard University Press, 1984; *Commodities and Capabilities*, Oxford: Oxford University Press, 1985; *The Standard of Living*, Cambridge: Cambridge University Press, 1987; *Inequality Reexamined*, Oxford: Clarendon Press, 1992; "Gender Inequality and Theories of Justice," in Martha Nussbaum and Jonathan Glover, eds., *Women, Culture and Development*, Oxford: Clarendon Press, 1995; *Development as Freedom*, New York: Knopf, 1999.

functionings, that is, a person's capabilities. In other words, a capability is a potential functioning, and all capabilities of a person together form her capability set, which represents her real freedom to be and to do what she wants. Distinguishing between achieved functionings and capabilities allow for people to make their own plan of life and decide for themselves what they want to be and to do. What counts in Sen's framework is primarily that people have the genuine, real, effective opportunities to achieve those beings and doings. The different constituents of the capability approach and the role that commodities have to play are perhaps best represented schematically as in Figure 1.

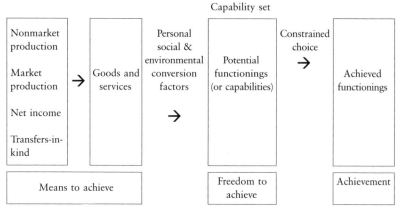

Figure 1: A schematic representation of the capability approach.

Resources, or goods and services, enable certain functionings. However, the relation between goods and the functionings to achieve certain beings and doings is influenced by three types of *conversion factors*. Firstly, *personal conversion factors* (e.g., metabolism, physical condition, sex, reading skills, intelligence) influence how a person can convert the characteristics of a commodity into a functioning. If a person is handicapped, or in a bad physical condition, or has never learned to cycle, then the bicycle will be of limited use in enabling the functioning of mobility. Secondly, *social conversion factors* (e.g., public policies, social or religious norms, discriminating practices, gender roles, societal hierarchies, power relations) and *environmental conversion factors* (e.g., climate, infrastructure, institutions, public goods) play a role in the conversion from characteristics of the good to the individual functioning. If there are no paved roads, or if a society imposes a social norm that women are not allowed to leave the house without being accompanied by a male family member, then it becomes much more difficult or even impossible to use the good to enable the functioning. It is obvious that many of these social conversion factors will be social processes that are sources of misrecognition. Cultural sources of injustices such as heterosexist, androcentrist or religious biases can narrow a person's capability set. This stylized representation of Sen's capability approach makes clear that resources are only part of the story. What ultimately counts is what real opportunities people have to be and to do, and resources are only one input in this process. In other words, the capability approach judges social justice in terms of the real or effective (in contrast to formal) opportunities that people have to lead the life they have reason to value, that is, to do the things that they want to do, and be the person that they want to be.

Sen has formulated the capability approach first as a critique of Rawls's theory of justice.[28] He argued that a focus on primary social goods "seems to take little note of the diversity of human beings" and does not capture what these goods enable human beings to do.[29] Sen also argued that "non-exploitation or non-discrimination, requires the use of information not fully captured . . . by primary goods."[30] Whereas the social bases of self-respect is a (Rawlsian) primary good, self-respect itself is a (Senian) functioning of a person.[31] Sen has criticized Dworkin's equality of resources along similar lines.[32] Sen has always phrased his critique of resources-based theories of distributive justice in terms of the pervasiveness of human diversity: what can be done with a bundle of goods depends on who is utilizing it. The intrinsic attention in the capability approach to human diversity and the impact of social, environmental and individual factors on a person's well-being allow us to incorporate aspects of distributive justice, as well as issues of recognition. In conclusion, it seems obvious to me that the capability approach can accommodate both recognition and redistribution.

Two remarks are in order. Firstly, I fully grant that it is not easy to reconstruct an exact account of Amartya Sen's capability approach. Sen's articles on the capability approach are dispersed over a wide range of journals and books, which cut across the disciplines. Moreover,

---

28 Sen, "Equality of What?" Sen also formulated the capability approach initially as a critique of utilitarianism, but that is not relevant in the present discussion.

29 Ibid., p. 366.

30 Ibid., p. 367.

31 Sen, "Rights of Capabilities," pp. 320–1.

32 Sen, "Rights of Capabilities."

depending on the disciplinary audience that he has been addressing, Sen has put stress on different aspects of the approach, which makes a careful interpretation of his work even more difficult. In addition, Sen has developed his approach gradually, hence to understand the capability approach one would need to go back to read from the earliest to the most recent of Sen's papers on the capability approach, as there is no clear overview paper by Sen that neatly describes the approach. The second remark concerns the difference between Sen's and Nussbaum's work on the capability approach.[33] It falls beyond the scope of this paper to describe in detail the differences between Sen's and Nussbaum's capability approaches. For the present context it is important to point out that while Sen's capability approach is a general normative framework that allows a lot of flexibility in how and where it can be applied, Nussbaum's capabilities approach makes much stronger normative claims. In addition, while Sen holds that one cannot specify all the capabilities that will be relevant in an ad-hoc fashion, and that this needs to be done in a democratic procedural way, Nussbaum has defended a universal list of capabilities. In my view, Nussbaum's approach thereby loses political legitimacy.[34]

4.2. The capability approach and the gender division of labor

To illustrate how and in what way the capability approach can account for both redistribution and recognition, I will briefly analyze the case of the gender division of labor in Western societies. According to feminist analyses, the current gender division of labor in Western societies is unjust. The interaction and accumulated impact of social norms, social institutions (such as schools and the tax system) and features of the labor market make it easier and often also financially beneficial for heterosexual couples to choose for a traditional gender division of labor, with the man working full-time in the labor market, and the woman being primarily responsible for the household, possibly combining housework and care labor with a part-time job. Building on earlier feminist research and studies in the social sciences, I have argued elsewhere that this is an unjust situation, both if judged in terms of fair

---

33 Martha Nussbaum, *Women and Human Development*, Cambridge: Cambridge University Press, 2000; "Capabilities as Fundamental Entitlements: Sen and Social Justice," *Feminist Economics* 9: 2–3, 2003, pp. 33–59.

34 Ingrid Robeyns, "Sen's Capability Approach and Gender Inequality: Selecting Relevant Capabilities," *Feminist Economics* 9: 2–3, 2003, pp. 61–92.

outcomes, as well as if judged in terms of fair procedures and opportunities.[35] I will take this injustice as my starting point, and ask what
a critical use of the capability approach would recommend us to do
to make the gender division of labor more just.[36]

Take a heterosexual couple with children. In a situation with the
traditional gender division of labor, the capability set of the man
would contain the capability to work on the labor market, uncon-
strained from responsibilities for care labor or household work. His
capability set would not contain the option to be a houseman, or to
work primarily at home and perhaps hold a small part-time job. The
welfare state and social institutions would not allow both parents to
combine work with care labor, and social norms would encourage the
mother to take up this role, not the father. The capability set of the
woman would contain symmetrical capabilities, that is, she could
be a housewife but she could not search for a job in the labor market
assuming that someone else would take care of her kids and the
household.[37]

In Europe, there have been many different ways in which governments have tried to respond to feminist claims that such an arrangement
is not fair. The Swedish model looks roughly as follows: all parents
are assumed to work—any women work about 35 hours in the public
sector. Childcare facilities and other provisions that make the combination of market work with care easier are provided at low cost by
the government. As a consequence, direct and indirect taxation is
high, and therefore the general price level is also high. To reach a
decent material standard of living, both parents need to hold a job.
Both fathers and mothers are encouraged to take parental leave. Policies
are thereby trying to transform identities of both mothers and fathers
into working parents. Choosing to be a mother or father at home
comes at a very high price in terms of opportunity cost, hence being

---

35 Ingrid Robeyns, "Gender Inequality: A Capability Perspective," doctoral
dissertation, Cambridge University, 2002, Chapter 2.

36 I add the words "critical use of" because in principle the capability approach
can also be used in a stripped-down version that only advocates a focus on multi-
dimensional ends of well-being (capabilities) instead of other dimensions of advantage
such as utility, resources or another dimension. However, given Sen's wider work, it
seems obvious to me that the capability approach needs to be used in a critical-
feminist-liberal fashion, and not in an androcentric libertarian fashion. Any other use
of the capability approach would be a reductionist interpretation.

37 An outcome-based justice evaluation would then need to show that this stylized
man's capability set is less attractive than this stylized woman's capability set. I shall
not try to argue that here, but see Robeyns, "Gender Inequality," Chapter 2.

a homemaker ceases to be an option except for the very rich. Non-market care work does not seem to be particularly valued in the Swedish society.[38]

The Dutch model is roughly the reverse. Domesticity is highly valued in the Netherlands, and the prevailing mother ideology praises mothers who are homemakers, and reprimands mothers who bring their children to day care for more than three days a week. The short school hours and the lack of after-school facilities are based on the assumption that one parent (or a grandparent) does not have a full-time job. Day care for babies and toddlers is insufficiently available, poorly subsidized and to a considerable extent the responsibility of the employer. State-funded nursing schools are only available from the age of four. To a large extent, the Dutch situation still reflects the traditional gender division of labor, except that state policies support homemakers. For example, every person who has legally resided in the Netherlands for at least fifteen years receives a state pension that is unconditional upon earlier employment status, and in the 2001 tax reform a small uncon-ditional individual tax credit has been introduced. Taxation is moderate; hence it is not practically unaffordable to be a homemaker, at least not to the extent that it is in Sweden. Dutch mothers are more supported in their capability to be a homemaker, but institutional design and policies do little to enlarge and support mother's capabilities to be a working parent, nor to divide the unpaid labor more equally between both parents.

The capability approach could provide a useful framework when we want to restore the injustice created by the gender division of labor. The norm should be to search for policies or institutional reforms that can enlarge men's and women's capability sets without simultaneously contracting the set in some other dimensions. The capability set should be enlarged without making certain existing options unavailable.

At the same time, the cultural and social non-material constraints on choice that determine which options a person will choose from her capability set must also be made just. For example, women should not feel social or moral pressure to prioritize their families over their other activities any more than men do, whereas cultural notions of masculinity should change to make it easier for men to effectively engage in equal sharing of care and market work, without losing social status or respect. This is a very important condition that makes the

---

38 Mary Daly and Katherine Rake, *Gender and the Welfare State*, Cambridge: Polity Press, 2003, p. 152.

capability approach quite different from other liberal theories of justice. Suppose both partners would have the option to choose from exactly the same capability set. A (left) libertarian, such as Van Parijs, will now argue that justice is reached.[39] However, a critical liberal such as Sen would insist on scrutinizing the constraints on the choices that people make. This is a tricky question, which leads us to difficult debates on what counts as a "real, "voluntary," or "free" choice and what doesn't. It is also here that additional aspects of identity, diversity and (mis-)recognition are taken into account, as unjust identity formation and social norms can lead to choices from one's capability set that therefore result in unjust inequalities. Similarly, often people don't make individual choices, but collective choices are made (for example within a household) that impact on people's well-being. Thus, power relations within collectivities such as the household need to be taken into account in a capability analysis.[40] And as is obvious from the work of Fraser and other theorists who have worked on normative aspects of identity and recognition, it is crucial to pay attention to power relations when one wants to develop a critical stand towards different identity claims.

5. Sen's capability approach and Fraser's participation parity

Now one might remark that the kind of transformation of the gender division of labor that a critical use of the capability approach would advocate comes close to Fraser's proposals of a transformative politics of redistribution.[41] There are differences in the details, but in the broad spectrum of normative political theorizing about just policy changes, Fraser's proposals and a critical use of the capability approach lie close to each other. This provides support for my claim that had Fraser examined the theories of Rawls, Dworkin and Sen more carefully, she

---

39 Philippe Van Parijs, "Real Freedom, the Market and the Family: A Reply to Seven Critics," *Analyse und Kritik* 23: 1, 2001, pp. 106–131.

40 Vegard Iversen, "Intra-household Inequality: A Challenge for the Capability Approach?" *Feminist Economics* 9: 2–3, 2003, pp. 93–115. Sen has himself contributed to the literature on intra-household inequalities ("Gender and Co-operative Conflict," in Irene Tinker, ed., *Persistent Inequalities*, New York: Oxford University Press, 1990), and has recently argued that he holds it very important to pay sufficient attention to power aspects of social relations ("Continuing the Conversation").

41 Nancy Fraser, "After the Family Wage: Gender Equity and the Welfare State," *Political Theory* 22: 4, 1994, pp. 591–618; "Social Justice in the Age of Identity Politics," pp. 57–67.

would have noted that they are far from the same, especially Dworkin's and Sen's theories.[42]

But more importantly, this triggers the question whether Sen's capability approach is identical to Fraser's proposal of participatory parity. Do these two accounts of justice advocate the same thing, but in a different language? In what follows I want to describe four differences between Sen's capability approach and Fraser's participatory parity, which all show that Sen's framework is broader and is able to handle some cases of justice that are difficult to fit in Fraser's theory. In other words, Sen's capability approach has a wider scope and pays attention to human diversity even more radically than does parity of participation.

Let us first look at the differences between the two approaches at the most abstract and theoretical level. This is not a straightforward task, as so far Fraser has not developed her proposal of participatory parity in much detail. What does it mean exactly "to participate on a par with others in social life"?[43] As I interpret this, it means that independent of the collectivities to which people belong, they should have the same access to take part in society. In terms of the capability approach, participatory parity seems to include those capabilities that are the *doings* of people, and not their beings. One could plausibly argue, that in so far as beings are instrumentally valuable for doings, they will also be included in Fraser's account. However, this would still leave us with two differences with the capability approach. Firstly, the capability approach would include those beings that are necessary for doings *not only* because they are instrumentally important, but also because of their intrinsic importance. In addition and more importantly, the capability approach would also include beings that cannot be said to enable participation in society. For example, in the Netherlands a child can receive the name of its mother, or its father, but cannot receive both names. In my opinion, this is an injustice toward both the parents and the child, but especially toward the mother, because due to gendered social norms and hegemonic notions of masculinity and femininity, it is much more likely that the child will receive the father's name. The capability approach would argue that as a matter of respecting a parent, he or she should be able to pass on his or her name to the child, and as a matter of respect towards

---

42 Indeed, in a recent debate on the difference between Dworkin's equality of resources and Sen's capability approach, Dworkin stated that he does not see on what basis one could judge that in the traditional gender division of labor men fare better than women. Dworkin, "Sovereign Virtue Revisited," *Ethics* 113, 2002, p. 137.

43 Fraser, "Social Justice in the Age of Identity Politics," p. 36.

the child, she should be able to enjoy having both her parents' names. Allowing the possibility of double names increases the capability set, especially those of mothers, and it is clear that some women value this capability strongly. I do not see how such a change could be advocated by taking participatory parity as the norm, even though I would assume based on Fraser's wider writing on gender and justice that she would agree that such an affirmative transformative policy contributes to gender justice. But would the norm of participatory parity support this claim?

A second difference between the capability approach and participatory parity is their reliance on some *notion of "normality."* One of the attractive features of the capability approach is that it can apply to all people. This includes "non-normal" cases, such as severe mentally and physical disabled people or inmates. Rawls's justice as fairness starts from a notion of an "average," "standard," or "normal" person, and determines the amount of primary social goods that people should have based on this norm. This is a major difference with Sen's capability approach, which does not presuppose such a "normal" case.[44] In addition, the capability approach can also be used to think about justice or the development of transformative policies toward babies, toddlers, and children.[45] For example, we might have to accept that blind people might never be able to see, and we do not think an injustice has happened because there will never be equality in the capability to see. Similarly, we accept that severely mentally disabled people might not be able to make reflective opinions and judgments regarding national politics and therefore will never be equal with respect to the capability to participate in politics. But for blind or mentally disabled people a different list of capabilities that society should aim to enable can be drawn up. In Sen's framework, one would aim to expand their capability set as much as possible, in terms of enabling them to make as many day-to-day decisions by themselves, enabling them to undertake interesting and enjoyable activities, making sure they are well sheltered, well fed, well cared for.

Fraser's normative concept of participatory parity seems, just like Rawls's "Justice as Fairness," to assume a notion of a "normal" person who has the mental capacities and legal rights to participate in society as peers with other people. This seems to exclude severely physically

---

44 Sen, "Equality of What?" pp. 365–6.

45 Madoka Saito, "Amartya Sen's Capability Approach to Education: A Critical Exploration," *Journal of Philosophy of Education* 37: 1, 2003, pp. 17–33.

and mentally disabled persons. Once again, Fraser's notion of participatory parity is not very much developed, and in further writing she might explain how these "special cases" are to be treated in her thinking about social justice. However, at a normative-philosophical level it seems more appealing to try to develop a normative account that includes all people, and that doesn't treat the disabled, the weak, the ill, the young, the frail elderly and inmates as "special cases."

A third difference between the capability approach and participatory parity lies in what they consider the *genuine and intrinsic reasons for redistribution and recognition*. Take the example of pervasive, structural and widespread poverty in a rural part of India. Many people work sixteen hours a day, have absolutely no leisure, and are predominantly concerned with their survival in terms of food intake and maintaining health levels that keep them alive. What is the use of judging this situation in terms of participatory parity? Of course, more material provisioning, more food, better shelter, less labor and more rest *are* necessary if these people ever want to participate in the wider Indian society as peers with urban inhabitants who have reached a minimal standard of living. But that's not the point, really. The point is that these people lack minimum levels of basic capabilities such as being healthy, enjoying some minimum amount of rest, having enough nutritional intake, and so forth. What is really important in such a desperate situation is in the first place these people's beings, and not so much their doings. Independent of whether participatory parity will ever be a realistic option for these people in the near future, the moral case for redistributing resources to them, and trying to structurally improve their living conditions, rests on their basic capabilities to function.

A final advantage of the capability approach in comparison with participatory parity lies in its ability to be applied to a *wide variety of cases*. This variety expresses itself both in terms of geographical situatedness, and in the kind of policy or political situation one is considering. The capability approach is not just about justice, but about all aspects of societal changes. For example, Sabina Alkire applied the capability approach as an expanded cost-benefit analysis to investigate how Oxfam might allocate its funds in Pakistan.[46] She argued that from a purely financial perspective Oxfam ought to invest its funds in a goat-rearing project. A rose-garland production project

---

46 Sabina Alkire, *Valuing Freedoms: Sen's Capability Approach and Poverty Reduction*, New York: Oxford University Press, 2002.

was not so successful in financial terms, but enabled capabilities that could not be quantified or expressed in material terms, such as being able to offer roses in religious ceremonies, enjoying the beauty and the smell of the roses, feeling that one had gained much self-respect and self-esteem, and having better social relations in the village. Another project, literacy classes for Muslim adult women, had no financial returns at all (as the markets for female labor in this area are nonexistent), but it created significant effects of self-development and empowerment among the students. In Alkire's study the capability approach is applied in a very pragmatic and messy development project, which lies a long way from theoretical reflections on criteria of justice in normative political philosophy. But this is what I find so attractive about Sen's capability approach: while it can be read as a theory of social or distributive justice, it is in fact much wider, and has over time developed in a sort of paradigm to think about normative issues. In contrast, it is not at all clear that the general criteria of participatory parity can eventually be developed into such a general normative frame-work, which could be used to analyze such a wide variety of normative problems, and develop policies and politics to deal with them.

In conclusion, on my reading everything that is being advocated by the norm of participatory parity is included in the capability approach, whereas the capability approach also points at some morally relevant information and considerations that are not included in participatory parity. In addition, the scope (both geographical as well as in terms of kinds of normative uses) of the capability approach seems to be wider than the scope of participatory parity.

6. Conclusion

Nancy Fraser has made a substantial contribution to critical normative thinking by arguing that social justice requires both redistribution and recognition, and that social justice thinking should take place in an integrative manner. While I agree in broad terms with her substantive analysis, I have argued in this paper that she has been unfair to theorists of distributive justice by not acknowledging their differences. More importantly, I hold that Fraser's critique of Amartya Sen's capability approach is misconceived. By incorrectly assuming that Sen's capability approach cannot accommodate issues of recognition, Fraser has not appreciated that the capability approach can actually meet all the requirements that she holds a theory of social justice should meet. In addition, I have suggested that Sen's capability approach might be more promising as a framework for integrative thinking on social justice that pays due attention to both issues of economic inequalities as well as cultural injustices. Given that the literature on the capability approach has been expanding extremely rapidly in recent years, and is slowly maturing as a normative paradigm, there is a case for participatory parity theorists to show what the added value or distinctiveness of their approach is. If it turns out that all claims advanced by the norm of participatory parity are also being advanced by capability theorists, then there is a case to be made for forming coalitions, and learning from the arguments and empirical studies in the capability paradigm.

One note of caution is in place. In this paper I have discussed the capability approach to contrast it with Fraser's proposal of participatory parity. In my opinion, the capability approach is promising as a broad theory of social justice that can encompass both the cultural and the economic. However, while the capability approach has developed considerably in recent years, much work needs to be done, and I certainly would not want to claim that it is a framework that is ready to give us guidance on any question of justice. But I do feel that it is the most promising framework that we have at present, and a rapidly increasing number of scholars, activists and policy makers feel the same. If Nancy Fraser thinks that her proposal of participatory parity is really different from the capability approach, and is offering us something that the capability approach cannot offer, then it would be helpful if this would be clarified.

RESOURCE EGALITARIANISM AND THE POLITICS OF RECOGNITION

Joseph Heath

I would like to begin with a little anecdote. I have in-laws who live in small-town Taiwan. Their attitude toward most foreigners is characterized by the kind of casual ethnocentrism that inhabitants of culturally homogenous communities generally exhibit. Their attitude toward white people—"pointy noses"—is somewhat more ambivalent. It was summarized for me very nicely a couple years ago by one of my wife's aunts. White people, she said, used to get a lot of face, because they were so *rich*. They could come into town and buy anything they wanted. This made everyone feel inferior. But nowadays, many Chinese people are just as rich as the visiting foreigners. So people realize now that whites are just ordinary, and they no longer give them special treatment.

This is the kind of story that proponents of the politics of redistribution take very seriously. Social status and recognition—"face"—tend to follow money and power. As long as one group exercises greater command over resources than another, that group will also inspire feelings of inadequacy and inferiority among those who are not members. Any program to redress such an imbalance that fails to correct at least the grosser underlying inequalities will be cold comfort. Getting recognition without redistribution is like winning the consolation prize.

Unfortunately, this insight is one that has a tendency to fade from view, particularly in societies where the baseline level of wealth is extremely high. Contributing to this tendency, however, has been the desire of many theorists on the "cultural Left" to downplay the importance of distributive issues, largely for political reasons. This is because many early advocates of the politics of redistribution jumped from the valid insight that an equal distribution of wealth was a necessary condition for equality of status and recognition, to the invalid conclusion that such a distribution would be both necessary and sufficient. Crudely put, they thought that solving distributive problems would make all other social problems go away.[1] In this respect, they failed to take seriously the way that misrecognition can both impede redistribution and perpetuate injustice even in the absence of significant material inequality.

However, the attempt to correct this overly naïve faith in the restorative powers of redistribution has generated its own excesses. It has sometimes been suggested that the correct relationship is exactly the reverse—that all injustices flow from failures of recognition. Solve the problem of recognition and distribution will work itself out.[2] This is no more helpful. The problem is not simply that neither dimension of social justice is easily reducible to the other; it is that they often pull in opposite directions. Nancy Fraser has argued, in my view persuasively, that principles of distribution and recognition should constitute analytically distinct dimensions of any general theory of social justice. The task that she sets is to figure out how the two can be fit together in such a way that they cease to work at cross-purposes, or at least such that conflicts between them can be resolved in a principled fashion.

In this paper, I would like to suggest a particular way of understanding the relationship between these two principles. I take as my guiding idea the view that a general theory of social justice must have at its core some conception of equality. This is because a theory of justice has as its goal some specification of what constitute fair terms of interaction, or terms that no party to the interaction could reasonably reject. Every cooperative endeavor "is marked by a conflict as well as by an identity of interests," since agents must decide how the benefits of cooperation are to be enjoyed and by whom.[3] A politics of distribution arises, according to this view, because some set of principles must be deployed in order to resolve this conflict. Since any proposed arrangement will be acceptable to all just in case the benefits

---

1 This idea was clearly aided and abetted by certain Marxian ideas about base-superstructure relations. The desire to put as much distance between themselves and Marx as possible is clearly what motivates many theorists to reject issues of redistribution entirely, and focus on questions of recognition and symbolic power. It also often leads them to assume that anyone who does raise the issue of distribution is some kind of vulgar Marxist.

2 Axel Honneth, *The Struggle for Recognition*, trans. Joel Anderson, Cambridge: Polity Press, 1995.

3 John Rawls, *A Theory of Justice*, Cambridge, MA: Belknap, 1971, p. 4.

of cooperation are distributed in a way that treats everyone equally, one might expect that equality will play a prominent role among any such set of principles. A politics of recognition is then required, I will argue, because recognition must be achieved in order to specify the demands that the principle of equality imposes in particular circumstances. Thus fair terms of interaction cannot be achieved without recognition, because appropriate standards of equality cannot be specified in the absence of particular information about the cultural traditions and social practices of the groups involved in the cooperative arrangement.

1. Problems with the politics of recognition

Before moving on to the details of this argument, I would like to expand briefly on what I take to be the motivation for Fraser's position. The most controversial claim she makes is that the "politics of recognition" constitutes an inadequate basis for a general theory of social justice. She has two reasons for making this claim, one of which is more subtle than the other. Her first claim is that certain groups exist only because of past injustice and discrimination. Under such circumstances, what these groups need is not recognition of their differences, but rather to have these differences abolished—they need to be "put out of business" as a group.[4] The second claim—the more subtle one— is that in a market economy, many social interaction patterns are "decoupled" from the cultural value system.[5] As a result, the way a particular group is represented or "valued" by the culture does not directly determine its entitlements. The upshot of the first argument is that the Left, in seeking both equality of distribution and recognition of difference, has often tried to have its cake and eat it too. The second argument suggests that the Left has often fallen prey to empty cultural criticism, deconstructing "ideologies" and symbol systems that have no functional role in the reproduction of any key economic or political systems. But whereas Fraser makes both of these suggestions in the gentlest manner possible, I am inclined to be somewhat more emphatic.

With respect to the first claim, I agree with Fraser that the politics of recognition often entrenches group differences that would be better off forgotten. Most obviously, a set of group-differentiated rights and

---

4 Nancy Fraser, in this volume, p. 22.

5 Nancy Fraser, in this volume, p. 67. Incidentally, I say "market economy" and not "capitalism" because the salient phenomenon is the decentralization of economic decision-making power, not the specific structure of ownership.

entitlements is of value only if the group being recognized wants to preserve its integrity as a group, or has some serious prospect of doing so. This is a problem, for example, with many groups defined by race or ethnicity, but which lack territorial concentration or national sovereignty. A glance at population statistics shows that, unless there is a huge backlash against interracial marriage in the next little while, the United States and Canada will evolve into post-racial societies within a few generations.[6] Already somewhere between 75 and 90 percent of the population in the United States that identifies itself as black is of mixed African and European heritage.[7] Even an attempt to *slow* this trend would require the kind of racism that most Americans no longer have the stomach for. As a result, the African-American community is only able to retain its numbers by applying the formerly racist "one-drop" rule, a practice that is making individuals of mixed ancestry increasingly uncomfortable.[8] So not only does the politics of recognition perpetuate an unhealthy level of race-consciousness, it also institutionalizes a classification system that is becoming increasingly retrograde.

Fraser's second point, which I identified as the more subtle one, deserves somewhat further elaboration. There is a marked tendency among proponents of the politics of recognition toward a form of cultural determinism. They tend to view all social practices as merely the expression of some underlying system of values or beliefs.[9] They forget that individuals do not merely act out culturally prescribed roles. Cultural values often get institutionalized in the form of social norms that impose fairly broad constraints on the range of acceptable or appropriate conduct. Not only do individuals exercise considerable discretion with respect to how they carry out these obligations, but the overall normative framework leaves open fairly extensive room for strategic action.[10] When individuals act strategically, the outcomes they get are not directly prescribed by the normative system; they are simply

---

6 See Michael Lind, *The Next American Nation*, New York: Free Press, 1995, pp. 294–8.

7 F. James Davis, *Who Is Black?*, University Park: Pennsylvania State University Press, 1991, p. 21.

8 Consider, for example, the displeasure Tiger Woods expressed when he was labeled the first "black" to win on the PGA Tour.

9 One can see this idea articulated very clearly in Charles Taylor's "Legitimation Crisis?" in his *Philosophy and the Human Sciences: Philosophical Papers*, Volume 2, Cambridge: Cambridge University Press, 1985, pp. 278–88.

10 This point has been emphasized by, among others, Pierre Bourdieu, *Outline of a Theory of Practice*, trans. Richard Nice, Cambridge: Cambridge University Press, 1977.

the aggregate outcome of a plurality of individual actors choosing their own best course of action. As a result, strategic action often generates consequences that are unplanned, and often undesired, from the standpoint of each individual actor.[11] This is especially true in markets, where individuals are given significant latitude to engage in maximizing behavior, often subject only to the requirement that they respect the property rights of others.

In a market economy, the overall pattern of wealth distribution is determined by the *factors* that individuals contribute to production and the price at which these factors trade. These prices are determined by the aggregate effects of millions of individual and corporate decisions, taken by people who have no idea, and usually no interest, in how their decisions affect others. As a result, the particular distributive share that an individual receives for a particular factor often says nothing at all about how the culture "values" that factor (a change in price may simply reflect the fact that others have stopped or started providing it). Garbage collectors make a fair bit of money, in part *because* their work is stigmatized—not many people aspire to be garbage collectors. So any attempt to "revalue" a factor, or grant increased recognition and status to its providers, will not necessarily increase the price at which it trades (and it may even have the perverse consequence of *lowering* it, since increased status may prompt more people to enter that market).

Consider how these facts relate to the problem of "pink ghettos" and the traditional devaluation of women's work. It is not because this work is not appreciated, or its value not recognized, that it is poorly paid.[12] Discrimination against women is, in most Western societies, seldom *directly* responsible for women's lower earnings. Workplace discrimination has the effect of preventing women from entering a wide range of occupations and from acquiring certain types of training. As a consequence of this exclusion, female workers are highly concentrated in particular sectors. Furthermore, primary child-care responsibilities give many women a preference for employment that they can enter and exit every few years, or that they can work part-time. This exacerbates the problem, leading to higher unemployment rates and more intense

---

11 See Joseph Heath, "Rational Choice as Critical Theory," *Philosophy and Social Criticism* 22, 1996, pp. 43–62.

12 For evidence against the "devaluation" hypothesis, see Tony Tam, "Sex Segregation and Occupational Gender Inequality in the United States: Devaluation or Specialized Training?", *American Journal of Sociology* 102: 6, 1997, pp. 1659–92.

wage competition in certain key sectors. As everyone who has nego-
tiated a salary knows, the amount of bargaining power one has is very
closely tied to how easily one can be replaced. As a result, "revaluing"
women's work may make women feel better about their jobs, but it is
not going to make them any richer unless it decreases the number of
people seeking this type of employment. Furthermore, revaluing their
work, or elevating wages to above-market rates, may have the perverse
consequence of decreasing the incentive that younger women have to
avoid these sectors and demand entry into the traditionally male
professions. (For example, the fact that nurses are badly paid has
something to do with the flood of women entering medical schools
in the past decade.)

Similarly, women's work in the home—childrearing, household
maintenance, etc.—is not "unpaid" because its value is not recognized
(although it is no doubt true that the value of these services is often
not recognized). People do not get paid to raise their own children for
the same reason that they do not get paid to repair their own fences,
or mow their own lawns. It has nothing to do with the fact that the
value of the labor is not recognized; it is because it is in the agent's
self-interest to engage in these activities. Anyone willing to raise someone *else's* children, or clean someone *else's* house, can secure payment
for these services (just as one can be paid to fix someone's else's fence,
or mow someone else's lawn). In any case, the idea that these activities
are unpaid is itself something of an illusion. In deciding whether to
care for their own children, or fix their own fences, most people do
a straightforward cost-benefit calculation, weighing the cost of hiring
someone else to do it against the inconvenience (including foregone
earnings), of doing it oneself. If a person saves $15,000 in daycare
expenses by shifting from full-time to part-time employment, that
person effectively earns $15,000 (after-tax) income during the time
that she spends at home.[13]

---

13 Taxation is a significant consideration in this regard. Most market transactions
are taxed, as are salaries. High taxation rates make it more attractive to do things
yourself, rather than hire someone else to do them. So using the tax system to achieve
distributive objectives can encourage the growth of the "unpaid" sector. (Perhaps this
is why Ikea comes from Sweden.) As to calculations concerning the transition from
full-time to part-time employment, these fall prey to the same confusion that lies
behind the commonly held view that while it costs money to rent a home, living in
one that you own is "free." The error comes from only counting money transactions
as costs, while ignoring opportunity costs. (Living in a home that you own means
foregoing the income stream from the equity.)

What these examples have in common is that in both cases there is a serious issue of injustice, but in both cases the injustice is at best indirectly connected to issues of recognition. The focus on cultural valuations tends to obscure the mechanism through which these injustices are generated. In both cases, low pay (or no pay) is associated with a low-status activity. This has led many people to think that the pay is low *because* the status is low. This is clearly false, and distracts from the real issue. Wages in pink ghettos are low not because women are discriminated against in these sectors, but because they are discriminated against in *other sectors* of the economy. This is what creates the large pool of women competing against each other for a small number of jobs (and not competing against men for other jobs—which has the effect of increasing average male earnings). In the case of housework, the problem is not that women's work is unpaid, the problem is that women are often unable to reclaim a fair portion of the surplus that their labor generates. This is usually because they have very little bargaining power in their relationships. In this case, the best way to solve the problem is for women to, in Rhona Mahoney's memorable phrase, "train up and marry down."[14] Altering the cultural valuations associated with traditional "women's work" may simply dull the incentives that young women have to adopt this strategy.

All of this invites the question, what reason do people have for thinking that misrecognition is at the heart of these various forms of social inequality? What kind of mechanism would connect these distributive effects up with a lack of recognition? Here many theorists are less than fully explicit. The most common view seems to be that misrecognition generates inequality because it undermines individual *motivation*. Some kind of causal connection of the following type is usually assumed: misrecognition and discriminatory attitudes are internalized by oppressed groups, who develop low self-esteem, low self-esteem produces decreased motivation, and decreased motivation produces lower achievement levels. This is of course an empirical claim about human psychology, but it is often treated by proponents of the politics of recognition as if it were a priori. It is remarkable, given the amount that has been written on recognition and personal identity, how seldom the question of whether a connection of this type actually obtains is addressed.

The empirical evidence for this claim is, in fact, not encouraging. For example, a number of studies in the United States have shown

---

14 Rhona Mahoney, *Kidding Ourselves*, New York: Basic Books, 1995.

that educational underachievement by African-Americans cannot be explained as the result of low self-esteem. In part, this is because numerous studies have shown that African-American students have, on average, higher self-esteem than white students, even when their level of academic achievement is lower.[15] Furthermore, African-American students are, on average, more likely to have high "expectancy of goal attainment" and are less likely to become discouraged by failure.[16] In short, there is no solid empirical evidence to support the claim that ambient discriminatory attitudes generate poor self-esteem in African-American students, or that self-esteem plays any causally efficacious role in academic achievement.

Here is an example of how the politics of recognition can distract from more obvious distributive problems. Americans have spent an enormous amount of time and money trying to increase the self-esteem of their schoolchildren, despite any evidence that this improves academic performance.[17] Meanwhile, the obvious problem with American schools is that they are funded in most states through municipal taxation—a system that allows for outrageous inequalities to arise between neighboring school districts, and which directly promotes the residential dynamic that segregates American cities into wealthy suburbs and poor ghettos. All that is needed to implement a redistributive solution is a change in the way that existing tax revenues are shared between state and local governments. It is very difficult to avoid the impression that the enormous energy spent fighting over the curriculum could have been better spent addressing simple funding issues of this type.[18]

---

15 See the helpful survey by Sandra Graham, "Motivation in African Americans," *Review of Educational Research* 64, 1994, p. 98.

16 Ibid., p. 95. Graham notes: "If anything, the data show that black research subjects remain remarkably optimistic about the future even in the wake of achievement failure. Researchers who study (or refer to) expectancy among African-Americans have not adequately grappled with this counterintuitive set of data. The preferred approach has been to either ignore the empirical findings and assume low expectancy or to focus on the dysfunctional (i.e. delusional) aspect of high expectations in the face of perceived barriers."

17 The state of California went so far as to set up a special "Task Force to Promote Self-Esteem and Personal and Social Responsibility." Some of the material presented to the task force is collected in Andrew Mecca, Neil Smelser and John Vasconcellos, *The Social Importance of Self-Esteem*, Berkeley: University of California Press, 1989. Despite the title, the papers are distinctly downbeat when it comes to the evidential connection between self-esteem and a variety of social problems, from academic underachievement to welfare dependency.

18 For a more detailed argument to this effect, see Todd Gitlin, *The Twilight of Common Dreams*, New York: Metropolitan Books, 1995.

A lot of what motivated the turn toward the politics of recognition was a general sense of dissatisfaction with the politics of redistribution. However, the limitations outlined above might invite us to look back at theories of justice that emphasize distribution, to reconsider the seriousness of the problems that generated this dissatisfaction. Does the "problem of difference" constitute a pervasive difficulty for egalitarian theories, or does it just present a set of tricky cases? If it turns out to be the latter, the question will then be whether we need to overturn the entire egalitarian-redistributive framework in order to handle these cases.

2. Welfare and resource egalitarianism

The traditional objection to the politics of distribution is that it is based on egalitarianism, and that egalitarianism is insensitive to difference. Treating people equally is often thought to mean treating them in exactly the same way (being "color-blind"). And treating everyone in the same way fails to recognize differences in individual circumstance that should be relevant to determining entitlements. So not only may egalitarianism fail to remedy injustice, this insensitivity to difference may help to perpetuate it. To use the old Marxian terminology, "formal" equality may become a mask for substantive inequality.

As has been widely noted, the extent to which this is true depends entirely upon the particular version of egalitarianism under consideration.[19] More specifically, it depends upon what the particular conception of equality under consideration takes to be the appropriate *equalisandum*. If a particular conception of equality takes as its goal the equalization of welfare (or well-being), then the charge is clearly false. Under welfare egalitarianism, each individual is entitled to whatever resources are needed to achieve his or her own goals and projects, up to a certain target level. The distributive regime, in this case, must be maximally sensitive to difference, because it must give each individual a bundle of resources that is exactly tailored to satisfy that individual's particular needs and aspirations. In this case, the individual's entitlement would be almost entirely determined by his or her particular circumstances and tastes.

This suggests that if everyone were a welfare egalitarian, there

---

19 Will Kymlicka has argued that "the colour-blind ideology has only a contingent relation to the Western liberal tradition." See *Liberalism, Community and Culture*, Oxford: Oxford University Press, 1989. The prestige of this doctrine, he argues, is to be traced back to the success of the American civil rights movement.

wouldn't really be a "problem of difference." In fact, the argument against egalitarianism formulated above tacitly appeals to welfare-egalitarian intuitions. There is nothing intrinsically wrong with failures of recognition; the problem is that such failures *harm* those whose identities are denied, because they reduce their welfare. "Egalitarianism" is being criticized, therefore, not because it is insensitive to difference, but because this insensitivity to difference makes it unable to achieve true equality. As a result, the debate over egalitarianism can more usefully be thought of as an intramural dispute among egalitarians over whether welfare is the appropriate *equalisandum*.[20] The question, then, is why many egalitarians, and in particular many proponents of the politics of redistribution, reject welfarism.

The most influential argument against welfarism in recent years comes from the work of Ronald Dworkin.[21] The centerpiece of this argument is the problem of *expensive tastes*. Dworkin points out that different individuals, given an identical bundle of resources, may achieve very different welfare levels. Sometimes this is because individuals have handicaps, or are subject to special circumstances that prevent them from achieving the same level of enjoyment as others. A person with severe food allergies, for instance, will not derive the same level of welfare from standardized food rations as someone without this condition. In such cases, welfare egalitarianism suggests the agreeable conclusion that this person should be given special and—if necessary—additional resources, in order to bring her up to the welfare level enjoyed by the others. But in other cases, this conclusion is not quite as agreeable. Often different individuals obtain different welfare levels from the same bundle of resources because their preferences differ. However, the resources needed to satisfy certain preferences may be intrinsically scarce, or very labor-intensive to produce. As a result, some individuals may have preferences that make them very inefficient at transforming resources into welfare. These people are said to have expensive tastes. The problem is that it is possible for individuals to cultivate such tastes intentionally. For example, people regularly expose themselves to fine wine and fussy cuisine in order to acquire a taste for it. Welfare egalitarianism has the counterintuitive consequences of

---

20 Amartya Sen, in *Inequality Reexamined*, Cambridge, MA: Harvard University Press, 1992, argues that a wide range of disputes in political philosophy can be usefully reconceptualized in this manner.

21 Ronald Dworkin, "What is Equality? Part 1: Equality of Welfare," *Philosophy and Public Affairs* 10, 1981, pp. 185–246; and "What is Equality? Part 2: Equality of Resources," *Philosophy and Public Affairs* 10, 1981, pp. 283–345.

suggesting that these individuals, by virtue of having acquired such tastes, should be entitled to additional resources in order to maintain their level of well-being.

What exactly is wrong with this kind of entitlement? Part of the problem, obviously, is that under a welfare-egalitarian regime, resources will be transferred away from individuals with moderate or frugal tastes in order to satisfy those who develop expensive ones. It would be question-begging, however, to say that such a redistribution is unfair, or unjust, since the definition of these terms is precisely what is at issue. For this reason, Dworkin advances two objections to this kind of compensatory arrangement, both of which avoid circularity.[22] The first is an argument from *moral hazard*, the second points to an objectionable form of *unilateralism*.

1. Moral hazard. There is an old French saying: "*l'assurance pousse au crime.*" The adage has its origins in the commonly noted fact that when, for example, landlords are able to buy fire insurance, their buildings begin to catch fire at a rate that exceeds the antecedent statistical probability. The problem is this: insurance allows a group of individuals to transform the risk of a large loss in the future into the certainty of small loss in the present (the premium). But if individuals have any control over the uncertain event that triggers the large loss, entry into the insurance scheme diminishes their incentive to ensure that the event does not occur. Because they are insured, they are able to engage in more reckless conduct, because the costs associated with this conduct are externalized, i.e. transferred to the other members of insurance scheme. Thus insurance often makes it more likely that unfortunate events will occur. This is referred to as moral hazard. (Anyone who doubts that people behave more recklessly when insured can conduct the following experiment: rent a car for a day, decline the damage insurance, and observe how carefully you drive.)

So how does this relate to welfarism? Welfare egalitarianism can be thought of as a giant insurance scheme, one that protects individuals against almost anything bad that could happen to them—or more specifically, one that insures them against unhappiness.[23] As a result,

---

22 Many commentators assume that Dworkin's view of responsibility is what does the work here. I intend to avoid this interpretation. The view that individuals should be *responsible* for expensive tastes is an example of a circular argument, since the force of the should must derive from some conception of what individuals are entitled to, which presupposes some conception of what is fair.

23 François Ewald, in *L'État Providence*, Paris: Grasset, 1986, makes the interesting claim that the private sector paved the way for the emergence of the welfare state by breaking down resistance to insurance, and pioneering new ways to control moral hazards.

it has the capacity to generate a mind-numbing range of moral hazard problems. People would lose whatever incentive they have to ensure that they get an adequate level of welfare out of their resources. They thus lose the incentive that people normally have to *not* develop expensive tastes. (As Dworkin correctly notes, this is really an efficiency problem, not a problem with the theory of justice per se.[24] If everyone exercises diminished caution in the way that they use resources, then everyone will still be equal, it is just that they will be equal at a lower level of welfare than would be obtainable without the equalization scheme. Since equality and efficiency are at least in principle distinct, this is not really a theoretical problem so much as it is an implementation problem. At the same time, it must be acknowledged that as implementation problems go, this one is especially serious.)

2. *Unilateralism.* The objection that Dworkin ultimately rests his case on is slightly different from the moral hazard one. Welfare egalitarianism generates moral hazard problems because it allows individuals to displace the costs that satisfying their preferences generates onto others. The problem for Dworkin is not the set of outcomes that allowing individuals to make this kind of choice would generate, but the very idea that they should be allowed to make such choices.[25] According to Dworkin, individuals should not, within the framework of cooperative relations, be able to unilaterally set the terms of interaction. This principle is very simple, yet it has far-reaching implications for the theory of justice.[26] By externalizing the cost of expensive preferences, agents are making decisions that impose costs upon others, without having to take these costs into consideration in their deliberations, and without having to consult those affected by their choice.

Thus the problem with welfarism, in Dworkin's view, is that it violates the idea that cooperation should be governed by terms of interaction that all could accept (or at very least, the idea that individuals should not be able to unilaterally dictate these terms). Welfare cannot generate entitlement, because individuals are able to modify their preferences and thus control the level of welfare they get out of any given bundle of resources. If they can modify their preferences, and these preferences in turn generate entitlements, it gives individuals the ability to unilaterally expand their entitlements. This allows them to modify the terms of cooperative interaction *ex post*. And certainly

24 Dworkin, "What is Equality? Part 1: Equality of Welfare," p. 235.

25 Ibid., p. 237.

26 See, for example, the theory of punishment developed by Arthur Ripstein in *Equality, Responsibility and the Law*, Cambridge: Cambridge University Press, 1998.

any individual could reasonably reject a cooperative arrangement that allowed any one person to unilaterally modify the distributive consequences of that arrangement at a later date.

These arguments suggest that the only acceptable principle of equality will be one that favors cooperative arrangements that are immune to subsequent unilateral revisions. According to Dworkin, this means that the only general principle for deciding distributive questions will be one that equalizes the distribution of *resources*, because only resources provide a basis for "tamper-proof" cooperative agreement. Under such a scheme, resources will be distributed out equally, and individuals will then "convert" them into welfare in their own time. The level of welfare they achieve will be determined by the type of preferences they have. People with expensive tastes will get less satisfaction, in general, than those with inexpensive ones. Thus resource egalitarianism has the effect of "internalizing" the costs associated with the acquisition of expensive preferences, thereby discouraging individuals from acquiring them, and preventing individuals from imposing the costs of these preferences on others.

It is important to note that this version of resource egalitarianism is still quite sensitive to individual differences. Dworkin argues that there is one particular distribution of resources that satisfies the demands of equality in being envy-free, i.e. one in which no one prefers the bundle that someone else receives to her own.[27] As a result, envy-freeness will usually be satisfied only if all individuals get a bundle of resources that is tailored to their specific needs. The kinds of differences that are not accommodated are simply those that would require a larger than average stock of resources (in terms of aggregate value) to satisfy. As a result, this type of resource egalitarianism is not obviously insensitive to difference, and where it is insensitive, there are principled reasons for believing that it should be. In order to see where the "problem of difference" arises, then, it is necessary to look a bit more closely.

---

27 See William J. Baumol, *Superfairness*, Cambridge, MA: MIT Press, 1986. Notice that Dworkin's use of an auction or a market to allocate the resources is entirely superfluous. The initial allocation of clam-shells is what generates the envy-free allocation. See "What is Equality? Part 2: Equality of Resources," p. 287. The auction just takes it to efficiency. The fact that an auction can be used in this way is a trivial consequence of the Second Fundamental Theorem of welfare economics (and as such, obtains only under the highly restrictive set of assumptions needed to prove that theorem).

3. Cultural differences

Resource egalitarianism handles the problem of expensive tastes in an intuitively correct manner, and therefore avoids one of the weak points of welfarism. However, it may be recalled that one of the key intuitions underlying welfarism was the idea that individuals are sometimes inefficient at converting resources into welfare due to circumstances entirely outside their control. Resource egalitarianism, as formulated so far, would give individuals with handicaps the resources needed to address their specific needs, but it would not give them a bundle of resources of greater aggregate value than anyone else's. This appears to be unmotivated. After all, the reason for denying individuals who are inefficient at converting resources into welfare a larger share of society's resources is that doing so would allow any individual to unilaterally alter the terms of interaction, by changing her conversion rate. A person with a handicap, however, is inefficient due to circumstances beyond his control. Allowing him a greater share of resources therefore does not pose any significant unilateralism (or moral hazard) problems.

The easiest way to correct this is to treat handicaps as a kind of "negative" resource. The envy-freeness principle will then automatically compensate individuals who suffer from them. The tricky part is to distinguish between handicaps and expensive tastes. In principle, the distinction is clear-cut. The objection to blanket compensation for all conversion inefficiencies is that, in cases where individuals exercise *control* over their rate of conversion, it gives them an objectionable form of control over the terms of interaction. It is because tastes can be *voluntarily incurred* that they present a problem for welfarism. As a result, the difference between a handicap and an expensive preference is simply the difference between a voluntarily and an involuntarily acquired conversion inefficiency.

Unfortunately, this distinction, while clear-cut in principle, is much messier in practice. It is in the gray region between the two that the problem of insensitivity to difference can arise. According to the resource-egalitarian view, any condition that lowers the welfare level that the agent can derive from an equal share of society's resources is in principle open to compensation. In order to merit compensation, however, it must be the case that this condition is involuntarily incurred. In certain cases, this is unproblematic. For instance, resource egalitarianism is clearly not inconsistent with the practice of employers offering a superior benefit package to female employees in order to accommodate childbirth. This merely reflects the fact that the reproductive physiologies of men and women differ generally making greater demands on women. Since reproductive physiology is not something that people generally choose, there is no unilateralism problem. In the same way, there are many kinds of differences that are clearly *not* candidates for compensation. For instance, an employee with a taste for extreme sports would generally not thereby be entitled to an improved medical benefits package. Given that leisure-time activities are freely chosen, there is no particular reason that other employees in the firm should be required to subsidize one person's preferences. This is the kind of difference that shouldn't make a difference. There are, however, a number of cases that seem to fall somewhere right in between. It is here that resource egalitarianism can seem hostile to difference, because it does not incorporate a presumption in favor of compensation.

Consider the case of someone who speaks a minority language. This person will be at a disadvantage in society, in a variety of different ways, and so may need a larger aggregate bundle of resources in order to achieve a welfare level comparable to that of the median majority-language speaker. But the level of voluntariness associated with this linguistic preference is very difficult to ascertain. On the one hand, people do not choose their mother tongue, and so there is clearly an element of sheer bad luck associated with learning a language that turns out not to be widely used. On the other hand, people are capable of learning new languages, so continuing to use a particular language, even though it results in systematic disadvantage, is sometimes a choice that people make. In this respect, the only bad luck seems to be that one must invest in some second-language education courses. It is unclear, therefore, how far egalitarians must go in compensating individuals who choose not to take this course of action.

Dworkin suggests that the distinction between voluntary and involuntary preferences can be determined by which preferences the agent in question *identifies* with. In the background of this view is a hierarchical conception of agency, along the lines developed by Charles Taylor. According to this model, agents have both first-order desires (preferences) and second-order desires (strong evaluations). The latter determine what kind of desires the agent wants to have. These strong evaluations are an important component of the agent's personal identity, since the kind of desires one wants to have define roughly the kind of person one wants to be. Dworkin suggests that in cases where the agent wants to have the kind of first-order desires that she has, or identifies with these preferences, they can be classified as voluntary. An agent with a genuine handicap, on the other hand, will experience it as an impediment and imposition, and so not identify with it. Dworkin claims that individuals should be compensated for conversion inefficiencies only in cases where they do not identify with them.

Using this criterion, it seems fairly obvious that linguistic preference is going to show up as voluntary. As a result, Dworkin's version of resource egalitarianism would make only minimal arrangements for linguistic minorities—they would be offered subsidized second-language education, and otherwise expected to bear any costs associated with the decision to continue using the mother tongue. The problem with this line of reasoning is that people speak a particular language not just because they can, but because they are committed to doing so. The language that one speaks is intimately connected to one's culture and values, and so is often an important component of personal identity. Furthermore, speaking a language makes one a member of an historical community, which many people feel an obligation to reproduce.[28] Thus it seems inadequate to think of patterns of language-use as expressions of mere preference.

When looked at from this point of view, it becomes clear that language use is a special case of a more general phenomenon. What makes it difficult to ascertain the level of voluntariness associated with language use is that it is not just a pattern of behavior, it is a *practice*. A practice is a pattern of behavior that is normed and often under-written by a set of shared values that agents are committed to maintaining and reproducing. As a result, individuals often experience the demands of practices in which they participate as involuntary. They do, however, identify with the preferences that the practice induces. This is because the strong evaluations are themselves reflections of the value system that underwrites the practice. Their personal identity is tied up with the cultural system that is institutionalized in the practice. It is central to reproduction of these practices that agents identify with the associated set of values. As a result, all culturally prescribed forms of behavior are likely to show up as voluntary on Dworkin's account.

Still, there is something strange about treating cultural practices as voluntary. The point of requiring agents to shoulder the costs of intentionally cultivated preferences is to prevent them from imposing costs upon others without taking these effects into account in their

---

28 Consider the case of Lucien Bouchard, the former separatist premier of Quebec. He speaks English better than most Canadians, and his wife, who is from California, speaks English to their children at home. It clearly would be much *easier* for him just to speak English with his family. The only explanation for his decision to use the French language is that he feels an obligation to maintain the continuity and integrity of Québecois culture.

deliberations. Individuals are not capable of conducting such deliberations until they have been fully socialized into some culture or other. As a result, holding individuals responsible for the preferences that this socialization process induces seems to have little justification. Furthermore, the intimate connection between culture and personal identity makes the level of voluntariness associated with different practices very difficult to ascertain. Values and role-expectations that are internalized through socialization become important building blocks in the development of personal identity, and so are often difficult to revise. Even if cultural patterns have a strong conventional element to them, this does not mean that individuals can change them overnight.

On the other hand, just standing back and treating all culturally entrenched practices as involuntarily is not a live option. First of all, it fails to recognize the fact that, over time, cultures can be extremely dynamic and adaptive. The fact that individuals may be strongly committed to particular ways of doing things does not mean that they will raise their children in the same way. Fully compensating individuals for cultural patterns that have become dysfunctional takes away this incentive, and so can lead to arrested cultural development. At the level of principle, however, the most significant problem is that compensating individuals for welfare losses that stem from culturally induced preferences allows one cultural group to unilaterally set the terms of interaction. There is something wrong with the idea that one group could be automatically entitled to compensation for its practices where providing such compensation would impose significant burdens on the rest of the community. If no individual member of a community should be able to dictate the terms of interaction, then no subset of that community should be able to do so either. Cooperation requires consultation of *all* parties.

Thus the problem of group differences presents something of a dilemma for egalitarians. With respect to practices, the salient distinction seems not to be between voluntary and involuntary preferences, but between essential practices—practices that are constitutive of personal or group identity—and inessential ones. Some practices can be abandoned without groups or individuals feeling significant dislocation or loss of self, others cannot. Determining fair terms of interaction will require finding an accommodation under which no group's essential practices result in serious, uncompensated welfare losses.

In everyday politics, the problem of group differences can often be put off by having people with significantly different practices form their own political communities. The doctrine of national sovereignty specifies, in effect, that the "terms of interaction" for a particular political community can be specified without consulting anyone outside its own membership. Within such political communities, less significant differences in practices can be accommodated through some kind of federalism, or the devolution of powers to subordinate political units. Finally, simple freedom of association at an individual level allows people to form whatever groups or associations that they like. This allows individuals to interact preferentially with those who share their particular values and habits.

These three types of liberty—national self-determination, regional autonomy, and freedom of association—have been enormously success-ful at managing the problem of specifying fair terms of interaction among individuals with different practices. The problems arise when, for one reason or another, this kind of institutional pluralism is not possible, and where an organization (the state, a corporation, etc.) needs to institutionalize one set of practices as authoritative.[29] Whenever there is a need for a uniform legal code, a shared language, a public education system, etc., a structural conflict between the prac-tices of different groups can arise. The conflict is most obvious in the situation of multinational states like Canada. In these cases, incom-patibility between practices can generate disadvantages, by virtue of the fact that institutions need to enforce just one. Since there is no reason why, in principle, one group's practices should be adopted over another's, whichever group is the loser has reasonable grounds for complaint.

This is the kind of situation in which negotiating group differences becomes important. As Jürgen Habermas correctly notes, the problem of difference does not primarily concern "the pluralism of conflicting life ideas and value orientations, of competing comprehensive doctrines." The problem involves reconciling "the harder material of institutions and action systems."[30] In the terms of the present discussion, the trick is to designate one set of procedures as authoritative, then compensate those whose essential practices put them at a disadvantage under this regime. The exact demands that that norm of equality imposes in this context will therefore be largely determined the kinds of practices that get counted as essential.

---

29 This is the point emphasized by Ernst Gellner, *Nations and Nationalism*, Oxford: Blackwell, 1983.

30 Jürgen Habermas, *Between Facts and Norms*, trans. William Rehg, Cambridge, MA: MIT Press, 1996, p. 64.

4. The politics of recognition

The problem of distinguishing essential from non-essential practices is in many ways similar to that of distinguishing voluntary from involuntary preferences. In both cases, a relatively clear conceptual distinction becomes quite murky when applied in practice. (In this context, it is worth noting that any compensation scheme for handicaps creates an incentive structure that makes it advantageous for agents to represent all conversion inefficiencies as involuntary. Similarly, an egalitarian scheme that compensates groups for engaging in practices that disadvantage them, when these practices form an integral part of their personal identity, can have the perverse consequence of encouraging the sort of fundamentalism that treats every minute detail of every practice as a matter of paramount significance for the continuity of the relevant community. In both cases, these incentive problems could make the distinction useless, for all practical purposes.)

The solution that Dworkin proposes to this problem is instructive. Recognizing that it will be difficult to tell when an agent truly identifies with her preferences, he develops a *revelation mechanism*, designed to induce agents to *report* which preferences each believes herself to be in control of. Roughly speaking, a revelation mechanism is an institutional structure that induces agents to self-select into groups according to private information that they hold. The advantage of such a mechanism is that it relieves the theorist of the need to specify how a particular distinction is to be drawn with respect to a given population. Instead, it provides a mechanism through which members of that political community can draw it for themselves.

I would like to make a similar proposal with respect to practices. The politics of recognition, I will argue, can be thought of as a revelation mechanism, one which allows members of a political community to determine which of the practices that its members participate in should be regarded as essential, from the standpoint of distributive justice. In order to see how this works, it is helpful to examine Dworkin's proposal in somewhat greater detail.

For his purposes, what Dworkin needs is a mechanism that will induce agents with handicaps to step forward and identify themselves as such, *without* inducing individuals with expensive preferences to claim handicaps. One way of doing this is through an insurance market. If individuals are able to take preventative action to eliminate the risk of a loss, then it generally will not be in their interest to purchase insurance against that loss (or if it is, they will not be willing to purchase it at the same premium level as those who have no control over the risk). Thus insurance markets often function as a revelation mechanism—they induce behavior in individuals that reveals the extent to which they believe that they have control over future events. As a result, the only type of conversion inefficiencies against which agents will purchase insurance are those whose incidence they consider to be genuinely outside of their control.

It should be clear from the previous discussion that this particular revelation mechanism will be of no help in resolving problems of group difference. The most general flaw in this proposal is that individuals often acquire preferences and handicaps before they are in a position to purchase insurance. Dworkin therefore suggests that compensation levels should be determined by the outcome of a "hypothetical insurance market," which would be a kind of thought-experiment that members of the society would run. This clearly creates problems for mediating group practices. Individuals would only be in a position to make such judgments after they are fully socialized, and so all compensation arrangements for cultural groups would need to be determined by speculation about which choices would be made under hypothetical conditions. More importantly, the idea of an insurance market only makes sense if individuals can "stand back" from their particular preferences and evaluate them. But when these preferences are dictated by a certain set of values, "standing back" would require that individuals evaluate their second-order desires, or strong evaluations. This is incoherent, since there is nothing "beyond" or "outside" culture that could be used to evaluate these values.[31]

This problem does, however, suggest a direction for determining the kind of revelation mechanism that would be required. In order to draw a distinction between essential and non-essential practices, individuals must adopt a reflective stance toward their own culture and identity. Since they cannot adopt a stance outside of culture to effect this evaluation, the only option is for them to examine their own practices from the standpoint of other cultural possibilities. It is only by situating their own practices and identities within what Taylor calls a "shared horizon of significance," that individuals can gain an appreciation of what is important in their own system of values. But the mechanism through which this kind of self-consciousness is achieved at the same time allows different groups to achieve appreciation of one another's values. As a result, the attempt to articulate a set of goods, and situate them in a shared discursive space, functions

---

31 Dworkin is aware of this; see "What is Equality? Part 2: Equality of Resources," p. 298.

as a revelation mechanism. Individuals come to see what is important in their system of values by helping others who do not share these values to see why they are so important.

When it comes to matters of social practice, no external incentive mechanism can be designed that will induce agents to directly reveal the seriousness of their value-commitments. Whether a particular practice is really essential to a particular group can only be determined if members of that group can articulate the commitments that underlie that practice and communicate their significance to others. (This need not occur just through argument, but may involve literature, art, music and so on.) Individuals must achieve a "fusion of horizons." This does not mean that, at the end of the day, they will all share some conception of the good. But it does mean that they will be able to see how the full range of goods matter to those who regard them as the most serious. And understanding the way that these goods are articulated through the relevant practices provides the foundation for an agreement on the relative *significance* of these practices.

An example may help to illustrate this mechanism at work. A number of very high-profile public disputes in Canada have been sparked by Sikh religious observances. Sikhs have sought modifications to a variety of official uniforms, so that they no longer conflict with the wearing of a turban.[32] In some cases, this has required modification of significant national symbols, such as the Royal Canadian Mounted Police uniform. In all such cases, a process of dialogue helped non-Sikh Canadians to appreciate the reasons for these changes. The fact that wearing a turban is an important religious obligation for Sikh men, and not a mere sartorial preference, was sufficient to overcome most resistance. On the other hand, a number of controversies involving the wearing of ceremonial daggers have gone the other way. In these cases, a similar process of dialogue made it clear that the practice enjoyed only lukewarm support in the Sikh community, and that many of the more controversial incidents were fundamentalist provocations. (In other cases, the practice was modified—the fully functional seven-inch dagger was replaced by a smaller, more symbolic version.) The important point is that it was only by learning something about the Sikh religion, and the rationale for these practices, that members of the broader community were able to start thinking about what would constitute reasonable forms of accommodation.

---

32 For general discussion, see Will Kymlicka, *Finding Our Way*, Toronto: Oxford University Press, 1998, p. 45.

This example also illustrates another fact about the politics of recognition. In order to achieve a genuine fusion of interpretive horizons, each party must put its own ideas and opinions "at risk." As Taylor puts it:

> It will almost always be the case that the adequate language in which we can understand another society is not our language of understanding, or theirs, but rather what one could call a language of perspicuous contrast. This would be a language in which we could formulate both their way of life and ours as alternative possibilities in relation to some human constants at work in both. It would be a language in which the possible human variations would be so formulated that both our form of life and theirs could be perspicuously described as alternative such variations. Such a language of contrast might show their language of understanding to be distorted or inadequate in some respects, or it might show ours to be so (in which case, we might find that understanding them leads to an alteration of our self-understanding, and hence our form of life—a far from unknown process in history); or it might show both to be so.[33]

As a result, grounding redistributive policies in a politics of recognition allows egalitarians to make special accommodations for particular groups, without at the same time allowing that group to unilaterally set the terms of interaction. This is because the mutual recognition that is achieved through a fusion of interpretive horizons is one that incorporates at least a potential for movement on all sides. Any group making a claim for recognition must be willing to give up that claim, if they come to see that it is unwarranted, or that it imposes unreasonable burdens on others. Too often, models of recognition are presented that treat recognition as a one-way street: one group makes a claim, after which it becomes incumbent upon others to recognize it. This leads to an objectionable form of unilateralism. Taylor makes it clear that any group may have to abandon its claims, if these prove to be unwarranted within the "language of perspicuous contrast." (This does not necessarily mean that the associated practices must be abandoned, but it does mean that the group will have to shoulder whatever costs the practice generates.)

---

33 Charles Taylor, "Understanding and Ethnocentricity," in his *Philosophy and the Human Sciences: Philosophical Papers*, Volume 2, Cambridge: Cambridge University Press, 1985, pp. 125–6.

What the politics of recognition allows a society to do is carve out some space between offering blanket respect to an entire value system and treating everything that people do as a matter of individual preference. The former would allow groups to show unreasonable disregard for the interests of others, while the latter fails to take seriously the obligations that group affiliations often impose upon individuals. The politics of recognition brings to light areas of shared concern, values that determine how individuals choose to live their lives. Within the context of a pluralist society, one cannot demand that individuals come to *share* these values and concerns. The most one can demand is that they develop some appreciation of how those values animate the practices of others. Once this is done, it becomes possible to specify the demands that the norm of equality imposes. It becomes possible to specify terms of interaction that allow individuals to integrate into a common set of institutions while offsetting any disadvantages that the particular character of these institutions may generate.

In the theory of justice outlined here, the politics of recognition plays a role that is complementary to the politics of redistribution. The primary concern of the theory of social justice is to specify terms of interaction that treat individuals equally. In a pluralistic society, in which individuals disagree over questions of the good life, and under conditions of personal autonomy, in which individuals are free to pursue whatever goals and projects they like, the only form of equality that can provide terms of interaction that are generally acceptable is one that equalizes the distribution of resources. Resource egalitarianism, however, must make a "cut" between preferences for which the individual will be held responsible, and those for which society in general is liable. The politics of recognition provides the mechanism through which this "cut" can be drawn in situations where the preferences in question are ones that individuals endorse due to aspects of their socialization or group membership.

III. BRINGING THE POLITICAL BACK IN:
A THIRD DIMENSION OF JUSTICE?

STATUS INJUSTICE:
THE ROLE OF THE STATE
Leonard Feldman

By reinterpreting and transcending some of the recurrent divisions between "the old Left" and "the new Left," between defenders of a politics of class and proponents of a politics of identity, and between theorists operating in a Marxian tradition and theorists developing the concepts of poststructuralism, Nancy Fraser's recent work on redistribution and recognition has yielded new insights and sparked new debates on the nature of justice. Fraser's work has examined the conditions under which claims for recognition of an identity interfere with claims for economic redistribution, and it has demonstrated surprising affinities as well—such as the resonances between socialist forms of redistribution and deconstructive forms of recognition.

There are three lines of thought in Nancy Fraser's recent work on the politics of redistribution and recognition that I would like to bring together and extend. The first concerns decisions about recognition strategies. Should a stigmatized group seek recognition of a distinctive group identity or minimize difference via an appeal to inclusion in universal categories? Should the very binary opposition between a privileged identity and a demonized other be deconstructed? While Fraser's initial account of redistribution and recognition endorses a "deconstructive" politics of recognition over its deficient alternatives, in later accounts she argues that different recognition strategies are required in different contexts and that what is needed is "a pragmatism informed by the insights of social theory."[1] To make a stab at some of these theoretically informed pragmatic judgments, I turn to two other lines of thought: I turn to Fraser's claim that the concept of

---

1 Nancy Fraser, "Recognition Without Ethics?" *Theory, Culture and Society* 18: 2–3, 2001, p. 30.

status gives us a better handle on contemporary justice struggles than the category of *identity* and I discuss the (only partially developed) idea that political exclusion may constitute an independent dynamic of injustice.

In developing these three strands of thought, I examine what it means in a liberal political community to have a *political status*. I argue that, paradoxically, affirmative state recognition of a supposedly prepolitical "social" or "personal" status can work to produce a subordinate political status: what looks like a form of recognition results in a form of political exclusion. As a result, I argue that pragmatic judgments concerning recognition strategies need to be informed not only by social theory, but also by *a critical theory of the state*. I explore these dynamics of political and legal status creation through two case studies: homeless criminalization and the military's policy on sexual orientation. Critical investigation of the liberal state's role in constituting hierarchical relations of identity/difference, and the tendency for such state production of status to become disguised as the recognition of an already existing social difference lead me to conclude that a *deconstructive* politics of recognition is key to confronting status-based injustice.

Different strategies: Evaluating the politics of recognition

In initial analyses of the politics of recognition, Fraser describes a tension between certain forms of cultural politics aimed at recognition and certain forms of economic politics aimed at redistribution. Fraser says, "in my diagnosis . . . the split in the Left is not between class struggles, on the one hand, and gender, 'race,' and sex struggles, on the other. Rather, it cuts across those movements, each of which is internally divided between cultural currents and social currents."[2] Collectivities such as those formed on the basis of gender and race classification and oppression face both economic injustice and cultural injustice. These "bivalent collectivities" find themselves in a bind: the attempt to combat misrecognition by, for instance, revaluing femininity, comes into conflict with the attempt to eliminate economic injustice by, for instance, eliminating the gendered division of labor. For bivalent collectivities, cultural politics often interfere with progressive economic restructuring. For instance, an affirmative politics of identity that celebrates and revalues a previously stigmatized identity, what Fraser terms mainstream

---

2 In this volume, p.108.

multiculturalism, undercuts transformative efforts at economic redistribution, which tend to eliminate the structured position of a group within the division of labor. Such forms of cultural politics as cultural feminism's revaluing of the feminine, a celebration of black pride, and the construction of a gay identity on the ethnic group model of American pluralism do not combine well with a "social politics of equality."[3]

The redistribution-recognition dilemma can be "finessed," however. Not all forms of cultural recognition impede progressive efforts to restructure economic relations. Fraser ends up endorsing the twin projects of economic socialism and cultural deconstruction over their deficient counterparts: the liberal welfare state and mainstream multiculturalism. A "transformative" politics of economic redistribution (socialism) and a transformative politics of cultural recognition (deconstruction) both engage the deep structures of injustice, avoid reinforcing the flows of resentment, and undermine group differentiation by transforming exploitative relations of production and deconstructing the hierarchical binary oppositions that sustain practices of cultural misrecognition. In so doing, these transformative politics promote "participatory parity" in society. Thus, a queer politics that destabilizes the hetero/homo binary opposition by, for example, bringing to light the homoerotic undercurrents of mainstream society would fit well with a socialist politics aimed at transforming control over production: rather than seeking simply to reallocate goods or esteem within a given (economic or cultural) order, such politics engage an underlying structure (of distribution or signification).

In more recent work, however, Fraser complicates her account of recognition politics. Fraser provides an analytical diversification of the recognition framework, and softens her stance towards non-deconstructive forms of cultural politics. The earlier versions appeared predominantly critical of an affirmative politics of recognition, as interfering with transformative economic justice and generating perverse feedback loops of resentment when combined with liberal welfare state programs targeting disadvantaged groups. But in the *Tanner Lectures on Human Values*, Fraser argues that different recognition strategies are needed at different times and in different contexts, and judgments about the appropriateness of a deconstructive approach to cultural injustice or a multiculturalist approach cannot be made theoretically, and a priori:

---

3 In this volume, p. 12.

> In some cases [misrecognized groups] may need to be unburdened
> of excessive ascribed or constructed distinctiveness. In other cases,
> they may need to have hitherto underacknowledged distinctive-
> ness taken into account. In still other cases, they may need to
> shift the focus onto dominant or advantaged groups, outing the
> latter's distinctiveness, which has been falsely parading as
> universality. Alternatively, they may need to deconstruct the very
> terms in which the attributed differences are currently elaborated.
> Finally, they may need all of the above, or several of the above
> . . . and in combination with redistribution.[4]

Thus, while at the end of the essay Fraser appears to advocate one
particular redistribution/recognition combination above others ("The
need . . . is to think integratively—by seeking out transformative
approaches to redistribution and deconstructive approaches to recognition"[5]), here Fraser pluralizes the possibilities of justice struggles.
In a subsequent essay, "Recognition Without Ethics," Fraser again
emphasizes that different recognition strategies are needed depending
on the form of injustice encountered, and that conflicting approaches
to remedying misrecognition are, at least "in principle" equally justice-
promoting—having the potential to promote "participatory parity" in
society. For instance, on the issue of whether the subordination of
gays and lesbians should be challenged by promoting legal recognition
of gay marriages or by decoupling benefits from heterosexual marriage
and attaching them to the individual, Fraser says, "Although there may
be good reasons for preferring one of these approaches to the other,
both of them would serve to foster participatory parity between gays
and straights; hence, both are justified in principle."[6]

The status versus identity model of recognition

One of the most compelling dimensions of Fraser's recent revisions
of the redistribution/recognition theory is the reconceptualization of
misrecognition in terms of *status subordination* as opposed to *identity
stigmatization*. Fraser argues that an identity-centered approach to the
politics of recognition displaces attention from social institutions and
towards the internalization of cultural stigmas within the psyche of

---

4 Fraser, "Social Justice in the Age of Identity Politics: Redistribution, Recognition,
and Participation," *Tanner Lectures on Human Values*, Volume 19, Salt Lake City:
University of Utah Press, 1997, p. 35.

5 Ibid., p. 67.

6 Fraser, "Recognition Without Ethics?" p. 34.

the damaged subject. Furthermore, an identity-based politics tends to assume a homogeneous group identity, promoting a separatist politics of withdrawal from mainstream society and ignoring complexity and power struggles within the cultural group. Therefore, rather than understand the politics of recognition in terms of identity, stigma and self-esteem, Fraser asserts that we ought

> to treat recognition as a question of *social status* . . . [W]hat requires recognition is not group-specific identity but rather the status of group members as full partners in social interaction. Misrecognition, accordingly, does not mean the depreciation and deformation of group identity. Rather, it means *social subordination* in the sense of being prevented from *participating as a peer* in social life.[7]

The status model, in other words, re-embeds the patterns of meaning that produce stigma in social institutions and social relations: "from this perspective, misrecognition is neither a psychic deformation nor a free-standing cultural harm but an institutionalized relation of social subordination."[8]

Because this status approach to understanding injustices of misrecognition emphasizes the role of institutionalized meanings, it directs attention to state institutions. For instance, the legal restriction of marriage to heterosexuals constitutes a state-sponsored form of status subordination, "the institutionalization in law of a heterosexist pattern of cultural value that constitutes heterosexuals as normal and homosexuals as perverse."[9] Status subordination is frequently accomplished through state law and policy: "In some cases, misrecognition is juridified, expressly codified in formal law; in other cases, it is institutionalized via government policies, administrative codes or professional practice."[10]

However, the specific modalities of state-constitution of status are occluded in Fraser's status model. Rather than develop an account of *political* status, Fraser returns to the language of civil society and the "social": "the status model situates the problem of recognition within a larger social frame. From this perspective, societies appear as complex

---

7 Ibid., p. 24.
8 In this volume, p. 135.
9 Ibid., p. 136.
10 Ibid., p. 135.

fields that can encompass not only cultural forms of social ordering but economic forms of ordering as well."[11] "Status" thus appears in Fraser's argument as a broad term that might signify something like "standing in society." Status is to be distinguished from class insofar as one's status is constituted by institutionalized patterns of meaning and value. Status is not reducible to economics. The two categories implicate two analytically separable dimensions of justice:

> The recognition dimension corresponds to the status order of society, hence to the constitution, by socially entrenched patterns of cultural value, of culturally defined categories of social actors —status groups . . . The distributive dimension, in contrast, corresponds to the economic structure of society, hence to the constitution, by property regimes and labor markets, of economically defined categories of actors, or classes.[12]

In this conceptualization, "formal law . . . government policies, administrative codes, or professional practice" are interchangeable locations for the production of social statuses.

Political exclusion

In "Rethinking Recognition," Fraser points toward a specifically political form of injustice. In a footnote, Fraser writes that maldistribution and misrecognition may not exhaust the dimensions of social justice comprehended by her framework:

> I have in mind specifically a possible third class of obstacles to participatory parity that could be called political as opposed to economic or cultural. Such obstacles would include decision-making procedures that systematically marginalize some people even in the absence of maldistribution and misrecognition [and] might be called political marginalization or exclusion.[13]

Fraser leaves this dynamic of injustice undeveloped.[14] In the next section I bring together the idea of a specifically political form of injustice

---

11 In this volume, p. 138.

12 Ibid., p. 137–138.

13 Ibid., p. 137–138, note 1.

14 "I do not develop this possibility here, however, but confine myself to maldistribution and misrecognition, while leaving the analysis of political obstacles to participatory parity for another occasion." (Ibid., p. 138, note 1)

with the concept of status subordination by examining what it means to have a political status in a liberal political community.

Political status and the liberal state

Fraser's brief discussion of political exclusion as an independent dynamic of injustice points obliquely to an older sense of "status": the legal standing of a person in the political community by virtue of his or her membership in a particular state-defined class of persons. One of the ways in which the *Oxford English Dictionary* defines status is "a person's standing or position such as determines his or her legal rights or limitations, as citizen, alien, commoner, etc.; condition in respect of marriage or celibacy, minority or majority."[15]

In Greek or Roman law, status was something possessed only by full citizens. Citizenship, in the civic republican tradition, is a status. Hannah Arendt describes legal status as a kind of protective artifice of citizenship:

> The distinction between a private individual in Rome and a Roman citizen was that the latter had a *persona*, a legal personality, as we would say; it was as though the law had affixed to him the part he was expected to play on the public scene, with the provision, however, that his own voice would be able to sound through . . . Without his *persona*, there would be an individual without rights and duties, perhaps a "natural man"—that is, a human being or *homo* in the original meaning of the word, indicating someone outside the range of the law and the body politic of the citizens, as for instance a slave—but certainly a politically irrelevant being.[16]

And in medieval England, "legal statuses served as the formal basis for each person's legal powers and obligations."[17] Liberalism, so the story goes, transforms membership and obligation "from status to contract" and liberates individuals from the confines of state-defined status categories.[18] The "classic liberal rejection of state involvement

---

15 *Shorter Oxford English Dictionary*, New York: Oxford University Press, 2007.

16 Hannah Arendt, *On Revolution*, New York: Penguin, 1990, p. 107.

17 Judith Failer, *Who Qualifies for Rights?*, Ithaca: Cornell University Press, 2002, p. 59.

18 "We may say that the movement of progressive societies has hitherto been a movement *from Status to Contract*." Henry Sumner Maine, *Ancient Law: Its Connection with the Early History of Society and Its Relation to Modern Ideas*, New York: Henry Holt, 1906, p. 165.

in the management of statuses"[19] produces a vision of political order as constituted by contracting individuals to secure *natural* rights that human beings have by virtue of birth, not as a result of their status as citizens.[20]

As contracts come to mediate human relationships, the contracting individual has no legal status; people now only have a status if they differ from the invisible norm of full citizenship, because of some incapacity.[21] Liberalism, in other words, marks the end of political statuses like lord and serf that are legally ascribed and define one's specific rights and obligations. As persons are freed from ascriptive political categories, states turn to the regulation of (freely chosen, harmful) conduct, not status. The normal citizen may have a social status, but, in contrast to the republican tradition, politically, the normal citizen is *freed from legal status.*

Thus it is liberalism that makes it possible to think of status as something social or cultural but not political. The idea that people are *politically* free and equal, but *socially* differentiated and hierarchically ordered is a consequence of liberalism's fundamental distinction between state and civil society, a distinction analyzed famously by Karl Marx. As Marx argues in "On the Jewish Question," the liberal state emancipates itself from those status categories that had, in the feudal era, mediated people's political relations. Class, religion, property, and so on, become "nonpolitical" distinctions. In other words, they become a matter of social status, not political status. Marx showed how the privatization of status as a matter of civil society, not the state, tended to naturalize those practices of differentiation by depoliticizing them and furthermore how the abstract universalism of the state and formal citizenship were constituted in opposition to those privatized elements.[22]

However, the liberal state is not completely free from the production

---

19 Janet E. Halley, *Don't: A Reader's Guide to the Military's Anti-Gay Policy*, Durham: Duke University Press, 1999, p. 29.

20 Giorgio Agamben writes that rights "are attributed to man (or originate in him) solely to the extent that man is the immediately vanishing ground (who must never come to light as such) of the citizen." *Homo Sacer: Sovereign Power and Bare Life*, Stanford: Stanford University Press, 1998, p. 128.

21 See Failer, *Who Qualifies for Rights?*, pp. 57–63, for an extended discussion of this transformation.

22 Marx writes that the "state permits private property, education, and occupation to *act* and manifest their *particular* nature as private property, education, and occupation in their *own* ways. Far from overcoming these *factual* distinctions, the state exists only be presupposing them; it is aware of itself as a *political state* and makes its *universality* effective only in opposition to these elements." Marx, "On the Jewish Question," in Karl Marx, *Selected Writings*, ed. Lawrence H. Simon, Indianapolis: Hackett, 1994, p. 8.

of political status, rhetorics of contracts and the natural rights of human beings notwithstanding. "Husband" and "wife" are political statuses.[23] And so too are "felon" and "child." These categories are partially state-defined, and they define, in Judith Failer's words, a particular set of rights, obligations and capacities. Indeed, most political statuses in the liberal state are on the order of felon and child: they indicate a restricted or protected category of persons that deviates from and is subordinate to the full citizenship enjoyed by the normal individual. As a result, Failer writes, "Anglo-American jurisprudence reserves the term for individuals who *differ from* the legal norm."[24] So, if the liberal state has not *fully* divested itself of the business of constituting political statuses, it has, at the same time, done two peculiar things: first, in the liberal state, a legal status is something one has when one *deviates* from the norm of full citizenship. Full membership in the political community is not considered a status at all; it is an unmarked norm. To have a political status is to be marked out as different from this norm.

Second, it is not just the unmarked norm of full citizenship that is hard to perceive—those subordinate political statuses are also difficult to perceive *as political* because legal and policy discourses in the liberal state treat them as social differences "out there" which the state simply re-cognizes. If the state grants children an expanded set of entitlements (state funded education, for instance) but a restricted set of rights (no right to vote), it does so because it recognizes certain relevant facts about children that require a subordinate political status. And when the state restricts the voting rights of convicted felons, even after their release from prison, presumably it is doing so on the basis of certain social facts about convicted felons. However, as Failer points out, felons "are not necessarily different from non-felons by nature." Rather than simply re-cognizing a set of social facts within the law, then, legal status *actively constructs difference*: "Because it is something the law adds or creates, legal status is essentially a legal creation."[25]

We can get a better handle on this maneuver via a distinction made by Patchen Markell between the "cognitive" and "constructive" senses

---

23 As Jacqueline Stevens writes, "Marx incorrectly defines the fully developed, liberal state as one that has eliminated all political status relations. The modern state has eliminated the 'villain,' 'knight,' 'lord,' 'serf,' and 'peon,' but one juridical status relation remains: that of the 'husband' married to his 'wife.' " Stevens, *Reproducing the State*, Princeton: Princeton University Press, 1999, p. 214.

24 Judith Failer, "Homelessness in the Criminal Law," in *From Social Justice to Criminal Justice*, ed. William C. Heffernan and John Kleinig, New York: Oxford University Press, 2000, p. 249.

25 Failer, "Homelessness in the Criminal Law," p. 250.

of recognition. Recognition is understood as *cognitive* in the sense that a person be respected based on a true knowledge of that person or group's identity or situation. (In this sense, mis-recognition is a kind of mistake, a failure to see the "real me.") But recognition also has a *constructive* dimension, and Markell gives the example of the chair of a meeting recognizing a speaker: "When the chairperson . . . recognizes a speaker . . . she is not acknowledging a status that already really exists; instead, the privilege of speaking is itself a product of the chairperson's institutionally authorized act of recognition."[26] In this example recognition is not cognitive but performative: the act of recognition produces the status itself. Markell points to a dynamic in recognition politics whereby constructive practices appear to be cognitive: "the act of recognition *does* construct identity, but it does so precisely by seeming only to cognize what it constructs; it is a performative whose conditions of felicity include that it seem only to be a constative."[27]

Nowhere is this "self-obscuring" aspect of recognition more clear, I argue, than in the state's approach to status. The state *appears* to be simply re-cognizing a relevant difference between persons "out there" in society, but in so doing, it is *actively constructing* the terms and terrain of status differentiation. State recognition of a social status is thus a performative act masquerading as a constative act. In other words, the liberal state does not produce status in a simple way: rather it constitutes political distinctions between full members and subordinate members, with full members becoming an unmarked norm, and then eliminates the evidence of its own constituting power, treating its production as, rather, a re-cognition of a social or personal difference. The liberal state obscures its own difference-making practices, obscures its own power to produce (subordinate) political statuses. State practices of recognition are an example of what Markell describes as an element of misrecognition central to the politics of recognition more generally: "the pursuit of recognition comes to be bound up with a certain sort of *misrecognition*—not the misrecognition *of identity* . . . but an even more fundamental *ontological* misrecognition, a failure to acknowledge the nature and circumstances of our own activity."[28] When "the state fade[s] into the background," as Markell

---

26 Patchen Markell, "The Recognition of Politics: A Comment on Emcke and Tully," *Constellations* 7, 2000, p. 496.

27 Markell, "Recognition of Politics," p. 503.

28 Patchen Markell, *Bound by Recognition*, Princeton: Princeton University Press, 2003, p. 59.

puts it, the state's identity and difference-making practices appear as the cognition of prepolitical social statuses.[29] Markell contends that this misapprehension of construction-as-cognition marks the politics of recognition as such; I wish to suggest (in part drawing on Markell's own analysis) that the tension between cognition and construction is particularly acute in the context of the modern liberal state.

Clarissa Hayward illustrates the self-obscuring role of state recognition practices in her analysis of racialized political boundaries in American cities. Hayward writes, "calls for state recognition of social difference are . . . reactive; they imply that the challenge for the democratic state is to respond to those differences it innocently happens upon." The paradigm of state recognition of a pre-existing social difference "deflects attention from the political processes through which identity\difference categories are defined, institutionalized, and ordered."[30] Liberalism's distinction between state and society, and the insistence that the state be neutral, universal and freed from the business of status regulation, means that the status-constructing power of the state becomes a problem, contradicting its commitment to universality and obscured through a rhetoric of cognition and the social.

The complexity of the state's role in status politics produces dilemmas for justice struggles. On the one hand, when the state recognizes a social difference, it may grant certain rights, exemptions or privileges in the process. On the other hand, when the state recognizes a difference, it also marks out a group from the norm of full citizenship. It may sound as though I am treading over very familiar ground: the "equality/difference" debate. The issues I am exploring are indeed connected to the long-standing issues of whether or not an oppressed social group should seek recognition of its own distinctiveness (difference) or assimilation to dominant norms (equality). However, the equality/difference debates tend to treat all venues, institutions and practices as equivalently structured by dilemmas of assimilation and difference. What I am suggesting is that dilemmas of inclusion and recognition are sometimes structured by *the specific dynamic of the state's self-concealing production of status*.

This self-concealing production of political status can be seen in two areas of law and policy: the rights of the homeless in the context of punitive public space laws, and the rights of gays and lesbians in

---

29 Ibid., p. 26.

30 Clarissa Rile Hayward, "The Difference States Make: Democracy, Identity, and the American City," *American Political Science Review* 97: 4, November 2003, p. 506.

the context of the military's 1993 revised policy on homosexuality. In both cases, I argue, government discourses treat status (sexual orientation, homelessness) as a social or personal characteristic, granting apparent recognition of that status while simultaneously criminalizing conduct linked to that status and producing a subordinate political status.[31] In both cases, a certain kind of supposedly personal or social status is granted legal recognition, while in so doing the state manages to produce very different statuses via the criminalization of conduct: when homosexual orientation as personal identity is recognized by Department of Defense policy, the state affirms heterosexuality as the fragile, protected norm of the military's public culture, and produces in a disguised way a completely contained, closeted, privatized homosexuality as a "recognized difference." And when cities turn to punitive policies criminalizing public sleeping, sidewalk sitting and panhandling, claiming to avoid the pitfalls of status-based vagrancy law, they end up affirming a vision of the normal citizen as home-dwelling consumer and producing in a disguised way the status of homeless outlaw.

"Homosexual conduct" and the military

The military policy on sexual orientation, implemented in 1993, proclaims that "homosexual orientation" is not itself a barrier to military service. The first version of the Clinton-era policy read as follows:

> Sexual orientation will not be a bar to service unless manifested by homosexual conduct. The military will discharge members who engage in homosexual conduct, which is defined as a homosexual act, a statement that the member is homosexual or bisexual, or a marriage or attempted marriage to someone of the same gender.[32]

While the old military policy made *being* homosexual itself grounds for discharge, the newer policy proclaims a focus on conduct, not

---

31 It must be acknowledged that the case of the military policy is really a case of a subordinate political status being constituted within an already subordinate political status. As Judith Butler writes, "The military is already a zone of partial citizenship, a domain in which selected features of citizenship are preserved, and others are suspended." Butler, *Excitable Speech: A Politics of the Performative*, New York: Routledge, 1997, p. 103.

32 "The Pentagon's New Policy Guidelines on Homosexuals in the Military," *New York Times*, July 20, 1993, p. A16.

status. The policy appears to recognize homosexual status by protecting it from criminalization. As Janet Halley observes, "gay-rights advocates were disarmed, even co-opted, when advocates of the 1993 revisions promoted them on grounds that they took government out of the business of regulating status." The Defense Department policy presumes that homosexuality is a private status, "a type of personal character that inheres so deeply within a person that it constitutes a pervasive personal essence."[33] By turning status into a private, personal essence, the state can "recognize" homosexual orientation as a protected status while at the same time making homosexual conduct grounds for discharge.

The Defense Department regulations create an expanded net of legal prohibitions surrounding "conduct that would manifest, to a reasonable person, a propensity to engage in homosexual acts." The end result, Halley says, is not a better policy but a worse one: "What actually emerged from the legislative process was a complex set of new regulations that discharge people on grounds that tie status to conduct and conduct to status in surprising, devious, ingenious, perverse and frightening ways."[34] The policy establishes a broad range of behaviors that constitute "homosexual conduct" (and thus grounds for discharge) including hand-holding and kissing "that a reasonable person would understand to demonstrate a propensity or intent to engage in homosexual acts."[35] Even coming-out statements are grounds for discharge, but again, not because they are a constative declaration of homosexual status but because they indicate a propensity to engage in same-sex erotic behavior. According to the Defense Department's clarifications of the policy in December 1993,

> A statement by a member that demonstrates a propensity or intent to engage in homosexual acts—such as a statement by the member that he or she is a homosexual—is grounds for separation *not because it reflects the member's sexual orientation, but because the statement indicates a likelihood that the member engages in or will engage in homosexual acts.*[36]

---

33 Halley, *Don't*, pp. 29–30.
34 Ibid., p. 4.
35 "The Pentagon's New Policy Guidelines," *New York Times*.
36 "Pentagon's New Rules on Homosexuals Isn't the Last Word for Troops," *New York Times*, December 24, 1993, p. A1, emphasis added.

According to Valdes, "The bottom line of the new policy is identical to that of its predecessors. The admitted brinkmanship of this policy is geared toward targeting members of sexual minorities without appearing to be unconstitutional."[37]

Halley shows how the move from status to conduct-based regulation is really a "bad faith" claim that enables the regulation of status to proceed "with new subtlety . . . to regulate status under the sign of conduct."[38] Halley argues that it is neither correct to say that these regulations forswear regulation of status and identity nor right to say that such "conduct" regulations are *really nothing more* than status regulation in disguise: "To describe the policy . . . as a regulation of conduct-not-status, or of status-not-conduct, is to distort it." Halley suggests that "the overarching mechanism of the new military anti-gay policy is not status *or* conduct, but a newly volatile, artifactual relationship between them."[39]

The end result is not recognition of a private, personal, homosexual status so much as it is the legal construction of the public status of heterosexuality and the constitution of a normalized homosexual who, as Ann Goldstein writes, "must be not merely celibate, but untouching and untouched."[40] While homosexual status, as an intrinsic core of personhood, is apparently recognized and protected by the regulations (a cognitive recognition of homosexuals "as they really are"), by regulating and prohibiting homosexual conduct the state (a) produces the status of the untouching and untouched homosexual (a disguised performative construction of legal status); and (b) protects the fragile status of heterosexuality (a disguised performative construction of the unmarked legal norm). When the military policy states that "sexual orientation is a personal and private matter," it appears to be offering a kind of cognitive, affirmative recognition of gays and lesbians.[41] However, read against the context of the elaborate conduct and propensity clauses of the policy, this statement turns out to be a performative, constructive act of misrecognition: homosexual orientation has been redefined as a private, inner essence that ought not to be publicly

---

37 Francisco Valdes, "Sexual Minorities in the Military: Charting the Constitutional Frontiers of Status and Conduct," *Creighton Law Review* 27, 1994, pp. 473–4.

38 Halley, *Don't*, pp. 68, 23.

39 Ibid., p. 126.

40 Ann B. Goldstein, "Reasoning About Homosexuality: A Commentary on Janet Halley's 'Reasoning About Sodomy: Act and Identity in and after *Bowers v. Hardwick*,' " *Virginia Law Review* 79, 1993, p. 1802.

41 "Pentagon's New Rules," *New York Times*.

declared or acted upon.[42] The state actively constructs gay identity here (as a private essence) and misrecognizes its act of construction as an act of discovery. Privatizing identity then is not simply the act of the liberal state getting out of the business of status and returning identity to its original or proper place but is a constituting act.[43] This sleight of hand works (and the emancipatory or constraining consequences of it become so difficult to read) as a result, in part, of two conflicting senses of the public/private dichotomy. In terms of the distinction between the sphere of state regulation (public) and the sphere of negative liberty (private), the military's declaration of sexual orientation as a private matter seems to grant recognition to gay people by protecting them from prosecution and harassment for their orientation. However, in terms of the distinction between a public sphere of intersubjective communication and citizen dialogue, and a private sphere of individual secrecy and withdrawal, the military's declaration works to performatively misrecognize and constrain homosexual identity by confining it to the point of disappearance. Furthermore, *heterosexuals*, as Halley maintains, do not benefit from the new policy, which enables surveillance of all service members for any acts or gestures that manifest a "propensity" to engage in homosexual conduct. Rather, it is *heterosexuality* as a public, legally enforced unmarked status that benefits from the new regulations.[44]

One way of criticizing the military's policy would be to suggest that a supposedly universalistic policy (allowing people to serve regardless of sexual orientation) is a sham; while the policy claims to take the state out of the business of discriminating against gays and lesbians, it in fact perpetuates that discrimination. But such an approach does not go far enough: it presumes that there is a prepolitical status group, gays and lesbians, which the state can either treat fairly (universalistic recognition via nondiscrimination) or unfairly (misrecognition via discrimination). But the policy, I am claiming, does much more than

---

42 Halley writes, "They disavowed any effort to regulate status as an intrinsic, prelegal personality structure while writing new rules enabling the state to regulate status as the public construction and maintenance of what would otherwise be a quite fragile personal type." *Don't*, p. 31.

43 Discussing Marx's "On the Jewish Question," Markell writes that "civil society and the state, Marx suggests, are not always independent entities that had only to be untangled through political emancipation; rather, the modern political state and civil society were *first constituted as such* through one and the same founding act of division." Markell, *Bound by Recognition*, p. 129.

44 Halley, *Don't*, p. 130.

this. It produces a political status—the gay or lesbian soldier, constituted by a private essence that may not be acted upon. This status is, in an important sense, different from the forces of social and cultural stigma that produce the "closet"; in this case the state not only produces the closet and its injunction of secrecy but also *claims to know* (and affirmatively recognize) what exists inside that closet. The state demands silence and inactivity in the course of providing recognition.[45]

Homeless criminalization and the production of status

Bad faith "recognition" of a private or social status coupled with a dense set of regulatory prohibitions surrounding conduct linked to that status is not restricted to issues of sexuality in the military. The invalidation of vagrancy laws (which were a classic example of the explicit production of legal status) has led to the emergence of a new set of conduct-based prohibitions targeting the homeless.[46] Cities across the United States have adopted public space "civility" laws such as public sleeping bans, sidewalk-sitting bans and the criminalization of various forms of panhandling, and turned to the "broken windows" approach to policing, emphasizing a crackdown on public "disorder." While vagrancy had been an explicit legal status, current anti-homeless policy produces a subordinate political status in a disguised way. For instance, public space restrictions banning urban camping, sitting on public sidewalks, and "aggressive" panhandling target, so the story goes, "conduct" and not "status." Thus, defenders of these ordinances claim that they have nothing to do with status at all; rather these policies uphold the liberal tradition's commitment to restricting individual liberty only in the context of freely chosen behavior that causes harm to others.

For instance, Kelling and Coles stress that their "order maintenance" approach to policing public space is different from older vagrancy law

---

45 State recognition of gay and lesbian soldiers is thus similar to what Patchen Markell describes as the contradictory nature of the nineteenth-century Prussian state's recognition of the Jews: "on the one hand, Jewishness (otherness) must be eradicated, in this case through a peaceful act of inclusion; on the other hand . . . the institutions of the state must maintain a vigilant surveillance of the Jews to be sure that they are conforming to the terms of their emancipation—and such a surveillance requires that Jews be recognizable. The imperative of emancipation becomes, paradoxically, that *the state must see at all times that each Jew has ceased to be Jewish.*" Markell, *Bound by Recognition*, p. 146.

46 The Supreme Court struck down a vagrancy law in *Papachristou v. Jacksonville* 405 US 156 (1972).

administration in so far as that order maintenance, done correctly, targets conduct, not the status of vagrancy, homelessness or poverty. "The *act* of panhandling, the *act* of public drinking, are disorderly behaviors of concern here—not being poor, or even being recognized widely as a prostitute or public inebriate. The issue is behavior."[47] This, they claim, is in sharp contrast to vagrancy laws, which "punished status—the poor and idle, able-bodied individuals who could work, but did not. No illegal act was required: vagrancy alone was sufficient cause for arrest."[48] Cities concerned to maintain civility in public spaces, and reduce fear, turn to narrowly targeted ordinances proscribing specific forms of conduct: "The permissible constitutional alternative to vague and overbroad status-based legislation was greater specificity and behavior-directed statutes and ordinances."[49]

These "conduct not status" laws work by simultaneously relying on our knowledge of who is really being targeted and our willingness to disavow such knowledge. On the one hand, laws targeting such "conduct" as sitting on the sidewalk carve out numerous exceptions —those instances when home-dwelling citizens may have reason to be sitting on the sidewalk. For instance, the city of Seattle's sidewalk ordinance contains numerous exceptions: people may sit on the sidewalk if they are suffering from a medical emergency, using a wheelchair, waiting for a bus, "operating or patronizing a commercial establishment conducted on the public sidewalk pursuant to a street use permit, or . . . participating in or attending a parade, festival, performance, rally, demonstration, meeting, or similar event . . . pursuant to a street use . . . permit."[50] As customers at espresso carts, and as spectators at parades, those included within the boundaries of the unmarked norm of citizenship are entitled to sit, and their activities must be distinguished, as exceptions, from the excluded behavior of homeless street dwellers and panhandlers.

Here is a case in which homeless and housed appear to have the same legal status, which is to say no status at all. However, as Failer argues, as a result of criminal laws targeting panhandling and sleeping in public, selective enforcement of other nuisance laws, and images of

---

47 George L. Kelling and Catherine M. Coles, *Fixing Broken Windows*, New York: Free Press, 1996, p. 40.

48 Ibid., p. 51.

49 Ibid. p. 57.

50 Seattle, Wash., Code 15.48.040-050. Cited in William M. Berg, "*Roulette v. City of Seattle*: A City Lives with Its Homeless," *Seattle University Law Review* 18, 1994, pp. 170–1, note 173.

homeless persons within legal discourse, homeless persons have, in practice, a subordinate legal status: "Whether looking at the enforce-ment of existing or new criminal laws, or at prohibitions on activities in which homeless people must engage, or at legal depictions of the homeless in judicial discourse, we can see that the criminal law gener-ates a different set of legal obligations for the homeless."[51] As Failer argues, homelessness as a legal status may produce not only subordi-nation, but also certain benefits (access to shelter, exemption from certain punitive laws).[52] Furthermore, homelessness is a disguised legal status: legal discourses appear to avoid regulating or criminalizing the *social* status of homelessness (and rather "recognizing" the right of homeless persons to be), while expanding the reach of conduct-regulation through punitive public space restrictions. And these laws, by criminalizing the conduct of homeless persons, do not simply target the already existing status of homelessness, they produce the status of the homeless-as-outlaw. Elsewhere, I have described this legal status (following Giorgio Agamben's account of the politicization of life itself) as the politically produced status of *bare life*.[53]

One way to respond to these new punitive laws is to insist that their supposed universality is a sham. These laws appear to regulate the conduct of all, and thus not stigmatize homeless difference, but their universality is false—formal universality is contradicted by practical discrimination. However, such an approach does not go far enough: it assumes an already existing social group, "the homeless," along with another already existing social group, "the housed," and a set of laws and practices that either produce injustices of misrecognition or not. But it is precisely these laws that help to constitute and preserve the boundary/difference between social groups in the first place. This is not to suggest that the state creates homelessness, but it *is* to suggest that the state does not "innocently happen upon" a pre-existing social divide between homeless and housed either.[54] As Samira Kawash writes, the "aim of the vengeful homeless policies of the last decade is not limited to the immediate goal of solving the problem of homelessness by eliminating the homeless. This 'war on the homeless' must also be

---

51 Failer, "Homelessness in the Criminal Law," p. 258.

52 "In some respects, this may be to their advantage. Homeless people, for example, may possess a right to shelter that full citizens do not possess." Failer, "Homelessness in the Criminal Law," p. 258.

53 Leonard C. Feldman, *Citizens Without Shelter: Homelessness, Democracy and Political Exclusion*, Ithaca: Cornell University Press, 2004.

54 Hayward, "The Difference States Make," p. 506.

seen as a mechanism for constituting and securing a public, establishing the boundaries of inclusion, and producing an abject body against which the proper, public body of the citizen can stand."[55]

Implications for the politics of recognition

This analysis of the state's role in status recognition has implications for our judgments about the desirability of particular recognition strategies, judgments which Fraser has grown increasingly reticent to make as her work on recognition and status subordination has developed. My claim is that a focus on the state's role in status production underscores Fraser's original critique of an affirmative or multicultural form of recognition: the political creation of status frequently renders an affirmative politics of recognition limited and counterproductive. When legal and policy discourses constitute differences and then treat those differences as already existing social facts to which the state merely reacts, the state shapes the terrain of recognition. In this context, movements for affirmative group recognition risk affirming their own subordinate political status by accepting the state's constitution of a so-called personal or social status. Demanding that this status be recognized and protected as opposed to criminalized does little to contest the liberal state's "self-obscuring" construction of status and it may do a great deal to affirm a subordinate position in the political order. Thus, I argue, it is not enough for recognition movements to insist that conduct-based regulations "really target status." This claim, while not incorrect, misses the important constitutive dimension—the state is not simply targeting a pre-existing social status but rather is producing the distinction between the normal citizen and subordinate status. Seeking protection for this subordinate status undermines efforts to promote citizen equality and the democratic contestation of state-produced status distinctions.

Responding to forms of state recognition that produce a subordinate legal or political status may require something other than an affirmative politics of recognition: it may require deconstructive and universalizing strategies. For instance, in opposing the injustices of the military's prohibition of homosexual conduct, one strategy (adopted by gay rights litigators) has been to make the claim that the policy really targets homosexual status, not conduct. This is the strategy of affirmative recognition. It accepts the military's distinction between "homosexual status" and "homosexual conduct" but seeks a recognition of that status which,

---

55 Kawash, "Homeless Body," p. 325.

it claims, the military policy fails to provide. Such litigation, contingent upon defending a closeted, celibate gay person who has been targeted because of her status and not her conduct reinforces institutionalized stigma against same-sex erotic acts, and reinforces the legally constructed status of homosexuality as a "secret inner core of personhood" that remains the same whether it is acted upon or not.[56] This form of litigation involves the claim that the military has really targeted status, not conduct, but entails the concession, as David Mazur argues, "that the military would be justified in discharging those gay service members with any intimacy in their lives."[57] Such a strategy seeks legal recognition of the celibate homosexual as a worthy soldier, thus seeking recognition within the demeaning status/conduct distinction put forth by the military's policy.[58]

On the other hand, a deconstructive strategy would show a shift of focus to the dominant identity, heterosexuality, and show how the policy, in the effort to prop up a fragile, public heterosexual status, ends up making all persons' sexual identity less secure, by involving the policing of acts, gestures, and conduct of everyone for signs of a "propensity" to engage in homosexual conduct. The specific litigation tactics to implement such a deconstructive strategy are beyond the scope of this paper. Perhaps such maneuvers work better as political criticism than as legal argument. However, as I argue below, a deconstructive form of legal recognition has proven compelling in undermining the legal status of homelessness.

Homeless criminalization is another area in which we can contrast affirmative with deconstructive forms of legal recognition. In the case of public space civility laws, the strategy for affirmative recognition—like the litigation on sexual orientation discussed above—stresses that the policies "in reality" target the status of homelessness, not the conduct of public sleeping, sidewalk-sitting and the like. In an extension of *Robinson v. California*, which made "punishment for status" a cruel and unusual punishment in violation of the eighth amendment, homeless rights litigators have had some limited success in convincing courts that public sleeping bans punish not conduct, but an involuntary status. Making the analogy to *Robinson*, in which the Supreme Court struck down a law that made it a crime to be addicted to narcotics,

---

56 Halley, *Don't*, p. 30.
57 Diane H. Mazur, "The Unknown Soldier: A Critique of 'Gays in the Military' Scholarship and Litigation," *UC Davis Law Review* 29, Winter 1996, p. 225.
58 Ibid., p. 249.

litigators argue that public sleeping bans punish an involuntary status (homelessness) and not freely chosen conduct. This strategy requires that homeless rights litigators demonstrate to courts that homelessness is a status in the sense that it is an involuntarily acquired social condition. When this account of the "social facts" of homelessness is taken up in the law, it has the unfortunate consequence of reinforcing a demeaning vision of the homeless as not citizens but dependent, helpless victims, defined by bodily needs. For instance, in the case of *Johnson v. City of Dallas*, a federal district court struck down a public sleeping ban, declaring it an unconstitutionally cruel and unusual punishment, punishing people not for freely chosen conduct but rather for their status as homeless. The court thus recognizes homelessness as a status and appears to grant it legal protection. However, by recognizing homelessness as a status, the court produces a vision of homeless persons as helpless "bare life," not citizens.[59]

The *Johnson* court claims that the ordinance under review does in fact target conduct, not status. Nevertheless, the court says, "maintaining human life requires certain acts, among them being the consuming of nourishment, breathing, and sleeping." After establishing that the conduct being regulated is that which sustains physical life, the court goes on to establish that the homeless plaintiffs are homeless involuntarily:

> at any given time there are persons in Dallas who have no place to go, who could not find shelter even if they wanted to—and many of them do want to—and who would be turned away from shelters for a variety of reasons. There are not enough beds available at the area shelter to accommodate the demand. Some persons do not meet particular shelter's eligibility requirements.[60]

The court reasons that since life requires sleeping, and since the homeless are involuntarily confined to public space, the homeless must sleep in public space. Therefore, punishing public sleeping in essence criminalizes the *involuntary status of homelessness*:

---

59 I take this term from Giorgio Agamben, *Homo Sacer*.

60 *Johnson v. Dallas*, 860 F. Supp 344 (N.D. Tex. 1994), p. 350. The analysis of *Johnson v. Dallas* and *Tobe v. Santa Ana* below repeats material from my *Citizens Without Shelter*, pp. 74–5, 142–3.

They have no place to go other than the public lands they live on. In other words, they must be in public. And it is also clear that they must sleep. Although sleeping is an act rather than a status, the status of being could clearly not be criminalized under *Robinson*. Because being does not exist without sleeping, criminalizing the latter necessarily punishes the homeless for their status as homeless, a status forcing them to be in public.[61]

The *Johnson* court, after establishing such an elaborate rhetorical weight of compulsion (it is as if the goal of the repetition of this "being forced" in all its permutations is to finally compel the agreement of the audience), the court remarkably explains what would be required to make public sleeping no longer an involuntary act committed by necessity by people who are involuntarily homeless:

> For many of those homeless in Dallas, the unavailability of shelter is not a function of choice; *it is not an issue of choosing to remain outdoors rather than sleep on a shelter's floor because the shelter could not provide a bed that one found suitable enough.* The evidence demonstrates that for a number of Dallas homeless at this time homelessness is involuntary and irremediable.[62]

The court here makes explicit what it would take to turn homelessness as an involuntary status into homelessness as a criminalizable choice: the presence of space on the floor of a shelter.[63]

The legal legitimation of space on a shelter's floor as an adequate response to the predicament of homelessness manifests what Samira Kawash describes as the "strategies of containment and constriction brought to bear on the homeless body."[64] The *Johnson* opinion, though,

---

61 *Johnson v. Dallas*, 860 F. Supp 344 (N.D. Tex. 1994), p. 350.

62 *Johnson v. Dallas*, 860 F. Supp 344 (N.D. Tex. 1994), p. 350, emphasis added.

63 As Wes Daniels argues, "Even when criminalization lawsuits are successful, the rights established are negative rights, in that at most they restrict the ways in which government can punish homeless people for engaging in certain types of behavior . . . And the state can remove the constitutional barrier to official punitive measures, a barrier cognizable only in the context of 'involuntary' homelessness, by offering homeless people even the most minimal of alternatives, such as 'beds' in emergency shelters, or even a 'shelter's floor.' " Wes Daniels, "Derelicts, Recurring Misfortune, Economic Hard Times, and Lifestyle Choices: Judicial Images of Homeless Litigants and Implications for Legal Advocates," *Buffalo Law Review* 45, Fall 1997, p. 731.

64 Kawash, "The Homeless Body," p. 331.

displays a specifically legal strategy of constriction and containment: discursively reducing homeless persons to the compulsions of life's necessities, and then authorizing their confinement in the most minimal of shelter. Thus, the *Johnson* court, while appearing to *recognize* and *protect* the involuntary *social* status of homelessness, at the same time *produces* the *political* status of homeless as those who, defined as helpless victims defined by biological necessity, may be legally confined in the most minimal or degrading conditions of the shelter system.

A deconstructive strategy, on the other hand, shifts the focus to the precarious identity of the public home-dwelling consumer-citizen who is being "protected" by the policy, *and* shows how all persons are potentially caught within the prohibitions. For instance, in *Tobe v. Santa Ana*, a California state appeals court struck down a public camping ban for being unconstitutionally vague and overbroad. The court showed how, read literally, the ordinance's prohibitions target all people, homeless and housed, who have reason to "store belongings" in public space at one time or another and who "live out of doors" in the sense that they occupy public space for some duration. This deconstructive strategy takes the "conduct not status" claims of the policy *seriously*, disavowing the background commonsense knowledge of the underlying status orientation (targeting the homeless).

For instance, the court says that the definition of camping—"to live temporarily in a camp facility or outdoors"—is unconstitutionally vague: "Most of us do that every day because all our activities are part of living."[65] And the prohibition against "storing" items in public spaces is struck down because the definition of the verb "to store" is overbroad: "The city may have been aiming at shopping carts and bedrolls; but it has hit bicycles, automobiles, delivery vehicles of every description, beach towels at public pools and wet umbrellas in library foyers."[66]

The appeals court gestures towards universality in a deconstructive direction, by drawing the domiciled into the category of the outlaw: "the statute is vague and overbroad as applied to anyone, be they homeless, picnickers, or scouts engaged in a field exercise."[67] By showing how

---

65 *Tobe v. Santa Ana* 27 Cal. Rptr. 2d 386 (Cal. App. 4 Dist. 1994), pp. 394–5. The decision was reversed by the California Supreme Court in *Tobe v. City of Santa Ana*, 27 Cal. Rptr. 2d 386 (Cal. App. 4 Dist. 1994), reversed, 40 Cal. Rptr. 2d 402 (Cal. 1995). I discuss the state Supreme Court's legal reasoning in *Citizens Without Shelter*.

66 *Tobe v. Santa Ana* (1994), p. 395.

67 Ibid., p.395, note 14.

homeless and housed are equally targets of conduct-based punitive policies, the court includes the homeless in the category of citizenship by, ironically, turning the "normal" home-dwelling citizen into a potential outlaw.

For the appellate court, taking the statute at face value means distancing ourselves from the common sense that the law is directly targeting the homeless: we *all* store belongings in public from time to time, and we *all* live temporarily out of doors to the extent that we are all residents of public space. The majestic equality of the law in forbidding the rich and the poor from sleeping under bridges has turned into the unconstitutional overreaching of the law that prevents the rich and poor alike from living temporarily outside.

This legal reasoning resists the call to convert homeless difference into absolute otherness. It attacks the political and material exclusion of the homeless not by referencing a common and abstract humanity that "deep down" binds us together, but rather by thinking through the connections between the dwelling activities of homeless persons and the dwelling activities of housed persons. The appeals court incorporates a recognition of *our common dwelling* into its reading of the law. By thinking of housed citizens as potential outlaws of public space, the court avoids some of the pitfalls of status crime arguments that protect homeless persons only by carving out a subordinate legal status of helpless bare life.[68]

Conclusion

How should we think of the liberal state's production of differential statuses? One way of understanding the status politics of the liberal state is in terms of leftover remains from medieval England. For instance, Failer describes subordinate legal statuses within the contemporary state as "relics of the law of persons" and "persisting echoes of the old system."[69] In this approach, it might be possible to envision a more complete liberalism that will liberate us from ascriptive identities so that we may live a politics of pure conduct. However, another way of understanding the status politics of the contemporary state is in terms of the political ordering of groups and statuses, practices that may become disguised within a liberal culture of

---

68 The appeals court in *Tobe* also made the eighth amendment a basis for striking down the camping ban, cursorily citing the *Pottinger v. Miami* case. However, its discussion of homelessness as an involuntary status is less well developed than is the overbreadth and vagueness discussion.

69 Failer, "Homelessness," p. 250.

contracts and individualism but will not disappear. If all political communities have their boundaries and frontiers, then they will inevitably be drawn into constructing categories of full members, subordinate members and nonmembers. Given such an understanding, the task is not to imagine an emancipation from status so much as it is to pursue conditions under which subordinate legal and political statuses can become legible as such. When subordinate statuses become visible, the unmarked norm of full citizenship becomes visible as well, and the political ordering of persons can be subject to democratic contestation and deconstruction.

In this respect, I endorse Fraser's guiding norm of participatory parity; my concern has been to explore how the obstacles to such parity may be concealed by the liberal state's approach to status, and how an affirmative politics of group recognition may exacerbate participatory inequality by further entrenching political subordination. In the context of the persistence of legal status, an affirmative politics of recognition often fails to enable such democratic contestation, because it seeks affirmation of a supposedly personal or social status, the contours of which have been shaped by state policy. Deconstructive recognition, on the other hand, may succeed in exposing the false universality of the unmarked norm of full citizenship, unsettling the boundaries that sustain potentially unjust forms of political status subordination.

PARTICIPATORY PARITY
AND DEMOCRATIC JUSTICE
Kevin Olson

Philosophy has had little success answering questions of justice. Theorists of distributive justice have vainly tried to find a norm for the equitable distribution of goods at least since Aristotle. More recently, difficult questions of cultural justice have arisen in disputes over identity, difference, and recognition, with similarly inconclusive results. These debates have produced important clarifications of the relations between cultural and economic justice, but no clear specification of what justice should mean in either domain. One promising strategy for resolving such problems is to tap the deep normative resources of democracy. A democratic theory of justice would allow the people themselves to decide what norms and values ought to regulate their lives. The problem, however, is to ensure that democracy is up to the task. After all, democratically generated norms and values are only as good as the political processes that create them.

In this essay I examine Nancy Fraser's important attempt to outline a democratic theory of justice. Fraser has recently claimed that norms of justice can be developed from a conception of democracy characterized by "participatory parity." Further, she has made programmatic remarks that culture and economy may not exhaust the analytical perspectives we can take on justice. Politics, she considers, may be a distinct and irreducible third perspective. I applaud this move, because I think that democracy provides the most normatively defensible way of evaluating claims to justice.

As a contribution to this project, I will provide a more forceful argument for its radical democratic elements and a clearer specification of some of the problems that this creates. I will begin by arguing that politics does in fact constitute a distinctive, third perspective on justice. Specifically, politics is normatively primary as a perspective on justice. It provides the basis for developing the norms and values that underpin justice itself. In spite of its great potential for solving problems of justice, however, this proposal conceals hidden problems. Normative appeals to political participation are potentially quite paradoxical. Participation resolves one set of problems but simultaneously raises a new one that I will call the paradox of enablement. The paradox arises out of the complex interconnections between politics, economy, and culture. The political sphere tends to be normatively decoupled from economy and culture even as it is empirically coupled with them. The paradox thus frequently goes unrecognized and plausible solutions to it are delegitimized. To resolve this problem, we need to think more deeply about the tensions between democracy and justice. I will explore solutions to this problem by focusing on the recursive character of political processes, the reflexive character of citizenship, and the relations between political theory and public deliberation. Perhaps surprisingly, I will argue that using democracy as a basis for justice puts limits on democracy while nonetheless resolving many unsettled issues of justice.

1. Politics as a third perspective on justice

Nancy Fraser's conception of justice is based on the idea of "parity of participation." She characterizes this as the notion that "justice requires social arrangements that permit all (adult) members of society to interact with one another as peers."[1] She further clarifies by saying that parity means "the condition of being a *peer*, of being on a *par* with others, of standing on an equal footing" in a given activity or interaction.[2] *Injustice* is correspondingly lodged in socio-material conditions that impede participation for some and not for others.

Fraser identifies two kinds of impediments to participatory parity. One of those violates its "objective condition."[3] That is defined as a distribution of material resources undermining participants' independence and voice. Fraser characterizes such circumstances as "maldistribution." When maldistribution violates the objective

---

1 Nancy Fraser, "Social Justice in the Age of Identity Politics," in Nancy Fraser and Axel Honneth, *Redistribution or Recognition? A Political-Philosophical Exchange*, London: Verso, 2003, p. 36. See also Nancy Fraser, "Rethinking the Public Sphere: A Contribution to the Critique of Actually Existing Democracy," in *Justice Interruptus: Critical Reflections on the "Postsocialist" Condition*, New York: Routledge, 1997, pp. 77–80; "Rethinking Recognition," in this volume; and "Recognition without Ethics?" *Theory, Culture, and Society* 18: 2–3, 2001, pp. 21–42.

2 Fraser, "Social Justice," p. 101, note 39. Emphasis in the original.

3 Fraser, "Social Justice," p. 36.

condition, some kind of economic redistribution is required. Injustices of this type occur within the *class* structure of society. A second form of injustice violates the "intersubjective condition." The intersubjective condition requires equal respect, particularly in the institutions and laws governing our practices. It focuses, then, on the ways that cultural understandings are coded into institutional structures. Fraser refers to such denials of equal respect as "misrecognition." Misrecognition is a form of injustice requiring changes in institutionalized systems of value that deny people full status in interaction. Injustices of this type occur within the *status* structure of society.

A focus on participatory parity moves away from narrow and potentially bifurcating definitions of justice solely based on goods distribution or valuations of personal identity. Instead, it provides a common normative standard for both of these dimensions, ruling social arrangements and institutions out of bounds when they violate either condition of participatory parity. Such a standard reveals underlying normative continuity between maldistribution and misrecognition: each describes one way that participation can be rendered inequitable.

Normative continuity in this case is a product of normative innovation. Fraser rethinks maldistribution and misrecognition as conditions that draw their normative weight from the injustice of participatory inequity. This framework focuses on the extent to which participation is basic to social membership and social interaction. Such a move has great importance to our understanding of social justice. It shows that economic and cultural inequalities are harmful for reasons beyond their immediate impact in their own domains. Economic inequality is distributively unfair, from this point of view, because it impedes participatory parity. Similarly, cultural stigmatization is a reprehensible status injury because it impedes participatory parity.

With this burden-shifting comes a need to make sure participation can bear the normative weight. We must be clear why participatory parity should be a persuasive basis for claims about justice. As a first step in this endeavor, I will try to trace its normative implications, outlining its relation to economic and cultural conditions and trying to give it the most robust characterization possible.

Nancy Fraser employs the notion of participatory parity in three distinct but interrelated senses. (1) The first of these is her exposition of participatory parity as having objective and intersubjective conditions. These mirror our familiar forms of economic and cultural justice, and follow a long tradition of analyzing social differentiation in terms of class and status. Participatory parity can be occluded in either domain, and is thus empirically linked to economy and culture.

One sense of participatory parity, then, is the compound, economic-cultural norm underlying two-dimensional forms of injustice.[4] Gender injustices, for instance, could be seen as having two moments that comprise one overall normative problem. One of those would be economic, violating the objective condition: differentials between men's and women's wages, second shifts of caregiving labor, and so on all conspire to make women economically unequal to men. The other would be cultural, violating the intersubjective condition: demeaning representations of women, sexual harassment, and rape, for example, undermine the equal cultural status of women. The overall problem from this perspective could then be seen as a double impediment to participation: women are hindered from participating as equals in both an economic and a cultural sense. This conception of participatory parity identifies the ways that culture and economy combine to create complex inequalities that are normatively problematic from both perspectives.

It is important to recognize, however, that the existence of economic and cultural conditions for participatory parity does not limit the norm of participatory parity *itself* to culture or economy. It may be tempting to read Fraser as claiming that the normatively important senses of participation are *solely* cultural and economic ones. Such an interpretation could result, for instance, from thinking that cultural and economic impediments to participation only have effects within their characteristic spheres. On that misreading, there would be two genres of participation just like there are two conditions of participation and two kinds of impediment. One might be tempted to imagine a new 2x2 matrix, similar in spirit to Fraser's original formulation[5]: (misrecognition and maldistribution) versus (participation in culture and participation in the economy). In this view, participation in culture could be impeded either by misrecognition or maldistribution. Either (or both) could prevent people from participating as equals in the social construction of norms and identities. Correspondingly, participation in the economy could be impeded either by misrecognition or maldistribution. Either (or both) could prevent people from participating as equals in the social production of wealth.

It is tempting to think of participation along these dual tracks, because it follows the analytic ethos of Fraser's earlier work. This is an overly narrow conception of participation, however. Here interaction

---

4 Fraser, "Social Justice," pp. 16–26.
5 Nancy Fraser, "From Redistribution to Recognition?" in this volume, pp. 33–4.

is reduced to its economic and cultural varieties. Even as a form of perspectival dualism, this kind of analysis leaves out many important domains of activity that are not distinctively cultural or economic, everything from innocuous civic activities like bowling leagues to formal participation in politics.

Further, this reading produces a bifurcated view of participation that could not serve as a unified basis for social justice. These two senses of participation describe fundamentally different kinds of activities. Economic participation paradigmatically means being an actor in markets. This includes participation in labor markets—as a worker or employer—and participation in goods and service markets as a consumer. Economic participation is thus commodified, non-linguistic, based on monological, subjective preferences, and instrumentally rational. Cultural participation, on the other hand, paradigmatically means being an actor in constructing the meanings, images, and representations through which we understand our common world. It is symbolic, linguistic, oriented toward creating dialogical, intersubjective preferences, and communicatively rational. These two senses of participation have almost nothing in common except the name. A unified theory of social justice cannot theorize participation solely in terms of culture and the economy, then. Rather, it must think of interaction more broadly. The set of activities that constitute partic-ipation extend far beyond the conditions that promote or hinder it.

(2) A second, more appropriate reading emphasizes the sense in which Fraser characterizes participation as *social interaction* or as occurring *in social life*.[6] Here the normatively important forms of parity range across a broad spectrum of social activities. On this reading, participation means being able to do all of the things that any other adult in one's society can do. One would have the same (or an equivalent set of) opportunities that anyone else has. This view strikes down many forms of discrimination that are simultaneously cultural and economic in character. One would be able to ride on the same bus seats, drink at the same fountains, patronize the same restaurants and hotels as anyone else. One would have an equal chance, *ceteris paribus*, at the same jobs, houses, neighborhoods, and schools. In short, this way of reading participatory parity theorizes it as a rich conception of equal opportunity. There would be no class of

---

6 Fraser, "Social Justice," pp. 29–31, 34–35, 38; and Nancy Fraser, "Distorted Beyond All Recognition: A Rejoinder to Axel Honneth," in Nancy Fraser and Axel Honneth, *Redistribution or Recognition?*, p. 232.

opportunities from which one could in principle be excluded. It would be correspondingly unjust to bar anyone's participation in any aspect of social life.

This interpretation spans the range of activities that adults undertake, providing a broad reading of what it means to participate in social life. Further, it covers a spectrum of historical cases in which participation *has* in fact been impeded. The social harms of discrimination, for instance, diminish people's ability to participate as equals in society in this broad and general sense. It is important to note, however, that this vision of participation is still narrower than we might like. By viewing social life as a domain in which people should have equal opportunities, possibilities, and choices, it frames a primarily *consumerist* vision of participation. Participation is the consumption of lifestyle options on this interpretation. Injustice, correspondingly, consists of having a narrower range of choices than others do. Such equality is certainly an important part of what it means to be an equal in society, particularly in modern, industrial societies in which consumption itself is an important indicator of status.[7] As a normative claim, however, this conception places weight on something like the classic, welfarist ideal of equal opportunity for preference satisfaction.[8] It is, ironically, a strongly subjective and individualist notion of participation that views social life merely as the domain in which individual projects are realized. Participation in social life here is distinctively non-social. This obviously does not exhaust the significance of participation as a normative concept.

(3) To develop a normatively sophisticated conception of participatory parity, we must describe its social dimensions in a more intersubjective sense. Participation often connotes working alongside other people to accomplish common goals, frequently with the ability to deliberate about the nature of the undertaking and the best means to accomplish it. This sense of participation implies some sort of cooperative activity. Further, it has connotations of opinion- or decision-making power, the kind of thing that Albert Hirschman refers to as voice.[9] Participation in this sense is not simply a matter of having a broad

---

7 Pierre Bourdieu, *Distinction: A Social Critique of the Judgement of Taste*, trans. Richard Nice, Cambridge, MA: Harvard University Press, 1984.

8 Richard Arneson, "Liberalism, Distributive Subjectivism, and Equal Opportunity for Welfare," *Ethics* 19, 1990, pp. 158–94; "Equality and Equal Opportunity for Welfare," *Philosophical Studies* 56, 1989, pp. 77–93.

9 Albert O. Hirschman, *Exit, Voice, and Loyalty: Responses to Decline in Firms, Organizations, and States*, Cambridge, MA: Harvard University Press, 1970.

and equivalent array of choices, but more richly, of being actively involved in some cooperative endeavor. In other words, it is an inter-active conception, not simply a voluntaristic one. This sense of participation is distinctively *political* in character.

The political meaning of participation is most obviously seen in activities within the official political sphere. Here participation allows people to vote for representatives, comment on the daily workings of government, and take part in decisions about policy implementation, legislation, rules, and budgets. Distinctively political forms of partic-ipation also occur outside of the official political sphere, however. They are characteristic of many different spheres of social life: voluntary organizations, civic groups, and workplaces.[10] Here political participation tackles issues of many different kinds. Take, for instance, the case of participatory decision-making in the workplace. Such processes can focus at times on wages and benefits. These are issues of justice as seen from the perspective of redistribution. Workplace decision-making also encompasses cultural issues, however. Discussions of family leave policies or the heteronormative character of spousal benefits invoke claims of justice from the perspective of recognition. It is clear, then, that distinctively political forms of participation can be used to raise and defend claims of justice in both an analytically economic and analytically cultural sense. This best captures Fraser's assertion that "participatory parity serves as an idiom of public contestation and deliberation about questions of justice. More strongly, it represents *the principal idiom of public reason,* the preferred language for conducting democratic political argumentation on issues of both distribution and recognition."[11]

It is important not to think of participatory parity solely as a means for adjudicating issues of distribution and recognition, however. Participation can have a distinctively *political* significance that is not reducible to either economic or cultural justice. In the workplace example, for instance, this would show up in discussions about the justice of participatory procedures themselves: who gets to speak, for how long, under what rules, and with what decision-making authority. It could span questions about the participatory equality of capital and labor, or the kinds of norms and arguments that can be invoked in

---

10 Robert Putnam, *Bowling Alone: The Collapse and Revival of American Community*, New York: Simon and Schuster, 2000; Carole Pateman, *Participation and Democratic Theory*, New York: Cambridge University Press, 1970.

11 Fraser, "Social Justice," p. 43. Emphasis in the original.

making claims about the organization of the workplace. Here participation is not about redistribution or recognition so much as about
participation itself. It addresses questions of justice inherent in the coor-
dination of cooperative decision-making. In such circumstances, political
participation is subject to claims of justice from its own unique perspective, not reducible to the perspectives of either economy or culture.

Consider, for example, the situation of a low-wage Latino worker as
seen from a multi-perspectival theory of justice. From one perspective
we can focus on the injustice of low wages. This is a redistributive issue
whose harm is registered in the way it undermines objective conditions
of participation. From another perspective we can focus on the injustice
of stigmatized Latino identities. This is a recognition issue whose
harm is registered in the way it undermines intersubjective conditions
of participation. We see, then, that this intersection of identities doubly
jeopardizes political participation. And in fact, both low-wage workers
as a group and Latinos as a group participate in politics much less
frequently than others in the contemporary United States.[12]

The question, however, is whether redistribution and recognition
tell us everything there is to know about this story. To be sure, impaired
participation is partly explained by maldistribution and misrecognition. However, a uniquely political dynamic is also at work. Political
procedures that determine citizenship typically do not distribute
political agency equally amongst citizens. Some groups wind up with
greater agency than others. When a particular group lacks political
agency, it lacks the very means required to make claims in the political
system. When a group is less effective making political claims, it cannot
fight the economic, cultural, and political circumstances that create
its marginality in the first place. Marginalization breeds marginalization, creating a downward spiral of unequal participation. This is a
uniquely political harm that is connected with, though distinct from,
injustices diagnosed from the perspectives of economy and culture.
Recognizing the distinctively political character of this problem, we
must extend what Fraser calls perspectival dualism[13] to a third
dimension—a perspectival trio of economy, culture, and politics.[14]

---

12 Sidney Verba, Kay Schlozman, and Henry Brady, *Voice and Equality: Civic
Voluntarism in American Politics*, Cambridge MA: Harvard University Press, 1995,
chaps. 7–8.

13 Fraser, "Social Justice," pp. 60–4.

14 Leonard Feldman draws a similar conclusion through an insightful analysis of
political harms. "Redistribution, Recognition, and the State: The Irreducibly Political
Dimension of Injustice," *Political Theory* 30: 3, 2002, pp. 410–40.

While this analytical scheme follows an orderly, three-part structure, the underlying empirical reality is much more complicated. Economy, culture, and politics are intertwined in ways that can undermine participatory parity for important segments of the populace. Parity of participation thus rests on three types of conditions: it requires a certain degree of economic equality (objective conditions), a certain degree of cultural equality (intersubjective conditions), and a certain degree of political equality, which we could call its *public-political* conditions. These conditions of participatory parity are connected in complicated ways. A person rarely experiences injustice *only* in an economic, a cultural, or a political sense. More likely is a scenario in which the same person is poor, disrespected, and politically marginalized.

Similarly, we can see that some important forms of social differentiation correspond neither to class nor status. The uniquely political harms I have described are most directly registered as matters of *citizenship*. This notion of citizenship is not limited to formal rights of political participation. It is a broader concept with many different qualities and degrees. The kinds of political agency a person enjoys can be more or less comprehensive. They can be blocked, occluded, or diminished in many ways, enhanced and strengthened in others.[15] Even when all citizens have formal rights to participate in politics, those rights can mean many different things for different people. Such differences become even starker when we focus on less formal political activities like contacting representatives or deliberating in community meetings. Here the impact of participation varies considerably. Citizenship is thus a highly differentiated form of identity that confers and foils political agency in many different ways. Some of those forms have rough parity with one another, while others are highly unequal. Most crucially, then, this conception of citizenship describes the differing senses in which parity of political participation is achieved.

We can draw this discussion together into a revised analytical framework. It illuminates the complexity of participatory parity and the conditions that support it by extending Fraser's work on the economic and cultural dimensions of justice:

---

15 Rogers Smith, *Civic Ideals: Conflicting Visions of Citizenship in US History*, New Haven: Yale University Press, 1997.

domains of justice	conditions for participatory parity	forms of social differentiation	forms of injustice	remedies
economic	objective condition	class	maldistribution	redistribution
cultural	intersubjective condition	status	misrecognition	recognition
political	public-political condition	citizenship	marginalization	inclusion

Beyond its analytical value, there are additional reasons to recognize political participation as a third perspective on justice. Like redistribution and recognition, it functions as what Fraser calls a folk paradigm of justice.[16] Social psychologists and experimental economists observe that people of many different cultures act on deeply embedded norms of participatory parity. In politics, for instance, people tend to see administrative and judicial decisions as more legitimate when they believe the rules regulating them are fair.[17] Impartiality and neutrality are important parts of this. They are norms of equal treatment that require treating citizens as peers. Further, people seem to attach great importance to participation for its own sake. A right to be heard before a decision is made is very important to people's estimation of its fairness, even when their opinion is not perceived to affect the decision itself.[18] These norms show that something like parity of political participation is normatively significant in our current folk conceptions of justice.

Now that we have established the analytic and normative independence of political participation, we can return to the question of how it relates to participation in social life in the broader sense outlined in (2) above. Social participation and political participation are rendered unequal by many of the same conditions. Although citizenship is legally encoded in universalist constitutional principles, it is importantly

---

16 Fraser, "Social Justice," pp. 11–16.

17 E. Allan Lind and Tom Tyler, *The Social Psychology of Procedural Justice*, New York: Plenum Press, 1988, chaps. 4, 7; Tom Tyler, *Why People Obey the Law*, New Haven: Yale University Press, 1990, Chapter 11; Tom Tyler and Steven Blader, *Cooperation in Groups: Procedural Justice, Social Identity, and Behavioral Engagement*, Philadelphia: Taylor and Francis, 2000, chapters 7–10.

18 Lind and Tyler, *The Social Psychology of Procedural Justice*, pp. 101–106, 170–172; Tyler, *Why People Obey the Law*, pp. 149–150; Tyler and Blader, *Cooperation in Groups*, pp. 96–101, 104–106.

influenced by status and class. Status has a large effect on the extent to which one is allowed to speak and receives uptake when speaking.[19] Class differences in wealth and income have a substantial influence on people's ability and willingness to participate in politics.[20] Moreover, the richer and more discursive the political activities, the greater the effect of status and class. In these senses, political participation functions in the same way as social participation: it has intersubjective and objective conditions—status and class. When these conditions are not met, political participation does not reach parity.

Although social and political participation have similar conditions, it is important not to conflate the two or try to reduce one to the other. Because political participation focuses on things like parity in speaking, being heard, and taking active part in coordinating cooperative endeavors, it is analytically distinct from participation in social life *sensu lato*. When one has equal voice, one can challenge forms of exclusion, renegotiate standards of justice, and demand changes in one's treatment by others. This interactive sense helps safeguard other kinds of participation, including the mundane, consumerist ones I described above. It allows people to make claims about the other forms of participation they find important. Parity of political participation is thus importantly connected with, but analytically distinct from, parity of participation in social life.

We can now draw some preliminary conclusions about participatory parity. (1) Political participation is *analytically* separable from broader senses of social participation. (2) Political participation is *normatively* separable from broader senses of social participation. (3) Citizenship is partially coupled with relations of status and class, and partly decoupled from them. (4) Parity of political participation constitutes a distinctive domain of claims about justice that can be made apart from misrecognition or maldistribution. It cannot be completely functionalized to economic and cultural justice.

2. Political participation as normatively basic

Now that we have established the analytical and normative separability of social and political participation, we can consider their interrelation in greater detail. In particular, it would be useful to know how the two are connected—or not—at a normative level. To answer this question, we must look deeper into the normative significance of each form of activity.

---

19 Bourdieu, *Distinction*, Chapter 8.
20 Verba, Schlozman, and Brady, *Voice and Equality*, Chapter 7.

First consider the idea of social participation in the broad sense. This idea is rich in normative connotations. Parity makes intuitive sense here: people should have equal opportunities to interact with others on equal footing and to do the same kinds of things that other people can do. It is important to note, however, that parity is underdetermined as a norm. It is not prima facie clear that parity should hold in any particular social domain or to any particular extent.

To use parity of participation as a normative standard in this sphere, we must devise some means of assessing *which domains of social life* demand participatory parity. Consider the following example, for instance. There is broad consensus that voting is a form of participation to which every citizen ought to be entitled. There is much less consensus, though, that participatory parity ought to require workplace democracy or citizen approval of new administrative regulations. The unresolved issue in this case is about the extent to which participation is normatively required in various domains of social life.

Once we have decided which domains demand participatory parity, we must also determine *what counts as a normatively significant impediment* to it. Consider the example again. Everyone agrees that participatory parity requires equal voting, but many would object to the idea that society ought to provide day care at polling places to ensure that voting is not unduly difficult for women or poor people. It isn't clear whether caregiving responsibilities really hinder people from voting, nor is it clear whether such a concern ought to be part of what we mean by political equality. The unresolved issue here is about which conditions impede participatory parity in a normatively significant way.

Each of the claims about participation I have just outlined enjoys some plausibility. Workplace democracy and citizen oversight would democratize important areas of social life and provide people with greater freedom to regulate their own actions. They could also be seen, however, as violations of capitalist property rights or over-politicization of government. Similarly, day care at polling places would ensure that full-time caregivers have equal opportunities to vote. It could also be seen, however, as an excess of political correctness or big government run amuck. The problem in these cases is finding some normative standard for participation. This must include both which areas of social life ought to have participatory parity and what counts as a morally significant impediment to it.

Mirroring Nancy Fraser's own discussion, I can imagine two strategies that might be useful for accomplishing this.[21] The first is an

---

21 Fraser, "Social Justice," pp. 70–72.

objectivistic assessment of participation and its problems. This would require some thoroughgoing theory of popular sovereignty that could spell out which areas of social life justly require input and which justly exclude it. It would have to make distinctions between different realms of participation, explaining, for instance, why selecting representatives requires participation but selecting federal judges does not. It would also have to distinguish different norms for different areas of social life, explaining why we should participate in government but not in corporate management. And it would have to explain how much participation is enough: why, for instance, a system of representative government exhausts what we mean by popular sovereignty.

Such a project is not absurd. It is, after all, one of the primary normative enterprises of political science. Strictly speaking, however, it has some troublesome problems. This approach displays a kind of normative schizophrenia. On one hand, it claims that legitimacy comes from the people and actual participation is necessary to secure that legitimacy. At the same time, this approach denies people the ability to decide about the extent and limits of their own participation. It attempts to answer questions about participation by ignoring or excluding the participation of those affected.

The second strategy is more normatively consistent because it is more radically democratic. This *deliberative* strategy says that participatory norms ought to be decided by those affected by them. It encourages deliberation and dialogue about participation itself, a self-referential practice of discussing the conditions under which discussion should occur. The principal advantage of this strategy is that it allows people to make claims about which forms of participation ought to exhibit parity and what counts as an impediment to it. In the examples I considered above, for instance, people would be able to deliberate over the relative merits of workplace democracy versus property rights, or whether day care ought to be part of the voting process. This strategy avoids normative problems because of its consistency. It upholds both the practice *and* the ideal of participation at the same time.

Because of its consistency and normative robustness, a deliberative conception is the best strategy for establishing norms of participation. I have argued for such a strategy in earlier discussions of Fraser's work.[22] Fraser also indicates a preference for a deliberative solution to

---

22 Kevin Olson, "Distributive Justice and the Politics of Difference," *Critical Horizons* 2: 1, 2001, pp. 5–32; "Recognizing Gender, Redistributing Labor," *Social Politics* 9: 3, 2002, pp. 380–410.

such questions. She says that "the norm of participatory parity must be applied dialogically and discursively, though democratic processes of public debate."[23] For all of these reasons, I believe that the participatory norms at the heart of social justice must be richly deliberative ones.

When we embrace deliberation as a means of decision-making, political participation acquires a special normative importance. It provides people with the means to interpret participatory norms and develop common agreements about the senses in which each individual should be able to participate as a peer. Whereas the broader, social sense of participation only describes the opportunities people have to do various activities, political participation additionally describes their ability to deliberate about the kinds of opportunities available to them. Thus it is normatively prior to participation in the broader sense, because it functions as a meta-category of participation *about* participation.

In sum, participation should be seen in a double sense: both as an interactive, political process of deliberation, and as the ability to take part in a broad range of (social) activities. Of the two, the political sphere is a privileged domain of participatory parity, because it safeguards and promotes other kinds of participatory parity and determines the extent and bounds of participation. In a complex, institutionally differentiated society, politics furnishes the basis for synthesizing norms and values. Our particular opinions about parity in other dimensions are politically formulated. Political participation thus takes pride of place in a trivalent theory of justice. This argument narrows the claim that parity of participation should be the normative basis for claims to justice. The normative weight of this conception rightly falls on parity of *political* participation.

3. The paradox of enablement

Shifting the normative burden from recognition and redistribution to parity of political participation has substantial advantages. Claims to justice can now be turned over to the actual deliberations of those affected by them. Norms and ideals thus arise from actual social contexts and the lived experience of real people. This conception of democratic justice is backed by intuitions similar to those of popular sovereignty. That ideal holds that people should be able to formulate the laws under which they live. A deliberative approach to justice takes much the same attitude towards norms. In so doing, such a conception considerably reduces the burden of justification that theorists need to

---

23 Fraser, "Social Justice," p. 43. More generally, pp. 42–5, 70–2.

shoulder when they talk about justice. There are significant philosophical challenges in staking out a satisfactory notion of justice, as the
debates over both redistribution and recognition have shown. Not least
of them is the daunting question of how a theoretically derived notion
of justice can bind actual people who may not recognize its validity.
A view like Fraser's solves that problem by turning justice over to the
people themselves. The theorist is left the more modest task of
establishing the conditions under which norms of justice can be justly
developed.

Although the theorist's role is reduced in this view, it is still important
and perhaps every bit as difficult. Justice is the quintessential normative
enterprise. If we are going to shift the normative basis of justice to
democracy, we must now ensure that democracy is up to the task.
Thus we must give careful consideration to the adequacy of politics
for formulating our most carefully considered norms and values.

Strictly speaking, the idea of participatory parity is separate from
the idea of its deliberative enactment. It is one thing to argue that
democratic politics should be characterized by participatory parity,
and another to use actual democratic processes to establish actual
norms. Nancy Fraser argues persuasively, however, that the two are
most normatively robust when they are joined together.[24] I strongly
agree with this claim. For ease of reference I will call that compound
proposition *the participatory ideal*. This refers to Fraser's overall thesis
that justice should be rooted in the norm of participatory parity *and*
that participatory norms should be deliberatively elaborated.

Unfortunately the juxtaposition of these two ideas creates substantial problems. Fraser notes that a circularity is inherent in the participatory
ideal.[25] Participation is to serve as a means for raising and adjudicating
claims to justice. People suffering from maldistribution, misrecognition,
or marginalization will be able to make claims about the injustice of
their situation, using participatory parity as the normative standard
for claims about what is unjust. Political participation gives citizens
not treated as peers the ability to make such claims. Moreover, it allows
them to argue for contextually appropriate policies that best match
their needs and interests. Here the irony of the situation becomes clear,
however. The people who most need to make claims about injustice,
those who are politically disadvantaged in a given society, are the ones

---

24 Fraser, "Social Justice," pp. 42–5, 70–2, 86–8; and "Distorted Beyond All
Recognition," pp. 207–11, 229–33.
25 Fraser, "Social Justice," p. 44.

whose participatory parity is most at risk. They are most in need of parity-promoting policies. By definition, though, people who cannot participate as peers are precisely the ones least capable of making such claims. The problem, in short, is that deliberation presupposes participatory parity at the same time that deliberation is supposed to set the standards for participatory parity. The participatory ideal is circular because it presupposes equal agency at the same time that it seeks to promote it. I will call this circularity the *paradox of enablement*. Enablement here refers to the participatory ideal's aim of *enabling* citizens to participate as equals. The paradox of enablement occurs when equally able citizens are both *presupposed* by deliberation and are its intended *product*.[26]

Fraser claims that such a circularity is not vicious. As an element of theory, it is merely a sign of what she calls the "reflexive character of justice as understood from the democratic perspective."[27] To the extent that the circularity is a problem in practice, she says, it can be abolished by distinguishing different levels of participation. A meta-discourse focusing on norms of participation should occur alongside the more direct, first-order claims about justice that make up the bulk of deliberation. Whereas first-order claims express opinions about justice directly, the second-order or meta-level countenances claims about discourse itself.[28] It is discourse about the norms and procedures regulating discourse. As such, it would allow marginalized people to make claims about the injustice of their own marginalization.

The idea of distinguishing levels of discourse seems a promising solution, because it shifts the normative burden away from generalized deliberation to a more specialized set of deliberations about deliberation. This solution only relocates the paradox to a new, meta-discursive level, however. At the new level, conditions of participatory parity must be met in order to reach normatively sound standards of justice. Before such standards can be met, however, we must know what they are. There is still a circular relationship between the conditions of participation and its results, then. The paradox is not resolved here, but only reiterated.

In contrast to Fraser, I believe that this circularity is problematic not only in practice but in theory as well. To get to the heart of the

---

26 Kevin Olson, *Reflexive Democracy: Political Equality and the Welfare State*, Cambridge, MA: MIT Press, 2006, Chapter 5.

27 Fraser, "Social Justice," p. 44.

28 Ibid., pp. 44–5.

problem, I will back up a step to examine its theoretical roots. The participatory ideal, as Fraser notes, is inherently reflexive. It specifies the procedures of its own creation and elaboration. As such, we cannot make a meaningful distinction between particular norms in their ideal state, on one hand, and their subsequent application to particular contexts, on the other. Upholding the participatory ideal means ensuring that all people in a given society can participate as peers in its political processes. The meaning of being a peer requires political elaboration, however: people must determine what dimensions of participation are important and to what degree. This is not a decision that *applies* a predetermined norm. Rather, the political process in question *formulates* the meaning and boundaries of that norm: what it means and what it applies to. This process performs fundamental conceptual work. Without it, there would be no norm to apply and no understanding of the domain to which it should be applied. Because norm formation and application cannot meaningfully be separated in this case, any practical problems that the participatory ideal encounters are also theoretical problems.

Keeping these cautions in mind, we can see that the paradox of enablement reveals an epistemological problem at the heart of the participatory ideal. Political participation is vital for expressing people's needs, circumstances, opinions, and preferences. It is crucial for communicating and processing information. The paradox of enablement prevents particular groups from fulfilling this function, however. It leaves them in a chronic condition of marginalization. Their political voice is diminished, reducing their ability to make political claims. Thus important voices are never heard and public policies often do not reflect the needs of those who could benefit from them most. Political marginalization deprives the political system of vital information, undercutting its ability to serve as an arbiter for claims to justice.

The epistemological problems created by political marginalization are particularly dire when they completely prevent people from making claims about their own political exclusion. In this case marginalization is not simply a violation of parity. It additionally deprives people of the means to demand inclusion. Such people become politically invisible, trapped in a political black hole from which no information can escape. The paradox is not merely a failure to treat others as peers in interaction, then. It is more profoundly a self-perpetuating trap for people and political information.

The paradox of enablement is exactly the kind of distinctively political harm I described above. It results from violating the public-political condition of participatory parity. Although this problem has important economic and cultural roots, it is ultimately political in character. We see this in its epistemological manifestations, which prevent citizens from lodging complaints through democratic means about their own marginalization. These epistemological problems are created by defects in a particular democratic regime. Marginalization is thus political in a way that goes beyond economy and culture. This is easily seen if we imagine trying to resolve the paradox solely by promoting economic and cultural equality. This would provide two of the conditions of participatory parity, but only in an objectivistic sense. It precisely ignores the political, deliberative basis of the paradox. Such a solution would lack the information provided by actual citizens in deliberation, failing to meet their needs and preferences and thus running aground on the epistemic problems I have just outlined. By attempting to resolve the paradox in a non-political fashion, it ignores a political harm that cannot be reduced to the objective and intersubjective conditions of participation.

The paradox I have described is not simply a failure to realize participatory parity in practice. It is inherent within the participatory ideal itself. Because the ideal contains a reflexive commitment to its own participatory interpretation and enactment, a clear line cannot be drawn between norms and their application. That distinction collapses in this case. In its place we are left with a conceptual problem created at the messy interface between ideas and the world. Participatory parity requires some means for promoting participation. If this mechanism is deliberatively formulated, it meets the requirements of participatory parity. Such a mechanism presupposes equal agency in the processes through which it is formulated, however. In order to promote participatory parity, it first requires participatory parity. If, on the other hand, a notion of participatory parity is paternalistically formulated by others, it normatively undercuts itself. This conception promotes equal agency while simultaneously marginalizing the people it is designed to help. We must conclude, then, that participation cannot be the solution to problems of participation. Paradox results when we do not heed this warning.

4. Integrating theory and politics

The paradox of enablement jeopardizes the project of democratic justice. It arises out of the tension between two commitments funda-mental to this project. On one hand, democratic justice is committed to the insight that justice requires participatory parity; on the other, it is committed to the idea that notions of justice can only be formulated by democratic citizens. Expert opinion about justice is in tension here with popular sovereignty itself. We must find a way to relieve this tension by devising a solution that is both theoretically acceptable *and* democratically legitimate. This is not just a matter of explaining the tension away in a theoretical sense, but of actually unifying theory and practice. To do this, we must explore the relationship between theory and actual democracy in greater depth. The key question, in the end, is how theorists' considered judgments can best be integrated with the folk norms and actual deliberations of real people.

In what follows I will outline several elements that may be useful for moving this project forward. They are building blocks that could be assembled in various ways, consistent with Fraser's work, to resolve the paradox.

Element One: Non-paternalist egalitarianism. A carefully thought-out democratic egalitarianism, drawing on insights of distributive justice, can considerably blur the line between objectivism and deliberation. This approach employs social science to characterize the connections between redistribution, recognition, and participation. It uses standard tools of data collection and statistical inference to identify the ways that political participation is rendered unequal. From this standpoint, it makes policy recommendations for ameliorating inequalities and promoting participatory parity.

Because such an objectivistic, social-scientific analysis stands outside the deliberative sphere of actual democratic citizens, there is a danger that it would establish paternalist, decontextualized solutions. To prevent this, we need to think in more detail about how democratic procedures could be formulated to promote participatory parity without simultaneously undermining democracy. Here distributive justice has some useful things to say. Social policy and social science become paternalistic when they use governmental power coercively to limit people's choices, or, even worse, to create specific kinds of subjects. This is very different from creating *opportunities*, which is not paternalistic as long as it expands the range of options available to people without foreclosing them in other ways.

A capability approach to political equality could be devised to create such opportunities.[29] In Amartya Sen's work, a capability is a metric

---

29 Olson, *Reflexive Democracy*, pp. 138–49; and "Distributive Justice." See also Ingrid Robeyns, "Is Nancy Fraser's Critique of Theories of Distributive Justice Justified?" in this volume; James Bohman, "Deliberative Democracy and Effective Social Freedom: Capabilities, Resources, and Opportunities," in *Deliberative Democracy: Essays on Reason and Politics*, ed. James Bohman and William Rehg, Cambridge, MA: MIT Press, 1997; and James Bohman, *Public Deliberation: Pluralism, Complexity, and Democracy*, Cambridge, MA: MIT Press, 1996, Chapter 3.

for distributive justice describing an actually equal opportunity to do some activity or be a particular kind of person.[30] Equal capabilities for political participation would create actually equal opportunities in the political sphere. If such a policy were sufficiently general and sufficiently rich in the opportunities it made available, it would not constitute a paternalistic imposition on popular sovereignty. Rather, it would simply reshape the structural environment in which popular sovereignty is realized. Equal opportunities to access the media or practice participatory skills might be examples of such a conception. Opportunities of this kind combine objectivistic analysis and deliberation in a fruitful way, creating a fair playing field for citizens to act as participatory peers in decision-making. In this sense, they erode the barriers between objectivistic and deliberative strategies.

Element Two: Recursive reflexivity. Nancy Fraser notes the reflexive character of democratic justice. When we stipulate that norms of justice should be deliberatively formulated, we invite citizens to develop norms that reflect back to inform their own condition. As Fraser notes, "In the democratic perspective, justice is not an externally imposed requirement, determined over the heads of those whom it obligates. Rather, it binds only insofar as its addressees can also rightly regard themselves as its authors."[31] This very reflexivity is the source of the paradox, of course. It allows fully capable citizens to author the laws to which they are subject, while leaving their less capable compatriots subject to laws that they are not peers in authoring. In spite of this, we might wonder whether reflexivity could serve as a solution rather than a source of problems.

One can imagine a process of norm formation in which reflexivity could be employed for constructive ends. Parity of participation specifies a status in which each citizen has means sufficient to participate as a peer in deliberation. Suppose for the moment that we simply hold out the *ideal* that citizens must be able to participate as equals in the processes that guarantee their participatory equality. They must be equally able to determine the meaning and content of citizenship. In this case citizens would be equally able to formulate the basis of their own, ongoing equality. When this happened, the legal status they share would become *reflexive*. It would endow citizens with the means to sustain their equality *as* citizens. That legal status is structured in such

---

30 Amartya Sen, *Commodities and Capabilities*, Amsterdam: North-Holland, 1985; *Inequality Reexamined*, Cambridge, MA: Harvard University Press, 1992; and "Capability and Well-Being," in *The Quality of Life*, ed. Martha Nussbaum and Amartya Sen, New York: Oxford University Press, 1993.

31 Fraser, "Social Justice," p. 44.

a way that it reflects back to support itself, as it were, sustaining its own grounds of possibility.[32]

Now suppose that this ideal is a public one. It is not simply a theorist's construction, but something that actual citizens see as important. It functions, in this sense, as a folk paradigm of justice. Suppose further that people use this standard as a reference point when considering various policy proposals dealing with political marginalization. When actual citizens ask, "what form of political parity do we need?" the answer they arrive at is "one giving each citizen an equal ability to determine the meaning and content of citizenship." This is an extravagant supposition in one sense. It assumes that actual citizens would see politics as a theorist does. In another sense, though, it simply assumes that they understand the importance of political participation in the same way that we do. They understand marginalization as a problem they need to solve, and they understand that reflexive citizenship would constitute an adequate solution to it.

When norms of reflexive citizenship become public, they allow actual citizens to see that the political process must be open to those whose participation is blocked. Further, *ex hypothesi*, these norms promote the realization that some people are rendered politically invisible by the paradox of enablement. Citizens must actively search for ways to expand the boundaries of reflexivity, then. If they are successful, the number of marginalized people decreases while the number deliberating as peers increases. This political dynamic consists in a *recursive* reformulation of the norms of participatory parity with an ever-increasing number of participants. It thus creates an evolutionary dynamic promoting participatory parity and reflexive citizenship.[33]

Reflexive participation would be the ultimate transformative solution. By definition, it establishes conditions of true political parity. This in turn allows all citizens to devise solutions that are in their eyes most acceptable given their institutional and social milieu. They could draw freely on redistribution, recognition, and inclusion to promote parity. Such a conception would cross the (artificial) boundaries between the three domains by playing on their empirical entanglement to solve a problem in which all are implicated. Such a solution is hybrid and flexible.

---

32 Kevin Olson, "Constructing Citizens," *Journal of Politics* 70:1, 2008, pp. 40–53; Olson, *Reflexive Democracy*, Chapter 6.
33 Kevin Olson, "Paradoxes of Constitutional Democracy," *American Journal of Political Science* 51: 2, 2007, pp. 330–43.

Of course, all of this is based on a large supposition: that norms of participatory parity could be introduced into public circulation, becoming the predominant understanding of social justice in an actual society. Because we can only envision such a situation, recursive reflexivity remains only an *element* of a possible solution.

Element Three: Implicit presuppositions. One way to promote the public acceptance of norms is to point out that people already *do* accept them. In their daily interactions, people often presuppose and draw on norms that they are not explicitly aware of. Such norms are implicitly presupposed by their own practices, but beyond their conscious grasp until they are identified as such.[34] We could take such an approach to democratic justice.

Consider, for instance, what the paradox of enablement teaches us about actual practices of democratic norm-formation. The fundamental lesson to be learned from this discussion is that participatory norms cannot be determined through deliberation in an open-ended manner. Not every decision about the meaning of being a peer is equally valid. Some such decisions are self-contradictory: those that undercut the conditions of participation, marginalize some citizens, and result in the paradox of enablement. Others, in contrast, avoid the paradox by sustaining participatory parity for everyone. To avoid the former and ensure the latter, some guarantee of enablement must be an integral part of democratic politics. Such a guarantee is justified directly as a solution to the paradox, and it is thus a corrective to the kinds of circumstances that give rise to the paradox in the first place. It is both implied by the democratic participation of actual citizens and justified against the background of their actual inequalities.

From this perspective, the paradox sows the seeds for its own solution. It is a problem in the worlds of both theory and practice. Any adequate solution must simultaneously satisfy theoretical diagnoses and resolve the real problems of actual societies. Citizens attempting to deliberate as peers about norms of justice will encounter such problems. Particular kinds of political rights, redistributive measures, and recognition are required to make their deliberations possible. Citizens who fail to establish such measures contradict their own goals and intentions. Such a solution is implicitly presupposed,

---

34 Jürgen Habermas, "What is Universal Pragmatics?" in *Communication and the Evolution of Society*, trans. Thomas McCarthy, Boston: Beacon Press, 1979; Kevin Olson, "Do Rights Have a Formal Basis? Habermas's Legal Theory and the Normative Foundations of the Law," *Journal of Political Philosophy* 11: 3, pp. 273–94.

then, in the deliberative practices of actual citizens. The need for parity in political participation sets limits on what can be democratically decided. It is something that such people can reject only on pain of self-contradiction.

This kind of approach justifies comprehensive guarantees of political agency. It has a public, rhetorical force, pointing out inconsistencies in the actual practices of an actual society. If people see themselves as formulating norms by democratic means, they presuppose participatory parity in an important sense. Solutions to problems of maldistribution, misrecognition, and marginalization are thus implicit *presuppositions* of democracy, not simply its conditions. An analysis of such presuppositions can function as an intervention in public deliberation. It provides a way for theorists to point out important social problems, actually existing paradoxes, and implicit resources for their resolution. This gets around the either-or dichotomy of justice *or* democracy. By giving theorists a role in the analysis of presently existing public commitments, it relieves the tension between objectivism and deliberation.

Element Four: Demystify relations between politics, economy, and culture. Theorists are also well equipped for the task of clearing obstacles to public deliberation. Above all, the paradox of enablement shows the need to resolve feedback relations between culture, economy, and politics. It requires us to undo the vicious circle connecting maldistribution, misrecognition, and marginalization. The paradox results precisely because these three spheres are empirically intertwined while also being normatively separated. Redistribution and recognition serve as conditions for participation as a result of the important empirical connections between economy, culture, and politics. At the same time, questions of economy and culture are often excluded from the political sphere. Political regulation of the economy is often portrayed as state interference, micromanagement, and a violation of property rights, legitimating a libertarian conception of separate economic and political spheres. Similarly, the idea that "you can't legislate culture" is often deployed both to isolate normatively suspect cultures from political interference and to mystify the cultural impact of political decisions. Again, the effect is to exclude culture from politics, at least from the official public sphere in which norms can be discussed. Both economy and culture are insulated from politics by these moves, isolating them from the normative context of popular sovereignty. The ideology of separate spheres prevents citizens from tackling the messy problems that come from the *de facto* empirical interconnection between these domains. As a result of empirical entanglement and normative separation, the paradox of enablement is often cut off from political solutions. Demystifying this situation, on the other hand, allows us to see the feedback relations between these spheres and find a way around them.

Element Five: Organic intellectuals and critical publics. The relation between expert opinion and public deliberation has been a constant theme here. A final element bridges the gap between these discursive spheres by highlighting their interconnection and rethinking the division of labor between them. It picks up where elements two, three, and four leave off, asserting that engaged work in political theory *does* in fact have practical effects. Work like Fraser's is not simply a contribution to theoretical discussions, but an intervention in actually existing public deliberation. From this point of view, intellectuals occupy an important role in public opinion formation and should not be treated as though they exist in a realm communicatively isolated from that in which political decisions are made. All intellectuals are organic in the sense that they are members of the populace and participants in the public sphere.[35]

These insights reframe the relation between theories of justice and actual deliberation. They explain how a practically oriented theory can be taken up by a critically sophisticated populace. Theorists' assertions about impediments to participatory parity function as claims to justice. They are indeed "contributions to the critique of actually-existing democracy," ones providing a theoretically informed perspective within public deliberation.[36] They thus help to collapse the distinction between objectivistic and deliberative strategies.

Although this approach seems quite promising, it does have limitations. It could be said to emphasize democracy over justice by leaving the ultimate normative warrant with the public. Theorists can make more or less persuasive suggestions within the public sphere, but their claims do not have any particular privilege. It is an open question, then, whether what counts as justice from a theorist's perspective would have any public traction.

This approach may also be accused of over-emphasizing the role of intellectuals in public deliberation. To some extent it ignores the differentiation of expert spheres out of public life. Academic opinion—

---

35 Antonio Gramsci, *Selections from the Prison Notebooks*, ed. Quintin Hoare and Geoffrey Nowell Smith, New York: International Publishers, 1971, pp. 5–23.

36 Fraser, "Rethinking the Public Sphere: A Contribution to the Critique of Actually Existing Democracy."

particularly of a non-quantitative sort—is often isolated from spheres of political decision-making. Academics address one another more than the public at large, their opinions are often disqualified as elitist or narrowly theoretical, and academic argumentation often meshes poorly with the emotive, semi-rational character of public discourse. There is an extent to which academic life renders intellectuals inorganic, then, whatever their social origins may be. Organic intellectuals and critical publics do not fit together perfectly, so this element has both promise and limitations.

5. Democratic justice within its own limits

We are now in a better position to assess the lessons that this discussion has produced for democratic justice. I have argued that politics should be seen as a separate, irreducible, and normatively prior perspective on justice. Political participation is a privileged genre of participation in this view, because it allows us to make and adjudicate claims of justice. Parity of political participation is in turn the key norm in the project of democratic justice.

When parity of political participation moves to center stage, the entwinement of the economic, cultural, and political realms becomes crucially important as well. Characteristically economic, cultural, and political harms can undermine parity of political participation in normatively problematic ways. The paradox of enablement is a particularly troublesome cluster of such harms. It is created and reproduced when a political system becomes recursively exclusionary. In this situation, a vicious spiral of marginalization occurs. Marginalized people become more and more removed from the sphere in which they might make claims about the injustice of their own marginalization. Democracy and justice thus grow further and further apart.

To put democracy and justice back together again, we must devise some way of bringing the economic, cultural, and political conditions of democratic participation into harmony with one another. This is best done, I have argued, through democracy itself. It requires a conception of democratic politics that can promote inclusion on an ongoing basis. To advance that project, I will close by sketching more clearly how the elements I have detailed could fit into Nancy Fraser's conception of justice.

The paradox of enablement shows that some carefully rethought political processes are needed to safeguard parity of political participation. Some "public-political condition" must ensure the dimensions of parity needed to prevent paradox. Because Fraser's conception of democratic justice suffers from this paradox, it commits us to equalizing agency.

Parity of political participation is, in this sense, an implicit presupposition of the theory. There is considerable room to argue about the form such parity should take, but it would be functionally similar to what I have called non-paternalist egalitarianism—a policy creating equal capabilities for political participation. Such limitations narrow the scope of deliberation in beneficial ways. By specifying the need for particular kinds of equality, they prevent democratic citizens from disenfranchising one another.

With these insights in the background, we can imagine how norms of participatory parity could be deliberatively developed within a society marked by misrecognition, maldistribution, and marginalization. In such a situation, parity of participation must function above all as a folk paradigm of justice. It is a genre of claim that actual people can make about their own concrete social situation. As such, it would likely not start out as the kind of norm that theorists might prefer. Rather, the folk form might be some inchoate, poorly developed intuition that is egalitarian only in an embryonic sense. Elaborating on this norm until it becomes a full-blown conception of participatory parity is an inherently political process: it requires people to deliberate over normative claims. Moreover, it is a *recursive* process, because each regime of norms and procedures provides the basis for deliberation about the *next* generation of norms and procedures.

As I have shown, though, parity of political participation is not *simply* a folk paradigm of justice, but also a norm implicit in the practice of democratic justice. Any society hoping to develop norms of justice through democratic means presupposes a very particular form of parity. This is the one that I have called reflexive citizenship. That norm says that people should be able to control the laws that sustain their own political agency. Such a norm of parity is presupposed in any society in which questions of justice are democratically raised.

This implicit fact is not a rhetorical trump card that theorists can use to impose their will on the populace. It does, however, provide anyone who cares to use it with powerful leverage to criticize existing states of affairs and suggest how they might be otherwise. Because parity of political participation is presupposed by democratic justice, claims for parity have added force in public discourse. Parity in this case is not simply a good idea, but an implicit part of a particular practice. Anyone who thinks democratic justice is a good idea is also implicitly committed to parity of political participation. As a result, the norm of parity enjoys a presumption of acceptability not shared by others. Attempts to introduce such a norm in dialogue will thus "make sense" in ways that others might not. Anyone arguing in favor of such a norm would fight a downhill battle rather than an uphill one.

Over time, through many years of political discourse, inegalitarian folk norms will have to compete against this argument. They will have to be justified against the background of a political system that is paradoxical because it is exclusionary. They will have to be further justified against competing views like the one I have described: views that "make sense" as solutions to paradox. Even when the populace is not wise or insightful, notions of reflexive citizenship enjoy the advantage of being better solutions to the paradoxes experienced by actual citizens. Theorists may not have a privileged authority in the public sphere, but they do sometimes have the advantage of suggesting solutions that are better suited to the problem at hand. As folk norms of equality are recursively applied and elaborated, quiet voices with good solutions to offer may, in the end, be the most convincing.

This argument shows that to *pose* questions of justice in terms of democracy is also to *answer* a substantial number of them. Turning such questions over to democratic deliberation narrows the range of what can be decided through deliberation itself. A theory of democratic justice like Fraser's answers many questions about the scope and character of justice. Somewhat surprisingly, it answers those questions with greater specificity and less reliance on actual deliberation than many deliberative democrats might suppose.

Nancy Fraser's ideas about participation provide a valuable entrée for thinking about justice from a new perspective. From this standpoint, justice becomes a process rather than a particular end state. It is based in democracy and the concrete normative horizons of actual societies, rather than theorists' armchair argument. My discussion tries to broaden such horizons by thinking about their implicit normative possibilities and problems. It discovers points of connection between socially embedded normative views and theorists' more abstract ideals. In this view democratic justice is not a union of contradictory opposites, but a project that gains energy from its internal tensions.

REFRAMING JUSTICE IN A
GLOBALIZING WORLD
Nancy Fraser

Globalization is changing the way we argue about justice. Not so long ago, in the heyday of social democracy, disputes about justice presumed what I shall call a "Keynesian-Westphalian frame." Typically played out within modern territorial states, arguments about justice were assumed to concern relations among fellow citizens, to be subject to debate within national publics, and to contemplate redress by national states. This was true for each of two major families of justice claims—claims for socioeconomic redistribution and claims for legal or cultural recognition. At a time when the Bretton Woods system facilitated Keynesian economic steering at the national level, claims for redistribution usually focused on economic inequities within territorial states. Appealing to national public opinion for a fair share of the national pie, claimants sought intervention by national states in national economies. Likewise, in an era still gripped by a Westphalian political imaginary, which sharply distinguished "domestic" from "international" space, claims for recognition generally concerned internal status hierarchies. Appealing to the national conscience for an end to nationally institutionalized disrespect, claimants pressed national governments to outlaw discrimination and accommodate differences among citizens. In both cases, the Keynesian-Westphalian frame was taken for granted. Whether the matter concerned redistribution or recognition, class differentials or status hierarchies, it went without saying that the unit within which justice applied was the modern territorial state.[1]

---

1 The phrase "Keynesian-Westphalian frame" is meant to signal the national-territorial underpinnings of justice disputes in the heyday of the postwar democratic welfare state, roughly 1945 to the 1970s. The term "Westphalian" refers to the Treaty of 1648, which established some key features of the modern international state system. However, I am concerned neither with the actual achievements of the treaty nor with

To be sure, there were always exceptions. Occasionally, famines and genocides galvanized public opinion across borders. And some cosmopolitans and anti-imperialists sought to promulgate globalist views.[2] But these were exceptions that proved the rule. Relegated to the sphere of "the international," they were subsumed within a problematic that was focused primarily on matters of security, as opposed to justice. The effect was to reinforce, rather than to challenge, the Keynesian-Westphalian frame. That framing of disputes about justice generally prevailed by default from the end of the Second World War to the 1970s.

Although it went unnoticed at the time, this framework lent a distinctive shape to arguments about social justice. Taking for granted the modern territorial state as the appropriate unit, and its citizens as the pertinent subjects, such arguments turned on *what* precisely those citizens owed one another. In the eyes of some, it sufficed that citizens be formally equal before the law; for others, equality of opportunity was also required; for still others, justice demanded that all citizens gain access to the resources and respect they needed in order to be able to participate on a par with others, as full members of the political community. The argument focused, in other words, on exactly what should count as a just ordering of social relations within a society. Engrossed in disputing the "what" of justice, the contestants apparently felt no necessity to dispute the "who." With the Keynesian-Westphalian frame securely in place, it went without saying that the "who" was the national citizenry.

Today, however, this framework is losing its aura of self-evidence. Thanks to heightened awareness of globalization, and to post–Cold War geopolitical instabilities, many observe that the social processes shaping their lives routinely overflow territorial borders. They note, for example, that decisions taken in one territorial state often have an

the centuries-long process by which the system it inaugurated evolved. Rather, I invoke Westphalia as a political imaginary that mapped the world as a system of mutually recognizing sovereign territorial states. My claim is that this imaginary informed the postwar framing of debates about justice in the First World, even as the beginnings of a post-Westphalian human-rights regime emerged. For the distinction between Westphalia as "event," as "idea/ideal," as "process of evolution," and as "normative score-sheet," see Richard Falk, "Revisiting Westphalia, Discovering Post-Westphalia," *Journal of Ethics* 6: 4, 2002, pp. 311–52.

2 It might be assumed that, from the perspective of the Third World, Westphalian premises would have appeared patently counterfactual. Yet it is worth recalling that the great majority of anti-colonialists sought to achieve independent Westphalian states of their own. Only a small minority consistently championed justice within a global framework—for reasons that are entirely understandable.

impact on the lives of those outside it, as do the actions of transnational corporations, international currency speculators, and large institutional investors. Many also note the growing salience of supranational and international organizations, both governmental and non-governmental, and of transnational public opinion, which flows with supreme disregard for borders through global mass media and cybertechnology. The result is a new sense of vulnerability to transnational forces. Faced with global warming, the spread of HIV-AIDS, international terrorism and superpower unilateralism, many believe that their chances for living good lives depend at least as much on processes that trespass the borders of territorial states as on those contained within them.

Under these conditions, the Keynesian-Westphalian frame no longer goes without saying. For many, it has ceased to be axiomatic that the modern territorial state is the appropriate unit for thinking about issues of justice, and that the citizens of such states are the pertinent subjects of reference. The effect is to destabilize the previous structure of political claims-making—and therefore to change the way we argue about social justice.

This is true for both major families of justice claims. In today's world, claims for redistribution increasingly eschew the assumption of national economies. Faced with transnationalized production, the outsourcing of jobs, and the associated pressures of the "race to the bottom," once nationally focused labor unions look increasingly for allies abroad. Inspired by the Zapatistas, meanwhile, impoverished peasants and indigenous peoples link their struggles against despotic local and national authorities to critiques of transnational corporate predation and global neoliberalism. Finally, WTO protestors directly target the new governance structures of the global economy, which have vastly strengthened the ability of large corporations and investors to escape the regulatory and taxation powers of territorial states.

In the same way, movements struggling for recognition increasingly look beyond the territorial state. Under the umbrella slogan "women's rights are human rights," for example, feminists throughout the world are linking struggles against local patriarchal practices to campaigns to reform international law. Meanwhile, religious and ethnic minorities, who face discrimination within territorial states, are reconstituting themselves as diasporas and building transnational publics from which to mobilize international opinion. Finally, transnational coalitions of human-rights activists are seeking to build new cosmopolitan institutions, such as the International Criminal Court, which can punish state violations of human dignity.

In such cases, disputes about justice are exploding the Keynesian-

Westphalian frame. No longer addressed exclusively to national states or debated exclusively by national publics, claimants no longer focus solely on relations among fellow citizens. Thus, the grammar of argument has altered. Whether the issue is distribution or recognition, disputes that used to focus exclusively on the question of *what* is owed as a matter of justice to community members now turn quickly into disputes about *who* should count as a member and *which* is the relevant community. Not just the "what" but also the "who" is up for grabs.

Today, in other words, arguments about justice assume a double guise. On the one hand, they concern first-order questions of substance, just as before. How much economic inequality does justice permit, how much redistribution is required, and according to which principle of distributive justice? What constitutes equal respect, which kinds of differences merit public recognition, and by which means? But above and beyond such first-order questions, arguments about justice today also concern second-order, meta-level questions. What is the proper frame within which to consider first-order questions of justice? Who are the relevant subjects entitled to a just distribution or reciprocal recognition in the given case? Thus, it is not only the substance of justice, but also the frame, which is in dispute. The result is a major challenge to our theories of social justice. Preoccupied largely with first-order issues of distribution and/or recognition, these theories have so far failed to develop conceptual resources for reflecting on the meta-issue of the frame. As things stand, therefore, it is by no means clear that they are capable of addressing the double character of problems of justice in a globalizing age.[3]

In this essay, I shall propose a strategy for thinking about the problem of the frame. I shall argue, first, that theories of justice must become three-dimensional, incorporating the political dimension of *representation* alongside the economic dimension of distribution and the cultural dimension of recognition. I shall also argue that the political dimension of representation should itself be understood as encompassing three levels. The combined effect of these two arguments will be to make visible a third question, beyond those of the "what" and the "who," which I shall call the question of the "how." That

---

3 I have discussed the elision of the problem of the frame in mainstream theories of justice in my first Spinoza Lecture, "Who Counts? Thematizing the Question of the Frame," in *Reframing Justice: Spinoza Lectures*, Amsterdam: Van Gorcum, 2005. See also Fraser, "Two Dogmas of Egalitarianism," in Nancy Fraser, *Scales of Justice: Re-imagining Political Space in a Globalizing World*, New York: Polity Press and Columbia University Press, 2008.

question, in turn, inaugurates a paradigm shift: what the Keynesian-Westphalian frame cast as the theory of social justice must now become a theory of *post-Westphalian democratic justice.*

For a three-dimensional theory of justice: on the specificity of the political

Let me begin by explaining what I mean by justice in general and by its political dimension in particular. In my view, the most general meaning of justice is parity of participation. According to this radical-democratic interpretation of the principle of equal moral worth, justice requires social arrangements that permit all to participate as peers in social life. Overcoming injustice means dismantling institutionalized obstacles that prevent some people from participating on a par with others, as full partners in social interaction. Previously, I have analyzed two distinct kinds of obstacles to participatory parity, which correspond to two distinct species of injustice. On the one hand, people can be impeded from full participation by economic structures that deny them the resources they need in order to interact with others as peers; in that case they suffer from distributive injustice or maldistribution. On the other hand, people can also be prevented from interacting on terms of parity by institutionalized hierarchies of cultural value that deny them the requisite standing; in that case they suffer from status inequality or misrecognition.[4] In the first case, the problem is the class structure of society, which corresponds to the economic dimension of justice. In the second case, the problem is the status order, which corresponds to its cultural dimension. In modern capitalist societies, the class structure and the status order do not neatly mirror each other, although they interact causally. Rather, each has some autonomy vis-à-vis the other. As a result, misrecognition cannot be reduced to a secondary effect of maldistribution, as some economistic theories of distributive justice appear to suppose. Nor, conversely, can maldistribution be reduced to an epiphenomenal expression of misrecognition, as some culturalist theories of recognition tend to assume. Thus, neither recognition theory nor distribution theory alone can provide an adequate understanding of justice for capitalist society. Only a two-dimensional theory, encompassing both distribution and recognition, can supply

---

4 This "status model" of recognition represents an alternative to the standard "identity model." For a critique of the latter and a defense of the former, see Fraser, "Rethinking Recognition," in this volume.

the necessary levels of social-theoretical complexity and moral-philosophical insight.[5]

That, at least, is the view of justice I have defended in the past. And this two-dimensional understanding of justice still seems right to me as far as it goes. But I now believe that it does not go far enough. Distribution and recognition could appear to constitute the sole dimensions of justice only so long as the Keynesian-Westphalian frame was taken for granted. Once the question of the frame becomes subject to contestation, the effect is to make visible a third dimension of justice, which was neglected in my previous work—as well as in the work of many other philosophers.[6]

The third dimension of justice is *the political*. Of course, distribution and recognition are themselves political in the sense of being contested and power-laden; and they have usually been seen as requiring adjudication by the state. But I mean political in a more specific, constitutive sense, which concerns the nature of the state's jurisdiction and the decision rules by which it structures contestation. The political in this sense furnishes the stage on which struggles over distribution and recognition are played out. Establishing criteria of social belonging, and thus determining who counts as a member, the political dimension of justice specifies the reach of those other dimensions: it tells us who is included in, and who excluded from, the circle of those entitled to a just distribution and reciprocal recognition. Establishing decision rules, the political dimension likewise sets the procedures for staging and resolving contests in both the economic and the cultural dimensions: it tells us not only who can make claims for redistribution and recognition, but also how such claims are to be mooted and adjudicated.

Centered on issues of membership and procedure, the political dimension of justice is concerned chiefly with *representation*. At one level, which pertains to the boundary-setting aspect of the political, representation is a matter of social belonging. What is at issue here is inclusion in, or exclusion from, the community of those entitled to

---

5 For the full argument, see my "Social Justice in the Age of Identity Politics," in Nancy Fraser and Axel Honneth, *Redistribution or Recognition? A Political-Philosophical Exchange*, trans. Joel Golb, James Ingram, and Christiane Wilke, London: Verso, 2003.

6 The neglect of the political is especially glaring in the case of theorists of justice who subscribe to liberal or communitarian philosophical premises. In contrast, deliberative democrats, agonistic democrats and republicans have sought to theorize the political. But most of these theorists have had relatively little to say about the relation between democracy and justice; and none has conceptualized the political as one of three dimensions of justice.

make justice claims on one another. At another level, which pertains to the decision-rule aspect, representation concerns the procedures that structure public processes of contestation. Here, what is at issue are the terms on which those included in the political community air their claims and adjudicate their disputes.[7] At both levels, the question can arise as to whether the relations of representation are just. One can ask: Do the boundaries of the political community wrongly exclude some who are actually entitled to representation? Do the community's decision rules accord equal voice in public deliberations and fair representation in public decision-making to all members? Such issues of representation are specifically political. Conceptually distinct from both economic and cultural questions, they cannot be reduced to the latter, although, as we shall see, they are inextricably interwoven with them.

To say that the political is a conceptually distinct dimension of justice, not reducible to the economic or the cultural, is also to say that it can give rise to a conceptually distinct species of injustice. Given the view of justice as participatory parity, this means that there can be distinctively political obstacles to parity, not reducible to maldistribution or misrecognition, although (again) interwoven with them. Such obstacles arise from the political constitution of society, as opposed to the class structure or status order. Grounded in a specifically political mode of social ordering, they can only be adequately grasped through a theory that conceptualizes representation, along with distribution and recognition, as one of three fundamental dimensions of justice.

If representation is the defining issue of the political, then the characteristic political injustice is *misrepresentation*. Misrepresentation occurs when political boundaries and/or decision rules function to deny some people, wrongly, the possibility of participating on a par with others in social interaction—including, but not only, in political arenas. Far from being reducible to maldistribution or misrecognition, misrepresentation can occur even in the absence of the latter injustices, although it is usually intertwined with them. At least two different levels of misrepresentation can be distinguished. Insofar as political decision rules wrongly deny some of the included the chance to

---

7 Classic works on representation have dealt largely with what I am calling the decision-rule aspect, while ignoring the membership aspect. See, for example, Hanna Fenichel Pitkin, *The Concept of Representation*, Berkeley: University of California Press, 1967, and Bernard Manin, *The Principles of Representative Government*, New York: Cambridge University Press, 1997.

participate fully, as peers, the injustice is what I call *ordinary-political* misrepresentation. Here, where the issue is intra-frame representation, we enter the familiar terrain of political science debates over the relative merits of alternative electoral systems. Do single-member-district, winner-take-all, first-past-the-post systems unjustly deny parity to numerical minorities? And if so, is proportional represen-tation or cumulative voting the appropriate remedy? Likewise, do gender-blind rules, in conjunction with gender-based maldistribution and misrecognition, function to deny parity of political participation to women? And if so, are gender quotas an appropriate remedy? Such questions belong to the sphere of ordinary-political justice, which has usually been played out within the Keynesian-Westphalian frame.

Less obvious, perhaps, is a second level of misrepresentation, which concerns the boundary-setting aspect of the political. Here the injustice arises when the community's boundaries are drawn in such a way as to wrongly exclude some people from the chance to participate *at all* in its authorized contests over justice. In such cases, misrepresentation takes a deeper form, which I shall call *misframing*. The deeper character of misframing is a function of the crucial importance of framing to every question of social justice. Far from being of marginal significance, frame-setting is among the most consequential of political decisions. Constituting both members and non-members in a single stroke, this decision effectively excludes the latter from the universe of those enti-tled to consideration within the community in matters of distribution, recognition, and ordinary-political representation. The result can be a serious injustice. When questions of justice are framed in a way that wrongly excludes some from consideration, the consequence is a special kind of meta-injustice, in which one is denied the chance to press first-order justice claims in a given political community. The injustice remains, moreover, even when those excluded from one political community are included as subjects of justice in another—as long as the effect of the political division is to put some relevant aspects of justice beyond their reach. Still more serious, of course, is the case in which one is excluded from membership in any political community. Akin to the loss of what Hannah Arendt called "the right to have rights," that sort of misframing is a kind of "political death."[8] Those who suffer it may become objects of charity or benevolence. But

8 Hannah Arendt, *The Origins of Totalitarianism*, New York: Harvest Books, 1973, pp. 269–84. "Political death" is my phrase, not Arendt's.

deprived of the possibility of authoring first-order claims, they become non-persons with respect to justice.

It is the misframing form of misrepresentation that globalization has recently begun to make visible. Earlier, in the heyday of the post-war welfare state, with the Keynesian-Westphalian frame securely in place, the principal concern in thinking about justice was distribution. Later, with the rise of the new social movements and multiculturalism, the center of gravity shifted to recognition. In both cases, the modern territorial state was assumed by default. As a result, the political dimension of justice was relegated to the margins. Where it did emerge, it took the ordinary-political form of contests over the decision rules internal to the polity, whose boundaries were taken for granted. Thus, claims for gender quotas and multicultural rights sought to remove political obstacles to participatory parity for those who were already included in principle in the political community. Taking for granted the Keynesian-Westphalian frame, they did not call into question the assumption that the appropriate unit of justice was the territorial state.

Today, in contrast, globalization has put the question of the frame squarely on the political agenda. Increasingly subject to contestation, the Keynesian-Westphalian frame is now considered by many to be a major vehicle of injustice, as it partitions political space in ways that block many who are poor and despised from challenging the forces that oppress them. Channeling their claims into the domestic political spaces of relatively powerless, if not wholly failed, states, this frame insulates offshore powers from critique and control.[9] Among those shielded from the reach of justice are more powerful predator states and transnational private powers, including foreign investors and creditors, international currency speculators, and transnational corporations. Also protected are the governance structures of the global economy, which set exploitative terms of interaction and then exempt them from democratic control. Finally, the Keynesian-Westphalian frame is self-insulating; the architecture of the interstate system protects the very partitioning of political space that it

---

9 See, in particular, Thomas Pogge, "The Influence of the Global Order on the Prospects for Genuine Democracy in the Developing Countries," *Ratio Juris* 14: 3, 2001, pp. 326–43; and "Economic Justice and National Borders," *Revision* 22, 1999, pp. 27–34; Rainer Forst, "Towards a Critical Theory of Transnational Justice," in Thomas Pogge, ed., *Global Justice*, Oxford: Blackwell, 2001, pp. 169–87; and "Justice, Morality and Power in the Global Context," in Andreas Follesdal and Thomas Pogge, eds., *Real World Justice*, Dordrecht: Springer, 2005.

institutionalizes, effectively excluding transnational democratic decision-making on issues of justice.

From this perspective, the Keynesian-Westphalian frame is a powerful instrument of injustice, which gerrymanders political space at the expense of the poor and despised. For those persons who are denied the chance to press transnational first-order claims, struggles against maldistribution and misrecognition cannot proceed, let alone succeed, unless they are joined with struggles against misframing. It is not surprising, therefore, that some consider misframing the defining injustice of a globalizing age.

Under these conditions, the political dimension of justice is hard to ignore. Insofar as globalization is politicizing the question of the frame, it is also making visible an aspect of the grammar of justice that was often neglected in the previous period. It is now apparent that no claim for justice can avoid presupposing some notion of representation, implicit or explicit, insofar as none can avoid assuming a frame. Thus, representation is always already inherent in all claims for redistribution and recognition. The political dimension is implicit in, indeed required by, the grammar of the concept of justice. Thus, no redistribution or recognition without representation.[10]

---

10 I do not mean to suggest that the political is the master dimension of justice, more fundamental than the economic and the cultural. Rather, the three dimensions stand in relations of mutual entwinement and reciprocal influence. Just as the ability to make claims for distribution and recognition depends on relations of representation, so the ability to exercise one's political voice depends on the relations of class and status. In other words, the capacity to influence public debate and authoritative decision-making depends not only on formal decision rules but also on power relations rooted in the economic structure and the status order, a fact that is insufficiently stressed in most theories of deliberative democracy. Thus, maldistribution and misrecognition conspire to subvert the principle of equal political voice for every citizen, even in polities that claim to be democratic. But of course the converse is also true. Those who suffer from misrepresentation are vulnerable to injustices of status and class. Lacking political voice, they are unable to articulate and defend their interests with respect to distribution and recognition, which in turn exacerbates their misrepresentation. In such cases, the result is a vicious circle in which the three orders of injustice reinforce one another, denying some people the chance to participate on a par with others in social life. As these three dimensions are intertwined, efforts to overcome injustice cannot, except in rare cases, address themselves to just one of them. Rather, struggles against maldistribution and misrecognition cannot succeed unless they are joined with struggles against misrepresentation—and vice versa. Where one puts the emphasis, of course, is both a tactical and a strategic decision. Given the current salience of injustices of misframing, my own preference is for the slogan, "No redistribution or recognition without representation." But even so, the politics of representation appears as one among three interconnected fronts in the struggle for social justice in a globalizing world.

In general, then, an adequate theory of justice for our time must be three-dimensional. Encompassing not only redistribution and recognition but also representation, it must allow us to grasp the question of the frame as a question of justice. Incorporating the economic, cultural and political dimensions, it must enable us to identify injustices of misframing and to evaluate possible remedies. Above all, it must permit us to pose, and to answer, the key political question of our age: How can we integrate struggles against maldistribution, misrecognition and misrepresentation within a *post-Westphalian* frame?

On the politics of framing: from state-territoriality to social effectivity?

So far I have been arguing for the irreducible specificity of the political as one of three fundamental dimensions of justice. And I have identified two distinct levels of political injustice: ordinary-political misrepresentation and misframing. Now, I want to examine the politics of framing in a globalizing world. Distinguishing affirmative from transformative approaches, I shall argue that an adequate politics of representation must also address a third level: beyond contesting ordinary-political misrepresentation, on the one hand, and misframing, on the other, such a politics must also aim to democratize the process of frame-setting.

I begin by explaining what I mean by "the politics of framing." Situated at my second level, where distinctions between members and nonmembers are drawn, this politics concerns the boundary-setting aspect of the political. Focused on the issues of who counts as a subject of justice and what is the appropriate frame, the politics of framing comprises efforts to establish and consolidate, to contest and revise, the authoritative division of political space. Included here are struggles against misframing, which aim to dismantle the obstacles that prevent disadvantaged people from confronting the forces that oppress them with claims of justice. Centered on the setting and contesting of frames, the politics of framing is concerned with the question of the "who."

The politics of framing can take two distinct forms, both of which are now being practiced in our globalizing world.[11] The first approach, which I shall call the *affirmative* politics of framing, contests the boundaries of existing frames while accepting the Westphalian

---

11 In distinguishing "affirmative" from "transformative" approaches, I am adapting terminology I have used in the past with respect to redistribution and recognition. See, inter alia, Nancy Fraser, "From Redistribution to Recognition?" in this volume, and "Social Justice in the Age of Identity Politics."

grammar of frame-setting. In this politics, those who claim to suffer injustices of misframing seek to redraw the boundaries of existing territorial states or in some cases to create new ones. But they still assume that the territorial state is the appropriate unit within which to pose and resolve disputes about justice. For them, injustices of misframing are not a function of the general principle according to which the Westphalian order partitions political space. They arise, rather, as a result of the faulty way in which that principle has been applied. Thus, those who practice the affirmative politics of framing accept that the principle of state-territoriality is the proper basis for constituting the "who" of justice. They agree, in other words, that what makes a given collection of individuals into fellow subjects of justice is their shared residence on the territory of a modern state and/or their shared membership in the political community that corresponds to such a state. Thus, far from challenging the underlying grammar of the Westphalian order, those who practice the affirmative politics of framing accept its state-territorial principle.

Precisely that principle is contested, however, in a second version of the politics of framing, which I shall call the *transformative* approach. For its proponents, the state-territorial principle no longer affords an adequate basis for determining the "who" of justice in every case. They concede, of course, that that principle remains relevant for many purposes; thus, supporters of transformation do not propose to eliminate state-territoriality entirely. But they contend that its grammar is out of synch with the structural causes of many injustices in a globalizing world, which are not territorial in character. Examples include the financial markets, "offshore factories," investment regimes and governance structures of the global economy, which determine who works for a wage and who does not; the information networks of global media and cybertechnology, which determine who is included in the circuits of communicative power and who is not; and the biopolitics of climate, disease, drugs, weapons and biotechnology, which determine who will live long and who will die young. In these matters, so fundamental to human well-being, the forces that perpetrate injustice belong not to "the space of places," but to "the space of flows."[12] Not locatable within the jurisdiction of any actual or conceivable territorial state, they cannot be made answerable to claims of justice that are framed in terms of the state-territorial principle. In their case, so the

---

12 I borrow this terminology from Manuel Castells, *The Rise of the Network Society*, Oxford: Blackwell, 1996, pp. 440–60.

argument goes, to invoke the state-territorial principle to determine the frame is itself to commit an injustice. By partitioning political space along territorial lines, this principle insulates extra- and non-territorial powers from the reach of justice. In a globalizing world, therefore, it is less likely to serve as a remedy for misframing than as a means of inflicting or perpetuating it.

In general, then, the transformative politics of framing aims to change the deep grammar of frame-setting in a globalizing world. This approach seeks to supplement the state-territorial principle of the Westphalian order with one or more *post-Westphalian* principles. The aim is to overcome injustices of misframing by changing not just the boundaries of the "who" of justice, but also the mode of their constitution, hence the way in which they are drawn.[13]

What might a post-Westphalian mode of frame-setting look like? Doubtless it is too early to have a clear view. Nevertheless, the most promising candidate so far is the "all-affected principle." This principle holds that all those affected by a given social structure or institution have moral standing as subjects of justice in relation to it. On this view, what turns a collection of people into fellow subjects of justice is not geographical proximity, but their co-imbrication in a common structural or institutional framework, which sets the ground rules that govern their social interaction, thereby shaping their respective life possibilities in patterns of advantage and disadvantage.

Until recently, the all-affected principle seemed to coincide in the eyes of many with the state-territorial principle. It was assumed, in keeping with the Westphalian world picture, that the common frame-work that determined patterns of advantage and disadvantage was precisely the constitutional order of the modern territorial state. As a result, it seemed that in applying the state-territorial principle, one simultaneously captured the normative force of the all-affected principle. In fact, this was never truly so, as the long history of colonialism and neo-colonialism attests. From the perspective of the metropole, however, the conflation of state-territoriality with social effectivity appeared to have an emancipatory thrust, as it served to justify the progressive incorporation, as subjects of justice, of the subordinate classes and status groups who were resident on the territory but excluded from active citizenship.

---

13 I owe the idea of a post-territorial "mode of political differentiation" to John Ruggie. See his immensely suggestive essay, "Territoriality and Beyond: Problematizing Modernity in International Relations," *International Organization* 47, 1993, pp. 139–74.

Today, however, the idea that state-territoriality can serve as a proxy for social effectivity is no longer plausible. Under current conditions, one's chances to live a good life do not depend wholly on the internal political constitution of the territorial state in which one resides. Although the latter remains undeniably relevant, its effects are mediated by other structures, both extra- and non-territorial, whose impact is at least as significant. In general, globalization is driving a widening wedge between state-territoriality and social effectivity. As those two principles increasingly diverge, the effect is to reveal the former as an inadequate surrogate for the latter. And so the question arises: Is it possible to apply the all-affected principle directly to the framing of justice, without going through the detour of state-territoriality?[14]

This is precisely what some practitioners of transformative politics

---

14 Everything depends on finding a suitable interpretation of the all-affected principle. The key issue is how to narrow the idea of "affectedness" to the point where it becomes an operationalizable standard for assessing the justice of various frames. The problem is that, given the so-called butterfly effect, one can adduce evidence that just about everyone is affected by just about everything. What is needed, therefore, is a way of distinguishing those levels and kinds of effectivity that are sufficient to confer moral standing from those that are not. One proposal, suggested by Carol Gould, is to limit such standing to those whose human rights are violated by a given practice or institution. Another, suggested by David Held, is to accord standing to those whose life expectancy and life chances are significantly affected. My own view is that the all-affected principle is open to a plurality of reasonable interpretations. As a result, its interpretation cannot be determined monologically, by philosophical fiat. Rather, philosophical analyses of affectedness should be understood as contributions to a broader public debate about the principle's meaning. The same is true for empirical social-scientific accounts of who is affected by given institutions or policies. In general, the all-affected principle must be interpreted dialogically, through the give-and-take of argument in democratic deliberation. That said, however, one thing is clear. Injustices of misframing can be avoided only if moral standing is not limited to those who are already accredited as official members of a given institution or as authorized participants in a given practice. To avoid such injustices, standing must also be accorded to those nonmembers and non-participants significantly affected by the institution or practice at issue. Thus sub-Saharan Africans who have been involuntarily disconnected from the global economy count as subjects of justice in relation to it, even if they do not actually participate in it. For the human-rights interpretation, see Carol Gould, *Globalizing Democracy and Human Rights*, Cambridge: Cambridge University Press, 2004; for the life expectancy and life-chances interpretation, David Held, *Global Covenant: The Social Democratic Alternative to the Washington Consensus*, Cambridge: Polity, 2004, p. 99ff; and for the dialogical approach, Nancy Fraser, "Two Dogmas of Egalitarianism" and "Abnormal Justice," both in Fraser, *Scales of Justice: Reimagining Political Space in a Globalizing World*, New York: Polity Press and Columbia University Press, 2008.

are attempting to do. Seeking leverage against offshore sources of maldistribution and misrecognition, some globalization activists are appealing directly to the all-affected principle in order to circumvent the state-territorial partitioning of political space. Contesting their exclusion by the Keynesian-Westphalian frame, environmentalists and indigenous peoples are claiming standing as subjects of justice in relation to the extra- and non-territorial powers that impinge on their lives. Insisting that effectivity trumps state-territoriality, they have joined development activists, international feminists and others in asserting their right to make claims against the structures that harm them, even when the latter cannot be located in the space of places. Casting off the Westphalian grammar of frame-setting, these claimants are applying the all-affected principle directly to questions of justice in a globalizing world.

In such cases, the transformative politics of framing proceeds simultaneously in multiple dimensions and on multiple levels. On one level, the social movements that practice this politics aim to redress first-order injustices of maldistribution, misrecognition, and ordinary-political misrepresentation. On a second level, these movements seek to redress meta-level injustices of misframing by reconstituting the "who" of justice. In those cases, moreover, where the state-territorial principle serves more to indemnify than to challenge injustice, transformative social movements appeal instead to the all-affected principle. Invoking a post-Westphalian principle, they are seeking to change the very grammar of frame-setting—and thereby to reconstruct the meta-political foundations of justice for a globalizing world.

But the claims of transformative politics go further still. Above and beyond their other demands, these movements are also claiming a say in a post-Westphalian process of frame-setting. Rejecting the standard view, which deems frame-setting the prerogative of states and transnational elites, they are effectively aiming to democratize the process by which the frameworks of justice are drawn and revised. Asserting their right to participate in constituting the "who" of justice, they are simultaneously transforming the "how"—by which I mean the accepted procedures for determining the "who." At their most reflective and ambitious, accordingly, transformative movements are demanding the creation of new democratic arenas for entertaining arguments about the frame. In some cases, moreover, they are creating such arenas themselves. In the World Social Forum, for example, some practitioners of transformative politics have fashioned a transnational public sphere where they can participate on a par with others in airing and resolving disputes about the frame. In this way, they are prefiguring the possibility of new institutions of *post-Westphalian democratic justice*.[15]

The democratizing dimension of transformative politics points to a third level of political injustice, above and beyond the two already discussed. Previously, I distinguished first-order injustices of ordinary-political misrepresentation from second-order injustices of misframing. Now, however, we can discern a third-order species of political injustice, which corresponds to the question of the "how." Exemplified by undemocratic processes of frame-setting, this injustice consists in the failure to institutionalize parity of participation at the meta-political level, in deliberations and decisions concerning the "who." Because what is at stake here is the process by which first-order political space is constituted, I shall call this injustice *meta-political misrepresentation*. Meta-political misrepresentation arises when states and transnational elites monopolize the activity of frame-setting, denying voice to those who may be harmed in the process, and blocking creation of democratic arenas where the latter's claims can be vetted and redressed. The effect is to exclude the overwhelming majority of people from participation in the meta-discourses that determine the authoritative division of political space. Lacking any institutional arenas for such participation, and submitted to an undemocratic approach to the "how," the majority is denied the chance to engage on terms of parity in decision-making about the "who."

In general, then, struggles against misframing are revealing a new kind of democratic deficit. Just as globalization has made visible injustices of misframing, so transformative struggles against neoliberal globalization are making visible the injustice of meta-political misrepresentation. In exposing the lack of institutions where disputes about the "who" can be democratically aired and resolved, these struggles are focusing attention on the "how." By demonstrating that the absence of such institutions impedes efforts to overcome injustice, they are revealing the deep internal connections between democracy and justice. The effect is to bring to light a structural feature of the current conjuncture: struggles for justice in a globalizing world cannot

---

15 For the time being, efforts to democratize the process of frame-setting are confined to contestation in transnational civil society. Indispensable as this level is, it cannot succeed so long as there exist no formal institutions that can translate transnational public opinion into binding, enforceable decisions. In general, then, the civil-society track of transnational democratic politics needs to be complemented by a formal-institutional track.

succeed unless they go hand in hand with struggles for *meta-political democracy*. At this level, too, then, no redistribution or recognition without representation.

Paradigm shift: post-Westphalian democratic justice

I have been arguing that what distinguishes the current conjuncture is intensified contestation concerning both the "who" and the "how" of justice. Under these conditions, the theory of justice is undergoing a paradigm shift. Earlier, when the Keynesian-Westphalian frame was in place, most philosophers neglected the political dimension. Treating the territorial state as a given, they endeavored to ascertain the requirements of justice theoretically, in a monological fashion. Thus, they did not envisage any role in determining these requirements for those who would be subject to them, let alone for those excluded by the national frame. Neglecting to reflect on the question of the frame, these philosophers never imagined that those whose fates would be so decisively shaped by framing decisions might be entitled to participate in making them. Disavowing any need for a dialogical democratic moment, they were content to produce monological theories of social justice.

Today, however, monological theories of social justice are becoming increasingly implausible. As we have seen, globalization cannot help but problematize the question of the "how," as it politicizes the question of the "who." The process goes something like this: as the circle of those claiming a say in frame-setting expands, decisions about the "who" are increasingly viewed as political matters, which should be handled democratically, rather than as technical matters, which can be left to experts and elites. The effect is to shift the burden of argument, requiring defenders of expert privilege to make their case. No longer able to hold themselves above the fray, they are necessarily embroiled in disputes about the "how." As a result, they must contend with demands for meta-political democratization.

An analogous shift is currently making itself felt in normative philosophy. Just as some activists are seeking to transfer elite frame-setting prerogatives to democratic publics, so some theorists of justice are proposing to rethink the classic division of labor between theorist and *demos*. No longer content to ascertain the requirements of justice in a monological fashion, these theorists are looking increasingly to dialogical approaches, which treat important aspects of justice as matters for collective decision-making, to be determined by the citizens themselves, through democratic deliberation. For them, accordingly, the grammar of the theory of justice is being transformed. What could once be called the "theory of social justice" now appears as the "theory of *democratic justice.*"[16]

In its current form, however, the theory of democratic justice remains incomplete. To complete the shift from a monological to dialogical theory requires a further step, beyond those contemplated by most proponents of the dialogical turn. Henceforth, democratic processes of determination must be applied not only to the "what" of justice, but also to the "who" and the "how."[17] In that case, by adopting a democratic approach to the "how," the theory of justice assumes a guise appropriate to a globalizing world. Dialogical at *every* level, meta-political as well as ordinary-political, it becomes a theory of *post-Westphalian democratic justice.*

The view of justice as participatory parity readily lends itself to such an approach. This principle has a double quality that expresses the reflexive character of democratic justice. On the one hand, the principle of participatory parity is an outcome notion, which specifies a substantive principle of justice by which we may evaluate social arrangements: the latter are just if and only if they permit all the relevant social actors to participate as peers in social life. On the other hand, participatory parity is also a process notion, which specifies a procedural standard by which we may evaluate the democratic legitimacy of norms: the latter are legitimate if and only if they can command the assent of all concerned in fair and open processes of deliberation, in which all can participate as peers. By virtue of this double quality, the view of justice as participatory parity has an inherent reflexivity. Able to problematize both substance and procedure, it renders visible the mutual entwinement of these two aspects of social arrangements. Thus, this approach can expose both the unjust background conditions that skew putatively democratic decision-making and the undemocratic procedures that generate substantively unequal outcomes. As a result, it enables us to shift levels easily, moving back and forth as necessary between

---

16 The phrase comes from Ian Shapiro, *Democratic Justice*, New Haven: Yale University Press, 1999. But the idea can also be found in Jürgen Habermas, *Between Facts and Norms*, Cambridge, MA: MIT Press, 1996; Seyla Benhabib, *The Rights of Others*, Cambridge: Cambridge University Press, 2004; and Rainer Forst, *Contexts of Justice*, Berkeley: University of California Press, 2002.

17 None of the theorists cited in the previous note has attempted to apply the "democratic justice" approach to the problem of the frame. The thinker who has come closest is Rainer Forst, but even he does not envisage democratic processes of frame-setting.

first-order and meta-level questions. Making manifest the co-implication of democracy and justice, the view of justice as participatory parity supplies just the sort of reflexivity that is needed in a globalizing world.

All told, then, the norm of participatory parity suits the account of post-Westphalian democratic justice presented here. Encompassing three dimensions and multiple levels, this account renders visible, and criticizable, the characteristic injustices of the present conjuncture. Conceptualizing misframing and meta-political misrepresentation, it discloses core injustices overlooked by standard theories. Focused not only on the "what" of justice, but also on the "who" and the "how," it enables us to grasp the question of the frame as the central question of justice in a globalizing world.

IV. PHILOSOPHICAL FOUNDATIONS:
RECOGNITION, JUSTICE, CRITIQUE

STRUGGLING OVER THE
MEANING OF RECOGNITION
Nikolas Kompridis

*My knowledge of myself is something I find, as on a successful
quest; my knowledge of others, of their separateness from me,
is something that finds me.*

Stanley Cavell

A *matter of justice or self-realization?*

In my view, the question at the center of the debate between Axel
Honneth and Nancy Fraser is not the redistribution or recognition
question. The decisive question of their debate is the question of what
recognition means, what it does, and for what and for whom it is
done. Very early in their exchange, Nancy Fraser puts it this way: "Is
recognition really a matter of justice, or is it a matter of self-
realization?"[1] This is more or less to acknowledge that we are still
struggling with the social and political *meaning* of recognition—what
it means to be "recognized," and so what it is that we are purportedly
doing when we are "recognizing" individuals or groups or asking to
be "recognized." Struggles for recognition also initiate struggles over
the contested and shifting meaning of recognition.[2]

On the face of it, Fraser's and Honneth's views of recognition could
not be more discordant. For Axel Honneth, as for Charles Taylor,
recognition is a "vital human need,"[3] a deep-seated *anthropological*

---

1 Nancy Fraser and Axel Honneth, *Redistribution or Recognition? A Political-
Philosophical Exchange*, London: Verso, 2003, p. 27.

2 Here I am trying to supplement James Tully's reformulation of the struggle for
recognition as a struggle *over* the norms of recognition. Even when actors challenge a
norm of (typically legal) recognition because they experience it as unbearable, they are
not only challenging the specific harm that the particular norm facilitates, they are also
implicitly attempting to redefine what recognition is or should be. I am indebted to Tully
for helping me with my own (ongoing) struggle over the meaning of recognition.

3 Charles Taylor, "The Politics of Recognition," in Amy Gutmann, ed., *Multiculturalism: Examining the Politics of Recognition*, Princeton: Princeton University
Press, 1994, p. 25.

fact of the matter about "the intersubjective nature of human beings."[4]
We do not just *desire* recognition, we *need* multiple kinds of recognition—respect in the political sphere, esteem in the social sphere, and
care in the intimate sphere of the family. Lacking these interlocking
experiences of recognition, we cannot achieve full "self-realization":
we cannot become who we want to be, cannot realize the kind of life
we want for ourselves. For Honneth, the harm done by non-recognition
and misrecognition is the worst form of social injustice; indeed, it is
the key to unlocking social injustice as a whole.[5] Experiences of non-
recognition or misrecognition violate putatively transhistorical
normative expectations geared to the social confirmation or affirmation
of our identity claims. Lacking such confirmation we will be unable
to develop "intact" personal identities, and so, by implication, unable
fully to function as self-realizing agents. Below the threshold of public
recognition struggles, below the level of this or that contingent historical configuration, there lies a stratum of "prepolitical suffering,"
claims Honneth, which can serve as an empirical reference point and
a normative resource both for moral theory and for social criticism.
Out of this material, Honneth fashions an all-encompassing theory
of justice and critical social theory.

For Nancy Fraser, on the other hand, recognition plays an important
but limited role in a theory of justice, normatively enlarging the meaning and practice of equality. That endeavor requires a shift from an
"ethical" normative framework of justice at the center of which is the
hyper-good of self-realization, to a deontological framework at the
center of which is the moral-democratic ideal of "participatory parity."
Rather than treating recognition as instrumental to individual self-
realization, she treats it as instrumental to acquiring status as a full
partner in social interaction. Recognition, she argues, is best treated
as an issue of social status, not as an anthropological constant that
functions as the necessary (and apparently sufficient) condition for
the formation of an "intact" personal identity. What we should be
paying attention to are patterns of cultural value that constitute some
individuals and groups "as inferior, excluded, wholly other, or simply
invisible." In such cases, we can legitimately speak of "misrecognition
and status subordination."[6] The "remedy" for injustice in these cases
will require the "deinstutionalization" of those patterns of cultural

---

4 Fraser and Honneth, *Redistribution or Recognition?*, p.145.
5 Ibid., p. 133.
6 Ibid., p. 29.

value that foster misrecognition and status subordination. The redress that is called for here is not the repair of the distorted subjectivities or damaged identities of social actors, but the restoration of their status as full partners in social interaction.

Honneth and Fraser find little if anything to endorse in each other's views. Fraser's criticisms are particularly sharp, expressing total skepticism about Honneth's project. She considers it to be overly ambitious, monistic, and foundationalist. I am largely sympathetic to some of the criticisms she makes, having made similar or complementary criticisms elsewhere.[7] However, I also have some serious concerns about Fraser's own approach. Just as it is unwise to reduce justice either to recognition or to redistribution, it is also unwise to reduce recognition struggles either to justice or to identity. Both of these either/ors are based on false antitheses. Nothing is gained by reproducing them. Moreover, since the very meaning of recognition is itself contestable, not just in theory but in practice, it may be wiser to resist defining it too strictly in relation to this or that normative ideal.

Misrecognition without a suffering subject

I want now to look closely at two interconnected features of Fraser's account of recognition that she believes make it normatively preferable to Honneth's: the incorporation of standards of (1) impartiality and (2) publicity. Because she treats recognition as a matter of justice within a deontological moral framework in which the right is separated from and rendered prior to the good, Fraser does not need to make any controversial or sectarian appeals to a historically or culturally specific idea of the good, as Honneth's notion of self-realization must. All the work is being done by the deontological non-sectarian norm of participatory parity. Thus, she believes, her account of recognition can appeal to an impartial normative standpoint that is compatible with value pluralism and deep diversity. I do not see, however, how evading one controversial normative standpoint by taking on another *necessarily* makes her view of recognition superior to Honneth's. After all, the day has long since passed when the sharp distinction between the right and the good upon which her standard of impartiality depends can simply be taken for granted. Compelling arguments have been circulating for some time as to why such strong notions of impartiality

---

7 "From Reason to Self-Realization? On the 'Ethical Turn' in Critical Theory," *Critical Horizons* 5: 1, 2004. Reprinted in John Rundell et al., eds., *Contemporary Perspectives in Critical and Social Philosophy*, Leiden: Brill, 2004.

may be part of the problem, not part of the solution to the challenges of value pluralism and deep diversity. One of those arguments makes clear that any struggle for recognition, and therefore over what it means and what it demands, "always implicates the right and the good in complex ways that we are just beginning to understand."[8] The thought that we can shield the right from the good, immunizing it against the challenges of pluralism and diversity, is self-defeating. And so we need to resist the still-seductive idea that there is some uncontroversial, ever-ready norm of impartiality that can serve as the single best problem-solving and conflict-resolving procedure for settling recognition claims and the "claims of culture." That idea too remains in the grip of normative monism, even if it is of a kind less obvious than Honneth's.

The standard of publicity to which Fraser appeals is also beset with difficulties. Although Fraser accepts that misrecognition can have the negative, disabling "ethical-psychological effects described by Taylor and Honneth," she nonetheless wants to insist that "the wrongness of misrecognition does not depend on the presence of such effects." For Fraser, "a society whose institutionalized norms impede parity of participation is morally indefensible *whether or not they distort the subjectivity of the oppressed*."[9] But does this mean that the effects of misrecognition are morally irrelevant to judging its wrongness? Certainly it would be hard to imagine genuine cases of misrecognition, cases which typically have a significant history, in which such disabling effects were not present. And just as certainly it is hard to imagine how anyone could ever make sense of misrecognition, their own or someone else's, without the presence of such effects. The very intelligibility of the concept, and so its place in the moral language in which it plays such an important role, is inconceivable without access to the suffering misrecognition can cause. Would Fraser be prepared to endorse institutionalized norms that produced disabling "ethical-psychological" effects so long as they were consistent with the principle of participatory parity (supposing this were a *real* possibility)? Wouldn't the presence of such effects be an indication that there is something wrong with the current institutionalization of our norms of equality? And isn't that, in part, why recognition has become part

---

8 James Tully, "The Practice of Law-making and the Problem of Difference: One View of the Field," in Omid Payrow Shabani, ed., *Multiculturalism and Law: A Critical Debate*, Cardiff: University of Wales Press, 2006.

9 Fraser and Honneth, *Redistribution or Recognition?*, p. 32.

of the normative vocabulary of contemporary democracies? So what is driving Fraser to make the ethical-psychological effects of misrecognition irrelevant to judging its wrongness?

Evidently, it is an issue of objectivity. For Fraser, "misrecognition is a matter of externally manifest and publicly verifiable impediments to some people's standing as full members of society." If we are to conceptualize "what really *merits* the title of injustice, as opposed to what is merely *experienced* as injustice," we have to reject appeals to an independent and "pristine" realm of subjective experiences that cannot be publicly verified.[10] What we require is an altogether different strategy, which begins not with unmediated subjective experiences, but with decentered, depersonalized discourses of justice and social criticism. Such "subjectless" discourses offer a far more plausible and objective empirical reference point for evaluating recognition claims than "inarticulate suffering." Unlike the latter, the former is not "sheltered from public contestation," but has the distinct advantage of "being subject to critical scrutiny in open debate."[11]

I must confess, however, that I find the distinction between "what really merits the title of injustice, as opposed to what is merely experienced as injustice" quite worrisome. While subjective experience is notoriously unreliable as a source of justification, it is also an irreplaceable and absolutely necessary source of *intelligibility*. The suffering in question is inescapably first-personal. Even if we set aside the point that in matters of justification the criteria of valid public justification are themselves always up for grabs, never settled, and perpetually subject to crises, it seems to me rather hard to deny that successful identification of misrecognition has to pass through *both* subjective experience *and* subjectless discourses. Just as subjectless discourses must act as a corrective or check against subjective experience, so subjective experience must act as a check or corrective against subjectless discourses. We want to make sure that there is a reciprocal looping or feedback process between subjective experiences and subjectless discourses. Indeed, subjective experience must *permeate* subjectless discourses in order to insure that the content of those discourses is not empty, that they do not serve as one more source of alienation: the misrecognized must be able to recognize themselves in, must be able to make sense of their suffering through, those subjectless discourses of recognition. That Fraser is prepared to privilege the latter

---

10 Ibid., pp. 31, 205.
11 Ibid., p. 205.

at the expense of the former reveals a certain positivist residue in her thinking, as though we could give an account of misrecognition without need of a suffering subject.[12]

There is something else that is quite worrisome about the distinction between what merits the title of injustice and what is merely experienced as injustice, and that has specifically to do with the underlying assumption that only an experience that is "externally manifest and publicly verifiable" can count as a valid case of misrecognition. What is assumed here is that currently available claims-making vocabularies and subjectless discourses are all the vocabularies and discourses we need to *express* and *justify* recognition claims. And that assumes, as well, that misrecognition will take an already familiar public form. But if what needs to be claimed cannot be made "externally manifest and publicly verifiable" in currently available vocabularies and discourses, and if the required discourses and vocabularies can't simply be created overnight *ex nihilo*, how much trust can we actually place in standards of public verification that presuppose the adequacy of currently available discourses and vocabularies of evaluation and justification?

I am somewhat puzzled by Fraser's position here, since she has acknowledged in her previous work the need of those suffering from maligned identities to transform inherited vocabularies of identity "in order to expand their field of action," and so turn a disabling identity into "an enabling identity, an identity one could want to claim."[13] How could one ever become aware of the need to do so if one did not experience first-personally the voice-erasing and agency-disabling effects of these inherited vocabularies of identity? This is precisely why we cannot presume the justificatory adequacy of our current discourses and vocabularies, and why subjective experience must always be an ineliminable normative reference point of resistance, contestation, and transformation.

Yet another questionable assumption underlying Fraser's standard of publicity is the assumption that recognition claims are *fully explicit and determinate* claims, much like straightforward truth claims and

---

12 For complementary criticisms of Fraser and an illuminating view of misrecognition and suffering from an Adornian perspective, see Jay Bernstein, "Suffering Injustice: Misrecognition as Moral Injury in Critical Theory," *International Journal of Philosophical Studies* 13: 3, 2005, special issue on "Rethinking Critical Theory," Nikolas Kompridis, guest editor, pp. 303–25.

13 See Nancy Fraser, "From Irony to Prophecy to Politics: A Response to Richard Rorty," *Michigan Quarterly Review*, 30: 2, Spring 1991.

certain kinds of moral claims. And that is just how Fraser's status model of recognition must treat them. However, because recognition claims cannot be strictly a matter of justice alone, but are also interwoven with our identities and the various goods we associate with them, they are shot through with indeterminacy. Thus, it is highly unlikely that any currently available vocabulary in which recognition claims can be stated is going to be fully adequate to what wants or needs recognition. For there to be any claiming in the first place, "inarticulate suffering" must be made *articulate*. Therefore, there will be cases in which what needs to be claimed cannot precede its successful articulation or expression. These are cases in which "right is not assertible; instead something must be shown."[14] What will determine the "success" of any articulation is the degree to which it shows what we were unable to see as injustice *prior* to its articulation. By disclosing a morally relevant but previously unthematized or unnoticed feature of our public practices of (mis)recognition, of our institutional rules and arrangements more generally, such an articulation also illuminates why right could not be asserted prior to what needed to be shown.

Once we see that recognition claims are highly indeterminate claims, and that their inarticulacy is internal to the nature of such claims, we may become more sensitive to an aspect of that inarticulacy that we might call the experience of *aphonia*, of voicelessness or inexpressiveness. This is also one of the disabling effects of misrecognition, and it is one that speaks against, if I may put it this way, Fraser's standard of publicity. The problem here is not an unwillingness to risk public contestation and critical scrutiny; rather, it is the more immediate problem of lacking a voice, more precisely, *one's own voice*, for no other voice will do, in which to state, and, so, make sense of one's suffering and misery. It is not just that what we lack the right words adequately to articulate our experience of injustice; it is also that we have been rendered literally and figuratively speechless. Finding our own voice in which to voice that injustice, and to give it a name, may be the only way open to us to turn what is merely experienced as injustice into what rightly merits the title of injustice. In this way our struggle to find that voice, and to give a name to that for which we did not heretofore have a name, enlarges the horizon of moral significance, and reminds us that public reason is *not* reducible

---

14 Stanley Cavell, *Conditions Handsome and Unhandsome: The Constitution of Emersonian Perfectionism*, Chicago: University of Chicago Press, 1990, p. 112.

to justificatory discourse: it necessarily entails a semantically innovative problem-solving dimension (i.e., the problem of making inarticulate suffering articulate) if injustice is to be seen *as* injustice. It should also alert us to how the light of publicity can be blinding as well as illuminating. We may fail to see some morally relevant feature of an issue or conflict *because* of the light publicity sheds—which is why we need continually to adjust the lighting by disclosing what the light of publicity itself obscures. And that means that we have to incorporate a role for disclosure and articulation in the public exercise of practical reason.[15]

Turning away for a moment from my discussion of Fraser, I want to draw out an implication for Honneth's recognition theory of the semantic-political struggle to bring new articulations of injustice and identity into being. The struggle to overcome our voicelessness, to regain *our* voice once we see that it is our voice itself that is at stake, is, *pace* Honneth, a struggle that cannot be sufficiently explained, not even motivationally, as a struggle for recognition, since it is also and perhaps more fundamentally a struggle *for* or *over* one's voice. The question of one's own voice may arise in contexts of misrecognition, but it is not going to be resolved by any appropriate form of recognition through which we will be finally reassured that it is our own voice that is speaking, our own agency that is at work. Our attempts to reassure ourselves that our words and actions are indeed our own can be only *partially* satisfied. Even under the most favorable social and political conditions, the "satisfaction" we seek will be provisional, subject to recurring normative challenge and self-induced doubt, since we must find "satisfaction" in the place from which the "desire" for it first arises: under the conditions of intersubjectivity where recognition is both conferred and denied, where "satisfaction" can easily turn into or be displaced by "dissatisfaction."

Honneth's theory of recognition exaggerates the degree to which we *need* recognition in order to exercise our agency, in order to speak in a voice of our own. Although I cannot go into detail here, Hegel's analysis of the "master/slave" dialectic proves to be an embarrassment for Honneth, since the "slave" is able to exercise a newly won agency and achieve a new self-understanding under conditions of inequality and misrecognition. He proves able, at least partially, to resolve the "epistemological crisis" set in motion by his unsatisfied (and unsatisfiable

---

15 On the "world-disclosing" role of reason, see Nikolas Kompridis, *Critique and Disclosure: Critical Theory Between Past and Future*, Cambridge, MA: MIT Press, 2006.

desire) for recognition without receiving the kinds of recognition Honneth regards as necessary and sufficient conditions of successful agency and personal identity. Indeed, it was the denial of due recognition and the ensuing epistemological crisis that forced the "slave" to reconceive and transform his basic self-understanding. The point of all this is not that misrecognition is really good for us, and so we need not worry so much about being misrecognized; the point is that recognition and misrecognition *underdetermines* our identities and our sense of ourselves as agents. Our power to shape our identity and exercise our agency does not strictly depend on receiving in advance the appropriate form of recognition. We are able to do so, over and over again, despite the denial or absence of such recognition. Furthermore, as I interpret Hegel, the experience of misrecognition does not *necessarily* entail a form of injustice. It can be the occasion of a transformative and critical encounter with an other. In this case, the other we encounter challenges the recognition we claim for ourselves, not in order to maintain conditions of domination and asymmetry but in order to initiate a change in self-understanding, and a change in our own relation to one another.[16]

Another implication follows from this: all the recognition in the world can neither guarantee nor serve as a substitute for our own voice. There is missing in Honneth's account of recognition the "perfectionist" concerns thematized by Emerson, Nietzsche, Heidegger and, more recently, Cavell. What is missing is an awareness or sufficient appreciation of the "internal" impediments to self-realization, those called "conformity" and "consistency" by Emerson, "*ressentiment*" by Nietzsche, and "*das Man*" by Heidegger.[17] Not all impediments to the

---

16 I make this point in greater detail in "From Reason to Self-Realization? On the 'Ethical Turn' in Critical Theory," *Critical Horizons* 5: 1, Summer 2004, pp. 346–9.

17 Ralph Waldo Emerson, "Self-Reliance," *Essays: First and Second Series*, New York: Vintage, 1990; Friedrich Nietzsche, *On the Genealogy of Morals*, trans. Walter Kaufmann and R. J. Hollingdale, New York: Vintage, 1969; Martin Heidegger, *Being and Time*, trans. John Macquarrie and Edward Robinson, New York: Harper and Row, 1962, Part 1, Chapter 4. For elaboration of this point, see Part 2 of my *Critique and Disclosure: Critical Theory Between Past and Future*, Cambridge, MA: MIT Press, 2006, and "Intersubjectivity, Recognition, and Agency," in *The Critical Theory of Axel Honneth*, ed. Danielle Petheridge, Leiden: Brill, 2006. Now this is another reason why I think Fraser is wrong to dismiss outright approaches that focus on the self, on identity, and on so-called experiences of "prepolitical" suffering. The dichotomy between self and society has surely outworn its welcome. It is an effect of a metaphysical picture that is based on questionable and prejudicial distinctions between inner and outer, subjective and objective, private and public. For one line of critique of this picture, the writings of Heidegger, Wittgenstein, Taylor, and Cavell are exemplary.

free exercise of our agency, or to a freer, practical relation to ourselves, can be understood as "external" impediments. We can find that we have become unintelligible to ourselves, obscure to ourselves, "as if we are subject to demands we cannot quite formulate, leaving us unjustified, as if our lives condemn themselves."[18] This situation is not one that can be remedied by receiving due recognition, for it is relations of recognition themselves which make urgent and ineliminable the struggle for and over our own voice.

On the other hand, I do think Honneth is right to claim that we are in need of a phenomenology of suffering. So long as it is not playing a foundationalist role, there is nothing wrong with such an undertaking, and much may be learned from it, namely, a greater sensitivity to forms of suffering for which no public language is currently adequate, and so of previously unnoticed aspects of our practices and institutions that might not otherwise merit the title of injustice. Unfortunately, Honneth doesn't provide such a phenomenology. What he provides instead is a taxonomy of suffering that he derives *ex ante* from an overambitious attempt to conceptualize the normative space within which *all* struggles against injustice must take place. However, even a modest phenomenology of suffering would have to be complemented and balanced by a Nietzschean genealogy of suffering, in light of which we could better understand the deeper motivations and the deeper complexities underlying our need for recognition.[19]

Instrumentalizing recognition

Thus far I have only thematized the deep disagreement between Fraser and Honneth, but, as it turns out, their views of recognition share a few common assumptions. I want now to look at one of these. Both Honneth and Fraser have an instrumental view of recognition; that is, they both regard it as a means to an end, whether that end is an intact personal identity or full social participation. And they both regard recognition as an *explicit* or *overt* act, something over which we can dispose, something that can be mobilized by an act of state or of individual will. For them it is as though once a recognition claim is publicly justified, it is then a matter of *administering* the right kind of recognition in the right dose. Recognition is thus construed as a "remedy" for injustice, as Fraser likes so often to put it.

---

18 Stanley Cavell, *Conditions Handsome and Unhandsome*, pp. xxxi–xxxii.

19 Wendy Brown, "Wounded Attachments," in *States of Injury*, Princeton: Princeton University Press, 1995, pp. 52–76.

I have two problems with this instrumentalist construal of recognition. And here again I want to focus on Fraser. First of all, an instrumental view of recognition *medicalizes* the issues of recognition, identity, and justice, as though we are dealing with a malady in the body politic for which the appropriate drug must be administered.[20] Second, it seeks to instrumentalize what is ultimately not instrumentalizable. Recognition is not something over which we can dispose, or which we can mete out in the appropriate amounts to the appropriate people at the appropriate time. While one can redistribute economic resources through the machinery of the state, recognition is not something that can be "redistributed." This is partly because it is not a thing, easily measurable and redeployable. To be sure, legal forms of recognition do institute norms of recognition in order to combat illegitimate forms of exclusion and inequality. Yet, as important as legal mechanisms are for instituting changes in practices of recognition, I think that the struggle for legal recognition is not a sufficiently complex model for understanding what is at stake in recognition struggles as a whole, and not only because legal norms of recognition are always themselves contestable.

Whatever recognition is, if indeed it is a circumscribable practice, it seems to figure importantly in a process of reeducation, in an alteration of our cognitive orientations and normative expectations. It is a part of a larger learning process, the outcome of which, to the extent that it is a genuine *learning* process, will be both unforeseeable and unpredictable. Institutional measures are *one* way to facilitate such learning processes; but even legal forms of recognition, necessary as they may be, are not in themselves sufficient to bring about the required symbolic and cultural change at the level of everyday practice. Moreover, as Fraser and others have pointed out, legal mechanisms for producing such change can be resisted and can be met with a severe backlash. So the question that Fraser needs to answer is just what kind of change she has in mind when she talks about the "deinstutionalization of patterns of cultural value." Is this change to be achieved by "institutional" means alone, e.g., by legal mechanisms? Are we using the right normative and conceptual language here to get at a more complex process of normative and cultural change?

These questions are particularly pertinent when considering

20 This medicalizing tendency is especially pronounced in Honneth. See "From Reason to Self-Realization?" for criticism of this tendency in Honneth.

what Fraser means by "deconstructive recognition" and precisely what practical role it is supposed to play. Although Fraser shares with Honneth the conventional view of recognition as consisting in an explicit act of affirmation that can be expressed in various ways in various social contexts, she is also of the view that some kinds of misrecognition call for an altogether different kind of recognition, where the "remedy" that is called for is not the affirmation of unjustly maligned group identities but the deconstruction of the very terms in which group differences are elaborated. Whereas recognition as affirmation leaves everyone's identity more or less unchanged, recognition as deconstruction would "change *everyone's* social identity."[21]

Obviously, the practice of deconstructive recognition is supposed to be the "radical" counterpart of the "conservative" practice of affirmative recognition, but just what it means *in practice* is anything but obvious. Deconstructing a text is one thing; deconstructing our identities is something else altogether. In the first case, the operation can be done without having to put anything of one's own at stake; indeed, once the operation is started the outcome is automatic and fairly predictable. But in the second case, most everything that matters to us is at stake, and we have no idea how to proceed or what to expect. After all, deconstructing our identities is not something we could ever get really good at, a practice we can master, for mastery in this domain would signal failure, not success. It is not just that our identities resist their deconstruction, or that we are both the "subject" and "object" of the deconstruction; it is that the process and the outcome is not something we can actually control or foresee.

So the question naturally arises as to whether "deconstructive recognition" can even constitute a social practice. Surely, if it is going to be a practice that we can normatively endorse, it will have to be a *democratic* practice, requiring the cooperation and consent of all concerned. But that will introduce an even higher level of indeterminacy to a process that looks highly indeterminate to begin with. Furthermore, were "deconstructive recognition" somehow to become a democratic practice, the "radical" ambition of bringing about a change in "everyone's social identity" might have to be tempered by a genuine confrontation with pluralism—that is, with the fact that some people will wish with good reason to preserve and continue

---

21 Fraser and Honneth, *Redistribution or Recognition?*, pp. 13, 15, 75.

aspects of their identity, will wish to pass them on and not just let them pass away.[22]

What I have just described is rather different from Fraser's attempt to make the deconstructive type of recognition viable as a social practice. She proposes the idea of "reformist reform" as a "*via media* between an affirmative strategy that is politically feasible but substantively flawed and a transformative one that is programmatically sound but politically unfeasible."[23] But I do not think the idea of deconstructive recognition is "programmatically sound" at all; to the contrary, I think its conceptualization as a possible practice is deeply flawed by Fraser's assumption that recognition is instrumentalizable, and so she misconceives how cultural change can and ought to take place.[24]

If we now note that with the notion of "deconstructive recognition" Fraser unintentionally reconnects the question of recognition to issues of identity, the very issues from which she wanted it strictly separated (call it a return of the repressed), we can say that we have come full circle. We see that recognition as we currently understand it is as much a matter of equality as it is of identity, as much a matter of justice as of agency. However, we are still unsure what to make of recognition—neither what it means to us nor what normative and political role(s) we would like it, or need it, to play in social life.

Discourses and counter-discourses of recognition

For some time we have been working with an essentially therapeutic discourse of recognition that distinguishes between good and bad kinds of recognition, and conceives of the good kind as unequivocally good, the sure remedy for the harm done by the bad. More or less simultaneously a much more skeptical counter-discourse of recognition has emerged for which recognition is implicated in a complex process of social construction that has to be continually and relentlessly deconstructed. Admirably, if unsuccessfully, Nancy Fraser has tried to combine both of these discourses, in order to get beyond their respective limitations.

---

22 Nikolas Kompridis, "Normativizing Hybridity/Neutralizing Culture," *Political Theory* 33: 3, 2005, pp. 318–43. On the issues raised in this paper, see Seyla Benhabib, "The Claims of Culture Properly Interpreted: Response to Nikolas Kompridis," *Political Theory* 34: 3, 2006, pp. 383–8, and my reply to Benhabib, "The Unsettled and Unsettling Claims of Culture: Reply to Seyla Benhabib," *Political Theory* 34: 3, 2006, pp. 389–96.

23 Fraser and Honneth, *Redistribution or Recognition?*, p. 79.

24 I should add that I find the application of the idea of "nonreformist reform" to redistribution far more promising.

But perhaps what we are dealing with are practices and expectations that are actually heterogeneous, far more indeterminate, and far less stable, than recognition theorists like Axel Honneth generally believe, united more by contingent historical circumstances than by an underlying and unchanging anthropological-normative core. If this impression is correct, then we need a more pluralistic and contextualist account of recognition, not a monistic account, no matter how complex and internally differentiated it may be. Honneth's account of recognition is skewed by an orientation to a formal theory of the good at the center of which is a very disputable and flawed ideal of self-realization that molds the practice of recognition for its own purposes.

I think that James Tully takes an important step in the right direction when he recasts the struggle for recognition not as a struggle for the recognition of one's legitimate identity claims but as a struggle *over the norms of recognition*. By shifting the focus to the norms of recognition themselves, Tully connects the struggle over intersubjective norms of recognition to the struggle over how we wish to be governed. Thus, recognition becomes a matter of *freedom* and not just a matter of justice or identity, and misrecognition an unjustifiable curtailment of our freedom to govern ourselves. Since the struggle over the norms of recognition is at the same time a struggle over what it means to recognize and be recognized, there can be no final or perfect state of recognition in whose projected normative light we should understand the shortcomings or imperfections of our current practices or forms of recognition. As Tully points out, like all moral and political norms, norms of recognition have a normative and normalizing function, both of which can provoke resistance and contestation. No matter how well meant or intentioned, no matter how mutual or reciprocal norms of recognition are, the effects in practice will always be contestable and questionable. Indeed, we may need to be just as worried about the coercive force of mutual and reciprocal norms of recognition.[25]

It might be time to ask just what it is we expect from recognition, for it may be that we have normativized and normalized recognition to such an extent that we have overburdened it with too many social and political demands. It might be time to think not only about what recognition does for us, but also what it can't do; what we can get from recognition and what we can't get. It might be time to think about the limits of recognition. I think we can safely say that full and complete recognition is a chimera. All recognition, even the very good

---

25 Tully, "The Practice of Law-Making and the Problem of Difference."

kind, is *partial*, both incomplete and one-sided. Because we don't fully know what we are doing when we are doing it, and because our motivations and our actions can never be fully transparent to us or fully foreseeable by us, the possibility of misrecognition is built into each and every act of recognition. This possibility is made actual in the practices by which we interpret and apply our current norms of recognition, for better and for worse.

I am not only suggesting that we may be overworking recognition theoretically and practically, but also that we may have partly misconstrued the good it represents, and is supposed to effect. There may be good reason to question our *craving* for recognition, to question the desire it is supposed to satisfy. Our desire for recognition may turn out to be a desire for which "we can't get no satisfaction," not even from equals, and the reasons for that may be worth understanding better than we currently do. It seems to me that this kind of questioning marks a new direction in the discourses on and of recognition.[26]

Perhaps we need to imagine different practices of recognition, practices that do not neatly divide between affirmative and deconstructive practices. Perhaps we need to work towards practices of recognition that do not already have form or place in our social life, expressive practices that are nonetheless continuous with self-criticism, engaging the misrecognized and misrecognizers in ways we can't yet describe. I can't say much more about this now—I wish I could. While I agree that critical theory requires a normative foothold in empirical reality, it requires even more the power to disclose alternative possibilities, possibilities not already available to us.[27]

---

26 In addition to the work of James Tully, here I am thinking of the work of Wendy Brown, *States of Injury*, Princeton: Princeton University Press, 1995, and Patchen Markell, *Bound by Recognition*, Princeton: Princeton University Press, 2003. See also James Tully, "On Reconciling Struggles over Recognition: Toward a New Approach," in *Equality and Diversity: New Perspectives,* ed. Avigail Eisenberg, Vancouver: University of British Columbia Press, 2006, "Exclusion and Assimilation: Two Forms of Domination," in *Domination and Exclusion*, ed. Melissa Williams and Stephen Macedo, Princeton: Princeton University Press, 2004, and "Recognition and Dialogue: The Emergence of a New Field," *Critical Review of International Social and Political Philosophy* 7: 3, Autumn 2004, pp. 84–106. In this vein of counter-discourses of recognition, see also Andrew Schaap, "Political Reconciliation through a Struggle for Recognition?" *Social and Legal Studies* 13: 4, 2004, pp. 523–40.

27 For a systematic statement of this alternative conception of critical theory, see Kompridis, *Critique and Disclosure.*

FIRST THINGS FIRST:
REDISTRIBUTION, RECOGNITION
AND JUSTIFICATION
Rainer Forst

I.

The debate between Nancy Fraser and Axel Honneth presents the two most advanced attempts to construct what we could call a comprehensive *critical theory of justice*. And the antagonism of their respective approaches reminds us of an ancient "schism of critique," so to speak, i.e., of the divergence of two strands of theory, having roots in the critical discourses of the Enlightenment as well as the Marxist tradition. The first strand is the one that primarily aims at overcoming economic, social and political relations of *inequality*; with respect to the sphere of political economy, "exploitation" was and is the central topic. The other strand mainly denounces the *impoverishment* of personal and cultural life under modern, capitalist modes of production; here, the main term of critique was and is "alienation" rather than exploitation.

These forms of critique have been, to be sure, connected in many ways,[1] yet the search for an integrated contemporary theory goes on, for the theoretical difference between the two approaches is clear enough: whereas the former critique has as its basis a notion of *justice* that aims at the establishment of social and political relations that are free from grave power asymmetries and unjustified forms of domination, the other uses much more qualitative, ethically substantive terms as the tools of critique: "true" *self-realization*, a "meaningful" form of life, or being *aufgehoben* in various forms of mutual recognition and social esteem.

One could be tempted to analyze this difference with Ernst Bloch, who reconstructed such a divergence as one between teachings of natural right focusing on the idea of human *dignity* and social utopias

---

1 The works of Rousseau provide illuminating examples of their combination.

aiming at the realization of human *happiness*.[2] This, however, is not quite adequate, for neither is the latter form of qualitative ethical critique necessarily in any sense "utopian," nor is it devoid of a concept of dignity. As Honneth makes clear in his work, the reconstruction of various forms of misrecognition so as to construct a positive notion of recognition is supposed to provide a rich and historically textured notion of human dignity, arising out of social struggles. Still, the juxtaposition between dignity and happiness captures something of the theoretical difference we encounter in this debate, for it reflects a difference between a basically Kantian and a Hegelian way of understanding the critical enterprise. And this is not just in light of the fact that theorists of the first tradition, like Nancy Fraser, keep reminding those of the second that happiness or "the good life" is a contested term that cannot ground justice claims in pluralist and postmetaphysical times, whereas proponents of the second tradition, like Axel Honneth, keep reminding the others that the overall aim of struggles for justice ultimately is having the possibility of leading a fulfilled and good life. More than that, the debate between the two reflects, I think, deeper issues about how to see human beings in relation to their society, i.e., issues of social ontology. In fact, one could say that representatives of the first tradition already start from a more "alienated" social-ontological view than those of the second, and that those who are mainly concerned with alienation and other phenomena of "bad" forms of life start from an ethical view that expects "nonreduced" social life to be one of a certain unity—if not *identity*—of individual and society.[3]

It is only from that vantage point that we see why representatives of the first approach like Nancy Fraser do not frame their critique of society as a critique of its "pathologies," trying to avoid carrying the burden to prove what a "healthy" form of social life would be—a burden that Axel Honneth tries to reformulate and make less metaphysically weighty in his comprehensive theoretical endeavor, yet one he believes one must carry in order to avoid settling for a reduced mode of critique that does not address the totality of a "false" form of life.[4] This difference, it strikes me, may be the basic issue we are confronted with when we look at the debate about "recognition" and

---

2 Ernst Bloch, *Natural Law and Human Dignity*, trans. D. Schmidt, Cambridge, MA: MIT Press, 1987.

3 See Axel Honneth on the Hegelian idea of a "rational universal" in "A Social Pathology of Reason: On the Intellectual Legacy of Critical Theory," trans. J. Hebbeler, in *The Cambridge Companion to Critical Theory*, ed. Fred Rush, Cambridge: Cambridge University Press, 2004, pp. 336–60.

"redistribution"; it is more, I want to say, than just another debate about justice. It is, to borrow a phrase from Fraser's recent work (out of context), a debate about the proper "frame" of critical thinking.[5] And then if, as she argues, debates about the frame of justice are a sign of "abnormal" discourse (as opposed to, in neo-Kuhnian language, "normal justice"), then here we find a debate of another form of "abnormality": not just one where the political frame of justice is at issue, but one where the basic methodological and normative questions of thinking about justice are contested. Furthermore, this may also be a debate about the question whether justice should be what we mainly focus on when we practice critical theory. These are the issues I want to address in my following brief remarks.

II.

To regard the theories of Fraser and Honneth as "advanced" implies that they each attempt to overcome the traditional schism of critique I mentioned, yet in quite different ways. Nancy Fraser starts from the diagnosis that contemporary Western capitalist societies are marked by two dominant forms—and subjective experiences—of injustice, often connected: suffering from a lack of resources due to economic and political inequality and suffering from a lack of social and cultural recognition for what one is—one's identity. Hence she suggests a two-dimensional theory of justice that aims at "transformative" strategies of redistribution as well as recognition, united in the aim of establishing a social basic structure in which there is *participatory parity* among all members with respect to the most important aspects of social life. This ideal of parity, however, is not based on substantive notions of the good life in mutual recognition; rather, it is meant to be a form of a "thick deontological liberalism"[6] that aims at establishing equal chances of leading an autonomous life (without providing an ethical interpretation of the meaning of "autonomy").

Axel Honneth, on the other hand, suggests a "monistic" theory of recognition that is, however, based on an analysis of three dimensions

---

4 See Axel Honneth, "Pathologien des Sozialen," in his *Das Andere der Gerechtigkeit: Aufsätze zur Praktischen Philosophie*, Frankfurt/M.: Suhrkamp, 2000, pp. 11–69.

5 Nancy Fraser, "Abnormal Justice," in *Critical Inquiry* 34: 3, 2008, pp. 393–422; reprinted in Nancy Fraser, *Scales of Justice: Reimagining Political Space in a Globalizing World*, New York: Polity Press and Columbia University Press, 2008.

6 Nancy Fraser and Axel Honneth, *Redistribution or Recognition? A Political-Philosophical Exchange*, trans. J. Golb, J. Ingram, C. Wilke, London: Verso, 2003.

of recognition—and of *self-realization* enabled through that recognition. On that basis, he claims, we can not only identify forms of suffering that we could not address with the help of a theory such as Fraser's, we will also better understand the social dynamics of the various struggles for recognition that are far from being simply struggles for "cultural" recognition. Rather, debates about economic redistribution are at their core debates about how to evaluate and to recognize certain forms of work and contributions to the economic social process. Finally, in his eyes the lack of a substantive ideal of recognized life in the three spheres of love, equal rights and social esteem makes a theory of justice empty and formal, doomed to forget what justice is really about: the good life.

But his theory, as I indicated, is not just one more attempt to bring out a teleological point about procedural justice, or the substantive side(s) of it; rather, there is a different comprehensive framework of thinking about individuality, sociality and normativity at work here. For in stressing that his approach relies on a stronger view both of the *immanence* and of the *transcendence* of social critique, Honneth implies that a recognitional account has access to a dimension of social and individual life that exhibits "a normative potential that reemerges in every social reality anew because it is so tightly fused to the structure of human interests."[7] According to his view, there is an anthropological as well as moral logic built into the very fabric of society that can lead to experiences of misrecognition that only a nuanced recognitional view can identify; approaches like Fraser's thus are doomed to remain bound to conventional paradigms of thinking about justice, especially to "goals that have already been publicly articulated," thereby neglecting "everyday, still unthematized, but no less pressing embryonic forms of social misery and moral injustice."[8] Against this charge, Fraser insists on the normatively mediated form of our access to experiences of subjective suffering, and she also stresses the "nonfoundational," pragmatist character of her approach, which critically reconstructs current "folk paradigms of justice"—as judged from an idea of participatory parity that according to her view represents a pivotal point of contemporary struggles for justice.[9]

---

7 Ibid., p. 244.
8 Ibid., p. 114.
9 Ibid., pp. 204–9.

III.

Given the many important aspects and dimensions of that debate, I cannot pretend to be able to do justice to it in what follows. Rather, my way to address the issues I find most important will be to develop a third, alternative approach to a critical theory of justice in dialogue with both Fraser's and Honneth's theories. I call it the "first-things-first" approach—or, more technically, an approach of *justificatory monism and diagnostic-evaluative pluralism.*[10] From that perspective, I might be able to explain why I (still[11]) think that recognitional accounts provide an indispensable *sensorium* for experiences of social suffering generally and of injustice more narrowly, yet that when it comes to the question of the criteria of the *justification of justice* claims, a procedural-deontological, discourse-theoretical account is necessary (which does not mean that we have to restrict ourselves to a "purely" procedural account of justice devoid of any substantive components). In matters of justice, we have to use a specific normative grammar of justification which cuts deep into the realm of the normative judgments we make: it works like a filter to sort out justifiable from unjustifiable claims, one that opens up and at the same time restricts the possibility of justice claims. If one understands justice in a critical way, not only this kind of opening but also the moment of restriction do serve an emancipatory purpose. Ultimately, this is what practical reason—and the respect for others—demands in this context.

Let me explain why I think that there is such a peculiar grammar of justice. When we talk about political and social justice, we talk about the ("perfect," in Kantian terms) duties of members of a given social and political context to establish institutions on the basis of norms that can legitimately claim to be generally and reciprocally valid and binding: a *context of justice* always is a specific *context of justification* in which *all* relevant basic social and political relations—including basic economic relations—are in need of mutual and general justification. Hence the criteria of reciprocity and generality turn, reflexively speaking, from criteria of validity into criteria of discursive justification. Seen in that way, contexts of justice are contexts of justification based on these criteria; from a realistic perspective, however,

---

10 I develop this approach more fully in my *Das Recht auf Rechtfertigung: Elemente einer konstruktivistischen Theorie der Gerechtigkeit*, Frankfurt/M.: Suhrkamp, 2007. English translation forthcoming from Columbia University Press.

11 For an earlier version of that argument, see my *Contexts of Justice: Political Philosophy beyond Liberalism and Communitarianism*, trans. J. Farrell, Berkeley: University of California Press, 2002 (German orig. 1994), p. 280.

most often contexts of justice are contexts of *injustice* first, and out of a critical analysis of such various forms of injustice an account of justice has to be constructed. Thus every theory of justice requires a complex theory of injustice, not just as a normative account, but also in the form of a social analysis. Still, even if such an account has to be complex and multi-dimensional, by way of a recursive argument we can formulate one *overarching reflexive principle of justice*: there must be no social and political relations that cannot be reciprocally and generally justified to all those who are part of a political-social context.

Justice, according to this view, is not primarily about *what you have* (or do not have); rather, it is first and foremost about *how you are treated*. Justice is not a teleological notion, for first, it rests on deontological duties of what persons owe to one another in a context of justice, and second, its critical part is not about persons *lacking* something that it would be good for them to have; rather, it is about persons *being deprived* of something they have reciprocally and generally non-rejectable reasons to claim. Justice is first and foremost about ending domination and unjustifiable, arbitrary rule, whether political or social in a broader sense; it is about citizens' status as equals in political and social life, i.e., as persons with what I call a *basic right to justification*.[12] The most fundamental principles of justice do not require specific patterns of distributing certain goods; rather, they demand that every such distribution has to proceed in the most justifiable way. It is important to see that we can call quite different and competing arrangements just or fair, depending on whether all affected have participated properly in the way they came about and had a sufficient chance to influence the results. Seen in this reflexive, higher-order perspective, there is an emancipatory priority of democratic justice that focuses on the equal standing of members in a context of justice.

This account suggests, unlike (at least one reading of) Fraser's theory, a monistic approach to justice, yet unlike Honneth's theory, it is not an approach based on a substantive account of recognition and self-realization, though it does presuppose one basic form of recognition: the recognition of the basic right of every member of a basic social structure to be respected as an equal participant in procedures of

---

12 See my "The Basic Right to Justification: Towards a Constructivist Conception of Human Rights," trans. J. Caver, *Constellations* 6, 1999, pp. 35–60; and "Towards a Critical Theory of Transnational Justice," in *Global Justice*, ed. Thomas Pogge, Oxford: Blackwell, 2001, pp. 169–87.

effective social justification. This is what the respect for human "dignity" means in this context. (I will come back to this point.)

There is an interpretation of Fraser's approach that also reads her theory as a monistic one, i.e. as based on the (single) general principle of "participatory parity." In her theory, however, that notion seems to serve different purposes.[13] On one reading, participatory parity is the *telos* of establishing just social and political structures, an end-state of justice:

> Redistribution claimants must show that existing economic arrangements deny them the necessary objective conditions for participatory parity. Recognition claimants must show that the institutionalized patterns of cultural value deny them the necessary intersubjective conditions. In both cases, therefore, the norm of participatory parity is the standard for warranting claims.[14]

On another reading, and this is the preferred one (also in light of Fraser's more recent work), participatory parity is not the *goal* of justice but its main *means*. It secures the necessary political and social standing of citizens in democratic debates about justifiable policies of redistribution or recognition: "Fair democratic deliberation concerning the merits of recognition claims requires parity of participation for all actual and possible deliberators. That in turn requires just distribution and reciprocal recognition."[15] This interpretation, however, implies a stronger theoretical agnosticism as to the aims of justice than Fraser at other times allows for.

To overcome ambiguities and circularities at this point, I suggest we distinguish conceptually between *fundamental* (or *minimal*) and *maximal justice*, based on the (above mentioned) reflexive principle of justice.[16] Fundamental justice calls for the establishment of a *basic structure of justification*, i.e. one in which all members have sufficient status and power to decide about the institutions they are to live under. Maximal justice then means the establishment of a *fully justified basic structure*, i.e., of a basic structure that grants those rights, life chances and goods that citizens of a just society could not reciprocally deny

---

13 See also Honneth's critique in Fraser and Honneth, *Redistribution or Recognition?*, p. 261.

14 Ibid., p. 38.

15 Ibid., p. 44.

16 See in particular my "Towards a Critical Theory of Transnational Justice."

each other. Obviously, "participatory parity" means quite different things in the fundamental and in the maximal mode. In the fundamental mode, it means having an effective right to justification in "reflexive," democratically self-transforming social and political institutions. Essentially, this includes the power to decide about the basic institutions of the way goods are *produced* and *distributed* in the first place. Hence if we argue—with Nancy Fraser (who agrees with that point[17])—for a "transformative" approach to social justice, we have to talk about fair institutions of production and distribution, not primarily of *re*distribution. The "re-" gives the false image that some "natural" first distribution has already taken place and that we want a second, less "natural" one. Rawls stresses this in his ideal of "pure procedural justice," and I will come back to that point.[18] In the maximal mode, "participatory parity" could be a general, though vague term for the possibility of really and fully living a socially integrated life without suffering any kind of structural social injustice; though given the required agnosticism about this, I am not sure we should give this idea of a just society a teleological name.

I conclude this discussion of Fraser's approach by questioning whether, seen in that light, "participatory parity" is a sufficient *criterion* of justifying justice claims, and also whether the conceptual tools she suggests for analyzing phenomena of *injustice* are sufficient. These are two large questions, and I can only hint at answers here. As for the first, I am not sure how (socially unavoidable) conflicts between different interpretations of what "participatory parity" means will be resolved; I assume that a notion of equality will be decisive here and not some more substantive idea of "participation." But if that is so, it seems that reciprocity and generality might be more adequate normative criteria, for they place the burden of justification on anyone who is trying to justify a social privilege of some sort, and it is here where the notion of reciprocity has sufficient bite. When it comes to questions of gay marriage, for example, the denial of equal rights is reciprocally non-justifiable, at least not with heavily contested religious or traditional ideas about the meaning of marriage. And when it comes to injustices in the systems of providing education or meaningful and decently paid work, social privileges of some groups are likewise indefensible. Hence with respect to criteria for claims to "recognition"

---

17 Fraser and Honneth, *Redistribution or Recognition?*, p. 95 note 8.

18 John Rawls, *Justice as Fairness: A Restatement*, ed. E. Kelly, Cambridge, MA: Harvard University Press, 2001, p. 50.

or "redistribution," we move from "parity" to "equality" in the sense of reciprocally non-rejectable justifications for certain social structures and relations.

Regarding the question of analyzing phenomena of injustice, I would say that injustices can have many faces, and that economic exploitation or exclusion or a lack of cultural recognition definitely are among those. But I am not sure we have to restrict our social-analytic language to these forms; if, for example, we criticize forms of manipulation in the media or forms of political exclusion, we might want to say that they are violations of democratic principles due to certain influences of power and interest politics, but it is not clear that the basic phenomenon is to be analyzed either in the economic or the cultural register, for these phenomena could also be products of a malfunctioning representative system; the *political* itself seems to be a broader and more independent realm than the two-dimensional theory allows for.

IV.

Let me now turn to Axel Honneth's theory, reiterating the two questions I just posed. As I argued, theories of recognition play an important role in identifying forms of injustice, but again I do not think that we need to restrict our explanatory tools in such a way. Take, for example, issues of distributive (in)justice. In some cases, misrecognition clearly can be the cause of unjust economic relations, and in such cases the remedy may not only be an institutional change (such as fair structures of economic compensation for socially impor-tant work) but also require a cultural change. But sometimes, it seems, injustice is not primarily linked to questions of recognition, for some professions with extremely high compensation are precisely not held in high esteem, such as being a manager of a large corpo-ration or a real estate agent. It is true, as Honneth says, that the economic realm is part of the general cultural realm of recognition, but many phenomena of injustice in that realm seem to have other causes and follow a different market or "systemic" logic that needs to be identified and criticized.[19]

To add one further point: even if it is correct that a change in the recognitional social structure is called for by way of a re-evaluation of some group's "contribution," such change might very well only be the *means* to the *end* of justice, not the end itself—the end would not

___

19 Fraser and Honneth, *Redistribution or Recognition?*, p. 142.

be to be socially esteemed but to have equal social standing and chances and be no longer the object of discrimination (which is different from being especially valued). Thus I question Honneth's charge that a deontological theory necessarily gets the means/ends relations the wrong way around and is blind with respect to the goals of social justice.

As for the question of whether criteria of recognition are sufficient to identify claims to justice (and to just recognition) that are *justifiable*, I have certain doubts. For any such claim needs to be justifiable with the criteria of reciprocity and generality: all those forms of "misrecognition" fall under the category of "injustice" that cannot be reciprocally and generally justified. Call that the *a priori of justification*. I do not in fact think that this is far from Honneth's own argument, for when it comes to translating a phenomenon—or subjective experience—of misrecognition into one of injustice and again translating this into a justice claim, he is generally using terms like "justified," "fair" or "equal": claims to recognition must be "well-founded," and injustice is an expression of "unjustified relations of recognition."[20] With respect to the justification of such relations or claims, I think equality—or reciprocity, in my language—clearly is the major criterion, even, I would venture to say, the only one. In the sphere of legal recognition this is explicitly so, but it is also true for claims to cultural recognition that must, according to Honneth, "pass through the needle's eye of the equality principle," since "the sort of social esteem that would be entailed in recognizing a culture as something valuable is not a public response that could be appealed for or demanded."[21] I would add that what can be "demanded" reciprocally in the third sphere, i.e., that of the evaluation of individual contributions to economic-social cooperation, also follows the logic of reciprocal justification regarding unjustified privileges as *unfair*. Here is Honneth's reconstruction of Hegel with respect to that point:

> With the three new forms of social relations that in my view prepare the way for the moral order of capitalist society, distinct principles of recognition develop in whose light the subject can assert specific experiences of undeserved, unjustifiable disrespect, and thus produce grounds for an expanded kind of recognition.[22]

---

20 Ibid., p. 114.
21 Ibid., pp. 140, 164, 168.
22 Ibid., p. 144.

Yet the critique of existing and "unjustifiable" forms and standards of recognizing "contributions" is most commonly expressed in terms of "fairness":

> And the fact of social inequality can only meet with more or less rational agreement because, beyond all actual distortions, its legitimating principle contains the normative claim to consider the individual achievements of all members of society fairly and appropriately in the form of mutual esteem.[23]

Thus the logic of reciprocal recognition, in translating subjective experiences into claims of justice, is dependent upon the criteria of reciprocity and generality: the substance of the sphere and the kind of particular recognition entailed do *not* transfigure into different criteria for justifying justice. And likewise, the multidimensional sensorium for phenomena of injustice does not either. This then also allows for a more radical critique of the "historically established recognition order" persons have to orient themselves toward—and possibly also for a critique of the problematic idea of "contribution" itself.[24]

In sum, normatively I argue for a basically *monistic* approach with respect to the overarching principle of justice, which is to be spelled out substantively with respect to the basic social structure of justification first, yet with respect to the question of what "maximal justice" means I opt for a radically *pluralistic* approach. Here, if you think for example about the question of how goods such as "work" or "health" should be distributed, we can think of a number of normative aspects that could be combined in an argument about (maximal) justice, and I see no reason why we should restrict that to a "dualistic" or a "monistic approach" in Fraser's or Honneth's sense. Once you had a structure of fundamental justice in place (which is quite demanding in terms of *substantive* justice), and once you had in play the criteria of reciprocity and generality that rule out arguments that unjustly favor one party, the argument should be open to a *wide* range of normative considerations, from the tradition of a political community to general human needs or particular capabilities, questions of effectiveness, specific ethical values, etc. In all these discourses, however, a discursive version of Rawls's difference principle should be in place, giving the "worst off," as

---

23 Ibid., p. 148.
24 Ibid., p. 137.

Rawls says, a "veto" against unjustifiable distributions: "Taking equality as the basis of comparison, those who have gained more must do so on terms that are justifiable to those who have gained the least."[25]

V.

The maxim "first things first" does not just have a normative meaning, with respect to the a priori of justification. For based on that, we should say that in matters of justice *power* is the most important of all goods, a true "hyper-good," for it is the good that is required to set up a justified basic structure in the first place—and to keep it going. Hence a critical theory of (in)justice has to be first and foremost a critique of the existing *relations of justification* (or of "justificatory power"). Such a critique, speaking in "diagnostic" terms, has three essential aspects.[26] *First*, by way of critical social analysis it aims at *exposing unjustifiable social relations*, not just political ones in a narrow sense, but also those of an economic or cultural nature—i.e., all those relations, in more or less institutionalized form, that fall short of the standard of reciprocal and general justifiability and are marked by forms of exclusion or domination. *Second*, it implies a discourse-theoretical (also in part genealogical) *critique of "false"* (possibly ideological) *justifications* for such relations, i.e., justifications that veil asymmetrical power relations and traditions of exclusion (say, along gender or class lines). And *third*, it implies an account of the *failure (or non-existence) of effective social and political structures of justification* to (a) unveil and (b) change unjustifiable social relations.

In normative-institutional terms, a justificatory approach of that kind suggests that only if a fair structure of justification is set up can more particular perspectives of justification be adopted. A just social structure will have many aspects, but it will in essence be *one* thing: a reciprocally and generally justified basic structure. And thus the first thing to aim at is a power structure of effective justification. Hence, I argue for a political turn within the theoretical discourse of justice, for there can be no proper account of distributive justice without first

25 John Rawls, *A Theory of Justice*, revised edition, Cambridge, MA: Harvard University Press, 1999, p. 131.

26 I can only list these aspects here; to spell them out, a normative account of justification needs to be completed by a theory of discursive power and a social theory of justification. For an attempt at the latter, see Luc Boltanski and Laurent Thévenot, *On Justification: Economies of Worth*, trans. C. Porter, Princeton: Princeton University Press, 2006.

addressing the political issue of power relations in a society: persons should not primarily be *recipients of justice*, rather, they should be *agents of justice*, i.e., autonomous agents who co-determine the structures of production and distribution that determine their lives—given, of course, the constraints of social systems that have developed within modern societies. And even though Rawls does not take such a turn and does not explicitly argue for political power being the most important of all primary goods, his argument for a form of "pure background procedural justice," which he explains in the following way, is essential here: "The basic structure is arranged so that when everyone follows the publicly recognized rules of cooperation . . . the particular distributions of goods that result are acceptable as just (or at least as not unjust) whatever these distributions turn out to be."[27] He spells this out by distinguishing welfare-state capitalism from his version of "property-owning democracy":

> The background institutions of property-owning democracy work to disperse the ownership of wealth and capital, and thus to prevent a small part of society from controlling the economy, and, indirectly, political life as well. By contrast, welfare-state capitalism permits a small class to have a near monopoly of the means of production. Property-owning democracy avoids this, not by the redistribution of income to those with less at the end of each period, so to speak, but rather by ensuring the widespread ownership of productive assets and human capital (that is, education and trained skills) at the beginning of each period, all this against a background of fair equality of opportunity. The intent is not simply to assist those who lose out through accident or misfortune (although that must be done), but rather to put all citizens in a position to manage their own affairs on a footing of a suitable degree of social and economic equality.[28]

My argument for the priority of the good of power and for an effective basic structure of justification implies that a two-dimensional view of justice between redistribution and recognition is insufficient if it does not stress the important *political* question of exercising power. This is in line, however, with a recent development of Nancy Fraser's theoretical enterprise; she now—in the context of second-order debates

---

27 Rawls, *Justice as Fairness*, p. 50.
28 Ibid., p. 139.

about the right frame or context of justice (national or transnational) —argues for a "three-dimensional" theory of justice, stressing the dimension of political representation as a third one, not reducible to the others.[29] "The political dimension sets the procedures for staging and resolving contests in both the economic and the cultural dimensions: it tells us not only who can make claims for redistribution and recognition, but also how such claims are to be mooted and adjudicated."[30] I believe that this is not just the case in an age of "reframing" justice, but more generally, and I also believe, *pace* Fraser, that this turns the political into a "master dimension of justice."[31] If we rely on a principle of justification, the political question is necessarily a higher-order question of justice, for it is here (if we understand the political not in a narrow institutional sense) where unjust cultural and economic and political social practices can be challenged and where changes in these spheres can be brought about.

VI.

By way of summary, let me emphasize why I think that through the combination of justificatory monism and diagnostic-evaluative pluralism that I have suggested, a critical theory of justice (as well as of injustice) can be constructed that does contain a number of the important characteristics that Honneth as well as Fraser claim such a theory needs to have—and that avoids some of the problems I pointed out.

First, it does not rest on a "quasi-transcendental"[32] anthropological or social-ontological foundation but finds a recursive, transcendental grounding in the principle of justification and in the self-reflexive idea of what it means to be a person with the capacity for practical reason (i.e., somebody who understands and accepts that principle and is capable of using reasons accordingly). Thus I would not follow a "nonfoundationalist" (Fraser) path here. At this point, of course, Fraser could accuse me of foundationalism, while Honneth could raise the objection that my "first-things-first" approach gets things the wrong way around, for it also seems to rest—as I indicated—on an "a priori of recognition": the moral recognition of the other as a being whom

---

29 Nancy Fraser, *Reframing Justice: Spinoza Lectures*, Amsterdam: Van Gorcum, 2005, pp. 41ff., 49.

30 Ibid., p. 44.

31 Ibid., p. 49.

32 Honneth, in Fraser and Honneth, *Redistribution or Recognition?*, p. 245.

I owe respect given his or her basic right to justification. I cannot go into these issues at length here, but only answer, to the first critique, that I think that any critical theory of justice and justification such as Fraser's is in need of a strong moral foundation of the right and the duty of justification in order to be a "deontological" theory,[33] whereas the competition between the a priori of recognition and that of justification may be resolved by interpreting the "original" form of moral recognition as a "fact" of justificatory reason, to use Kant's (in)famous term, i.e., as both the cognitive and moral recognition of the other as a justificatory being and authority to whom I *owe* appropriate justifications (in given contexts)—*without* further (ethical, metaphysical, religious or self-interested) reason. This, I take it, is a basic—and autonomous—moral insight of practical reason, for it sees the other in the light of the capacity of reason we share: as someone who can use and is in need of reasons. Thus I do not think that this is an act of practical recognition alone, but also one of cognition: an insight of (justificatory) reason.[34] To learn to see yourself as a "rational animal," i.e., to be socialized into the space of reasons, presupposes that kind of insight that needs no further relation to my self-interest (broadly understood).

A second possible objection from the viewpoint of Honneth's theory could be that a justificatory approach is ahistorical, being based on an abstract principle of reason alone. But as I tried to show elsewhere —in my reconstruction of the discourse of toleration from the early Christians until today[35]—the claim for justice as the claim for mutually justifiable concrete social and political relations, i.e., the claim to be respected as an agent with a right to justification, was and still is an important and central driving force in social conflicts. People in very different historical circumstances, speaking different "thick" normative languages, questioned given justifications for the structures and norms they were supposed to live under, demanding other, better reasons. The struggle for justifications is, to use one of Honneth's own phrases, a deep "grammar" of social conflict and emancipatory movements, leaving the form in which this demand is phrased up to them and historical circumstance. The practice of justification then is to be seen

---

33 Fraser, from Fraser and Honneth, *Redistribution or Recognition?*, p. 30.

34 See my "Moral Autonomy and the Autonomy of Morality," trans. Ciaran Cronin, *Graduate Faculty Philosophy Journal* 26:1, 2005, pp. 65–88.

35 Rainer Forst, *Toleranz im Konflikt: Geschichte, Gehalt und Gegenwart eines umstrittenen Begriffs*, Frankfurt/M.: Suhrkamp, 2003. English translation forthcoming from Cambridge University Press.

as a basic *social and dynamic practice* with the inherent potential of opening up conventional and exclusionary forms of discourse. Reason, as I see it, is a critical and subversive force—but reason it must be to criticize its own "pathologies" of false practices and contents of justification. A critical theory is in need of a free-standing as well as situated conception of practical reason.

Hence, to address a third possible worry of a recognition theorist, as far as the psychological aspects of the "desire" for justice and/or recognition—in other words the "emancipatory interest"—are concerned, I believe that the desire to be respected as an autonomous agent to whom others, especially in a political context, owe good reasons is a deep and rational desire of human beings. Its basis is a moral sense of "dignity," which is violated by being "invisible"[36] and by being disregarded as a proper justificatory "authority." The insult of being treated unjustifiably is felt very deeply, yet the insult of not even being seen as someone others owe reasons to is worst of all. Autonomy (understood in the sense of having a right to justification) is not just a philosophical idea in the noumenal realm; it is basic to our individual self-understanding and our self-respect.

VII.

One last concern may remain, and it brings me back to my opening remarks. Could it be, as Jürgen Habermas once asked in his famous essay on Walter Benjamin, that such a vision of justice forgets something most important; could it be, in Habermas's words, that "one day an emancipated humanity would exist in an enlarged space of discursive will-formation and yet be bereft of the light in which it could be able to interpret its life as a good one"?[37]

As a first answer to this, I believe that a sufficiently pluralist approach to just institutions in the above mentioned sense would be capable of incorporating a great number of aspects of the "good" life based on the particular justice claims persons justifiably make. Yet as

---

36 See also Axel Honneth, *Unsichtbarkeit: Stationen einer Theorie der Intersubjektivität*, Frankfurt/M.: Suhrkamp, 2003.

37 "Könnte eines Tages ein emanzipiertes Menschengeschlecht in den erweiterten Spielräumen diskursiver Willensbildung sich gegenübertreten und doch des Lichtes beraubt sein, in dem es sein Leben als ein gutes zu interpretieren fähig ist?" Jürgen Habermas, *Philosophisch-politische Profile*, Frankfurt/M.: Suhrkamp, 1987, p. 375 (my translation). On the same page, Habermas also argues for a "first things first" approach to questions of emancipation, adding, however, some thoughts about (what we could call) the saving power of undistorted communication.

a second answer, I think that the first tradition I spoke of above, and in which I have placed my own thinking, has to pay some price for its ethical agnosticism: there are aspects of the good—contested ones, to be sure—that such an approach does not capture, and there are other forms of critique with particular conceptual tools to address the ways societies fail to provide certain forms of the good. An approach based on the notion of justice can only go as far as that concept allows for— which I think is what Nancy Fraser stresses. And yet I think that it is one of the virtues of Axel Honneth's theory of recognition that it enables him to formulate a rich critical theory of "pathological" and ethically "bad" forms of social practice that goes beyond what a critical theory of *justice* can and should do. His recent Tanner Lectures on the theme of reification—analyzed as "forgetfulness of recognition"— attest to that.[38] But it seems to me important, and no sign of conceptual poverty but rather of richness and clarity, to see that whenever such a critique uses the terms of injustice or justice, a certain kind of reciprocal recognition, materialized in the practice of reciprocal justification, is primary. That does not mean that other forms of critique are weak or misguided; they just use other tools, have other aims and might imply different claims to validity.

---

38 Axel Honneth, *Reification: A New Look at an Old Idea*, New York: Oxford University Press, 2008.

PRIORITIZING JUSTICE AS PARTICIPATORY PARITY: A REPLY TO KOMPRIDIS AND FORST

Nancy Fraser

Both Nikolas Kompridis and Rainer Forst examine the philosophical underpinnings of my attempt to reconstruct critical theory. In different ways, each probes the normative foundations and "social ontology" of my approach. Whereas Forst interrogates my participation-theoretic conception of justice, Kompridis objects more generally to its discourse-theoretical underpinnings. Thus, the issues they raise can be divided into two streams. In one stream, which I will call "intra-paradigmatic," the fundamental objectives of critical theory are taken as settled, and the primary question is: In what terms should the theory be formulated in order best to fulfill those objectives? In the second stream, which I will call "extra-paradigmatic," the very aims of critical theory are in dispute.

In what follows, I begin with the second, extra-paradigmatic stream of questioning, in which I locate Kompridis's concerns. Reading him as challenging my understanding of critical theory, I compare the latter's merits with those of some other possibilities, hinted at in Kompridis's essay. Here I consider the question: is there a defensible and desirable alternative to my view that critical theory should prioritize the critique of institutionalized injustice? Turning next to the intra-paradigmatic stream of questioning, I examine the principal issues between Forst and me. Premised on a shared under-standing of critical theory, these issues concern the best way to realize a project we jointly espouse. Here, accordingly, I weigh the relative merits of our respective answers to the following question: With which social-theoretical and normative conceptions can one best fashion a critical theory of institutionalized injustice for the present era?

The priority of justice: a rejoinder to Nikolas Kompridis

Nikolas Kompridis contends that the central issue in *Redistribution or Recognition?* is the meaning of recognition. Rejecting both Honneth's identitarian account of that concept and my own status model, Kompridis maintains that neither of those interpretations captures the full meaning of recognition. In his view, recognition belongs exclusively neither to the realm of justice nor to that of self-realization. An essentially contested concept, its meaning cannot be reduced to a single normative idea. For Kompridis, accordingly, the alternatives debated in *Redistribution or Recognition?* present a false antithesis. Far from wishing to contribute to that debate, he seeks to displace it in favor of a different set of questions. This larger, extra-paradigmatic agenda informs Kompridis's more specific objections to my approach—for example, his contention that I am so focused on justifying recognition claims relative to existing protocols of public reason that I neglect the disclosive role of language in articulating subjective suffering. This criticism and others like it point not only to another understanding of recognition but also to a different conception of critical theory, not primarily focused on institutionalized injustice.

Yet the nature of Kompridis's alternative remains unclear. At some points, he suggests that recognition implicates both justice and self-realization, thereby insinuating the need for a synthesis of Honneth and me. At other points, however, he contends that recognition is best understood as a matter of freedom in the Foucauldian sense, as it concerns "how we govern ourselves." At still other points, though, he alleges that any attempt to reduce such a rich and contested concept to a "normatively monistic" interpretation is inherently misguided. Then again, finally, he maintains that recognition is the focus of aspirations that are so intrinsically problematic that critical theorists would do better to question the concept than to accord it any normative validity.

As I see it, each of these four claims about recognition entails a different standard and model of critique. Yet all of them reject the premise, central to my approach, that a critical theory should accord priority to the critique of *institutionalized injustice*. In what follows, therefore, I shall examine each of Kompridis's claims about recognition with a view to determining whether it affords a viable alternative to that *justice-theoretic* conception. For the sake of argument, I shall assume the following thin definition of critical theory, which I take to be non-controversial: *a theory is "critical," as opposed to "traditional," only if it is guided by a practical, emancipatory interest in unmasking domination.* Supposing this definition to be sufficiently neutral to serve as a benchmark, I shall ask whether any of the alternatives intimated by Kompridis better satisfies its provisions than the approach I elaborated in *Redistribution or Recognition?* In this way, by comparing them with some other possibilities, I shall attempt to defend both my status model of recognition and my focus on institutionalized injustice against Kompridis's objections.

My strategy, I must add, will be dialectical. Borrowing a leaf from Hegel, I shall treat each of Kompridis's claims about recognition as a stage of thought, which leads when probed to an impasse and so gives way to the next. Beginning with the most radical, rejectionist view and proceeding in order of increasing proximity to the status model, the sequence reveals the latter's comparative strengths in step-by-step fashion. The end result will be to demonstrate the *conceptual priority of the justice-theoretic understanding of recognition and, by extension, of critical theory.* Defending the thesis that *justice is the first virtue of recognition,* I shall argue that it is only by imagining the overcoming of misrecognition as a genre of *institutionalized injustice* that we can conceive any positive form of recognition that can be considered a good beyond justice.

Let me begin, accordingly, with Kompridis's most radical claim about recognition and, by implication, about critical theory. The claim here is that the desire for recognition is inherently unrealizable and self-defeating. In fact, so deeply problematic is this craving that critical theorists should treat it not as an emancipatory aspiration, but as a vehicle of normalization and thus as an object of critique. Forswearing any effort to distinguish good from bad forms of recognition, they should abandon such mainstream "therapeutic" concerns and question the yearning for recognition. Read this way, as a recognition skeptic, Kompridis invites the thought that a genuinely critical theory would deconstruct, rather than reconstruct, recognition.

Kompridis himself stops short of such a conclusion. Yet its implications are worth examining for heuristic purposes. As I see it, the argument just sketched runs up against two objections, one conceptual, the other political. Conceptually, the claim that the craving for recognition is inherently self-defeating is question-begging. It assumes what needs first to be shown: namely, that the desire for recognition is best analyzed as a wish to be regarded and valued by others as one really is, which means, in effect, as one regards and values oneself. Certainly, if this is what is meant by recognition, then recognition is neither possible nor desirable, and the most radical thesis would be right: we should jettison recognition as a normative category of critical theory. In fact, however, recognition need not be interpreted in this way. Another (non-identitarian) possibility is the one I proposed in *Redistribution or Recognition?*: that we understand claims for recognition as protests against status subordination—hence, as claims for justice. In that case, such claims would point to the need for institutional change, specifically to the need to deinstitutionalize hierarchical patterns of cultural value and to replace them with patterns that foster participatory parity. Understood in this way, claims for recognition are no more self-defeating than other types of justice claims, including claims for redistribution and representation. Granted, they will not lead to perfect justice, even in the best-case scenario; and they may well miscarry in practice. But that is hardly a reason for critical theorists to eschew the category of recognition, which corresponds in this interpretation to a bona fide genre of subordination not reducible to distributive injustice. Absent a functional equivalent, able to expose such subordination, recognition remains indispensable to any critical theory that seeks to unmask domination.

Politically, moreover, the proposal to jettison recognition presupposes a god's eye view from which the theorist presumes to invalidate whole social movements in a single stroke. Premised on an authoritarian and elitist view of critical theory, it treats those who struggle for recognition as simple dupes. Thus, it fails to strike a proper balance between independence from and sympathy with struggling subjects. A better, more democratic approach would identify the emancipatory kernel of their aspirations and reconstruct their claims accordingly. Following this path in *Redistribution or Recognition?*, I reconstructed recognition claims as aiming to overcome status hierarchy. The point was to discern the legitimate core of identitarian social protest in order to separate the wheat from the chaff. Although it is disdained by Kompridis, this interest in distinguishing better from worse recognition claims is indispensable to any critical theory with a practical, emancipatory intent. On both counts, then, political as well as conceptual, the proposal to equate recognition with normalization fails to yield a defensible view of critical theory as a practically motivated inquiry aimed at unmasking domination.

It is fortunate, therefore, that this proposal is not the one closest to Kompridis's heart. A more likely candidate for that position is his second, less radical suggestion that recognition claims are unobjectionable in principle but so multifarious and contested that any "normatively monistic" account of them is bound to be reductive and inadequate. On this view, misrecognition covers a multitude of sins, including

violations of justice, impediments to self-realization, fetters on freedom, and so on. Thus, every attempt to associate recognition
exclusively with one single normative category can at best capture only
part of the story. Also doomed are efforts to subsume all of recognition's many facets within a single comprehensive account. For one
thing, the various parts are at odds with one another; like Weber's
polytheism of values, they cannot be harmoniously reconciled or
lexically ranked. For another, recognition's meanings continue to unfold
historically in novel and unpredictable ways; thus, they cannot be
definitively enumerated once and for all. It follows that critical theorists
should abandon efforts to conceptualize recognition along normatively
monistic lines. Instead, they should treat it as an essentially contested
concept, whose meaning will never be settled.

Although Kompridis may not subscribe to its full implications, this
view, too, is vulnerable to serious objections. First, the view that recognition cannot be comprehensively theorized is objectionably aprioristic.
Giving away the game at the outset, it forecloses the chance to develop
a viable theory of recognition by settling for a pluralism that could
be gratuitous. Second, the view that recognition is too inherently indeterminate to be theorized is hard to square with critical theory's
emancipatory intent. Counseling the theorist to throw up her hands
in the face of an unruly multiplicity of meanings, it positions her as
an impotent observer of an endless, irresolvable contest into which
she can offer no insight. Implying, too, that any account of recognition
is as good as any other, it replaces the wholesale negativity of the
previous view with an equally wholesale, and disabling, indifference.
Finally, and most important, this view overlooks another, more promising strategy, aimed at elaborating an account of recognition as one
dimension among others of a comprehensive theory of justice. Focused
on those aspects that pertain to justice, such an account need not
claim to encompass every facet of recognition. What it must do,
however, is establish the *conceptual priority of the justice-related
aspects* over the others.

To pursue this possibility, consider another, less problematic interpretation of the thesis that recognition is essentially contested. Suppose
this thesis is meant to endorse the democratic view that it is up to the
participants themselves to determine the meaning of recognition. In
that case the critical theorist would have to concern herself with the
fairness (or lack thereof) of the terms on which their contest is waged.
Do all concerned have equal chances to participate fully, as peers, in
the struggle to define what will count as recognition? Or are some of
them excluded or marginalized as a consequence of unjust social

arrangements? Clearly, this democratic view leaves open the precise content of the norms of recognition. But unless it interrogates the terms of the contestation that will settle that content, it does not deserve to be called a *critical* theory. To merit that title it must be prepared to do the hard social-theoretical work of exposing structural obstacles to fair participation. In principle, however, these can include institutionalized relations of recognition, which deprive some potential participants of the status of peers. If the critical theorist is to identify *these* impediments to a fair contest over the meaning of recognition, she must already possess a general, *justice-theoretic* notion of misrecognition. And *that* notion, of misrecognition as *status subordination*, must enjoy conceptual priority over the other, more specific meanings that emerge from the struggle, which may or may not be justice-related. Elaborated in *Redistribution and Recognition?*, this account offers the only way I can see to connect Kompridis's interest in valorizing contestation over recognition's meaning with critical theory's *emancipatory* aims. Without it, his second thesis about recognition fails to express the sort of practical interest in overcoming domination that distinguishes critical from traditional theory.

The same is true for the third claim I attributed to Kompridis: namely, that recognition is at bottom a matter of freedom. Contradicting both the view of recognition as normalization and the view of its meaning as essentially contested, this claim offers a positively valued, normatively monistic account of that concept. Yet the freedom-theoretic conception of recognition incorporates features of those previous views, especially a dislike of normalization and a fondness for contestation. Associated by Kompridis with James Tully's quasi-Foucauldian perspective, it values the *struggle* over recognition above the end to which the struggle aspires. On this view, when recognition is achieved, it coerces and constrains, even when it is reciprocal, while the struggle to achieve it is a practice of freedom. Thus, critical theorists should de-teleologize recognition, valorizing the freedom-incarnating process over the freedom-limiting result.

Despite its interest in promoting freedom, this view fails to generate a framework that is adequate for that purpose. The problem is that the only ideal of freedom that can be acceptable to a *critical* theory is an ideal of *equal* freedom. Social arrangements that enhance the freedom of some by restricting the freedom of others are unacceptable, as are arrangements that enable some to exercise their freedom at the expense of the freedom of others. Thus, a struggle over recognition cannot be considered a bona fide expression of freedom unless the antagonists are equally empowered to exercise their freedom in and through it. Failing that, the contest is better described as an exercise in domination. Like the previous view, therefore, this one must interrogate the terms on which struggles over recognition proceed. Asking whether social arrangements enable all to participate as peers, it must expose structural impediments to equal freedom, including those inhering in institutionalized relations of recognition. Thus, this view too must prioritize questions of justice in order to sustain its emancipatory intent. What appeared at first to be an independent rival view turns out on closer inspection to be parasitic on the justice-theoretic view. In general, then, the view of recognition as freedom maintains its critical-theoretical bona fides only insofar as it presupposes the view of recognition as a dimension of justice in the sense of participatory parity.

Let me pause to recap my reasoning to this point. So far, in discussing three of Kompridis's claims about recognition, I have returned again and again to a single point: while the status model does not capture every meaning of recognition, it is the interpretation critical theorists should prioritize so as to forward their emancipatory aims. Focused on status subordination as a genre of institutionalized domination, this model is justice-theoretic. As such, it is conceptually prior to other interpretations in the following sense: it is only by imagining the overcoming of misrecognition as a genre of *institutionalized injustice* that we can conceive any positive form of recognition that can be considered a good beyond justice. It follows, to paraphrase John Rawls, that critical theorists should regard justice as the *first virtue* of recognition—where "first" means not necessarily the highest virtue but the one that secures the enabling conditions for all of the others.[1] Seen this way, as a justice-theoretic conception, the status model does not so much exclude other meanings of recognition as set constraints on how they may be legitimately construed and pursued. Prioritizing justice, it rules out interpretations of recognition that require or promote institutionalized disparities of participation.

The thesis that justice is the first virtue of recognition bears as well on the fourth alternative hinted at in Kompridis's essay—namely, that recognition implicates both justice and self-realization. The least radical of his various suggestions, this claim implies that critical theorists should seek to combine Honneth's concern for self-realization with my concern for justice. Now, however, we can discern the specific

---

1 John Rawls, *A Theory of Justice*, revised edition, Cambridge: Belknap Press, 1999, pp. 3–4, 263–4, 266–7.

form such a combination must take: critical theory must prioritize the critique of institutionalized injustice in order to open a space for legitimate forms of self-realization. Treating justice as the first virtue, it must seek to equalize the conditions under which various interpretations of human flourishing are formulated, debated and pursued. Far from supplanting or demoting self-realization, then, the status model of recognition aims to establish the terrain on which it can be fairly pursued.

These considerations dovetail, I think, with the spirit of one of Kompridis's criticisms of Axel Honneth. Claiming that Honneth reduces self-realization to recognition, Kompridis contends that he overburdens the latter concept and impoverishes the former. The better course, I agree with Kompridis, is to disentangle self-realization from recognition so as to make room for a broader spectrum of perfectionist concerns. What Kompridis misses, however, is that the status model does just that. By prioritizing the critique of institutionalized injustice, which can be overcome by institutional change, this approach limits itself to a *political conception* of recognition. Effectively downsizing recognition, as Kompridis himself recommends, the status model clears a space in which social agents can legitimately pursue diverse perfectionist aims, freed from the straitjacket of identitarian recognition.

What I have said so far suffices, I trust, to defend my general conceptions of recognition and of critical theory. But by establishing the priority of the critique of institutionalized injustice, I hope also to have provided the basis for dispelling Kompridis's more specific objections. Let me conclude by responding to one such objection here, while leaving it to readers to work out the implications for the others.

Kompridis claims that I neglect the importance of linguistic innovation aimed at giving expression to heretofore unnamed injustices. Yet nothing in my approach entails that existing vocabularies of justification are adequate for disclosing harms that have not yet been publicly articulated. On the contrary, the justice-theoretic view is fully compatible with the claim, which I advanced more than twenty years ago, that a society's authorized "means of interpretation and communication" (MIC) are often better suited to expressing the perspectives of its advantaged strata than those of the oppressed and subordinated.[2]

---

2 Nancy Fraser, "Toward a Discourse Ethic of Solidarity," *Praxis International* 5: 4, January 1986, pp. 425–9; Nancy Fraser, "Talking about Needs: Interpretive Contests as Political Conflicts in Welfare-State Societies," *Ethics* 99: 2, January 1989, pp. 291–313; and Nancy Fraser, "Struggle over Needs: Outline of a Socialist-Feminist Critical Theory of Late-Capitalist Political Culture," in Nancy Fraser, *Unruly Practices: Power, Discourse and Gender in Contemporary Social Theory*, University of Minnesota Press and Polity Press, 1989.

As a result of this typical bias in signifying systems, the dominated shoulder an extra, asymmetrical burden in political argument. Impeding their ability to participate as peers, the bias built into the MIC is itself an institutionalized injustice. To unmask it requires the sort of justice-theoretic critique I have elaborated here.

For this reason, virtually every epochal struggle against injustice has involved the creation of new vocabularies for articulating injustices that previously lacked names. Second-wave feminism, which invented such expressions as "date rape," "sexual harassment," and "the double shift," as well as the language game of consciousness-raising, is exemplary but by no means unique. What Kompridis calls the struggle for voice is intimately linked to such linguistic innovation, as new political subjects literally talk themselves into existence, often creating their own subaltern counter-publics to amplify new need interpretations and situation definitions that cannot at first gain a hearing in mainstream public spheres.[3]

Moreover, when social movements succeed in expanding the range of publicly nameable injustices, the protocols of public reason change, too. In broadening the spectrum of intelligible claims, these movements also enrich the pool of potentially persuasive justifications and change the understanding of impartiality. Contra Kompridis, no paradigm better comprehends the historicity of public reason than the version of discourse ethics that informs my approach. Far from relying on rigid, predefined notions as to what counts as an impartial reason, that version invites the reflexive critique of all institutionalized rationality regimes, whose injustice it already suspects. And far from neglecting the disclosive dimension of signification, it valorizes the efforts of emancipatory social movements to invent novel significations that expand the meaning of justice.

In general, then, the account of critique I have been advocating here is informed by a version of discourse ethics. Although Habermas's version is sometimes thought to privilege justification at the expense of disclosure, mine accords due importance to both those linguistic practices, while clarifying the relation between them. What distinguishes this approach from all four alternatives intimated by Kompridis is its ability to link the disclosive use of language directly to the project of unmasking domination. On this point, too, it better expresses the practical, emancipatory intent of critical theory.

---

3 Nancy Fraser, "Rethinking the Public Sphere: A Contribution to the Critique of Actually Existing Democracy," in *Habermas and the Public Sphere*, ed. Craig Calhoun, MIT Press, 1991, pp. 109-42, reprinted in Fraser, *Justice Interruptus: Critical Reflections on the "Postsocialist" Condition*, New York: Routledge, 1997.

In replying to Kompridis I have pursued a quasi-Hegelian strategy. Examining a staged sequence of views about recognition—rejectionist, anti-monistic, freedom-theoretic and synthesizing—I have shown that each leads to an *aporia* whose sublation requires a shift to a justice-theoretic conception. The end result is to validate a specific answer to the extra-paradigmatic question about the social ontology of critical theory: such a theory best promotes its emancipatory aims when, construing misrecognition as status subordination, it prioritizes the critique of institutionalized injustice.

Justification or participation?
A response to Rainer Forst

Rainer Forst and I agree on the basic objectives of critical theory. For him, too, such a theory best fulfills its practical, emancipatory aims when it makes the critique of institutionalized injustice its priority. Unlike my dispute with Kompridis, then, my disagreements with Forst are intra-paradigmatic. Premised on a shared commitment to justice-theoretic critique, they concern the best way to realize that project. The core issue is categorial: With what categories should one formulate a critical theory of (in)justice?

In order to specify that core disagreement, I must first note the points of agreement, of which there are many. In fact, notwithstanding his carefully cultivated posture of evenhandedness, I read Forst as siding with me, and against Axel Honneth, on nearly all of the fundamental issues debated in *Redistribution or Recognition?* Aligning my position with the tradition of exploitation critique and Honneth's with that of alienation critique, Forst himself comes down in favor of the former. Thus, he agrees with me that Honneth's theory fails in two major ways to provide an adequate conceptual basis for critical theory. First, recognition monism is deficient as social theory, as it cannot identify the major genres of structural injustice in contemporary society. Because distributive injustices are not always forms or effects of misrecognition, a critical theory needs a multi-dimensional explanatory framework. Second, recognition monism fails to supply an adequate normative basis for critique. Because a teleological notion of recognition cannot justify binding obligations of justice in modern contexts of ethical pluralism, a critical theory needs a deontological moral philosophy, which should, moreover, be normatively monist. Thus, instead of distinguishing three spheres of recognition, each governed by a different norm, critical theorists should espouse a single overarching principle of justice, which *all* injustices can be shown to violate.

In general, then, Forst and I agree that a critical theory of contemporary society should be *social-theoretically multi-dimensional* and *normatively monist*.[4] Nevertheless, Forst does not endorse the theory I have proposed. On the plane of social theory, he appears to reject my account of three intertwined orders of subordination in favor of a "pluralism of evaluative notions." On the plane of moral philosophy, he proposes to replace my principle of parity of participation with a norm of justificatory fairness. The apparent result is to substitute a *justification-theoretic* conception of justice for my *participation-theoretic* conception.

Consequently, Forst's paper invites us to consider the question: Which of these two approaches should one prefer? Given the priority of (in)justice, should critical theorists conceive that notion in terms of justification or participation? But that is not the only possible interpretation of our exchange. Instead of reading Forst's and my views as rivals, one can read his norm of justificatory fairness as a special case of my principle of participatory parity, applied to one specific arena of social practice, namely, the practice of political argument. In what follows, I shall consider each of these interpretations. While devoting the bulk of my discussion to the relative merits of our respective views when construed as alternatives, I shall end by sketching a reading that incorporates elements of Forst's approach into mine.

Let me begin, then, by assuming that we are confronted with a choice between two competing conceptions of (in)justice, one justification-theoretic, the other participation-theoretic. How should one weigh their relative merits? Forst himself suggests an evaluative standard: does a given critical-theoretical framework succeed in putting "first things first"? Does it clarify the power asymmetries that simultaneously entrench injustices and hamper efforts to challenge them? I wholeheartedly endorse this evaluative standard. Construing Forst's theory and mine as rivals, I shall employ his standard to assess their respective strengths and weaknesses, asking: which does a better job of putting first things first in social theory and moral philosophy?

---

4 Forst suggests that my theory can be interpreted in two ways: as normatively monist or as normatively dualist. The first is interpretation is correct. Although I conceive distribution and recognition (and now representation) as two (now three) conceptually irreducible dimensions of justice, I subsume both (all) of them under the single overarching norm of participatory parity. For me, accordingly, all injustices violate a single normative principle. Thus, my view is two- (now three-) dimensional, but normatively monist.

I can deal briefly with the social theory side of the question, as Forst himself says little about that. In fact, I am not even sure whether his references to "evaluative pluralism" are really meant to refer to social theory at all, i.e., to a multi-dimensional *explanatory* account of the genres, mechanisms, orders, and sources of injustice. Because he offers no account of his own of these matters, nor any substantive arguments against mine, it not entirely clear whether he really does mean to reject my account of three intertwined orders of subordination (economic, cultural, political), corresponding to three intertwined genres of injustice (maldistribution, misrecognition, misrepresenta-tion). In any case, this account satisfies Forst's evaluative standard. Each of the three orders of subordination/genres of injustice names a type of institutionalized power differential that deprives some social actors of the chance to participate on a par with others in social life. Given Forst's failure to provide a comparable account of power asymmetries, one might conclude that my approach is better equipped to put first things first in social theory.

I turn now to the moral-philosophical aspect of our exchange, which requires more extended discussion. Beginning with the points of agree-ment, I note that both of our views belong to the family of discourse-theoretic approaches. Each of us holds that justice claims must be warranted discursively, via a deliberative process in which all potentially affected can participate on fair terms in the exchange of arguments and counterarguments. For both of us, moreover, that process is not conceived monologically, as an interior thought process, but rather dialogically, as a real democratic political process, which must be socially institutionalized. For both of us, finally, the process will be fair and the outcome legitimate only if all who are potentially affected are able to participate fully, as peers—which is to say, only in the absence of entrenched power asymmetries.

Nevertheless, our moral-philosophical views differ in four respects, which concern the *object, modality, scope,* and *social ontology* of normative critique. Let me consider each of these issues in turn, begin-ning with the problem of object. Here the question is: What does each theory take to be the principal focus of critical scrutiny? How does each construe the *object* to which its normative principle applies? As I understand it, Forst's justification-theoretic approach takes as its privileged object the *formal syntax of the reasons* the participants exchange. This, I take it, is what he means to assess when he invokes the criteria of generality and reciprocity. Those criteria are treated by him as attributes of reasons, as opposed to social relations. For Forst, accordingly, justifications cannot be cogent unless their syntax manifests formal properties of generality and reciprocity. The reasons offered must eschew special pleading and restricted, non-reciprocal codes and idioms.

In contrast, my participation-theoretic approach takes as its primary object the *social relations* among the interlocutors. The parity standard applies not to the syntax of the propositions they utter, but to the social terms on which they converse. Are these terms such as to permit all to participate fully, as peers, in political argument? Or do institutionalized power asymmetries deprive some potential interlocutors of the resources, standing, and voice that are needed for full participation? Thus, my approach applies its normative standard to the power relations in force, which can institutionalize obstacles to participatory parity in deliberation.

This difference in object bears importantly on Forst's suggestion that critical theorists put first things first. Unlike his, my approach provides a non-circuitous route to the question of power. Whereas he broaches power indirectly, through the proxy of syntax, my approach confronts power directly, tackling head-on the structural asymmetries that taint social practices of justification in unjust societies. As a result, it is better able to see through the ways in which dominant strata manipulate arguments—for example, by using reasons whose formal syntax is facially general and reciprocal to defend arrangements that injure the dominated, on the one hand, and by disqualifying the latter's protests as particularistic and non-reciprocal, on the other. By training scrutiny not on syntax but on social relations, my approach unmasks such strategies. Interrogating the social-structural context disregarded by Forst, it captures power asymmetries that are not reflected in justificatory syntax and that elude an approach that takes the latter as a proxy for the former. If the two theories are construed as rivals, then, mine has advantages over Forst's on the issue of object. Directly targeting differentials in power, it is better able to put first things first.

My second moral-philosophical difference with Forst concerns the *modality* of normative critique. What is at issue here is the mode in which our respective principles of justice operate. For each of us, does the principle function procedurally or substantively? Does it evaluate the *process* of deliberation, or does it serve rather to assess the *outcome*? As I understand it, Forst's principle of justificatory fairness is purely procedural. Applying exclusively to the input side of the dialogical exchange, it serves to evaluate the latter's procedural fairness—by scrutinizing the syntax of the reasons exchanged within it.

For me, in contrast, the principle of participatory parity is at once procedural and substantive. Applied to both the input and the output of deliberation, that principle serves to evaluate each of two major variables in the equation. First, it assesses the procedural fairness of dialogical processes—by interrogating the relations of social power that underlie them. Second, it also serves to assess the substantive justice of deliberative outcomes—by examining their consequences for future social interaction. In the first case, the principle directs us to ask whether the interlocutors are really able to participate as peers in exchanging arguments about justice and injustice. In the second case, it directs us to ask whether the political decisions that ensue from their discussions will really enhance the fairness of future encounters by reducing disparities in participation.

Once again, faced with two alternatives that appear to be rivals, we should ask: Which approach is better positioned to put first things first in the sense of exposing unjust asymmetries of power? To be genuinely critical, in my view, a theory of power must keep open the possibility of a gap between procedural fairness and substantive justice. Allowing for the possibility that a procedurally fair process can generate a substantively unjust outcome, such a theory should be able to criticize substantive injustice as well as procedural unfairness. Granted, any specific account of substantive injustice must be dialogically warranted. But the discussion, like the theory itself, should be informed by empirical research, which can reveal the likely impact of a contemplated policy decision on extant power relations in a given context. Thus, a critique of institutionalized injustice should encompass both consequentialist and procedural considerations. Sensitive to output as well as to input, such a theory best grasps the workings of power when it incorporates a normative principle that operates in both modalities, i.e., both procedurally and substantively—while taking care neither to confuse them with each other nor to blur the distinction between them.

Forst correctly notes, however, that my double use of participatory parity to evaluate both the input and the output of political argument raises the question of circularity. On the one hand, what exactly is needed to achieve parity of participation in a given case can only be determined dialogically, through fair democratic deliberation. On the other hand, fair democratic deliberation presupposes that participatory parity already exists. There is indeed a circularity here, but Forst's own view is circular in just the same way: one needs a fair structure of justification in order to determine the requirements of justice; but one needs just distribution and recognition in order to have a fair structure of justification. In no way specific to me, then, the circularity problem arises for *any* approach that envisions a transition to more just social arrangements via political processes that occur by definition in unjust circumstances. All such approaches must take steps to prevent the circle from becoming vicious.

Forst proposes an ingenious solution to this problem. Echoing James Bohman's idea of the democratic minimum, he distinguishes minimal from maximal justice.[5] Whereas the first refers to the existence of an institutionalized structure of justification, where participants can demand and receive justifications, the second denotes a fully justified basic structure of society. Although Forst suggests that this distinction redounds to the exclusive credit of his approach, I maintain that it sits equally well with mine. Elsewhere, in fact, I have proposed the analogous idea of *good enough deliberation*. A variation on D. W. Winnicott's notion of "good enough mothering," this expression refers to deliberation that, while tainted by power asymmetries and thus falling short of participatory parity, is "good enough" to generate outcomes that reduce disparities, so that the next round of political argument proceeds on terms that are somewhat more fair and can be expected to lead to still better outcomes, and so on.[6] This idea, like those of Forst and Bohman, aims to turn a vicious circle into a virtuous spiral. The difference between it and Forst's minimal justice is not a difference that makes a difference.

As I see it, therefore, when our two approaches are construed as rivals, mine comes out better than Forst's with respect to the issue of modality. No more liable than his to the charge of circularity, the participation-theoretic model is more critical of power asymmetries insofar as it interrogates both the input and output of deliberation. Operating substantively as well as procedurally, it is better able to put first things first.

Let me turn, then, to my third moral-philosophical difference with Forst, which concerns the *scope* of normative critique. The issue here is the range of social practices that each theory subjects to critical scrutiny. As I read him, Forst limits his core principle's scope of application to a single class of social practices—namely, practices of justification. It is to them alone (or to the reasons exchanged within them) that his criteria of generality and reciprocity apply. In contrast,

---

5 James Bohman, "The Democratic Minimum: Is Democracy a Means to Global Justice?", *Ethics and International Affairs* 18, 2004.

6 The phrase "good enough deliberation" was suggested to me by Bert van den Brink (personal communication). I develop the idea in Nancy Fraser, "Two Dogmas of Egalitarianism," in Fraser, *Scales of Justice: Reimagining Political Science in a Globalizing World*, New York: Polity Press and Columbia University Press, 2008.

my principle of participatory parity applies more broadly, to *all* major
social practices and arenas of social interaction. Included here are
practices of justification, to be sure, but also other major social arenas,
such as employment and markets; family and personal life; formal and
informal politics; public goods and services; and associations in civil
society. It is thanks to this wide scope of application that the parity
principle can serve as a substantive norm for evaluating the outcomes
of deliberation as well as a procedural principle for evaluating
deliberative processes.

Assuming here, too, that we are dealing with competing views, we
should ask: Which approach more thoroughly exposes the unjust asymmetries of power that pervade contemporary societies? On its face,
my approach is more critical, because it targets more types of power
asymmetries in more arenas of social life. Yet Forst maintains that he
is justified in limiting the scope of his principle to justificatory arenas
for two reasons: first, because the political is the master dimension of
social (in)justice; and second, because power is the hyper-good whose
distribution determines that of all other goods. What should we make
of these claims?

In my view, Forst mixes genuine insights with dubious conclusions.
I agree that the political is a fundamental dimension of justice, as my
revised three-dimensional framework makes clear. I also agree that
power has a special status, that it is a hyper-good. But it is a mistake,
in my view, to identify power exclusively with the political dimension
of justice. Rather, each of the three dimensions (economic, cultural,
and political) identifies a fundamental, irreducible dimension of social
power. Corresponding to a distinctive mode of subordination and genre
of injustice, each picks out an order of power asymmetry that poses
a distinctive type of obstacle to parity of participation. So what is so
special about the political?

Forst is right, I think, to insist that the political is always necessarily
in play, even when it is not the explicit focus of dispute. But this does
not entail that is the master dimension. For the same is true of the
other two dimensions of justice. In fact, the three dimensions stand
in relations of mutual entwinement and reciprocal influence. Just as
the ability to make claims for distribution and recognition depends
on relations of representation, so the ability to exercise political voice
depends on the relations of class and status. Thus, maldistribution
and misrecognition conspire to subvert the principle of equal political
voice for every citizen, even in polities that are formally democratic.
It follows that efforts to overcome injustice cannot, except in rare
cases, address the relations of representation alone. On the contrary,

struggles against misrepresentation cannot succeed unless they are joined with struggles against maldistribution and misrecognition—and vice versa. Where one puts the emphasis, of course, is a both a tactical and strategic decision. Given the current salience of injustices of misframing, my own preference is for the slogan "No redistribution or recognition without representation." But that priority is conjunctural, not conceptual. And even today the politics of representation appears as one among three interconnected fronts in the struggle for social justice in a globalizing world.

The upshot is that the political cannot be designated the master dimension of (in)justice. I say this even while endorsing Forst's view of power as a hyper-good and stipulating that the political enjoys a special salience today—for conjunctural, not conceptual, reasons. This is a difference that makes a difference. By refusing to treat the political as the master dimension of justice, my approach avoids the pitfalls of what I shall call reductive "politicism." Analogous to economism, on the one hand, and to culturalism, on the other, politicism is the view that the social relations of representation determine those of distribution and recognition. Ascribing a base-superstructure configuration to contemporary society, while installing the political as the "base," this view is no more adequate than vulgar economism or reductive culturalism. Like those discredited approaches, whose architectonics it faithfully mimics, politicism fails to do justice to the complexity of structural causation in capitalist society. Consequently, its practical implication, that one can overcome all maldistribution and misrecognition simply by overcoming misrepresentation, is deeply misguided. Politicism appears to follow from Forst's insistence that the political is the master dimension of justice. If so, it disables his approach from grappling successfully with the three dialectically entwined sources of power asymmetry in contemporary society.

What follows for the issue of scope? If the political cannot be deemed the master dimension, there is no justification for limiting normative critique to justificatory practices. Rather, critical theory should track the effects of power asymmetries across the entire range of social practices in contemporary society. On this count, too, then, the participation-theoretic approach puts first things first.

This brings me to my fourth moral-philosophical difference with Forst, which concerns the *social ontology* of normative critique. Here, too, it is necessary to separate out the points on which we differ from the views we share. Both of us eschew as sectarian the strategy espoused by Honneth, which purports to ground critical theory on a comprehensive (albeit "formal") account of human being. Rather, each of us follows John Rawls in correlating her or his theory with a more limited, "political" conception of the person, which picks out only those features of personhood that a nonsectarian theory of justice must presuppose.[7] On this general theoretical strategy we agree. Nevertheless, Forst and I hold different political conceptions of the person. His approach portrays persons as givers and receivers of justifications, who participate with one another in the social practice of exchanging public reasons. Mine, in contrast, depicts persons as co-participants in an indeterminate multiplicity of social practices, which emerge and disappear in a historically open-ended process, and so cannot be specified once and for all. In my approach, persons are socially situated but potentially autonomous fellow actors, whose (equal) autonomy depends on their ability to interact with one another as peers—not only in political reasoning, but in *all* the major arenas and practices that constitute their form of life. For me, accordingly, the practices of justification that Forst makes central are but one of the many social practices in which individuals ought to be able to exercise their free and equal personhood by participating with one another as peers.

Assuming they constitute rival social ontologies, which of these conceptions is better situated to put first things first? As I see it, my approach has at least two advantages over Forst's. First, by refusing to single out justification practices for special notice, it offers a more capacious, variegated, and historically open-ended view of social personhood. As a result, it is less vulnerable to the charge of excessive rationalism. Second, by affirming the ideal of participatory parity, my approach posits a close relation between the liberal value of individual autonomy and social belonging. According the latter a non-communitarian interpretation, it construes institutionalized obstacles to participatory parity as impediments not only to equal autonomy but also to full membership in society. As a result, this social ontology permits critical theory to address a major form of alienation—namely, *alienation from one's society and fellow actors*—even while prioritizing justice. Thus, the participation-theoretic view manages to recoup within a deontological theory of justice at least one important ethical concern that is usually deemed the exclusive province of teleological theories of self-realization.[8] In this way, it satisfies Forst's desideratum

---

7 John Rawls, *Political Liberalism*, New York: Columbia University Press, 1996, pp. 29–35.

8 I owe this point to Cristina Lafont (oral intervention in discussion of this exchange at session on "Redistribution or Recognition?" at the Central Division meetings of the American Philosophical Association, Chicago, April 2006).

that a critical theory avoid as far as possible sacrificing other ethical concerns, even as it rightly prioritizes the critique of institutionalized injustice.

In general, then, there are good reasons for preferring my approach to Forst's with respect to all four issues considered here: the object, modality, scope, and social ontology of normative critique. Thus, in moral philosophy, as in social theory, the participation-theoretic conception of justice appears to do a better job of putting first things first, assuming the two views are construed as rivals.

Suppose, however, we reject that interpretation in favor of one that regards Forst's view as a special case of mine. Read this way, his norm of justificatory fairness appears as an application of the principle of participatory parity within one important but restricted type of social practice—namely, the practice of demanding and receiving political justifications. No longer *the* fundamental principle of justice, Forst's norm now presents itself as one of several such applications, each of which specifies the meaning of parity in relation to a given type of social practice.

Certainly, this interpretation assumes the validity of my approach, but perhaps it captures the spirit, if not the letter, of Forst's as well. As I read him, he too envisions a maximally just society as one in which no one is disrespected as a result of institutionalized power asymmetries in *any* social practice that is essential to full membership. It follows, I think he would agree, that in such a society no one would be structurally excluded from or marginalized in *any* social arena of real significance. And Forst would agree, too, if I understand him, that a just society requires that no one be deprived of the resources, standing, and voice needed to avoid exclusion or marginalization in *any* major arena of social interaction. If that is right, then the equal right to justification serves in effect for him as a kind of synecdoche for society-at-large; it not only promotes but also *models* the sort of egalitarian social relations that justice requires more broadly, throughout the whole of social life.

Perhaps I read too much of myself into Forst. But the mere fact that I can imagine interpreting him in this way shows how close in spirit our views really are. Our disagreements, as I said at the outset, are intra-paradigmatic, premised on a shared understanding of the basic shape and point of critical theory. In defending my participation-theoretic view here, then, I have sought to forward objectives we hold in common.

·Conclusion

Let me conclude on a note of gratitude. It is a rare privilege to have the opportunity to respond to such interesting and intelligent essays. Different as their foci are, both Kompridids and Forst inspired me to think more deeply than I had before about key aspects of the view I elaborated in *Redistribution or Recognition?* Whether the primary focus was extra- or intra-paradigmatic, the result was the same: each of them pushed me to devise new formulations of my position that go beyond, and (I hope) improve upon those that appear in that volume. No author could ask for anything more.

ACKNOWLEDGMENTS

Judith Butler, "Merely Cultural" was originally published in *Social Text* 15, 1997, 265–277. The author is grateful to Duke University Press for permission to publish it here.

Rainer Forst, "First Things First: Redistribution, Recognition and Justification." An earlier version of this essay was presented at the Socialist Scholars Conference in New York City (March 2004) and at the meeting of the American Philosophical Association, Central Division, in Chicago (April 2006). The author thanks the participants of the respective panels for helpful comments and criticism, and especially Nancy Fraser and Axel Honneth for their constructive replies. This essay first appeared in the *European Journal of Political Theory* 6, 2007, pp. 291–304, and is published here with permission. Together with a reply by Honneth, a version of it will be published in *The Critical Theory of Axel Honneth*, ed. Danielle Petherbridge, Leiden: Brill, forthcoming.

Nancy Fraser, "From Redistribution to Recognition? Dilemmas of Justice in a 'Postsocialist' Age" originally appeared in *New Left Review* 1: 212, 1995, pp. 68–93. It is reprinted in Nancy Fraser, *Justice Interruptus: Critical Reflections on the "Postsocialist" Condition*, New York: Routledge, 1997. For generous research support, the author would like to thank the Bohen Foundation, the Institut für die Wissenschaften vom Menschen in Vienna, the Humanities Research Institute of the University of California at Irvine, the Center for Urban Affairs and Policy Research at Northwestern University, and the dean of the Graduate Faculty of the New School for Social Research. For helpful comments, she thanks Robin Blackburn, Judith Butler, Angela

Harris, Randall Kennedy, Ted Koditschek, Jane Mansbridge, Mika
Manty, Linda Nicholson, Eli Zaretsky, and the members of the
"Feminism and the Discourses of Power" work group at the Humanities
Research Institute of the University of California, Irvine.

————. "Heterosexism, Misrecognition, and Capitalism: A
Response to Judith Butler" was originally published in *Social Text* 15,
1997, pp. 279–89. The author thanks Laura Kipnis and Eli Zaretsky
for helpful comments.

————. "Why Overcoming Prejudice Is Not Enough: A Rejoinder
to Richard Rorty" was originally published in *Critical Horizons* 1,
2000, pp. 21–8.

————. "Against Pollyanna-ism: A Reply to Iris Young" was
originally published in *New Left Review* 1: 223, 1997, pp. 126–129.

————. "Rethinking Recognition: Overcoming Displacement and
Reification in Cultural Politics" was originally published in *New Left
Review* 2: 3, 2000, pp. 107–120.

————. "Reframing Justice in a Globalizing World" was originally
published in *New Left Review* 2: 36, 2005, pp. 69–88. First delivered
as a 2004 Spinoza Lecture at the University of Amsterdam, the text
was revised at the Wissenschaftskolleg zu Berlin in 2004–05. The author
conveys thanks to both institutions for their support, to James Bohman,
Kristin Gissberg and Keith Haysom for their assistance, and to Amy
Allen, Seyla Benhabib, Bert van den Brink, Alessandro Ferrara, Rainer
Forst, John Judis, Ted Koditschek, Maria Pia Lara, David Peritz, and
Eli Zaretsky for helpful comments and stimulating discussions.

————. "Prioritizing Justice as Participatory Parity: A Reply to
Kompridis and Forst" was first published in a symposium on Fraser's
work in the *European Journal of Political Theory* 6: 3, 2007. The
author thanks Nikolas Kompridis, who guest-edited the symposium,
and Amy Allen, Maria Pia Lara, Rainer Forst, and Eli Zaretsky, whose
comments proved very helpful.

Nancy Fraser would like to convey her gratitude to all those who
have granted permission for her work to be republished in this volume.

Joseph Heath, "Resource Egalitarianism and the Politics of
Recognition." The author would like to thank Will Kymlicka, Philippe
Van Parijs, Arthur Ripstein, and Daniel Weinstock for helpful
comments on an earlier version of the argument put forth in this essay.

Nikolas Kompridis, "Struggling over the Meaning of Recognition,"
was first published in the *European Journal of Political Theory* 6: 3,

2007, pp. 277–89. The author is grateful to the editors and publisher for permission to reprint it.

Kevin Olson, "Participatory Parity and Democratic Justice." The author would like to thank Nancy Fraser for several rounds of very beneficial dialogue as well as Kenneth Baynes, James Bohman, Cristina Lafont, and Christopher Zurn for their thoughtful comments.

Anne Phillips, "From Inequality to Difference: A Severe Case of Displacement?" was originally published in *New Left Review* 1: 224, 1997, pp. 143–53.

Ingrid Robeyns, "Is Nancy Fraser's Critique of Theories of Distributive Justice Justified?" was originally published in *Constellations* 10: 4, 2003, pp. 538–53. The author is grateful to the editors and publisher for permission to reprint it.

Richard Rorty "Is 'Cultural Recognition' a Useful Notion for Leftist Politics?" originally appeared in *Critical Horizons* 1, 2000, pp. 7–20. Nancy Fraser and Kevin Olson would like to thank the editors and publisher for permission to reprint it.

Iris Marion Young "Unruly Categories: A Critique of Nancy Fraser's Dual Systems Theory" was originally published in *New Left Review* 1: 222, 1997, pp. 147–60.

CONTRIBUTORS

Elizabeth Anderson is John Rawls collegiate professor of philosophy and women's studies at the University of Michigan, Ann Arbor. She is the author of *Value in Ethics and Economics* (Harvard University Press, 1993) and numerous articles on democratic theory, equality, political economy, value theory, and rational choice. She is currently writing a book about democracy and racial integration.

Judith Butler is Maxine Elliot professor in the Departments of Rhetoric and Comparative Literature and chair of the Department of Rhetoric at the University of California, Berkeley. She is the author of several books, including *Gender Trouble* (Routledge, 1990), *Bodies That Matter* (Routledge, 1993), *The Psychic Life of Power* (Stanford University Press, 1997), *Undoing Gender* (Routledge, 2003), *Precarious Life* (Verso, 2004), and *Giving an Account of Oneself* (Fordham, 2005).

Leonard Feldman is associate professor of political science at the University of Oregon. He is the author of *Citizens Without Shelter: Homelessness, Democracy, and Political Exclusion* (Cornell University Press, 2004) as well as articles on democratic theory. He is currently working on a book, *Governed by Necessity*. In 2007–2008, he was a visiting member of the Institute for Advanced Study in Princeton.

Rainer Forst is professor of political theory and philosophy at Johann Wolfgang Goethe-University in Frankfurt am Main, Germany. He is the author of *Contexts of Justice* (University of California Press, 2002), *Toleranz im Konflikt* (Suhrkamp, 2003, English translation forthcoming with Cambridge University Press), and *Das Recht auf Rechtfertigung* (Suhrkamp, 2007), editor of *Toleranz* (Campus, 2000), and coeditor of *Ethos der Moderne: Foucaults Kritik der Aufklärung* (Campus 1990).

Nancy Fraser is Henry and Louise A. Loeb professor of philosophy and politics at the New School for Social Research. Formerly coeditor of the journal *Constellations*, and currently the holder of a Chaire Blaise Pascal at the École des hautes études en sciences sociales in Paris, she is the author of *Scales of Justice: Re-imagining Political Space for a Globalizing World* (2008); *Redistribution or Recognition? A Political-Philosophical Exchange* (2003), with Axel Honneth; *Justice Interruptus: Critical Reflections on the "Postsocialist" Condition* (1997); *Feminist Contentions: A Philosophical Exchange* (1994) with Seyla Benhabib, Judith Butler, and Drucilla Cornell; and *Unruly Practices: Power, Discourse, and Gender in Contemporary Social Theory* (1989).

Joseph Heath is associate professor of philosophy at the University of Toronto. He is author of *Communicative Action and Rational Choice* (MIT Press, 2001), *The Efficient Society* (Penguin, 2001), and, with Andrew Potter, *The Rebel Sell* (HarperCollins, 2004). His primary research interests are in critical social theory and normative economics.

Nikolas Kompridis is assistant professor of philosophy at York University. He is the author of *Critique and Disclosure: Critical Theory between Past and Future* (MIT Press, 2006) and editor of *Philosophical Romanticism* (Routledge, 2006). He has also published numerous essays on contemporary social and political philosophy, German idealism and romanticism, critical theory, aesthetics, and the philosophy of culture.

Kevin Olson is associate professor of political science at the University of California, Irvine. He is the author of *Reflexive Democracy: Political Equality and the Welfare State* (MIT Press, 2006), as well as essays on popular sovereignty, citizenship, the cultural and material bases of democracy, social justice, the politics of diversity, and European social, political, and legal theory. In 2006–7 he was an Erasmus Mundus Scholar at Utrecht University, the Netherlands.

Anne Phillips is professor of political and gender theory at the London School of Economics and has written extensively on issues of democracy, equality, feminism, and multiculturalism. Her publications include *Engendering Democracy* (Pennsylvania State University Press, 1991), *Democracy and Difference* (Pennsylvania State University Press 1993), *The Politics of Presence* (Oxford University Press, 1995), and *Which Equalities Matter?* (Polity, 1999). Her most recent book,

Multiculturalism without Culture, was published by Princeton University Press in 2007.

Ingrid Robeyns received her PhD degree from Cambridge University for a dissertation on gender inequality and the capability approach. She is now professor of practical philosophy at the Erasmus University in Rotterdam, the Netherlands. She is especially interested in the capability approach, theories of justice, gender inequality, family justice, feminist economics and philosophy, and the reform of the welfare state.

Richard Rorty taught philosophy at Princeton University for twenty years, where he published the pathbreaking book *Philosophy and the Mirror of Nature* (1979). His subsequent career took him to the University of Virginia and Stanford University, and led to important works like *Consequences of Pragmatism* (1982), *Contingency, Irony, and Solidarity* (1989), and *Achieving Our Country* (1998), as well as several other books and four volumes of collected papers. His most recent work is *Philosophy as Cultural Politics* (2007).

Iris Marion Young was professor of political science at the University of Chicago until her untimely death in 2006. She authored many books and articles on feminist theory and political philosophy, including most recently *Inclusion and Democracy* (Oxford University Press, 2000), *On Female Body Experience* (Oxford University Press, 2004), and *Global Challenges: War, Self Determination and Responsibility for Justice* (Polity, 2007).

Christopher Zurn is associate professor of philosophy at the University of Kentucky. He is the author of *Deliberative Democracy and the Institutions of Judicial Review* (Cambridge University Press, 2007), as well as articles on democracy, law, recognition, distribution, and critical theory.

INDEX